Good Order and Safety

A History of the
St. Louis Metropolitan Police Department
1861–1906

Allen E. Wagner

Missouri History Museum
Distributed by the University of Missouri Press

This book is dedicated to Sally, my wife and best friend.

It is also dedicated to the brave and caring men and women of the St. Louis Metropolitan Police Department of the past, the present, and those who will follow.

Library of Congress Cataloging-in-Publication Data

Wagner, Allen Eugene.
Good order and safety : a history of the St. Louis Metropolitan Police Department, 1861/1906 / Allen E. Wagner.
p. cm.
Summary: "Examines the beginnings of the St. Louis Metropolitan Police Department, from 1861 to 1906, when St. Louis was the fourth-largest city in the United States"--Provided by publisher.
Includes bibliographical references and index.
ISBN 978-1-883982-63-8 (cloth : alk. paper)
1. Saint Louis (Mo.). Metropolitan Police Dept.--History. 2. Police--Missouri-Saint Louis--History. I. Title.
HV8148.S262W34 2008
363.209778'6609034--dc22
2008009243

Distributed by University of Missouri Press
Printed and bound in the United States by Thomson-Shore, Inc.
Designed by Madonna Gauding

Contents

Foreword

MOUNTED POLICE OFFICERS RIDE on horseback through Forest Park, and sometimes they pass below my office window in the Missouri History Museum. Pausing on their patrol, they welcome youngsters, and adults too, to come a little closer (but not too close) for a look at their horses, animals seldom seen now on the streets of St. Louis but a common sight once upon a time. Indeed horses a century ago had a significant role in fighting crime and keeping the peace. Looking at these handsome beasts, I can nearly see back across the years when their ancestors were ubiquitous.

In the forty-five years covered in Allen E. Wagner's *Good Order and Safety*, we find police company horses—and more. Here, we explore important decades in the story of the St. Louis police, a period of time that has an effect on the police of today and thus on our whole community as well. We find tales of bravery and heroic action, stories of behind-the-scenes maneuvering and questionable behavior, discussions of what to change and what to keep, instances of innovation side by side with hard-line resistance to change—the whole human adventure reflected in the history of St. Louis's official endeavors to bring order and safety to the streets of the city.

The Missouri History Museum is pleased to present this account of a civic institution that is essential to the story of our community. "The histories of the metropolitan police department and the city of St. Louis are inseparable," our author writes in his preface. I would also suggest that, just as I can see the police horses trotting elegantly through Forest Park and think about their predecessors' era, so we can look around at our twenty-first-century landscape and begin to know how it took shape.

"Good order and safety" is an old-fashioned phrase but an objective still current and commendable. What else from the past is worth preserving, and what shall we adjust to better accommodate what we have learned from the past? This is in essence what we seek from all of our exploring of the past, and, to quote T. S. Eliot, "We shall not cease from exploration," whether it be an era of the metropolitan police or the impulses within ourselves.

—Robert R. Archibald, Ph.D.
President, Missouri History Museum

Author's Preface

SOME OF THE LANDMARKS REMAIN: the site of the
United States Arsenal; the Old Courthouse; the Basilica of St. Louis,
King of France (the Old Cathedral); the Eads Bridge; the Cupples
warehouses; the warehouses along Second Street (now Laclede's
Landing); Union Station; and Forest Park. I'm sure there are many
others. These sites were familiar to patrol officers who worked at one
time or another between 1861 and 1906. The histories of the metropolitan police department and the city of St. Louis are inseparable,
so the reader will find some of the history of the city embedded in
accounts of police activities.

Many police policies and procedures established during that time
remain today. But that was a different time. By present standards,
the actions of some members of the police department, from the top
ranks to the bottom, seem to be less than laudable. Other actions
would be praiseworthy at any point in history. The reader must keep
the phrase "by present standards" in mind before making judgments
about some activities, especially where politics is involved. Politics
was involved in many decisions and was all important in the operation
of nineteenth-century states and big cities, including Missouri and
St. Louis.

The criminal law was in a continuous state of evolution. Missouri
was a rural state (St. Louis was the only large city), and the General
Assembly was dominated by rural legislators. This made it difficult
to pass criminal law statutes that were perceived to have little or no
consequence outside of St. Louis.

The city government of St. Louis had not yet evolved into what
we see today. At one time or another, the lack of the appropriate city departments turned police officers into sanitation officers;
street, building, privy, dairy, and meat inspectors; dogcatchers; cen-

sus takers; and enforcers of the city tax codes and licensing laws. Most of these duties dwindled as the twentieth century dawned and city government took over virtually all but the law enforcement responsibilities.

The reader should also remember that technology at the beginning of the era consisted of oil lamps and the heating of rooms by wood- or coal-burning stoves or fireplaces. The most modern invention available to the police department was the telegraph system. Through most of the period described in this book, there were no telephones, electric lights, central heating, automobiles, or inside toilet facilities. Rolled, perforated toilet tissue wasn't even marketed until the 1880s. Water came from wells, and, when city water was finally pumped into homes and businesses, it tended to be less than clear.

Good Order and Safety, then, is the history of a police department that was born at the beginning of the Civil War and, as the political era ended in St. Louis, was policing the fourth-largest city in the United States. The "good order and safety" part of the title was taken from the response of the Board of Police Commissioners to Mayor William Ewing's 1883 allegation that the city was "overrun with thieves." The board used the reports of the district commanders to state that "good order and safety prevailed in the city." I hope you enjoy this look back.

If you want the present to be different than the past, study the past.

—Baruch Spinoza

Introduction

THE MODEL FOR URBAN AMERICAN police departments was the London Metropolitan Police. When the first constables of the London Metropolitan Police began patrolling in September 1829, the event constituted both an evolution and a revolution. They were called the "new police" because, unlike their predecessors who simply reacted to offenses, the metropolitan police were organized to prevent them. In this respect, the new police represented an evolution necessary to keep pace with a growing metropolis and the crime and disorder that accompanied the growth. On the other hand, the police were revolutionary. Established by the home secretary, Sir Robert Peel, the force was the first twenty-four-hour, paid, uniformed, civilian police force in the English-speaking world.

The metropolitan police introduced three new elements to modern policing: a new mission, strategy, and organizational structure.[1] The new *mission* was crime prevention. The two commissioners appointed by Peel to oversee the "Met" sought to achieve this through a *strategy* of preventive patrol: the patrolling of designated beats. *Organizational structure* was based on the military model, including uniforms, ranks, and an authoritarian system of command and discipline.[2]

American authorities were aware of the new police in London. London was, however, different from the cities of the United States. As a result of industrialization, London already was a growing metropolis. Industrialization in the United States lagged behind that in England. Policing of American cities before the 1830s was "some combination of watchmen and constables, sheriffs and marshals, elected or appointed, paid by salary or fee."[3] Those on the watch in American cities usually reported to a constable or marshal. Watchmen, who worked at night, patrolled their areas watching for fires, proclaiming the hours of the night, reporting broken street lamps, and performing a host of other duties.

The period between the 1830s and the Civil War, however, saw rioting in many American cities. The causes of these riots varied, ranging from nativism and racism to election fraud and unemployment. Boston had three major riots between 1834 and 1837. In Philadelphia, anti-black riots occurred in 1838 and 1842; riots involving nativists and foreign-born citizens took place in 1844. New York City was also the scene of major rioting. So many riots occurred in 1834 that it became known as "the year of the riots."[4] Besides deaths and injuries, rioting led to a great deal of property damage and destruction. Putting down these riots was the job of the local detachment of the state militia or a quickly gathered group of citizens known as the posse comitatus. Both the militia and the posse required time to form and get to the scene of the rioting. Sometimes they arrived to find that the rioting had stopped of its own accord.

Crime was also a concern as the cities grew. Whether it increased in proportion to population growth is unknown; crime statistics in the first half of the nineteenth century were virtually nonexistent in the United States. The newspapers printed criminal incidents as they became known, but newspapers didn't keep crime statistics. The riots and disorder, however, eclipsed any concern about crime. "At best, one could say that the creation of the police force reflected a growing intolerance for riots and disorder, rather than a response to an increase in crime."[5]

The London Metropolitan Police force was a model, not a blueprint. There was some opposition to forming metropolitan police–style departments in the United States. First, new police departments would have to conform to the idea of "republicanism," an ideology that required decentralization of power and accountability to the voters.[6] An elected (not appointed) official had to be ultimately responsible for the actions of the department and its officers. Second, the idea of uniformed officers was most controversial. David R. Johnson describes the arguments of proponents and opponents of uniformed police. The basic principles of crime prevention, proponents maintained, dictate uniformed police; the visible presence of a police officer discourages criminal activity. Early American police, however, countered that the uniform would permit criminals to see them and get away before an officer could get to the scene of the crime. Another argument in favor of uniformed police addressed the viewpoint of crime victims: Police officers in uniform could be more readily found. Uniforms also prevented officers from shirking their duties—they could not easily ignore situations requiring police attention if citizens could see that they were police officers. The police replied that uniforms "smacked of subordination and tyranny" and denounced them as "un-American liveries which would destroy their sense of manliness and democracy."[7]

Eric Monkkonen argues that the issue was the point of convergence of urban American police departments. If the police in different cities began from completely different points, converging only with the completion of the move into uniforms, the police must have been shaped by similar external forces.[8] Monkkonen also believes that opposition to the new police style focused on the uniform, so much so that the date that a uniform was adopted by a city signaled that city's employment of the new style of policing: "The uniform concretely symbolizes the changed system of social control represented by the new police, asserting publicly and unequivocally the difference between the old and the new."[9] Monkkonen adds that whatever emotion the uniform evokes from the wearer or the viewer is not significant. What counts is that the uniform is a statement of power. And in the nineteenth century when a city took the step of uniforming its police, it clearly stated its power to control its inhabitants.[10]

Thus, says Monkkonen, the uniforming of the police is seen simply as a part of the growth of urban service bureaucracies. The uniform represented an important change, but its introduction and dispersion throughout the United States "was not a function of elite demands for class control, changing urban riots, or rising crime . . . [it] conformed to a simple rank-order dispersion model."[11] The larger cities began to selectively copy the London Metropolitan Police model, and other large cities followed as each government developed a new service orientation. Since New York City was, in 1845, the first to adopt the

London model (and to later add the wearing of uniforms), other cities looked to New York when they were ready to employ the model.

Riots and disorder, says Monkkonen, were largely responsible for the establishment of the new style of policing. The wearing of uniforms, however, was a separate issue, directly connected to the shift of a city to a more service-oriented form of government. Nineteenth-century urban police departments, then, began to take on similar appearances only after (1) it was determined that the present police arrangement was not effectively dealing with riots and disorder, (2) city administrators examined police departments in cities of similar size, (3) city government changed to a service-oriented construct, and (4) the police began wearing uniforms. In summary, says Monkkonen, "if each city had adopted a uniformed force only after a riot, changing crime rate, or the need for a new kind of class-control agency, many places would not today have a uniformed police force."[12]

As officials in large cities looked to cities of similar size for assistance in putting the new police concept into operation, smaller cities looked to larger cities. In retrospect, it can be seen that these transformations took place within generalized time frames.

George Kelling and Mark Moore have divided American policing into three identifiable time frames: the political era, the reform era, and the community problem-solving era.[13] The political era, which will be of concern in this book, began with the introduction of police into municipalities in the 1840s. The period was characterized by a close alliance of the police and local politicians, especially at the ward or neighborhood level. It was likely that police officers would patrol the ward or neighborhood from which they were selected. As a result, the police provided a wide array of services to the citizenry. And, while they were involved in crime prevention, crime control, and peacekeeping duties, they also provided a variety of social services. Police might operate soup kitchens or offer temporary lodging in station houses.

In some cities, the political philosophy took a democratic twist. In 1840, the citizens of each ward in Cincinnati elected the night-watch officers in their respective wards. Ten years later, the addition of a day watch was attended by the same manner of selecting officers.

Chiefs of police were elected in Chicago in 1851, Cleveland in 1852, and San Francisco in 1856.[14]

At the same time, the idea of police boards became fashionable. Local boards of police formed in Philadelphia in 1850, New York City and New Orleans in 1853, and Cincinnati in 1859. The police boards were administrative bodies whose composition and powers varied by city. The New York City board consisted of the mayor, the recorder, and the city judge. In Cincinnati, the mayor, police judge, and city auditor selected four citizens for the police board. San Francisco's board was composed of the police judge, president of the board of supervisors, and the chief of police, serving as an ex officio member. Some boards were partisan, some nonpartisan, and others bipartisan.[15]

The political era had strengths. Because of the closeness of the police with the community and the services provided to the community, the police had the support of many citizens. The police also were credited, in varying degrees, with keeping the neighborhoods safe. There were also weaknesses. The police were susceptible to selective enforcement of the laws and to interfering in elections. Strangers were often discriminated against; "curbstone justice" might await minority ethnic and racial groups. The political nature of many police appointments caused inefficiency and disorganization and led many citizens to view the police as bunglers.[16]

This book is a history of the first century of policing in St. Louis. Founded in 1764, the village soon hosted a diverse population that reflected its past, present, and future. It saw the revolution that spawned the United States to its east, just across the Mississippi River. It was part of the territory of a foreign power, then of the United States, and, finally, a town and then a city in the new state of Missouri. It would be almost forty-five years after its founding before any civilian policing was required. Another fifty years passed before a police department was organized. In 1861, as the Civil War began, the police department in this border city of this border state came under state control.

If law enforcement in the village, the town, and the city of St. Louis followed the postulates of the authors cited earlier in this introduction, which generally relied on the experiences of cities in the eastern portion of the country, we should expect to find several break points. First, the establishment of a police department should herald the beginning of the political era. Did police officers patrol the ward or neighborhood from which they were selected? Did they provide a wide array of services to the citizenry? What were the selection standards? Second, we would also expect to see riot and disorder in St. Louis, a phenomenon that the police would fail to effectively handle. We would also expect city administrators examining police departments in cities of similar size, city government changing to a service orientation, and the wearing of uniforms by the police. Finally, as the twentieth century dawns, we should expect to witness the movement into the reform era. Who began police reform in St. Louis? What did the police do with the emerging technologies?

The history of the police in St. Louis is the description of a journey that continues to this day. It had its beginnings in 1808.

Chapter One

The Formative Years

IN 1808, PEOPLE BEGAN MOVING TO St. Louis from states east of the Mississippi River and mixed with the Creoles, French, Spanish, Native Americans, slaves, and others who lived there. But with the increase in population, and the increasing diversity introduced by the settlers from the east, the crime rate increased. Fighting, political arguments, public drunkenness, thefts, and duels became more common. A few months after his arrival in 1807, acting governor Frederick Bates wrote to his brother in Virginia about the people he saw with weapons, "Pistols & Durks and sometimes with Rifles also...."[1]

By 1808, the village of St. Louis had found it necessary to form a patrol. The patrol consisted of four persons chosen from all male residents of St. Louis over the age of eighteen. They were referred to as the "constabulary." Service was compulsory, and there was a $1 fine for refusing to serve.[2] After serving for four months, without pay, they were replaced by another four men from the rolls. St. Louis was incorporated as a town the following year and, in 1811, expanded from the Mississippi River westward to Fourth Street.

The patrol was increased to six men and a night watch of two men in 1818. The term "constabulary" was dropped and a captain of the patrol was established. In 1820, Captain Henry W. Conway organized the St. Louis Guards, a volunteer militia whose purpose was to quell disturbances. In 1821, Missouri became a state. During the following year, the state legislature permitted St. Louis to incorporate as a city upon a majority vote of the residents of St. Louis. St. Louisans voted to incorporate in April 1823. A physician, Dr. William Carr Lane, was elected the first mayor. Population was rapidly increasing; the western city limits expanded to Seventh Street, and the city extended for two miles along the Mississippi River.[3] The city was divided into three wards.

In 1826, the St. Louis Board of Trustees compiled a list of residents of St. Louis. All free white males between the ages of eighteen and sixty years were enrolled to serve as peace officers, for one year, when requested. The patrol was not only to preserve the peace, but to ring church bells each evening as a signal for the slaves to retire. The church bells were rung at 10:00 p.m. from May 1 to October 1, and 9:00 p.m. the remainder of the year.[4]

A night watch was established in 1831 under the command of a constable, an elected official, who would be its ex officio captain. The night watch was specifically designed to prevent riots, apprehend suspicious persons, and sound the alarm in case of fire.[5]

By August 1837, the city had expanded to four wards. A new ordinance authorized the Board of Aldermen to elect four watchmen from each of the four wards for a six-month period. The ordinance also established a day watch. There would be one day-watchman for each ward.[6]

In 1839, the city of St. Louis successfully petitioned the state legislature for a new city charter that would establish the city council, to be composed of the Board of Aldermen and the Board of Delegates.[7] On December 19, 1839, the city council passed an ordinance establishing the city guard.[8] The men would be called "guards" rather than "watchmen." Beginning with the May 1840 commissions, city guard appointments lasted for one year.[9] Equal numbers of guards were to be selected from the four wards of the city. They would be under the command of the city marshal, who was ex officio captain of the guard.[10]

Each ward was provided with a number of sentry boxes (the number to be determined by each ward) that were furnished with "the requisite lamps and other furniture." The guards were required to make "the rounds assigned them" but had to be at their sentry box to "repeatedly proclaim the hour of the night . . . regulating themselves by the clock on the Catholic Cathedral, or such other clock as the mayor shall designate."[11] The 1839 ordinance, in listing additional duties of the guards, first used the term "police."

St. Louis Cathedral. Lithograph by J. C. Wild, 1840. Missouri History Museum.

In June 1841, a seemingly unrelated but important event occurred. The company of Moore and Ward set up a "Daguerrean Gallery" at Dennis's boardinghouse at Main and Market streets. Moore and Ward, who would only remain in the city for a few months, were the first to visit the city to demonstrate the daguerreotype likeness process developed in Paris by L. J. M. Daguerre and his associates two years earlier. Beginning in 1846, however, several photographic studios were established in St. Louis.[12] American police departments quickly realized the value of daguerreotypes in identifying criminals. Several rogues' galleries were instituted in various city police departments. There is some evidence to suggest that the first daguerreotype of a "rogue" taken for the St. Louis police was created in 1843.[13] Thus, the St. Louis police department was one of the earliest departments, if not the first, to establish a rogues' gallery.[14]

In 1846, the entire city administration was reorganized. The city guard was placed in a separate department called the police department.[15] The police department included the city marshal, the city guard, the day police, and the keeper of the calaboose. The police department was to consist of a captain, seven lieutenants, and forty-nine privates. The city guard, who patrolled at night, consisted of six of the lieutenants—one for each of the now six wards, or districts—and forty-two privates. (The seventh lieutenant and seven privates constituted the day police.) There was no mention in the 1846 ordinance of the city guard wearing any insignia, but the day police were required to wear a gilded star on the left lapel of their coats. The city guard reported for duty from 8:00 p.m. until sunrise the next morning, October through March, and from 9:00 p.m. to sunrise the remainder of the year. For the first time, rooms were rented in the First and Sixth wards to serve as "lockup rooms." Persons arrested and being held overnight in those wards were kept in the lockup room until the guard went off duty in the morning. The prisoners were then moved to the calaboose.[16]

In the early morning of March 24, 1849, a crime the *Missouri Republican* later called "one of the most daring burglaries on record" was taking place.[17] Burglars cut through wood, brick walls as thick as three feet, and one-inch-thick sheet iron to enter the banking house of Wm. Nesbit and Company, at Main and Olive streets, and enter the vault. Approximately $15,000 was taken. The *Missouri Republican* asked, "Where was the night watch? It almost requires a search warrant to find a policeman in the night."[18] Nesbit and Company offered a $1,500 reward. A captain of the city guard, John E. D. Couzins, and two companions tracked two of the burglars into Illinois and captured them and part of the loot. In 1861, Couzins would become the second chief of police of the newly organized metropolitan police department.

During the night of May 17, 1849, a strong northeasterly wind pushed into the area, where twenty-three boats, ranging along almost one mile of the levee, were tied up. The wind pushed them closer to shore. When fire was discovered aboard the *White Cloud,* the alarm sounded. Firemen arrived and sprayed water on the burning boat from another moored nearby, but the flames soon leaped beyond the range of the hoses. To prevent it from catching fire, the lines of the steamboat *Edward Bates* were cut and an attempt was made to push it into the current. The wind prevented that, however. Not being secured, the

Bates eventually began to drift downriver, crashing into other moored boats and setting them afire.

The flames jumped across the narrow levee, set fire to bales of hemp stored there, and then leaped to some shanties and warehouses along the narrow streets. All ten St. Louis fire companies (more than one thousand men) were on the scene. Then, the city water supply failed. The river couldn't be used as a source of water because of the almost one mile of boats burning at the shoreline. The city was beginning to burn, and there was no water. In desperation, a fire captain, Thomas Targee, sent soldiers to the U.S. Arsenal for powder and, upon their return, began to blow up buildings in an effort to create a fire-stop.

Great Fire at St. Louis, 1849. Lithograph by Nathaniel Currier.
Missouri History Museum.

Targee's efforts were successful, but he died when a keg of powder prematurely exploded. The cost of the fire was high. Three men were dead; many more were injured. Nearly fifteen blocks of commercial and residential buildings had burned to the ground. Twenty-three steamboats, three canal boats, and one barge had been destroyed. As a result of the fire, the narrow levee was expanded, downtown streets were widened, and a new business district was built of brick and cast iron along cobblestone streets with gutters, sewers, and gaslights.[19]

As if these disasters were not enough, 1849 saw the beginning of a wave of violence between some nativists and immigrants.[20] Many boats were laid up at the levee, and hundreds of deckhands, mostly Irish, were out of work. The hot summer weather, the large number of unemployed deckhands, and the lure of waterfront taverns combined to create problems. The Irish from northern Ireland even began quarreling with those from the south of Ireland. One riot on the levee left several bystanders injured, and a steamboat was commandeered and held for some minutes. The city marshal and the police did what they could, but their numbers were small.[21]

The worst of the violence occurred on July 29, when fire again started on a boat at the levee, resulting in the loss of five steamers. One fire company was waiting for a new supply of water when the firemen saw two dogs fighting. One fireman intervened, but an "Irish rowdy" struck him in the head with a piece of iron and ran into O'Brien's coffeehouse (saloon) on Battle Row, "a row of dilapidated buildings which extended from Fifth to Sixth on Green Street."[22] Some of the firemen went into the coffeehouse and grabbed the assailant, but once outside they were greeted with stones and gunfire from the second floor of O'Brien's. In spite of the protests of the mayor, the firemen went back into the building and demolished it.[23]

The mayor and the police arrived and arrested ringleaders from both sides. The Irish were now outnumbered, and the mob began to target other Irish-owned businesses. They destroyed the interiors and furniture of O'Brien's coffeehouse and Murphy's boardinghouse on Battle Row, Shannon's coffeehouse and Gilligan's on Cherry Street, and Terrence Brady's coffeehouse at Fifth and Morgan streets.[24]

Fifty volunteer police were quickly sworn in. Several more arrests were made, and the rest of the day was quiet. At about 9:00 p.m., however, the mob reassembled and returned to the levee with a six-inch howitzer loaded with scrap iron, which had been stolen from a local foundry. The mob intended to demolish the Battle Row rooming houses. The police were unsuccessful in attempts to seize the gun, but the mob moved to a firehouse where police finally captured it.[25]

By 1850, the population of St. Louis had grown to 77,860. An ordinance passed that year made the city marshal the ex officio chief of police. The police department was divided into a day guard and a night guard,[26] and the city was divided into three police districts: Wards 1 and 2 (the southern portion of the city) constituted the First District, Wards 3 and 4 (the central part of the city) made up the Second District, and Wards 5 and 6 (the northern section of the city), the Third District. A station house was to be provided for each district. The mayor, city marshal, and captain would select a building for the First and Third districts; the police office would serve as the Second District station. Each would have a temporary lockup to hold prisoners until they could be moved to the calaboose.

For the first time, the police department was authorized to "employ a suitable vehicle for the purpose of removing any person or persons arrested and confined in the first or third district station houses, to the Recorder's Court, or to the calaboose, or to prison, as the case may require."[27] The vehicle that was eventually used was an enclosed horse-drawn wagon that must have been painted black, for it was called the "Black Maria."[28]

In his second consecutive one-year term, 1854–1855, Mayor John How asked the city council to require the police to wear uniforms. In his address to the city council on May 18, 1854, the mayor asserted that "[a uniform] would be better adapted for designating their office than the star now worn, which, if one of the members from a lack of courage, or what is still more reprehensible, from false pride, desires, is easily concealed."[29]

The city council approved the wearing of a uniform beginning in November 1854. The captain of the night guard, James A. Guion, accompanied by six of his men, promptly walked to Mayor How's place of business on Main Street and resigned from the force. When How asked why, Guion replied, "It's because we won't wear uniforms. It's too much like soldiering. It's contrary to the spirit of American citizenship."[30]

In August 1854, the police department faced its first real riot— and lost. As the August 7 election approached, a new political party, the Know-Nothings, surfaced. Members of the Know-Nothings were opposed to both foreigners and the Catholic Church. St. Louis had a large immigrant population, many of whom were Catholic, and ill feelings had been brewing for some time. When the polls opened, foreigners were asked for papers before they could vote, and many were rejected. At the Fifth Ward polling place, an Irishman stabbed a boy and then fled into a boardinghouse. Bystanders pursued him and his group, smashing windows and furniture. Shots were fired from other houses, and within thirty minutes a mob of five thousand had gathered.[31] The mob went west from the levee, sacking Irish houses on two different streets. When they returned to the levee they were met by a group of Irish levee workers. In the ensuing fight, which included flying bricks and gunshots, the Irish fell back. The mob went on another spree, wrecking more Irish homes and then Irish saloons along several streets.

Mayor How appeared on the scene with the entire police force, sixty-three officers and men, who were identified only by the star on their lapels. There were not nearly enough police, so How called out the volunteer militia. The fighting continued through the night, with numerous casualties and at least two people shot to death.

On the morning of the second day of rioting, How called a public meeting. It was decided to suspend the police: Because of their small number, they were ineffectual, and many of them were Irish.[32] Instead, a volunteer police force of one thousand men was organized. While the volunteers organized, however, the rioting began to lose strength, completely stopping by midnight. Ten people were dead, thirty-three were wounded, and ninety-three buildings were damaged.[33] The regular police were restored to duty.

In his semiannual message in October 1854, Mayor How told the city council that many citizens had offered to help the city should other disturbances occur. Because he saw that a volunteer police force was more effective than the paid force, he was going to appoint a group of special police to call upon in similar circumstances.

Mayor How's one-year term (the term of most police officers as well) expired, however, and Washington King was elected mayor of St. Louis. In his May 1855 address to the city council, King told those assembled that he wished to reorganize the police department in the manner of the New York City Police Department. He also wanted to dissolve the relationship between the marshal and the police department and appoint a chief of police. He saw such an ordinance pass on April 5, 1856.

The new ordinance called for a chief of police appointed by the mayor, along with a total reorganization of the police department. The likely reason was another geographical expansion of the city limits. The western limits were extended from Eighteenth Street to Grand Avenue, a distance of about eighteen blocks. The northern and southern limits were also extended to increase the size of the city from 4.78 to 17 square miles.[34] The city was now divided into thirteen wards. The reorganization wasn't effective until June, however, almost two months after King's successor was sworn in. King's successor was his predecessor, John How.

How saw the reorganized police department become operational. The new ordinance, Regulating the Police Department of the City of St. Louis, had been approved on April 5, 1856, but it was to take effect on the first Monday in June. It called for 1 chief of police, 2 captains, and 4 assistant captains. The rank of lieutenant was eliminated and replaced by the rank of sergeant. The rank of private was also eliminated and replaced by the rank of policeman. The ordinance authorized 8 sergeants and 120 policemen divided into two divisions, the night guard and the day guard.[35]

All members of the department had to be citizens of the United States and the state of Missouri and had to live in the city. They had to read, write, and speak the English language and could have no interest in any "tavern, inn, coffee house, or dram shop."[36] All had to take an oath of office. All members had to be appointed by the mayor, with the approval of the Board of Aldermen, and they served for one year. The day guard and the night guard each worked twelve-hour watches.

The first chief of police was Daniel A. Rawlings.[37] Not much is known about Rawlings. St. Louis city directories before 1856 list his occupation as "wood merchant." Rawlings was chief of police until 1861, when he was appointed the U.S. marshal in St. Louis.[38] His name last appears in city directories in 1866.

Policemen were to give their names and numbers to all persons who asked. They "shall never use their clubs except in the most urgent cases of self-defence." There was a separate section in the ordinance dealing with lost children; those whose parents or guardians could not be located by 9:00 a.m. the next day were to be taken to the House of Refuge. While walking their beats, officers had to report unlit, dirty, and damaged gaslights to their commanding officers. They had to report all persons found "throwing ashes, offal, vegetables, garbage, straw, shavings, filth, dirt or rubbish of any kind whatever, in any paved or macadamized street, lane, alley or public place in this city." They also had to report stray horses and cattle so that they might be secured. Police department regulations placed additional duties on the day police. At least twice a week officers of the day police had to examine the streets, alleys, sidewalks, and gutters on their beats and report any "nuisances" to the chief of police. "Nuisances" included "ashes, vegetable matter, offal or filth of any kind or description."[39] Both top-ranking officers and policemen were required to wear a uniform and a star while on duty. Finally, the ordinance granted the mayor and the chief of police the power to detail no more than eight members of the police force "to act as Detective Police." Members so designated were not required to do regular police duty.[40] Because of the problems the police department and its predecessors had, off and on, for almost fifty years, the ordinance and the rules and regulations were specific and in writing. The duties and responsibilities of each rank were precise, and the discipline for violations was supplied in great detail.

For the first time, the St. Louis police department was now a paid, uniformed department that patrolled the city around the clock. The chief of police was the commander of both divisions of the police department, the day and night guards.

In the meantime, policing in London and the rest of the United States had taken a step in a different direction. The London Metropolitan Police force was directed by appointees rather than elected officials. In 1857, the New York City Police Department, which had begun a full-time uniformed force twelve years earlier, came under the control of appointed police commissioners, becoming a "metropolitan" police department. The American version of metropolitan police, designed to wrest control of police departments from mayors who allegedly misused the police or were from the wrong political party, stemmed from the passage of a state law that placed the police department under the control of the governor of the state. The governor would appoint a board, consisting of citizens of the city, to be responsible for the operation of the police department. The only involvement of the city was to provide the funds the citizen police board requested for operation of the police department.

It was against this backdrop that Charles D. Drake, a member of the St. Louis delegation to the Missouri General Assembly, began the move to enact a metropolitan police bill for St. Louis. Drake, a newly elected Democrat, obtained a copy of the New York bill. He

Charles D. Drake. Photograph, ca. 1863. Missouri History Museum.

had, in his words, "taken from the so-called obnoxious New York bill that which he found to be good, and applied it to remedy the fearful state of things as they existed, in the present corrupt Police system of St. Louis."[41] Drake's comments touched upon one possible reason for pursuing the metropolitan police bill, "the present corrupt Police system of St. Louis." There were claims that the police force was inefficient, ineffective, and even corrupt, but those making such claims were likely to be Democrats or the *Missouri Republican* newspaper, which, contrary to what its name might imply, supported the Democrats. It was clear that, as in New York, there was conflict between the political parties controlling the state and the city. The Missouri governor was a Democrat, and the Missouri General Assembly was controlled by Democrats. Yet St. Louis was dominated by the Republicans.

Drake's bill was introduced in the Missouri House of Representatives in November 1859.[42] It provided for a five-member police board (four appointed by the governor with the consent of the Senate, as well as the mayor of St. Louis as an ex officio member) and, as in New York City, a "Police Life and Health Insurance Fund." In addition, the bill gave the police board power to appoint all officers and members of the fire department. It also vested in the board the sole duty of quelling all riots using policemen and fire equipment.[43]

Drake's bill was withdrawn for several reasons. First, other bills were seen as more pressing. Second, there were disagreements among members of the select committee that would perfect the bill for the House. Finally, city officials made a strong lobbying effort to have the police board elected by the citizens of St. Louis.[44] The bill was, however, to set the stage for the next legislative session.

✳   ✳   ✳

Several significant events occurred between the close of the 1859–1860 legislative session and the beginning of the 1860–1861 session:

1. In August 1860, Missouri voters elected a Democrat, Claiborne F. Jackson, as governor. Jackson was sympathetic to the South. A Democrat-controlled state legislature, which did not *at first* appear to be in Jackson's camp, was also elected.

2. In November 1860, Abraham Lincoln was elected president of the United States. Although Lincoln won in St. Louis, he lost Missouri.

3. In December 1860, South Carolina became the first state to secede from the Union.

After the close of the 1859–1860 legislative session, but before the first of these three events occurred, St. Louis city councilman Erastus Wells, who was chairman of the city waterworks committee, traveled to several large eastern cities to examine their waterworks systems. Wells wanted his committee to recommend the most modern system for St. Louis. As later related by his son, Wells also had

Erastus Wells. Steel engraving by A. H. Ritchie, 1883.
Missouri History Museum.

another interest: having the best possible police department in St. Louis. As he visited with the eastern city mayors, he asked about their police systems. The mayors of New York City, Boston, and Philadelphia told Wells that the metropolitan police system recently enacted in Baltimore was the best. Wells was able to get a copy of the Baltimore metropolitan police bill and changed it to comply with Missouri laws and the city charter. Even though the city council was generally against placing the police department under state control, Wells personally took it to the state capital at Jefferson City.[45] Wells's ideal of having the best possible police department for St. Louis by bringing it under state control was to fall victim to the passion and politics of the times.

Chapter Two

The War Years

BEGINNING WITH SOUTH CAROLINA in December 1860, the Southern states that would form the Confederate States of America began seceding from the Union. Missouri was a border state both geographically and ideologically, and St. Louis was a border city in a border state. Missourians fell into three loosely defined groups: those who wanted to immediately secede from the Union; those who fully supported the Union and were against secession; and "conditional Unionists," those who supported the Union but believed that the Southern states should not be coerced.[1]

In his inaugural address on January 2, 1861, governor-elect Claiborne Jackson said, "Missouri will not be found to shrink from the duty which her position upon the border imposes, her honor, her interests, and her sympathies point alike in one direction, and determine her to stand by the South."[2] The 1860–1861 Missouri legislature convened on the last day of 1860; on January 2, 1861, "they elected avowed Secessionists as officers."[3] Charles Drake, who had written the ill-fated 1859–1860 metropolitan police bill, later wrote in his autobiography that "probably not one member of either House had, before the people, been an *avowed* disunionist; but when that body assembled, it soon appeared that a majority in each house was made up of men of that stripe, who were ready to follow Claib. Jackson's traitorous lead."[4]

1861

On January 18, 1861, Governor Jackson recommended that a state convention be held in order to determine whether Missouri should secede from the Union. Virtually all members of the legislature, except the St. Louis delegation, voted to convene. The state convention began on February 28 with delegates elected by the citizens of Missouri. The governor presumed that the same people who elected the current pro-South administration and legislature would select a similar group of delegates. His presumption proved inaccurate, as not a single secessionist was selected for the convention. On March 22, the convention adjourned with the decision that Missouri would not secede. The former chief justice of the Missouri Supreme Court, Hamilton R. Gamble, who had become a dominant figure at the convention, wrote the final report. It was decided that the convention would reconvene on the third Monday in December. However, a committee of seven was appointed, one from each congressional district, to whom the power was delegated to call the convention together earlier if exigencies demanded.[5]

In the meantime, bills hostile to St. Louis and the Union were rushed through the legislature. Bills were introduced to arm and equip the militia, to increase the power of the governor, and to decrease the powers of the mayor of St. Louis.[6] One of the bills designated to do that was the metropolitan police bill, formally titled "An Act Creating a Board of Police Commissioners, and Authorizing the Appointment of a Police Force for the City of St. Louis." It was introduced in the Missouri Senate by Senator Joseph O'Neil of St. Louis on February 26, 1861. After the second and third readings, the Senate voted twenty-eight to three in favor of the measure; five members were absent and one was excused from voting.[7] The House of Representatives received the bill on March 4.

The first reading of the bill in the House didn't occur until March 22, the same day the state convention adjourned after the decision to remain in the Union. A motion that the rules be suspended was approved, and the bill was read a second time.[a] On March 25, the

---

[a] Bills had to be read three times, with an interval between each reading. On motion, the rules were suspended to eliminate the interval, and the second reading came immediately after the first. It was probably a political, and time, consideration; the General Assembly session would end the next week and there was pressure to enact the police bill.

House resumed deliberation of the act. Representative John D. Stevenson of St. Louis offered amendments to the Senate version that called for the election of the police commissioners by the citizens of St. Louis rather than appointment by the governor. Stevenson's amendments also would stagger the terms of the board members. His amendments were defeated.

When deliberation of the police bill was resumed later that day, Representative Stevenson offered additional amendments. One amendment would require all persons arrested by the police to be brought before the recorder of the city of St. Louis or a justice of the peace in the county. That amendment (Section 17 of the bill) was approved. The bill was then read a third time and passed in the House, as amended, by a vote of fifty to thirty-two. The bill was immediately returned to the Senate.[8]

At the evening session of the Senate, Senator Thomas C. Johnson of St. Louis called the bill. The House amendments were read, the rules were suspended, and the amendments were read a second and third time and then approved. The "metropolitan police" bill was sent to Governor Jackson, who signed it into law on Wednesday, March 27, 1861. The key features were the following:

1. Appointment by the governor, with the advice and consent of the Senate, of four residents of St. Louis as police commissioners, with the mayor serving as an ex officio member, for a term of four years. Each commissioner would receive $1,000 per year, paid quarterly. (The member selected as treasurer of the board would receive an additional $500 per year.)

2. Authorization for the board to employ a permanent police force to be equipped and armed as it judged necessary.

3. A provision that persons appointed as police officers by the board would serve for four years, subject to removal for cause and only after a hearing by the board. At the end of the four years, any officer who had "faithfully performed his duty" and was otherwise qualified to serve, would "be preferred by the board in making their new appointments."

4. A requirement that all promotions, except to chief of police, be made from the next lower rank.

5. The establishment of a fund for the relief of police officers, and the families of such officers, injured or killed in the discharge of police duties. The fund would be financed through rewards given to individual policemen (which they were not allowed to keep), fines levied against police by the board, and monies received from the sale of unclaimed property.

6. The setting of the number of officers in the various ranks and their salaries.

7. The requirement that the city of St. Louis must pay the entire cost of the police department.[9]

Equally interesting, however, was that the metropolitan police bill altered the city charter of St. Louis, prohibiting the city council from passing any law that conflicted or interfered with the exercise of powers by the Board of Police Commissioners. It imposed a $1,000 fine and lifetime disqualification from holding any office or being employed by the city or the police department for those who obstructed the board in the performance of the duties imposed upon them by the statute. The bill also said nothing about a nonpartisan or a bipartisan board.

It also required that the sheriff of St. Louis County come to the aid of the Board of Police Commissioners, when ordered, for "the preservation of the public peace and quiet." The board could order the sheriff to summon a posse comitatus for that purpose. In addition, constables and "any military force lawfully organized or existing in said city" would come under the command of the board when so ordered, for the purpose of aiding the Board of Police Commissioners "in preventing threatened disorder or opposition to the laws, or in suppressing insurrection, riot or disorder at all times...."[10]

The reaction of St. Louisans to the metropolitan police bill's passage was varied. Before the bill passed and was signed into law, the board of the common council of St. Louis passed a resolution, thirteen to four (with three abstentions), setting forth its objections to the bill. The account of the meeting in the *Missouri Republican* indicates that the board of the common council seemed most concerned about the police commissioners doing whatever they wished while the city had to unquestioningly pay the bills.[11] The *Republican* also ran articles about the merits of the newly instituted metropolitan police systems in Boston and Chicago.[12] The *Missouri Democrat*, on the other hand, editorialized that the bill was an "iniquitous and tyrannical measure."[13]

Governor Jackson, with the consent of the Senate, appointed the first police board on April 4, 1861. The commissioners were John A. Brownlee, James H. Carlisle, Basil Wilson Duke, and Charles McLaran.[14] Brownlee was a prominent member of the community,

Charles McLaran. Photograph, ca. 1880. Missouri History Museum.

the founder and president of a bank and president of an insurance company. Carlisle and Duke were lawyers. Before coming to St. Louis just before the outbreak of the war, McLaran had been the president of the First National Bank of Columbia, Mississippi. He became involved in public affairs in St. Louis, and would become one of the principals involved in the building of the Southern Hotel and, after the war, the co-owner of a wholesale hardware business.

All of the board members were characterized as secessionists.[15] With the possible exception of bank and insurance company president Brownlee, Duke was the board member most likely known to the general public. Before his appointment to the police board, Duke

Basil Wilson Duke. Photograph by E. & H. T. Anthony, New York, ca. 1863. Missouri History Museum.

was one of eight organizers and leaders of the Minute Men, a group of about three hundred men formed to spy on and harass the unionist Home Guard (formerly known as Wide Awakes), a paramilitary group augmented by members of the German *Turnverein* led by Frank Blair, a lawyer and politician. Many years after the Civil War, Duke wrote that "the chief and primary object of this organization [the Minute Men] was the capture of the arsenal."[16] The "arsenal" was the United States Arsenal (also called the St. Louis Arsenal), the largest military storehouse in the slave states and the principal supplier of arms and munitions for the army's Department of the West, which extended from the Mississippi River to the Rocky Mountains. While different figures have been cited, the arsenal was the storehouse for approximately 30,000 to 60,000 muskets, rifles, and carbines; 1,500,000 cartridges; as many as 90,000 pounds of powder; and 35 to 40 pieces of artillery.[17] It was the view of the *Missouri Democrat* that "the new police will be nothing but the Minute Men under another name."[18] As Duke would later claim, "the Police Bill was in reality a war measure, adopted to enable our people to control St. Louis . . . I knew the meaning of the measure, . . . and tried to carry it into action."[19]

On April 10, Brownlee, Carlisle, and McLaran took the oath of office before a circuit court judge. The three members of the board, plus the ex officio member, newly elected mayor Daniel G. Taylor, immediately met for an organizational meeting. (Duke was not present; he would make his first appearance at the board meeting of April 15.)[20] At the organizational meeting, Brownlee was elected president of the board and Carlisle was selected as treasurer. Two persons were nominated for the position of chief of police of the new St. Louis Metropolitan Police Department: John S. Bowen and James McDonough. McDonough, about forty-four years of age, was selected as chief.[21]

James McDonough, Chief of Police. Photograph, ca. 1890.
Missouri History Museum.

McDonough learned the carpentry trade in his native Baltimore. He came to St. Louis in 1839 and was believed to have been employed as a carpenter in the building of the Planters House hotel. When John Wimer was elected mayor in 1843, he appointed McDonough, then twenty-six years old, captain of the city guard. He served in that position until 1846. It was in that year that McDonough and one of his former lieutenants, Louis DeBreuil, formed the Independent Police, a private detective service. Later that year, because the detective agency wasn't doing sufficient business, McDonough supplemented his income by being elected township constable. He was reelected to another one-year term in 1847. After he was unsuccessful in a bid for county marshal in 1848, McDonough opened a tavern and, sometime later, moved to the western states where he traded cattle and lumber. He returned to St. Louis in 1860 and became the county tax collector.[22]

The board met a second time on the evening of April 10 and then went to city hall where Mayor Taylor "turned the Police Force over to the control of the Board, and Mr. Brownlee as President of the Board accepted the charge and installed the new Chief of Police. The Secretary was directed to give public notice of the organization of the Board by advertisement in the 'Republican' and 'State Journal.'"[23]

Although not required by law, the board decided to meet daily. On April 12, the day that St. Louisans learned of the bombardment of Fort Sumter by the Confederacy, the board issued a series of orders, which were published in the local press:

1. A notice that the "Sunday law," prohibiting all shows, exhibitions, games, plays, and liquor sales, would be strictly enforced.

2. A notice that "negroes" would no longer be granted permits by the chief of police for "parties or other assemblages. All saloons, or public house of whatever character, kept or owned by negroes are forbidden and will be suppressed."

3. A notice that "crowds or assemblages of idlers, loafers, or others on the prominent thoroughfares of the city, interfering with the legitimate use of the public streets and sidewalks, and the safety

and security of the good and orderly citizens, are positively prohibited; and the Chief of Police is strictly enjoined to see that the
spirit of this order is enforced."

4. A notice that "churches for negroes, or churches wherein negroes
   or mulattoes officiate as preachers, will not be allowed to open
   unless an officer of the police is present and appointed to be there
   by the undersigned (the president of the Board, John Brownlee)
   or the Chief of Police."

5. A notice that "the requirements of law in regard to slaves hiring
   their own time, in violation of law, will be rigidly enforced."

6. A notice that "all free negroes" found within the city limits without a "license" would be dealt with according to the law. The chief
   of police was given the order to "arrest all free negroes, mulattoes,
   or slaves found selling liquor, or keeping any house where liquor
   of any kind is sold, and to disperse all unlawful assemblages of free
   negroes, slaves, and mulattoes." In addition, all persons "keeping
   public gambling-houses or rooms wherein gambling is allowed"
   would be arrested.[24]

On April 15, Chief McDonough posted a notice in the press that
"all negroes found in the street after the hour of ten o'clock without
a proper pass will be arrested and brought before the recorder."[25]
The apparent purpose of these rules was to prevent disorder after the
attack on Fort Sumter. They were, obviously, directed at blacks, both
slave and free. However, the orders might also have beeen intended
to include another part of the population that could be perceived
as a threat: the large German American population that lived in
St. Louis. The First Ward, in the southernmost part of the city, was
almost exclusively German American. They were Republicans and
opponents of slavery in a Democrat-controlled, pro-slavery state.
German Americans saw the control of the police department taken
from the Republican city administration and placed in the hands of
Governor Jackson, whose four commissioners, in the words of the
editor of a German-language newspaper in St. Louis, *Anzeiger des
Westens,* "were all committed secessionists."[26]

The German community was also agitated by enforcement of the Sunday law, which apparently had been loosely enforced before the issuance of the board's orders. That law struck directly at the German lifestyle. Henry Boernstein, the founder and operator of the St. Louis Opera House and publisher of *Anzeiger des Westens,* noted that "the German theater gave its most important performances on Sunday, and on this day it made the most profits, for since German citizens lived either in the far north or far south of the city, it was almost impossible for them to get to the German theater (located in the center of the city) after the end of work or once their businesses closed on most days."[27]

On Sunday, April 14, two days after the orders had been published in the newspapers, Boernstein wrote that police were sent throughout the city to close all taverns, especially German taverns: "At the same time all evening concerts were abolished, so that a police captain came to me at 6 PM, an hour before the performance, informing me that there could be no further performances on Sunday by order of the commissioners."[28]

Boernstein debated the legality of the order, but the captain told him that obedience would be compelled. In spite of this, Boernstein opened the box office and prepared for the performance. He was soon visited by Chief McDonough and forty policemen, who closed the box office and blocked the entrances to the theater.

Boernstein told his performers that there would be no performance that evening. In the meantime, the police blockade of the entrances to the theater and the assembled customers drew crowds of onlookers. The crowd grew larger and became hostile:

> All that was needed was a spark to move this heated mass to action. The chief of police and his forty police stood nervously in a little group in front of the theater, crowded in by the mass on all sides. They had ordered the doors of the theater closed behind them, so their escape route had been cut off. The police chief could certainly have called for assistance, but by the time this arrived and worked its way through the mass of people (several thousands), they would have been given up to the wrath of an enraged mob.[29]

Chief McDonough asked Boernstein to tell the crowd to go home, assuring him that he would present his protest to the commissioners and not enforce the ban in the interim. Boernstein considered that a riot would result in the police being "pounded to a pulp," and the commissioners would then call for armed assistance. The result "would have been a dreadful bloodbath." Boernstein climbed on a table and asked the crowd to disperse "and show by your conduct that you are peaceful, orderly, free citizens." The crowd slowly broke up without incident, and police assistance arrived to find an empty street. Nonetheless, the St. Louis Opera House did not reopen because, as Boernstein later recalled, "the bloody tragedy of the American Civil War was about to begin on the great stage of the world, and in this tragedy we Germans played a leading role."[30]

On Friday, April 19, the minutes of the board indicate that "Mr. [Basil Wilson] Duke" offered a resolution to create a twenty-man corps of "special Police," commanded by a captain of police, whose duties were to suppress riots, but to also act as "secret Policemen," gathering information about the illegal organizing and arming of individuals. (The commander of the special police, Captain Rock Champion, was, with Duke, another of the Minute Men organizers.) Champion reported directly to the chief of police unless the information was something the captain believed the board should know at once. In that case, he would report directly to the board.[31]

The following day, April 20, the board met at its room in Arnot's Building, at 46 Chestnut Street. The board, which had probably been meeting at Brownlee's home, rented the facility on Chestnut. It would later become known as the police office, and a few months later it would, in addition, become the station house for the Second District.

On April 21, the board authorized President Brownlee to send a letter to Brigadier General William Harney, commander of the Department of the West, who was posted in St. Louis.[b] In the letter,

---

[b] Harney was a native of Louisiana. While his loyalty to the Union was never questioned, there was some concern among Missouri Unionists that his southern roots ran deep.

Brownlee asked Harney (1) to assume command of the arsenal and establish his headquarters there; (2) to prohibit the issue or distribution of arms to the citizens of Missouri; (3) to prohibit any citizen or inhabitant of Missouri to be armed or sworn into the service of the United States, a violation of existing laws and the express orders of Governor Jackson; and (4) to refuse to send arms to any sister state "for the purpose of arming one portion of the U.S. against the other." The board requested these actions, "as City and State officers," to preserve the peace and protect the persons and property of the citizenry "from internal violence, and at the same time prevent any possible collision between them and the United States Forces."[32]

General Harney replied the next day. He said that, with reference to request number 1, he had taken temporary quarters at the arsenal just before receiving the letter. With regard to the remainder, he stated that he was bound by the orders of the War Department.[33]

The board met in April and issued an "Order of Police Commissioners" to be printed in three daily city newspapers for one week. This proclamation announced the formation of "companies," two in each ward, to be sworn into service to act under the orders of the board and the chief of police to more effectively "suppress mobs or riots, and to protect the lives and property of the people." The board, then, would have ten companies of militiamen under its command. The proclamation concluded that "all companies so formed are requested to report at once at this office, where instructions more in detail will be furnished."[34]

At the same time, a "Notice to Citizens" from the chief of police was printed under the board's proclamation. The notice explained that "in consequence of the numerous burglaries" that were occurring each night, police officers were being instructed to stop anyone on the street after 1:00 a.m. "and respectfully inquire of them their residence, and if necessary, so accompany them home. Persons not giving satisfactory answers, or against whom suspicions are aroused, will at once be taken to the Police office."[35]

The minutes of the board meeting from the following Saturday indicate that the board had received a letter from General Daniel Frost informing them that troops from the U.S. Arsenal had begun occupying and fortifying the heights around the arsenal.[c] The board ordered "that protest be made to the Commanding Officer at the Arsenal against any such proceeding."[36] While the board did not enter the contents of the letter to the commander of the arsenal (Captain Nathaniel Lyon) in the minutes of that meeting, a copy of the letter they sent was published in the *Missouri Republican* on May 4. It said, in part: "We therefore, solemnly warn you, that attempts to occupy positions outside of the Arsenal enclosure, and within the limits of the city, are without authority of law, useless for your own protection, and dangerous in the extreme; and if they are persisted in, you must assume all the grave responsibilities which may result from your unauthorized acts."[37]

Captain Lyon replied in a very courteous tone, explaining how the situation was legal and offering examples from other parts of the country. He added, however, "and any consequences against which you would warn me, thus arising, it will be my duty, as I trust, my power, to meet."[38] There were other, unstated, reasons why the police commissioners did not want the federal troops on the bluffs overlooking the arsenal. These were to become evident in May.

On May 1, the board announced that it would, on May 8, "proceed to make a permanent police force for the City of St. Louis, in pursuance of law, commencing at 10 o'clock a.m."[39] The board began to run newspaper announcements informing the public of the plan to accept applications for appointments to the police force. Applicants for captains, lieutenants, sergeants, turnkeys,[d] and "calaboose keepers" would report to the police office at 10:00 a.m. on May 8. Applicants for the position of private would report to the police office at noon, Wednesday through Saturday, depending upon the first initials of their last names. The alphabet was divided over the four days.

---

[c] General Frost, a U.S. Military Academy graduate, resigned from the U.S. Army in 1853 and, in 1861, was the commander of the First Military District of the Missouri Militia. He would later serve as a general officer in the army of the Confederate States of America.

[d] It is likely that the turnkeys performed duties similar to those performed by turnkeys in later years: standing guard over prisoners held at the district station houses and, later, transporting them to the calaboose.

Meanwhile, events were taking place that would have rippling effects ranging from the operation of the St. Louis Metropolitan Police Department to the conduct of the Civil War. It was customary for the state militia in Missouri to encamp in their local areas for one week of training. General Frost asked Governor Jackson to order a formal encampment of the state guard and, in the meantime, send south for artillery to lay siege to the arsenal. Frost had originally selected the bluffs south and west of the arsenal for the encampment; the arsenal was within artillery range from both directions. The failure of the police board to have the federal troops removed from the bluffs caused Frost to change the location.

Governor Jackson ordered the state militiamen in the St. Louis area to assemble on Monday, May 6, at a location at the western city limits. They would remain encamped in this area, known as Lindell Grove, for one week.[40] The encampment, which General Frost named Camp Jackson (in honor of the governor), was approximately three miles from the arsenal.[e] Estimates of the number of militiamen in Camp Jackson range from five hundred to seven hundred.

In the meantime, Basil Wilson Duke and Colton Greene, another of the co-organizers of the Minute Men, were dispatched by Governor Jackson to Montgomery, Alabama, with letters to Confederate president Jefferson Davis. In the letters, Governor Jackson requested that Davis provide Duke and Greene with certain pieces of artillery, pieces specified in attached letters from General Frost:

> We started on April 6th and proceeded via Cairo [Illinois] to Memphis, thence via Chattanooga to Montgomery. . . . When we reached Montgomery we sent our credentials to President Davis and he received us at a meeting of his cabinet. . . . The President very cheerfully granted Governor Jackson's request, and gave us an order on the commandant of the arsenal at Baton Rouge for the guns specified in the list prepared by General Frost. [The arsenal at Baton Rouge was a federal arsenal that had been captured by the Confederacy.]

---

[e] On the same day, May 6, a new militia unit, the Reserve Corps of the St. Louis Police (also known as the Brownlee Guards), met and elected officers.

Having procured, on our order to the commandant of the arsenal, two twelve-pound howitzers, two thirty-two pound siege guns, some 500 muskets, and a quantity of ammunition, we returned to New Orleans to make arrangements for their transportation to St. Louis, and for that purpose chartered the steam-boat *Swan* [sic].[41]

Detail showing Camp Jackson on the Military Map of St. Louis, 1863.
Missouri History Museum.

Greene took charge of the boat while Duke preceded him to Cairo, Illinois, by rail. Duke then crossed the Mississippi River to New Madrid, Missouri, where he was (ironically) jailed by Southern sympathizers as a suspected Union spy. He was released upon the arrival of the *J. C. Swon.*

St. Louis Dispatch. **Painting of** *J. C. Swon* **by Harold G. Stratton, 1998.**
Courtesy of Harold G. Stratton.

Duke never attended another board meeting. He later recalled
that

> We reached St. Louis on the morning of May 9th and turned over
> the guns and munitions to Major Shaler, sent by General Frost to
> receive and take them to Camp Jackson. [General] Blair and [Cap-
> tain] Lyon were doubtless almost immediately informed in some
> way of their arrival and the disposition made of them, for the latter
> promptly prepared to seize them.[42]

> On the evening of the 9th the board of police commissioners
> became convinced, by a report of the chief of police, that a move-
> ment against the camp was imminent. The chief reported that the
> regiments into which the Wide Awake (Home Guard) companies
> had been organized were mustering at their respective points of
> rendezvous, and that ammunition had been distributed to them;
> also, that a number of horses had been taken into the arsenal for the
> purpose, he thought, of moving artillery. I went to the camp that
> night, notified General Frost of this information, and urged him to

prepare for an attack, which I believed would be delivered early the next morning...I soon became convinced that he had not decided on any line of action.[43]

Duke and Greene continued to the state capital at Jefferson City and met with Governor Jackson. They described the situation to him and told Jackson that Frost should not await an attack on Camp Jackson, but should either go on the offensive (that is, lay siege to the arsenal) or retreat to some point less vulnerable to attack.[44] While they were meeting with Jackson, they were informed that Lyon had gone on the attack and that Frost's entire command had surrendered.

Indeed, Captain Lyon had known about the artillery and munitions arriving in St. Louis.[45] He might have seized them on the wharf, but obviously wanted them to reach their destination, Camp Jackson. Lyon, disguised in women's clothing, then toured Camp Jackson in a carriage. And, although he had been encouraged to serve a writ of attachment for the return of the stolen federal artillery in Camp Jackson, he declined to follow that route. Lyon was determined to capture Camp Jackson.

The following day, May 10, Lyon marched the three miles from the arsenal to Camp Jackson with his regulars and volunteer regiments composed of the now federalized Home Guard, virtually all of them German Americans. Lyon's troops numbered six thousand or more. When they reached Camp Jackson, they surrounded it and demanded unconditional surrender.

The sight of six thousand or so troops marching through the city drew a crowd. Once the destination of the troops was known, thousands of people descended on the site. They arrived by every mode of transportation. Some brought lunches. Some, including several secessionists, brought guns. Frost surrendered his entire command and they were taken prisoner and held on Olive Street, the northern edge of Camp Jackson, awaiting orders.

The wait turned into hours. Tensions mounted and taunts were hurled from the crowd; most of them were aimed at the heavily German Home Guards. The taunts became rock throwing and then someone fired a weapon from the crowd. A Home Guard captain fell wounded, and some of the Home Guard returned the fire. When the shooting stopped, twenty-eight persons, including children, had been killed and others wounded. None, it was later determined, had been shot by Lyon's regulars. The prisoners were eventually marched the three miles to the arsenal, fed, and bedded down for the night.

The day was not yet over. Groups of people gathered on the main thoroughfare in the city. Some carried banners espousing a variety of positions. There were fights and shouting, and sometimes a shot could be heard. Fearing a riot, some businesses closed; there was what was described as a "mass exodus" of citizens from the city; and the president of the police board made arrangements with General Harney to detach four hundred infantry and artillery regulars to the central part of the city. And, while there was no evidence of the police being anywhere near Camp Jackson at the time of the engagement, they were on duty that night:

> As the crowd rushed down Locust Street and across Second Street, they were greeted by a platoon of thirty policemen, who, with bayonets fixed, were in line extending across the street and facing the mob. The chief soon gave them to understand that his duty was to keep the peace, and he intended faithfully to discharge that duty. The crowd reflected, and hearing orders given, in case of resistance, to use both ball and bayonet, set up a shout of derision, but did not advance. Finally, convinced they were wasting time in that locality, they turned around, and shouting "Anzeiger!" "Anzeiger!" [*Anzeiger des Westens,* the Unionist German-language newspaper] moved off to attack that office. [Chief of Police] McDonough had some of his men there also, but they were strongly backed by a company or two of Sigel's soldiers.[46]

The crowd also intended to attack the offices of the *Missouri Democrat,* but the police were guarding that location as well. A gun store was broken into and fifteen to twenty guns were taken before Chief McDonough and the musket-armed police officers arrived to disperse the mob and secure the building. Chief McDonough and the police department received high marks from the public for the job they did on the night of May 10.[47]

The next day, May 11, all the materials captured at Camp Jackson were taken to the arsenal. Included were the howitzers, siege guns, muskets, and munitions that had been stolen from the arsenal at Baton Rouge. On that same day, the men taken into custody at Camp Jackson were offered an immediate parole if they swore that they would not again take up arms against the United States. Only one refused to take the oath of allegiance. Of those who did take it, most later joined the army of the Confederacy.[48]

Basil Wilson Duke never returned to St. Louis. While he and Colton Greene were in Jefferson City reporting to Governor Jackson, a high-placed lawyer friend in St. Louis sent a message to Duke that he would be arrested if he returned to St. Louis. Instead, Duke went to his home state of Kentucky where, in June 1861, he married the sister of Confederate cavalryman John Hunt Morgan. He enlisted in Morgan's rifle company and was elected to the rank of lieutenant. He would be wounded at the Battle of Shiloh, captured, exchanged, and rise to the rank of brigadier general.[49] Duke would later serve in the Kentucky legislature.

On May 21, the remaining three members of the Board of Police Commissioners met and swore in fifty-four more special police. The minutes of the meeting did not state whether they were, like the twenty appointed before them, "secret" police. Captain Champion, the commander of the original twenty special (secret) police, was ordered "stricken off the roll" for "having absented himself beyond leave."[50]

Basil Duke was appointed to the board to replace his cousin, Basil Wilson Duke. He attended his first meeting on May 25. A Kentucky native, Basil Duke received his undergraduate degree from Yale College and a law degree from Transylvania University in Lexington, Kentucky. Duke came to St. Louis and opened a law practice in 1848, remaining in St. Louis until his death in 1885.[51]

In the meantime, the board had interviewed all of the applicants for the permanent police force. On May 29, the board published a list of those appointed to the force. The list, which was published daily through June 1, included 3 captains, 3 lieutenants, 12 sergeants, 214 privates, 4 turnkeys, 1 clerk, and 1 calaboose keeper.

The officers and policemen of the permanent police force were sworn in by board president John Brownlee between 11:00 a.m. and noon on Monday, June 3. Chief McDonough gave a speech during which he presented the individual ranks their charges. The men then met with the captains to receive their assignments. St. Louis now had its metropolitan police.

Sadly, within the first sixty days of the new department, two policemen were killed, one in a bizarre incident. At 10:00 a.m. on June 17, policeman Nehemiah M. Pratt was standing on the outside second-floor balcony of the Recorder's Court on the east side of Seventh Street, between Olive and Pine streets. Pratt had been testifying in the Recorder's Court. When he and others in the court heard martial music, he stepped onto the balcony to see the troops, a battalion of Home Guards, as they marched south on Seventh Street. The clerk and the marshal of the Recorder's Court, a lawyer, and a reporter for the *Evening News* had also gone onto the balcony.[52] As they watched, they heard the sound of a gunshot.

The Home Guard battalion turned toward the east and fired a volley of shots into the homes and buildings along the entire block. (Later, seventy-two bullet marks were found on various buildings.) The volleys seemed to be concentrated on the balcony of the Recorder's Court. Officer Pratt, who had joined the police department in 1850, was shot through the left breast. Four other civilians, who were on the street, were also killed, two were mortally wounded, and there were several injuries.[53]

Pratt was taken back into the courtroom, where it was determined that he was still alive. He was then taken to his home on Eleventh Street, between Cass Avenue and O'Fallon Street.[54] It is not known whether he died en route or at home.

Because of the number of witnesses, an inquest lasted more than a week. On Friday, June 28, the coroner's jury returned its verdict. The jury found that those killed in the incident, including Officer Pratt, all died from gunshot wounds "by Minie musket balls, discharged by certain members of Companies C, E, F, B, and I, of the Second Regiment of the United States Reserve Corps, whilst they were marching down Seventh street, on the morning of the 17th inst."[55] The identities of the soldiers responsible for the killings could not be determined. On July 2, a criminal court grand jury was sworn in to investigate what was called the "Seventh Street Tragedy."[56] It was never determined, however, who had fired the ball that killed Officer Pratt.[57] The officer was interred in Bellefontaine Cemetery.

Since the Board of Police Commissioners had yet to institute the relief fund established by the metropolitan police bill, there were no funds for Pratt's widow and two children. Fellow police officers began to individually contribute money toward a goal of $300. The *Missouri Republican* reported that in the "central [second] district," officers had contributed $50.[58]

A second officer was killed on July 5. Officer Thomas Kirk learned that one Charles Zuckswart, who was wanted for a serious assault, was at his home in the area of Fourteenth and Biddle streets.[59] Kirk enlisted the aid of a fellow officer, Edward T. Davis, to assist him in arresting the wanted subject. Zuckswart, however, saw the officers approaching and locked his doors. While Kirk positioned himself at the front door, Davis walked around the house and opened a back window. Officer Davis had climbed partly through the window when Zuckswart pointed a loaded musket at him and pulled the trigger. The percussion cap exploded, but the weapon did not fire.

Officer Kirk, hearing the explosion of the cap, broke through the locked door and entered the house. Zuckswart rushed at him and ran him through with a triangular-shaped bayonet attached to the musket. Kirk pulled his pistol, but he was thrown to the floor and Zuckswart wrested the gun from him. Zuckswart was removing the bayonet when he heard Officer Davis quickly approaching from his rear. Zuckswart turned and fired at Davis, but the bullet just missed Davis's head. Before Zuckswart could fire another shot, Davis struck him two or three times with his club, knocking him to the floor. While Kirk was carried to Sisters Hospital, Davis applied pincers to Zuckswart's wrist and took him to the calaboose.

Officer Kirk died from the wound on July 10. He was buried in Calvary Cemetery on July 13 after a Mass at the Catholic cathedral at Second and Walnut streets. The funeral procession consisted of a long train of carriages headed by the Emmet Guard and the entire night police force. He was unmarried and believed to have been thirty-three years of age.

Charles Zuckswart was indicted for murder by the criminal court grand jury and was arraigned on July 21. Jury selection began on Saturday morning, July 27, and the trial began later that day. The case went to the jury on Monday, July 29. Criminal Court Judge Henry A. Clover instructed the jury to keep in mind that "police officers have no right to enter a man's house without a warrant except in cases where they are themselves immediate witnesses of the man's crime."[60] The jury deliberated for less than half an hour and returned a verdict of "manslaughter in the third degree." The jury recommended six months in the county jail.[61] Judge Clover followed the recommendation of the jury.

Meanwhile, the police board, which now met twice a week, busied itself with the affairs of a police department: permitting the chief to employ and pay detectives, making personnel transfers, hearing complaints against officers, and administering discipline. On some scheduled meeting days the minutes note that there was no business to conduct.

There were, however, others conducting business that would affect the metropolitan police. On June 11, Governor Jackson met with now General Lyon in St. Louis. (Lyon was appointed a brigadier general in May, succeeding General Harney as commander of the Department of the West.) Jackson offered to disband the state guard if the Union Volunteers were disarmed, federal troops from other states were kept out of Missouri, and Lyon's out-of-state recruiting activities were halted. Lyon exploded, stating that rather than concede to the state of Missouri the right to demand these things of the federal government, he would see Jackson and "every man, woman and child in the state dead and buried." He then told Governor Jackson, "This means war. In an hour one of my officers will call for you and conduct you out of my lines."[62]

Jackson and other state officials accompanying him got on a train for Jefferson City. Jackson then put out a call for militiamen, burned two bridges to the capital, gathered the state seal and some records, and went to Boonville, a small town on the Missouri River east of

the capital. Within forty-eight hours, General Lyon and two thousand troops had taken a steamboat upriver to Boonville and quickly
defeated Jackson's militia. The governor and the state guard retreated
southward.

In early July, under pressure from Hamilton R. Gamble, who
thought that Lyon was too inexperienced, President Lincoln replaced
Lyon with Major General John C. Frémont as commander of the
Department of the West.

Hamilton R. Gamble. Photograph by Scholten, 1860s.
Missouri History Museum.

With Governor Jackson gone, the state was without leader-
ship. On July 22, the state convention was reconvened to select new
state leaders. Jackson and other state officials were deposed, and the
group voted to establish a provisional government with Gamble

as governor. The convention passed a military bill to raise a loyal state militia. Gamble also needed to replace the police board with a more loyal board.[63]

Before he could do so, however, General Frémont made a decision bearing on the board. He declared martial law in St. Louis. On August 14 he proclaimed: "I hereby declare and establish martial law in the city and county of St. Louis. Major J. McKinstry, United States Army, is appointed Provost Marshal. All orders and regulations issued by him will be respected and obeyed accordingly."[64]

The *Missouri Republican,* which published Frémont's declaration, noted on the same page that "Major McKinstry has caused the arrest of John A. Brownlee, Esq. [the president of the police board], and he has been sent to the Arsenal." Brownlee was arrested for consorting with the enemy. In that same column the *Republican* also announced that "Bazil [sic] Duke, Esq., is appointed President of the Police Commissioners, and the laws of the State and city will be executed without any change."[65] There is, however, no mention in the board minutes of Duke being elevated to president of the board.

The board met on August 16. The minutes state that Charles McLaran, the vice president of the board, presided over the meeting; the same would be true throughout the remainder of the board's time in office. Board president Brownlee is not listed as attending any of the meetings after August 13, nor is there any explanation in the minutes for his absence.

Meanwhile, Provost Marshal McKinstry instituted strict penalties for carrying concealed weapons, and gunsmiths and dealers were not allowed to sell or give away any weapons without his permission. Theaters, dance halls, and concert halls had to close by 10:30 p.m. during the week and all day on Sunday. Street assemblages were not permitted and "spiritous liquors" could not be sold on Sunday. On August 26, McKinstry closed all saloons except those in major hotels. He also closed several local newspapers for anti-Union sentiments and banned the sale of several out-of-state newspapers for being "seditious."[66] The operations of the police department and other civil authorities would not be affected, but the line between military and civil authority would be blurred until the end of martial law in March 1865.

On August 18, Frémont wrote a letter to Governor Gamble in which he recommended that the current members of the police board be changed. Said Frémont:

> I mention the fact that, the freight on the arms brought from Baton Rouge and deposited at Camp Jackson was paid by the Police Commissioners and that Policemen superintended & guarded these arms in their transit from the Boat to the Camp ... these men should not any longer be allowed to wield power in our midst which enables them under the color of law to subvert all law and aid the traitors who are seeking to overthrow our Government.[67]

Frémont added that Gamble's failure to act would "compel" him, as military head of the Department of the West, to remove the board members. And, said Frémont, since the new board members would be interacting with him, he had the names of four people he thought would be "suitable."

The last board meeting held by the first Board of Police Commissioners was Friday, September 6, 1861. A week before, on August 30, they had seen the officers of the police department pin on their new stars. Unlike the first star, the new star had the "Missouri coat of arms worked upon it" to designate the department's state affiliation.[68]

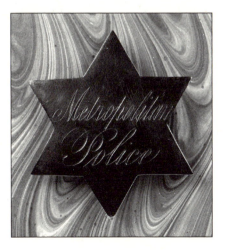

Early silver St. Louis Metropolitan Police star. Photograph by David Schultz, 1999. Missouri History Museum.

On Monday, September 9, Mayor Taylor, John How (the former mayor of St. Louis), and William Patrick met to serve as members of the second Board of Police Commissioners. (It is probably not coincidental that How and Patrick were two of the four names recommended by General Frémont.) The minutes of that meeting note that Brownlee had resigned, and Carlisle, Duke, and McLaran had been removed from office by Governor Gamble. How was elected president of the board; two appointments remained. The board continued to meet twice a week, usually on Tuesday and Friday.

John How. Photograph of a lithograph, mid-nineteenth century.
Missouri History Museum.

At their second meeting, on September 11, the minutes note that the chief of police had supplied the commissioners with the names of everyone employed on the force. On September 17, the board announced that the size of the force would be reduced. It then dismissed five policemen. Several more were later dismissed as the reduction in force continued. On September 24, Chief McDonough lost his job. The minutes of that date note the adoption of the following resolution: "Resolved that the confidence does not exist between the Board and its Chief that should exist. It is therefore declared that the office will be considered vacant on the First of October 1861."[69] The new chief of police was not announced until October 18. While there is no record of an interim chief, that duty probably fell to one of the captains.[70]

The minutes note that on October 18 a third police commissioner, John Riggin, joined the board.[f] The board then voted for a new chief of police. John E. D. Couzins was unanimously elected. To save

John E. D. Couzins. Photograph by William Brown, 1859–1867. Missouri History Museum.

money, the board paid Chief Couzins an annual salary of $1,500 per year, $500 fewer than authorized by the 1861 statute.

Couzins had been a member of the city guard beginning in the early 1840s, and in 1846 he became a lieutenant. He was demoted

---

[f] A fourth member was never appointed to this board. And, while the 1861 statute provided for staggering the appointments, the How board remained intact until January 1865.

to private in 1847. The city marshal then made Couzins one of his deputies so that he could pursue a line of work at which he was especially adept, detective work. In 1850, he was made captain of the city guard.[71]

Sometime between Abraham Lincoln's election in November 1860 and his inauguration in March 1861, Couzins and five other men were appointed by "the Union men" in St. Louis to become the Committee of Safety. One member of the committee was John How, now president of the Board of Police Commissioners.[72] James O. Broadhead, another of the six, later described the work of the committee and Couzins's participation in the organization. The committee was responsible, said Broadhead, for

> consolidating the Union strength in Missouri, and in organizing volunteer troops to be mustered into the service when called for . . . four regiments in St. Louis; we had to watch the movements of the enemy in the preparations they were making to take Missouri out of the Union; the headquarters of the rebel movement was in St. Louis until the taking of Camp Jackson by Gen. Lyon.

> Major Couzins was our Chief Executive Officer; he had a small detective force under him which was employed by us, *but his services were gratuitous;* he reported to us every night such facts as were important for us to know; his was an important and perilous service, and such as the Government at that time had no means for performing, on account of the small military force it had west of the Mississippi . . . Major Couzins performed services at that time which were invaluable to the Union cause. . . .[73]

The work of the Committee of Safety was formally recognized by President Lincoln in a special order of April 13, 1861. On October 1, 1861, Couzins was called to Washington, D.C., by Attorney General Edward Bates.[g] He apparently planned an intelligence mission that would send the two men he selected through the Confederate lines south of St. Louis. Couzins left Washington on October 7 and was appointed chief of police upon his return.

---

[g] Bates, a Missourian who was nationally known, was the brother-in-law and law

Not much is known about board treasurer William Patrick. The board minutes identified him only by name. City directories of the time list a William Patrick as a partner in the firm of Ladd, Patrick and Company, which owned the Mississippi Planing Mill at Thirteenth and O'Fallon streets. Patrick also apparently owned, with James Patrick, a lumberyard in the 1600 block of Washington Avenue.[74]

The third member of the board, John Riggin, owned, with his son, John Riggin, Jr., a real estate firm, John Riggin and Son, located at 43 Chestnut Street, just east of the central police office and Second District station house. During the Civil War, Riggin's son was a colonel in the U.S. Army and an aide to Major General Ulysses S. Grant.[75] All three appointed members of the board were known to be strong Union supporters.

On November 12, the board passed a resolution that all officers of police and patrolmen of the city would be required to produce evidence of their citizenship and subscribe to the oath that was required of each civil officer of the state. Meanwhile, the board continued to reduce the size of the police force. By April 1862, it would be reduced from 207 to 175. Those discharged in the reduction in force had expressed "loud and frequent expression of secession sentiments, and their sympathy with traitors and rebels, and for inefficiency (and so forth)."[76] Also, the first set of departmental rules and regulations for the new metropolitan police department were completed near the end of 1861.

A third police officer was killed in December. Late on the night of December 9, two burglars were leaving a house they had just plundered at Broadway and Jefferson, when they awakened the occupants. The burglars ran from the house as they were being pursued by at least one of the occupants. Police sergeant John Gilmore joined in the pursuit. The burglars dropped the items they had taken and made their escape. Sergeant Gilmore suspected Billy Wilson and Pat Malroy, alias Pat Burns, of being the burglars. Gilmore knew where the two suspects lived, and he and two other officers placed the rooming house under

partner of Missouri's provisional governor of 1861, Hamilton Gamble. Bates had been a member of the Missouri Constitutional Convention in 1820 and was a former congressman.

surveillance through the night. The next morning, while Gilmore sent the two officers for breakfast, he entered the rooming house and was in the kitchen when Wilson and Malroy appeared. Gilmore placed them under arrest.

As they were leaving, Sergeant Gilmore agreed to Wilson's request that he be allowed to get his coat. When Wilson returned, he attacked the officer with a "slungshot."[77] Gilmore tried to pull his pistol, but Wilson began striking him on the head with the slungshot while Malroy held him. Sergeant Gilmore was able to fight back while attempting to get outside the house. As they continued to fight in front of the house, one of the two shot Gilmore in the jaw and the two escaped. It is not known whether one of the suspects had a pistol or was able to get Gilmore's weapon.

On December 24, Sergeant Gilmore died, apparently from complications arising from the gunshot. On Friday afternoon, December 27, Gilmore's funeral and procession were attended by Chief Couzins, the three district captains, and 150 policemen. Based upon information from an informant, Billy Wilson and Pat Malroy were arrested in Pittsburgh, Pennsylvania, in December 1862. They were both tried and convicted of the murder of Sergeant John Gilmore and were hanged in the old St. Louis jail yard. A fund-raising ball was later held for the officer's widow; it was attended by a great number of people and netted $1,800.[78]

1862

The year 1862 was relatively quiet for the police department. On January 3, the board minutes noted approval of the payment of $213 to the *Republican* office for printing and binding five hundred copies of "Rules and Regulations of Police Department."[79] And, at the end of November, the board approved a $500 raise for Chief Couzins, bringing his salary to the $2,000 cap.[80]

Easily overlooked is a notation in the minutes of December 9. Under "bills paid" is a line noting that the board paid A. W. Wood (Woods) $35.50 "for daguerreotypes." A week later, the same amount was paid to Woods "for Rogues daguerreotypes."[81] These are the first official references to a photographic rogues' gallery for the eighteen-month-old metropolitan police department. According to a newspaper article, about 600 rogues' gallery daguerreotypes, ferrotypes (tintypes), and ambrotypes were still maintained by the police department in 1891.[82] Of these, 197 rogues' gallery ferrotypes and ambrotypes were mounted in a frame, with a label indicating that they dated from 1843 to 1867. The earliest dated photo is from October 3, 1857. Other recorded information, besides the date, "is the name, alias, physical description, and crime."[83]

1863

On March 27, 1863, exactly two years after Governor Jackson signed the metropolitan police bill into law, another policeman was mortally wounded. Sergeant John Sturdy and Officer Francis Hack arrested a man for disturbing the peace on Second Street, between Plum and Cedar. The two officers began walking south on Second Street with their prisoner, intending to take him to the First District station house. About a block from the scene of the arrest, two men described as companions of the prisoner attacked Sturdy and Hack in an effort to rescue him. One of them grabbed Sturdy's club and began striking him on the head with it. They disabled Hack by fracturing his left arm. The two then began kicking Sturdy, who had been knocked to the ground, and stopped only upon the approach of additional police officers. The three ran from the scene.

Sturdy was taken to his home on Fourth Street, where he was treated by two physicians. Hack, who lived near the arsenal, also was assisted home and treated for his fractured arm. Sturdy died from his injuries on April 10. He was about thirty-three years of age and had joined the police department before it became the metropolitan force. He left a wife and three children.

The 1863–1864 General Assembly amended the 1861 Metropolitan Police Act. The first amendment, approved on December 12, 1863, revised several sections of the 1861 statute. The mayor of

St. Louis was appointed ex officio president of the Board of Police Commissioners, with the vice president of the board serving as acting president in the absence of the mayor. The board was authorized to increase the size of the police force by one captain and thirty policemen and to give the members of the force a pay raise. The board was to estimate the cost of the additional men and the increases in pay and certify the amount to the common council of St. Louis for payment. The total cost of the police department for fiscal year 1863–1864 could not exceed $175,000.[84]

The second amendment, passed on February 5, 1864, was obviously a response to city fathers who wanted to know where the city was supposed to get the additional money for the police department. The statute ordered the common council, beginning with fiscal year 1864, to annually levy an additional tax of one-tenth of 1 percent on all property subject to state taxes. The money received was to be placed in a special fund to be used solely by the police department. Apparently in the spirit of a metropolitan police force (and lowering the overall expense to the city), the statute also ordered that, beginning in 1864, the county of St. Louis would be responsible for one-fourth of the expenses of the police department.[85]

1864

In January 1864, the board met to reorganize under the December 1863 statute that made the mayor the ex officio president. The board had invited Mayor Chauncey I. Filley to the first board meeting under the amended statute, but Mayor Filley did not attend.[h] Former board president John How was then elected vice president; William Patrick

---

[h] The minutes of the board fail to indicate the presence of Mayor Filley at any meeting during the remainder of his term. He became, in 1861, the first mayor to serve the new two-year term. He was reelected in April 1863, but had to leave office because of illness. James S. Thomas was elected to complete Filley's term, which ended in April 1865, but he did not attend any meetings of this board.

was reelected treasurer. In April 1864, the board began a new inspection policy. The chief of police, or someone designated by him, had to inspect each district monthly, with special attention directed at the condition of the uniforms worn by the men. Each officer was required to buy his own uniform, and those newly appointed to the force had to be in uniform during the second month of service.

When the board, on February 18, sent a requisition to the county of St. Louis for $7,000 (one-quarter of the expenses for January and February), the county refused to pay. The board then applied to the Missouri Supreme Court for a writ of mandamus. The court issued a conditional writ, and the county responded to it.

The opinion of the Supreme Court was read by Chief Justice Barton Bates, who found no validity to the arguments of the county. The county was ordered to pay one-quarter of the expenses of the St. Louis Metropolitan Police Department beginning with the requisition for January and February. The other two members of the three-member Supreme Court, Justices William V. N. Bay and John D. S. Dryden, concurred.[86]

1865

In January 1865, the board began to close out its term. It burned over $107,000 in counterfeit notes that had been seized during its tenure; ordered that all unclaimed property such as trunks, valises, and clothing be distributed to the Soldiers' Home, the Soldiers' Orphans' Home, and the Girls' Industrial School; and conducted an inventory of all police property in the city. The three district station houses were inspected and found in good order. The First District station house, at the junction of Fourth and Fifth streets near the South Market, would soon have to be vacated; it was scheduled to be torn down to make way for a new street, Chouteau Avenue. The How board held its last meeting on Wednesday, January 31, 1865.

Slavery was abolished in Missouri in January; martial law in St. Louis would end in March; and the Civil War would end in April. St.

Louis was now a city of sixteen square miles with a population that doubled between 1850 and 1860 and would double again by 1870. The police department could now expend its energies and resources policing the rapidly growing city.

Chapter Three

A Peacetime Metropolitan Police

AS 1865 BEGAN, THE CIVIL WAR was coming to an end; Abraham Lincoln was preparing for his second term as president; Missouri had a new governor, Thomas C. Fletcher; St. Louis City voters had reelected Mayor James S. Thomas; and Missouri was about to acquire a new constitution. The Missouri Constitutional Convention convened at the Mercantile Library in St. Louis in January. On January 11, following approval by the delegates of the Constitutional Convention, Governor Fletcher issued a proclamation of immediate emancipation of slaves in Missouri.

1865

Governor Fletcher was the first native Missourian and the first Republican elected to the office. He was a Radical Republican who appointed a new police board of Radical Republicans.[1] The new board members were approved by the Senate and took office on February 1. As mayor, James Thomas became the ex officio president of the board.[a] Thomas was also a Radical Republican.[2] The members appointed by the governor, Ferdinand Meyer, N. H. Clark, Bernard Laibold, and E. H. E. Jameson, were prominent members of the city, but each had different strengths. Meyer was a principal in the hide and leather firm of Meyer

---

[a] Mayor Thomas would be elected to another two-year term in 1867. His second term would be punctuated by an ongoing feud with the police board that resulted in the mayor boycotting police board meetings, two attempts to return the control of the police department to the mayor, and an investigation by a joint committee of the Missouri General Assembly.

and Braun, Clark owned a men's furnishings store, Laibold was a colonel with the Second Missouri Regiment, and Jameson was a partner in the land and claim agents firm of Moss and Jameson. At their first meeting, Meyer was elected vice president of the board, and Jameson was elected treasurer.

The election of Ferdinand Meyer as the vice and acting president of the board would prove to be a wise choice. He would be the one constant on a police board that, in the early postwar years,

Ferdinand Meyer. Photograph by Latour Photographers, Sedalia, MO, ca. 1870. Missouri History Museum.

would have a high turnover rate. Under Meyer, the Board of Police Commissioners would draw upon the greater experiences of the eastern police departments, would be innovative in its own right, and would be most controversial.

Martial law in St. Louis ended on March 9. The milestone was met with little fanfare. The police board continued to ready the metropolitan police force to serve in peacetime. The board appointed E. H. E.

Jameson to meet with a general officer of the U.S. Army to determine how to organize the police force like a military organization.

On March 16, John Couzins tendered his resignation as chief of police. The board passed resolutions citing his importance in suppressing crime in the city and aiding the Union cause, and his loyalty to both.[3] The board "then proceeded to ballot for the election of a new Chief of Police, to which office Col. Bernard Laibold was unanimously elected."[4] Laibold would be the third chief of the metropolitan police department and the first member of the Board of Police Commissioners to become the chief of police.

A summer police uniform was agreed upon late in March. The uniform was to consist of one blue blouse of flannel and trousers of heavy brown linen. A blue cloth cap would be worn. The cap would have a new silver-plated star in front with the raised letters "M.P." and the officer's number on it. No star was worn on the breast.

Turnkeys would wear the same uniform, but their star would have the word "Turnkey" on it. Officers of the rank of sergeant and

Star probably designed in March 1865. Courtesy of St. Louis Metropolitan Police Department (hereafter SLMPD).

higher (referred to as "officers" in the minutes of the board meetings) would have a blouse made of "finer cloth." All metal insignia, buttons, and belt plates would be gold, and the rank of the officer would be engraved on the star. The chief of police would wear a shield instead of a star, with "Chief of Police" engraved on it. Each police officer had to buy his uniform from the vendor authorized by the board. Insignia, belt plate, and buttons were furnished by the board. It was also decided that the police would display the new uniforms at a "public demonstration and parade" on the first day of May.[5] The demonstration and parade were to be a part of the dedication of Lafayette Park.

Before the end of March, the board authorized Commissioner Clark, Chief Laibold, and former Chief Couzins to "visit the principal cities of the United States." In this first-ever tour of the major cities east of the Mississippi River, the committee was to learn more about the operations of metropolitan police departments and other police systems to gain "such other knowledge as will be of benefit to the Police system of St. Louis."[6] Because the larger cities of the eastern part of the United States had been in operation for several years before the police department in St. Louis, eastern cities would be visited almost annually by board members, the chief, or both. The visits were an effort to stay abreast of technological and administrative improvements in policing and changes in law enforcement techniques. The committee would be gone more than three weeks.

On March 28, the board welcomed a new commissioner, James M. Corbitt, to replace now chief of police Bernard Laibold. Corbitt was a principal in the firm of Beck and Corbitt, iron merchants, with offices on the levee. He was also the chairman of the St. Louis school board.

At the end of March, the board named Detective John Eagan the first detective supervisor, with the title of sergeant of detectives. Eagan was provided with a desk in the police commissioner's room.

On April 9, General Robert E. Lee surrendered, ending almost five years of war. Governor Fletcher announced that Saturday, April 15, would be celebrated as a day of thanksgiving. Thanksgiving turned to grief, however, when the news filtered through the city that President Lincoln had been shot Friday night by an actor, John Wilkes Booth. Booth was known to many St. Louisans, having played a week's engagement in the city in January 1864.[7] The fact-finding committee of Commissioner Clark, Chief Laibold, and Couzins were en route to St. Louis from Chicago when the news reached them. While Clark and Laibold continued to St. Louis, Couzins left for Pennsylvania to assist in the search for Booth.[8] The board would later give Chief Laibold and Sergeant of Detectives Eagan leaves of absence to attend President Lincoln's burial in Springfield, Illinois.

As a result of the tour of the eastern cities, the committee made two major recommendations. First, it recommended a "police telegraph," which would be connected between the police stations and the residences of the mayor, chief of police, and the police commissioners. Second, the committee recommended that, instead of renting, the police buy or build its own police stations. Police authorities in New York City even loaned the committee the architectural plans used by that department to build precinct station houses.[9] A third recommendation was also considered. Clark, Laibold, and Couzins recommended that the board institute a Police School of Instruction such as they had observed in the police department of New York City. It would be another three years, however, before the actual establishment of such a school.

The reopening of Lafayette Park was delayed until Monday, May 15.[10] The police demonstration and parade were also postponed to coincide with the park opening. Following the event, on May 16, the *Missouri Democrat* allotted a great deal of space to describe the newly renovated park and the new uniforms of the police on parade: "The large white metal buttons—the silver stars of the first magnitude—the standing collars of the coats—the whitish linen pantaloons, and the short clubs excited the wonder of the good citizens, and all eyes were turned upon the moving constellation, as it proceeded like a portable 'milky way' up the crowded [Fourth] street."[11]

The police parade ended at the park. Speeches were made by the mayor, the chief of police, two police captains, a police sergeant, and an attorney. Afterward, Staehlin's Brewery, at Eighteenth and Lafayette streets, supplied the police with lunch and refreshments.[12]

The board also requested that all employers of private watchmen in the city have the watchmen report to the board on June 5. The private watchmen were sworn in by vice president Meyer, and the board ordered that all licensed private watchmen "procure and wear a star on duty with the words 'Private Watchman' engraved thereon."[13]

In April, the board acted on a provision of the legislation creating the metropolitan police that had not been addressed by the first two boards. The 1861 act required the establishment of a fund to assist officers and their families who were in need of relief. The board ordered that "all rewards, presents or compensations of any kind" for police service be given to the recipient's district captain. The captain would forward the proceeds to the board, which would be held by the treasurer in a special account.[14]

In June, the board established the Metropolitan Police Relief Fund and ordered that 20 percent of all reward monies presently held by the treasurer, and received in the future, be retained by the board and added to the proceeds of unclaimed property to create a relief fund as required by the act creating the metropolitan police. The remaining 80 percent would be returned to the recipient of the reward. Money in the fund (which was modeled on the New York City plan) was to be used for the benefit of sick and disabled members of the force, for defraying funeral expenses, and for assisting widows and orphans of deceased officers.[15]

In August, the board called for an election by ballot of one officer from each of the four police districts to join the board as a standing committee on the Metropolitan Police Relief Fund.[16] The newly elected members joined the board and established the rules and regulations of the relief fund. Fifty cents was to be deducted each month from the pay of all members of the department. The members of the board volunteered to furnish the same amount to the fund each month. The establishment of the fund was important; police officers had no days off and were not paid for days that they didn't work. Before initiation of the relief fund, officers injured in the line of duty or unable to work because of illness or injury, and families of officers who had died or been killed in the line of duty, had to petition the board for relief.

Also in August, the board reappointed all police officers in good standing to a four-year term, demoted some higher ranking officers to private, and transferred all district captains, lieutenants, and some sergeants to other districts.

Meanwhile, animals continued to roam about the streets of the city of St. Louis, which had an estimated 1865 population of 180,000 living in an area of sixteen square miles. While farm animals were sometimes a nuisance, the real problem was stray dogs. On July 6, a committee of the St. Louis Medical Society sent a letter to Mayor Thomas in which it discussed hydrophobia, described as an almost always fatal disease that is contracted when bitten by a "mad" dog.[17] The medical society committee recommended that dogs that bite people should be confined; dogs with hydrophobia would likely die within a week. Other recommendations included strewing poisoned meat about the streets and passage of an ordinance permitting the slaying of stray dogs.

The letter was sent to the city council, where it was referred to the Committee on Police.[18] The mayor asked the council to create an ordinance that would give the mayor authority to issue a proclamation each summer that would require owners to have their dogs muzzled and accompanied by a keeper when on the streets. It was hoped that the new law would reduce incidents of hydrophobia spread by dogs.

On Wednesday, July 19, the common council approved Ordinance 5604, which gave the mayor the authority he had requested to issue a proclamation notifying dog owners to keep their dogs secured on the premises or, when out walking, have them muzzled. Any dog found at large without a muzzle and a "keeper" would be immediately killed. The owner would be fined between $10 and $20, half of which would go the police officer or other officer who killed the dog, and the remainder to the city treasury.[19] The following day, Mayor Thomas issued the proclamation, which gave dog owners two days to come into compliance with the ordinance. Police officers would begin killing stray dogs and making arrests at dawn on Saturday, July 21.[20]

What the newspapers dubbed the "dog war" would be an embarrassment to Mayor Thomas and the beginning of a power struggle between the mayor and the other members of the board. It was the beginning of a relationship that Thomas treated with benign neglect, and one that would lead to the first investigation of the metropolitan police department.

The ordinance was quickly enforced by the police. One policeman was reported to have shot twelve dogs before breakfast "and would have killed as many more had he not run out of ammunition."[21] The *Missouri Democrat* reported that many valuable dogs had been sent out of town until "the Mayor's wrath was appeased." The same issue of the *Democrat* mused that "some of the policemen refuse to kill dogs at all, and many of them have dogs themselves which they value highly. A dog is useful to a policeman, for when the weary star sits down on a dry goods box and takes a nap, the dog [k]eeps his eyes open, and gives warning of the approach of the Sergeant in his rounds."[22]

The *Democrat* also printed accounts of dog shootings that went awry. One policeman fired at point-blank range only to have the "ball" go under the dog, ricochet off the pavement, and break a window on the third floor of a nearby building. No one was injured. Another policeman only succeeded in shooting off the tip of the dog's tail. Still another policeman chased a dog onto the levee. The dog jumped onto a raft in the river. The policeman also jumped onto the raft but then proceeded to fall into the Mississippi River and had to be rescued. Officers in the Third Police District (commanded by Captain William Lee) had shot about 150 dogs in less than a week, but had not arrested one owner. In a reference to the ordinance that permitted the arresting officer to claim half of the fine, one local newspaper reported that "Captain Lee's men say they don't want any such extra pay for doing their duty."[23]

Because of the negative publicity about the dog war, Mayor Thomas asked the Board of Police Commissioners, a week after his proclamation became effective, to instruct the members of the force to use their batons to kill the dogs "and to avoid the use of their pistols, except where no other means will prevail."[24] The board instructed the chief of police to issue orders prohibiting the shooting of dogs. Kill the dogs, said the order, "by some other means than shooting."[25] Although some of the antics demonstrated in the shooting of dogs caused an outcry in the city, the beating of dogs with clubs was seen as worse. The city later hired two men to capture the dogs.

Mayor Thomas attended one or two additional board meetings in August. On Tuesday, August 29, he wrote a letter to the board. He would later say that the letter was delivered to the office of the board that same day. The board, however, would not see the original letter until later in the week; it first saw a copy of the letter printed in the newspapers. (The newspapers, as was typically the case, had printed the letter the following day.)[26] A copy of the letter was also delivered on Tuesday to the chief of police and the captains of police, all of whom saw the letter before the board did. Because of the content of the letter, a special meeting of the board was held on Saturday, September 2, to prepare a reply to the mayor.

In the letter, Mayor Thomas first noted that he had received the police department payroll voucher for August and had approved it for payment. The mayor then accused the police department of not fully enforcing the dog law, adding in the next paragraph that he would do all in his power as chief executive of the city to see that the dog ordinance, and all ordinances, were enforced. Thomas ended the letter by stating that "if the police are not more vigilant in the discharge of their duties, I may consider it my duty to refuse to approve the requisition for the pay of the police for the month of September."[27]

In a lengthy reply, the board focused on three issues. First, the board was upset that it had first read the mayor's letter in the newspaper. The board thought such an act was discourteous and done without "a moment's reflection. . . ."[28] The board then attacked each of the mayor's statements, citing sections of the state law creating the metropolitan police to indicate that he had no power over the board nor the police department and could not have ordinances enforced "without our sanction or direction . . . you are either deficient in a knowledge of the law under which we act, or your action in so addressing us is reprehensible. In charity, we attribute it to the former."[29]

The third issue was the statement that the mayor would consider withholding approval of the September police payroll if the police were not more vigilant in the discharge of their duties. The board asked, "What duties? Killing dogs? It is an impossibility for them to devote all their time to the killing of dogs with their clubs, . . ."[30] With reference to withholding approval of pay, the board replied that, again, the mayor did not know the law. Sending the vouchers to the mayor for approval had been a courtesy; the state law did not require his approval. Finally, the board included the section of the state law creating the metropolitan police that prohibits the mayor of St. Louis from impeding, obstructing, hindering, or interfering with the board or anyone under its control.

That Mayor Thomas was not in favor of a gubernatorial-appointed Board of Police Commissioners was evident in his lengthy reply to the board. In a letter, the mayor said that he knew the law that created the metropolitan police, "but this damnable proof of the attempt of Claib Jackson's Legislature to paralyze the efforts of the loyal men of St. Louis to sustain the General Government is still too fresh in the minds of the people of St. Louis to admit of its being forgotten." He then cited eight instances (including the dog ordinance) where the police had not enforced the law. The eight included permitting houses of ill fame to operate, letting goats run at large on the streets, and allowing transportation companies to bring paupers into the city.

The mayor also took this occasion to recommend charges against Captain of Police Lee, commander of the Third Police District, for failure to properly see that a child was committed to the House of Refuge and for failing to enforce the dog ordinance. In the latter instance, the mayor claimed that he saw Captain Lee and three or four policemen standing outside of the station house. There were also several stray dogs present, and Mayor Thomas asked Lee why he did not have the dogs killed. Lee refused to answer the mayor. Thomas ended his letter with the statement that, had he not earlier vetoed the ordinance providing money for a new downtown police hall and station, he would not likely have received a reply to his original letter.[31]

The board called special meetings to deal with the charges Thomas made against Lee. Lee was charged with (1) delivering a child to Catholic nuns for care after the mayor had signed an order committing her to the House of Refuge and (2) showing disrespect to the mayor (who was also the president of the board) by failing to answer Thomas's question about his failure to enforce the dog ordinance. After hearing testimony at several different meetings, the board found Lee guilty of both charges. For failing to deliver the child to the House of Refuge,

Lee, who the board believed "acted from pure and humane motives," was to "be called before the Board and instructed in his future duties in such cases."[32] For turning away from the mayor and not making any reply, "thereby showing contempt to the President of the Board," the board ordered that Captain Lee "be reprimanded by the [vice president] of the Board. Disrespect to a superior officer will not be tolerated."[33]

Two weeks after the Lee hearings, Mayor Thomas sent a letter to the board asking it to inform him of its findings. Thomas, who had not attended a board meeting for three months, received a curt reply.

Drawing of Captain William Lee. *St. Louis Republic.*
Courtesy of Deborah VanDyke.

Vice President Ferdinand Meyer sent a letter to Mayor Thomas that said, in part, "the Board wishes me to say, that their decision in the Case of Capt. Lee, is recorded in the min. of Nov. lst 1865, to which you are respectfully referred."[34]

The investigations and trials held by the board in response to the mayor's charges were not, however, to end the matter. On December 4, the mayor attended his first board meeting since August 28. During the meeting, Mayor Thomas stated that he had heard a rumor concerning some misconduct on the part of Captain Lee that allegedly took place on Saturday night, November 25. He asked the board to set a meeting date to conduct an investigation to determine if there was substance to the allegation. Subpoenas were issued to witnesses.

The board reconvened on Friday, December 8. Witnesses were called and testified, but a decision was postponed until the following Monday. While the minutes of the board meetings do not indicate the type of complaint alleged by the mayor, a local newspaper reported that Thomas claimed that Lee "was drunk at a house of prostitution on Green street, and acted like a fool, and abused the inmates of the house, and, finally, arrested them and sent them to the Central Police Station."[35] This was on a Saturday night, said Thomas, and the women were not released on bail until Monday morning, when their trial was to take place. By then, he stated, "Captain Lee had got sober, and found out that he had done wrong, and that it would not do to have this matter come up before the Recorder, as that would bring the fact of his drunkenness and his actions before the public."[36] Thomas said that Lee went to the city attorney and asked that the cases be dropped as there were indictments against the two women, they would be convicted, and that would be enough. The cases were dropped, said the mayor, but only after police board vice president Meyer asked the city attorney to do so because the women were providing the police department with valuable information and would continue to do so.

The minutes of December 11 note: "It appearing from a list of Witnesses subpoenaed for the prosecution, that a majority of them were women having the reputation of prostitutes; it was decided by the Board that the finding in the case shall be governed by the custom under the law in regard to the testimony of such characters." The "custom" apparently was to place little credence in the testimony of prostitutes. The board—Mayor Thomas voting no, Meyer abstaining, and Jameson absent—found that "inasmuch as sufficient grounds have not been elicited from the investigation, on which to base a charge against Capt. Lee that the case be dismissed."[37]

Mayor Thomas attended one more meeting, in December 1865. In spite of the fact that he was the ex officio president of the board, he would attend only seven of the weekly meetings the following year and would attend none in 1867 and 1868.[38]

Almost lost in the feuding of Mayor Thomas with the Board of Police Commissioners and Captain Lee was the issuance of General Order 33 on November 13. General Order 33 instructed the commanding officers of each district to read pertinent parts of City Ordinance 4894 to the men under their commands. Ordinance 4894 dealt with the maintenance of sanitary conditions within the city. All violations of the ordinance were to be promptly reported by the police as soon as practicable to the street inspector of the district in which the violation occurred. The reason for the issuance of General Order 33 was contained in the first sentence of the order: "In consequence of the anticipated approach of the Asiatic Cholera. . . ."[39] That sentence was prophetic, for the deadly disease that led to the deaths of so many St. Louisans in 1849 would again visit the city.

The four captains appointed as district representatives to the Police Relief Fund were also chosen to assist the board in adopting winter uniforms for the police. The board had already communicated with the New York City chief of police regarding uniform styles and material. Ultimately, the winter police uniform for St. Louis police officers would emulate those of their counterparts in New York City.

Gambling and prostitution were a constant concern. There were numerous gambling houses. Most of the houses were in the central area of the city (the Second Police District), and most of those were on Fourth and Fifth streets. Keno, similar to bingo; faro, a game in which players bet on cards drawn from a dealing box; and poker were the most common games found in St. Louis gambling houses. Since the police could only arrest the proprietors after a citizen filed a formal complaint or a police officer actually observed the gambling, arrests were few. Raids were usually led by the Second District commander, Captain David Hopkins, assisted by Sergeant Maston Gore.[40] The board also employed three men for "secret service in the Police."[41] The three would work undercover to gather sufficient evidence about gambling houses to apply to the city recorder (judge) for writs that would permit police squads to "descend" upon the locations. The board met with all captains, lieutenants, and sergeants to arrange simultaneous descents on the gambling houses and other places that criminals might frequent.

The police could only raid houses of prostitution under the same circumstances. Means other than raids were devised to deal with prostitution. For example, Chief Laibold was ordered to detail one or two officers to list all of the bawdy houses between Third and Eleventh streets on Market Street with the names of lessees, landlords, or other agents. A copy of the list was subsequently posted in the Second Police District station house (also occupied by police headquarters), and another copy was sent to the sitting grand jury. The board also met with members of the common council, the city attorney, and the city recorder to discuss amendments to city ordinances that dealt with vagrancy and related situations so that the police would have more-effective tools with which to deal with the problem.

1866

In February 1866, the board began discussions with city officials to establish a police telegraph in conjunction with the existing fire alarm telegraph system. The fire and police telegraph system would become a reality within the next six months.

Also that year, the sergeant of detectives, John Eagan, was tried before the board for insubordination for using "threatening and insolent language to the Vice President of the Board."[42] The charge was made by Vice President Meyer after Meyer spoke with Eagan about the claims of two men arrested as suspects in the robbery of an express company messenger. The two men claimed that Eagan and two other detectives spoke with them about how much money the detectives might get for keeping silent and taking no action in the case. When Meyer told Eagan what the men had said, Eagan replied with a few words that resulted in the charge and trial.[43] After completion of his trial, at which he was represented by counsel, on February 25, Sergeant Eagan was terminated for insubordination.

In March, the board tried the other two detectives involved in the case on charges stemming from the claims of the two suspects. The detectives were acquitted, but in a strange twist, they were "dropped from the rolls" of the police department because, in the words of the board, "their usefulness and effectiveness as members of the Police Force is so much impaired. . . ."[44]

The robbery of the express company messenger led to another confrontation between Mayor Thomas and Second District Captain William Lee. Soon after the robbery on February 17, 1866, Lee had contacted the superintendent of the company to request that the company reserve a room on the top (fifth) floor of the Lindell Hotel. Suspects would be taken to the hotel and questioned.[45] On March 19, Mayor Thomas attended the board meeting and filed a complaint against Captain Lee:

> Saturday night, March 3rd, when meeting the agents of the United States Express Company at Room No. 12 Lindell Hotel, I found on entering the room that Capt. Lee was present, and he knowing the agents were strangers to me, and he having the confidence of the agents, and knowing the Board of Police Commissioners would support him, used very abusive and insulting language towards me, and of which I informed [Commissioner] Clark the next morning, and I am satisfied that [Commissioner] Clark has informed the other members of the Board.
>
> It was then I determined never to act as President with the present Board of Police Commissioners as long as they retained Capt. Lee on the police.[46]

Mayor Thomas also attended the board meeting of March 26. All of the board members were present. A letter from Thomas to the board was read. The mayor wanted to advance charges against Captain Lee for the "abusive, insulting, and threatening language" directed at the mayor in the Lindell Hotel, and for "insulting and abusive language" on an unspecified earlier date.[47] The board ordered that Lee be furnished with a copy of the letter and scheduled a hearing date of March 29.

At the March 29 board meeting, Captain Lee stated that he would not be ready to defend himself until the affidavits of the four express company investigators were received. Mayor Thomas objected to such one-sided testimony. The board then instructed the secretary of the board to send a letter to each investigator asking for his attendance before the board at his "very earliest convenience." It was decided that as each investigator came to St. Louis, any member of the board could hear the testimony and report it at the next regular board meeting. No further mention of the complaint of Mayor Thomas against Captain Lee, or any disposition in the case, is noted.[48]

In March, Governor Fletcher appointed Joseph Conrad to the Board of Police Commissioners to replace E. H. E. Jameson. While there is no mention in the board minutes of Jameson's resignation, the appointment of a new member was probably not unexpected; Jameson had not attended a board meeting since the meeting of October 13, 1865. Not much is known about Jameson's replacement. The *Missouri Democrat*, in announcing the appointment of the new police commissioner, simply stated that "Brigadier General Joseph Conrad;

Joseph Conrad, Brevetted Brigadier General, United States Volunteers. Photograph, 1864. Missouri History Museum.

formerly of the gallant 15th Missouri, has been appointed a police commissioner, in place of Col. Jameson, resigned. . . ."[49]

*   *   *

All of this, however, had little effect on the day-to-day life of a beat policeman. Beat policemen were responsible for the good order and condition of their beats. They had to report the conditions of streets and other thoroughfares, check the gas-fired street lamps for damage or failure, return lost children to their parents, and report any visible damage of the fire telegraph system.

There were also special details. A "proper force of police" was placed at the Keokuk Packet Company landing every morning to protect strangers and travelers "from imposition or violence."[50] At the request of Henry Shaw, one "suitable policeman" was to be detailed on Sundays and holidays at Shaw's horticultural gardens, described as "a place of public resort outside the City limits."[51]

Policemen worked twelve hours a day and had no days off or vacations. One of the results was that the department had a high turnover of personnel. In the fiscal year April 1, 1866, to March 31, 1867, for example, forty-five policemen resigned, six died, and forty-five were dismissed from the force. Thus, more than one-third of the police department had to be replaced in one year.

The board minutes listed two ways the police commissioners attempted to deal with the problem. In June, each commissioner was assigned a police district and had "the entire control and general superintention of the Office Book and papers."[52] In July, the board established the position of assistant sergeant, later referred to as acting sergeant. (The appointment of acting sergeants was stopped in September when, it was determined, such positions were not authorized by law.)

A second member of the Meyer board resigned on April 9. In his letter of resignation, James Corbitt explained that the duties of a member of the board required more time from his private business than he could spare. Corbitt praised the other board members and wished them well. Lucien Eaton was appointed by Governor Fletcher

Lucien Eaton. Photograph by J. A. Scholten, 1867–1868.
Missouri History Museum.

to fill the vacancy; he took his seat on the board the same day. Eaton was a lawyer and, at the time of his appointment to the board, was a register in bankruptcy for the Eastern District of Missouri. During the Civil War, he had attained the rank of major in the Union army.

At the same time, the board was looking for a "more suitable conveyance" for taking prisoners to the City Workhouse. The board received several proposals for building a Black Maria.[53] The board accepted the $500 bid of carriage manufacturers Jost and Yeakel.[54]

On June 16, the board issued an order prohibiting the wearing of stars by private watchmen and special policemen, substituting a badge with the words "Private Policeman" displayed on it. While the board minutes did not explain the reason for moving from a star to a badge, it is likely that the board had experienced some instances where private watchmen, who were permitted to wear police-style uniforms, were mistaken for policemen or purposely posed as policemen.

The cholera warned of in November 1865 was first noticed in St. Louis at the beginning of August 1866. Mention was first made by the board at a special meeting called on August 7; a private was appointed an acting sergeant (which was still considered legal at the time) and charged with the duty of reporting all cases of cholera in the Second District (the central part of the city) to the chief of police. More than 1,600 persons died in the first three weeks of August. At least 70,000 persons, more than 25 percent of the population, fled the city. When the plague passed in October, it had left 3,527 dead.[55]

* * *

On October 11, Chief Bernard Laibold tendered his resignation to the board. Chief Laibold was going to run for the position of St. Louis County marshal (to which he was later elected) and offered his resignation to comply (more or less) with a June directive of the board that policemen had to resign before accepting the nomination for a public office. Laibold had already accepted the nomination.[56] The board at first tabled Laibold's resignation, but accepted it October 18, simultaneously announcing the appointment of a new chief of police, William P. Fenn, effective October 22, 1866.

Little is known about Fenn. He came to St. Louis in 1838. City directories from the dozen or so years before the Civil War list him as being employed by the "dairy depot," also known as the "butter, cream and milk depot." Another source lists Fenn as the proprietor of the dairy depot.[57] Fenn served in the Civil War, rising to the rank of colonel in the Union army. In 1866, he was elected to the Missouri House of Representatives as a representative from St. Louis.

On the day Fenn was sworn in as chief of police, the board ordered the formation of the first posse comitatus, a power granted to the board under the 1861 act that created the metropolitan police. In a letter to St. Louis County sheriff John C. Vogel, the board noted that threats to disrupt the general election on November 6 had come to its knowledge and, in order to preserve the public peace, "you are hereby required to summon a 'Posse Comitatus' for that purpose consisting of not less than One Thousand men and to hold that force in readiness to act at a moments notice and especially upon the 6th day of November next that being the day of general election in the State of Missouri."[58]

In a meeting a week later, the board ordered five hundred tin stars and four hundred police clubs for the extra force. The board planned the placement of the police force and the posse comitatus for election day and informed Chief Fenn. Mayor Thomas issued a proclamation prohibiting the dispensing of liquor after six o'clock on election eve until midnight on election day. The show of force had its desired outcome. There were few problems; most of the arrests on election day were for selling liquor during the hours that sale was forbidden. Through the press, the board thanked the members of the posse comitatus for the job it had done.

Chief Fenn, meanwhile, prepared for the upcoming winter season. Because the four district station houses were routinely used to house the homeless overnight during the winter, he requested that the board purchase four dozen blankets for the use of lodgers.

1867

In January 1867, the board began planning to redistrict the city so that the Mississippi River would constitute the eastern boundary of each of the four police districts. A substation would be located in the western portion of each district. The board would have to establish some new station houses and substations.

On January 28, Charles W. Irwin took his seat as a member of the board, replacing Joseph Conrad. Conrad, appointed in March 1866, went on leave in October and didn't return to the board. Irwin was a partner in the firm of Cheever, Burchard and Company, a firm selling cutlery, hardware, and home furnishings. He had been a member of the Board of Education for six years, and a former judge of the county court. He would serve only a week before Governor Fletcher changed the appearance of the board. Ferdinand Meyer remained on the board, and Lucien Eaton was reappointed.[59]

The board meeting of February 4 was attended by two new police commissioners, John O. Codding and William A. Hequembourg. Codding owned a firm bearing his name that manufactured store and office equipment and showcases. Hequembourg was a partner in the firm of Hequembourg and Findley, listed only as "collecting agents."

One of the early tasks of the new board was to continue to amend the rules and regulations of the police force. One of its chief concerns was the ability of individual officers to physically perform police work. Accordingly, the board ordered that any member of the force who had failed to do duty for a total of sixty days in any consecutive three months be dropped from the rolls unless retained by special order of the board. The board also ordered that all applicants for the force present a certificate from a physician, who was designated by the board, "showing that the proposed appointee has been carefully and thoroughly examined, is of sound health, of vigorous constitution, and has no indications of any chronic disease or physical disqualification for police duty."[60] Doctor R. W. Oliphant was designated as the examining physician for the police department.

An act amending the 1861 police act was passed by the Missouri General Assembly on March 13, 1867. The new law was lengthy and covered a wide range of topics. It gave the policemen raises, but also eliminated the rank of lieutenant. Twelve sergeant positions were added to the authorized strength of the department to compensate for the loss of the higher rank. A mounted police patrol was created, the board being given the authority "to appoint, mount and equip not more than twenty policemen for duty in the outskirts and open portions of the city, and elsewhere in the city and county of St. Louis."[61] The city of St. Louis would continue, according to the act, to pay three-fourths of the costs of the operation of the police department, with the remainder being paid by the county of St. Louis.

Perhaps eclipsing these provisions of the new act, however, was the additional power given to the Board of Police Commissioners. In response to what the board viewed as the seriousness of the gambling problem in the city, the law gave the acting president of the board some of the authority of a magistrate. Given reasonable grounds to believe that there were gaming devices at some location, he was authorized to issue warrants to seize them, and police officers were given the power "to break open doors" to execute the warrant. The law required that the seized gaming devices be publicly destroyed "by burning or otherwise."[62]

The acting president was also given the authority to issue search warrants (upon reasonable grounds) for stolen or embezzled property in both the city and county of St. Louis. Any property recovered upon executing the search warrant had to be brought before a magistrate or justice of the peace in the city of St. Louis. The law required that judge to proceed in the case "as if such warrant had been by him issued." The amendment prohibited the collection of fees for issuing or executing such warrants. In the first fiscal year after the amendment became law, the board issued, and police officers executed, fifty-three search warrants for stolen or embezzled property. In addition, sixty-three warrants against gambling houses were issued and executed during the year.[63]

The amendment also resolved some lingering issues about the licensing and control of private watchmen by giving the board complete control over the licensing of private watchmen:

> The Board of Police Commissioners of the city of St. Louis shall have full power to regulate and license all private watchmen and private policemen serving or acting as such on any street, alley, wharf, or other public place in said city, and no person shall serve or act as a private watchman or private policeman in said city without the written license of said Board first had and [*sic*] obtained, on pain of punishment for a misdemeanor.[64]

In response to the new law, the board voided all private watchman licenses effective May 1. Those wishing to be relicensed by the board, and those seeking appointment as private watchmen, had to personally appear before the board for examination.

Finally, the act declared that "the members of the police force of the city of St. Louis, organized and appointed by the Board of Police Commissioners of said city, are hereby declared officers of the city of St. Louis, under the charter and ordinances thereof, and also to be officers of the State of Missouri, and shall be so deemed and taken in all courts having jurisdiction of offenses against the laws of this State or the ordinances of said city."[65]

✳   ✳   ✳

Two items of note occurred at the board meeting of April 8, 1867. First, an officer tried by the board for inefficiency was referred to as a "patrolman." This was the first time that such a designation appeared in the minutes; patrol officers were previously referred to as "privates." Second, the board approved the first police redistricting of the city.[66] Under the redistricting, all four police districts were to be bounded on the east by the Mississippi River and on the west by the city limits. The city limits extended from East Grand and the Mississippi River on the north, then south on Grand to Keokuk Street, and east on Keokuk to the river.[67] Later, a blacksmith's shop on Carondelet (Broadway) between Soulard and Lafayette streets was purchased for a First District station, and a two-story building at Twelfth and Monroe streets was leased for the Fourth District station. In July, at the request of the commissioners of Lafayette Park (and with their payment of half the costs), the board began construction of a police substation in that park.

At the meeting of June 1, Commissioner Eaton, who had been reappointed to the board in January, resigned.[b] Governor Fletcher appointed Otto C. Lademann, who took his seat at that meeting. Lademann, who was the tenth commissioner to serve with Ferdinand Meyer in just two and one-half years, emigrated from Germany in 1856 at the age of fifteen. In 1861, he enlisted in the Union army

---

[b] In November 1868, Lucien Eaton would be sworn in as U.S. commissioner. In 1869, he would serve as the attorney for the Board of Police Commissioners.

at the U.S. Arsenal and had been with Captain Nathaniel Lyon at Camp Jackson and at the Battle of Wilson's Creek. Lyon (then General Lyon) was killed at Wilson's Creek, and Lademann was captured. He later rejoined the army after a prisoner exchange. He returned to

Otto C. Lademann, Captain Company F, 3rd Regiment Infantry, Missouri Volunteers. Photograph, 1863. Missouri History Museum.

St. Louis after the war and married Josephine Uhrig, the daughter of Franz Uhrig, the pioneer St. Louis brewer. He joined his father-in-law in the brewing business.[c]

Later in June, the board approved new insignia for sergeants and captains, which had been designed by the members of those ranks. While there is no mention of the kind of insignia changes that were approved, it is believed that the designs were in the form of shields, to replace the gold stars that had been worn. At the same time, the board ordered that the stars (until now worn by all ranks except chief

---

[c] In 1893, the old Uhrig homestead on the southwest corner of Eighteenth and Market streets would be demolished to make way for the construction of Union Station.

of police) be removed from the hats and placed over the left breast. Patrolmen would wear a silver-plated, six-pointed star until 1923.

In September, Chief of Police William Fenn gave the board his resignation, effective October 22, exactly one year from his appointment as chief. The board took no action on Fenn's resignation until the meeting of October 7, when it was accepted to take effect on the date requested by Fenn. Two weeks later, Chief Fenn changed his mind and sent a letter to the board requesting that the board allow him to withdraw his resignation. In response, the board appointed him "Chief of Police Pro Tem" to take effect October 22 "and continue day to day till final action upon his application by the Board."[68]

At the meeting of October 23, the board unanimously reappointed Fenn as chief of police, effective October 22. Neither the minutes of the board nor a search of the local newspapers revealed any reason for Fenn's actions or the responses of the board, although, in his request to withdraw his resignation, Fenn referred to his intention to "withdraw all unpleasantness which may have existed. . . ."[69]

One of the first orders of business for the reappointed chief of police was to implement an order of the board that all members of the force were to wear their police uniforms both on and off duty. Any request to wear civilian clothing when off duty had to be approved by the officer's sergeant and captain, as well as the chief. The board took this action, it was later explained, "with a view of remedying as much as possible the sparsity in the numbers of the force."[70] In November, the board reiterated its stand, instructing Chief Fenn to enforce the order to wear uniforms off duty "to the letter."[71]

Also in November, the board made its first foray into helping the homeless and needy citizens of St. Louis beyond providing them with overnight lodging in the police stations. Commissioners Hequembourg and Lademann met with members of the St. Louis Provident Relief Association for the purpose of "devising ways and means by which the needy and homeless who may be thrown into the hands of the police during the coming winter may obtain the necessary relief."[72]

On November 19, Governor Thomas Fletcher came to St. Louis. He met with Mayor Thomas at his office, where the mayor outlined the problems he had been having with the police commissioners and Captain Lee for over two years. These charges were later put into the form of a "memorial" (a representation of facts) to the state legislature.[73] Thomas told the governor about Captain Lee and the House of Refuge case, and how Lee had been only reprimanded. He spoke of the arrests made by a drunken Lee at the house of prostitution on Green Street, and how the case against the women had been dropped at the behest of the vice president of the board, Ferdinand Meyer, because the prostitutes were providing the police with helpful information. Yet at the police board trial, the testimony of the women was not allowed because the testimony of prostitutes was not to be believed. He told Fletcher how Lee had verbally abused him and threatened him at the Lindell Hotel during the investigation of the express company robbery, and how he first preferred charges against Lee and then dropped them because it would be too expensive to hire a lawyer.

Mayor Thomas accused the police board of using its power to have him defeated in the city election of 1867 and even fired one policeman who was supposed to be a friend of the mayor. Yet, he told the governor, the metropolitan police concept was a good one: "I do not believe that we could get along without it."[74] But, he said, the department should be under the control and direction of city authorities, and he so relayed his thoughts to be included in the proposed amendment that was to be taken up by the state legislature. Mayor Thomas had other complaints that he discussed with Governor Fletcher, but all would be a part of the memorial the mayor sent to the state legislature in February 1868. The memorial would serve as the basis of an investigation by a joint committee of the Missouri General Assembly less than three months later.

In December, Chief Fenn was sent to observe the police departments of Boston and New York City. While no report of the information learned by the chief is included in the board minutes, he made an oral report to the board at the meeting of December 24, 1867.

1868

At the January 22, 1868, meeting of the board, three letters (or "communications," as they were called) from Chief Fenn were read. In light of the timing and the nature of the communications, it is likely that all three requests resulted from Fenn's eastern city trek. The first requested an increase in the size of the force; the second asked for an increase in pay for patrolmen (the present $75 a month being "insufficient for the comfortable support of a small family in this city . . ."); and the third recommended that the board establish "a school of instruction for policemen." The requests for more officers and an increase in the size of the force were denied by the board "owing to the general stagnation of business in our city for the past year, and the offensive taxation (both National, State & Municipal) pressing upon our citizens. . . ."[75] The request concerning a school of instruction was not acted upon at this meeting.

While the 1867 amendment to the Metropolitan Police Act gave the vice president of the police board the power of a magistrate regarding search warrants for gambling paraphernalia and for stolen property, the board had no such power with regard to prostitution and related crimes. One of the related crimes was a so-called social evil that had first emerged during the Civil War, the "beer jerking saloon." A "beer jerker" was a woman, usually a prostitute or "lewd woman," who served beer to customers in a saloon and might also be "employed in singing or dancing in a lewd or indecent manner . . . ."[76] Such a woman, according to the 1864 city ordinance, was to be considered a vagrant and subject to arrest. The police arrested most of an estimated seventy-five local beer jerkers numerous times, and many of them, according to the *Missouri Democrat*, "abandoned their haunts."[77]

Based upon the memorial Mayor Thomas sent to the state legislature on February 13, the Missouri General Assembly approved, on March 26, a joint resolution that a committee be appointed to investigate "the journal, books, and documents" in the possession of the Board of Police Commissioners, and also to examine "certain charges of fraud and corruption which have been made against said Board."[78]

The members of the joint committee (none of whom could be from the St. Louis area) were Senator Ellis G. Evans and Representatives P. G. Stafford and Martin Hickman.[79] Officially named the Joint Committee of the General Assembly Appointed to Investigate the Police Department of the City of St. Louis, the committee first met, in the rooms of the Board of Police Commissioners, on April 21, 1868. The minutes of the meetings were kept by Stafford until April 24, when a police sergeant was selected as a clerk and a patrolman was appointed his assistant. The journal, books, and documents were first audited. These documents included every record from the minutes of the meetings of the board, to the board treasurer's books, to the various records kept at the district stations.

The second phase, the investigation of charges of fraud and corruption against the board brought by Mayor Thomas, began on May 4. Thomas formally presented his list of allegations of corruption against the board but flatly denied ever having made any allegation of fraud. The joint committee would question the witnesses listed by Thomas and those of the Board of Police Commissioners, 126 in all. The committee concluded its work on May 30.

In its report to the General Assembly in August, the joint committee stated that it, with regard to its first charge, found the documents, books, and papers of the board in good order.[80] The minutes of the board meetings were found to be "very full," and the vouchers and treasurer's books were correct. The relief fund, created by the present board, was solvent. The records and books kept by the chief of police were noted as "evidence of the perfection that has been reached in this part of the system...."[81]

The joint committee questioned the size of the force, noting that the number of officers "seems inadequate for the demands of a city of two hundred and forty thousand inhabitants, and with the extended area of the great city of St. Louis."[82] Nevertheless, the report found, as a result of the committee's observations, "an efficiency that cannot easily be excelled."[83] The report credited the selection process of the Board of Police Commissioners for the efficiency.

The report then turned to the second part of the investigation, the charges of fraud and corruption brought by Mayor James Thomas.

The report concluded that "charges of 'fraud' were not only not made, but expressly denied, by Mayor Thomas, from whom they were supposed to emanate. Certainly no fraud on the part of the present Board has been detected by us, or cause for suspecting it disclosed, by the examination and the evidence taken."[84] The joint committee went on to state that "the same remarks apply to the charges of 'corruption'; we think that nothing of the kind is fairly suggested by the evidence . . . we are clearly and unanimously of the opinion that the charges are not sustained by the facts."[85]

The joint committee noted that during the course of the proceedings, the Board of Police Commissioners leveled charges against Mayor Thomas. The mayor was accused of neglecting his duty as president of the board by attending so few board meetings; "seeking ill of the Department from discharged policemen"; withholding valuable information from the force; seeking to injure and defame the police department; "and by pardoning criminals and vagrants, or granting stays of execution after conviction, thereby returning outlaws upon the citizens; and that the Mayor himself has violated both the laws of the State and of the United States."[86]

The committee learned that Mayor Thomas had attended "thirty-two or thirty-three meetings of the Board" in 1865, seven in 1866, none in 1867, and (at the time of the investigation) none in 1868.[87] George Gavin, secretary to the Board of Police Commissioners, testified that Thomas had not been cooperative with the board for the past eighteen months. This, said the committee, was corroborated by three other witnesses. The committee found that the mayor had pardoned thousands from the workhouse, causing some of them to "become impudent and defiant toward the Police Department. This power of the Executive undoubtedly works against the efficiency of the Police Department. . . ."[88]

The sentiments of Mayor Thomas about the findings of the joint committee quickly became evident. In a letter addressed to the committee, Thomas wrote that anyone who read the full proceedings of the joint committee would "be convinced that I have proved every charge against the Police Commissioners, and I even believe that I have proved fraud, a charge which never was mine, but which was one made by the Police Commissioners themselves, as having come from me."[89] Thomas concluded his letter to the joint committee by stating that, at the next session of the state legislature, he would make a statement of facts that would, he believed, "show that the Committee are just as corrupt as the Police Commissioners."[90] Thomas would not attend another police board meeting during his term of office.

In the meantime, in his annual report to the Board of Police Commissioners, Chief Fenn again recommended that a "school of the policeman" be established for every person appointed to the force to attend, as well as those presently on the force. Fenn suggested that the school be at least one month long and that, before a patrolman began full police duties, he had "to answer promptly and accurately any question in regard to any duty he may be called upon to perform in any case embraced within the limits of written law or instructions."[91] Fenn noted that the school of the policeman should not overlook the military aspect of the police. Each policeman "should also be instructed in the school of the soldier, the position and movements to qualify him to take rank in the school of the company when placed on full duty, as well as the proper use of the baton on established principles of the broadsword exercises."[92]

The two references Fenn made to objectives that had to be met by the new officer before being placed on full duty implied that the school of the policeman would be part of the officer's shift for the first month, with the officer being placed on a beat (presumably with an experienced officer) for the remainder of the shift. The Police School of Instruction would be established by the board in 1869. Fenn, however, would be unseated before that happened.

＊   ＊   ＊

Shortly after midnight on the morning of June 16, 1868, a fourth metropolitan police officer was killed while in the discharge of police duties. Patrolman John W. Skinner was shot to death by a man later identified as Daniel Rabenan, a saloon keeper, near the Fourteenth Street train depot. Skinner, who was on duty at the depot with Patrolman Miller awaiting the arrival of a train, told Rabenan, whom Skinner believed to be intoxicated, to go home. Rabenan began to leave and then stopped and turned toward the officers. Patrolman Skinner walked up to Rabenan and again told him to go home. He turned and began walking away, followed by Skinner. Patrolman Miller said that he saw both men stop between the two sets of railroad tracks, and then heard a shot. Miller began running toward the two, and Skinner came toward him and said, "Go for him, Miller." Miller fired a shot at Rabenan, who went down an embankment. Miller "gave a call," that is, rapped his club on a hard surface for assistance. Two other officers immediately responded to Miller's call and, while they searched for the subject, additional officers arrived. Meanwhile, a private watchman at the depot, James Birney, assisted the mortally wounded officer, who died at the scene.

An off-duty officer who lived near the depot, Thomas Smith, heard the first call rap and assisted for a time in the search for Rabenan. He returned to his home when, a short time later, a second call rap was heard. Smith was met at the depot by private watchman Birney, who told Smith that he thought that he had found the man who had shot Skinner. The man was lying in some weeds and was, according to Smith asleep and "about half drunk." Smith took the man to the station and "found a pistol on him." Rabenan later admitted to Smith that he had shot the officer.

Rabenan told a newspaper reporter the following day that he didn't know that the two were police officers, that he was very drunk at the time, and that he thought they were robbers.[93] They struck him and pulled his hair, said Rabenan, and he ran, warning the two not to approach. Rabenan said that he drew his revolver without intending to shoot, and when Skinner walked toward him, "the pistol went off by accident."[94] The disposition of the case could not be determined.

＊   ＊   ＊

At a special meeting called on Thursday evening, June 25, the four appointed members of the board heard testimony concerning Chief

Fenn's conduct in office. The Second District commander, Captain David Hopkins, testified, as did two sergeants, two detectives assigned to the chief's office, and others from inside and outside the police department.[95] In a letter dated June 25, the board asked for the resignation of Chief Fenn. Fenn replied to the board in a letter, dated June 30 and recorded in the board minutes, in which he acknowledged receipt of the board's order but declined to resign.

The board then rescinded the order of October 18, 1866, appointing Fenn as chief of police, and the order of October 22, 1867, that reappointed him chief, and declared the office of chief of police vacant. The board ordered that all property, papers, and so forth pertaining to the office "be turned over to the senior Captain of Police, who will take charge in accordance with existing orders."[96] Both Fenn and the senior captain of police, William Lee, received a copy of the order declaring the office vacant. Lee was appointed acting chief of police. One week later, at the meeting of July 7, Lee was appointed chief of police, with the effective date of July 1, 1868.

Lee had joined the old city police department on August 2, 1855. In 1858, Mayor Oliver D. Filley appointed Lee assistant captain, a post he held until the formation of the metropolitan police department in 1861, when the first Board of Police Commissioners appointed him captain of police. Being the senior captain, Lee had served as acting chief of police on many occasions during the absence or illness of the chief.

In the meantime, former Chief Fenn prepared a booklet of his own.[97] Fenn denied the testimony of Captain David Hopkins and one of the sergeants, that he "was acting as a friend and protector of gamblers, . . ."[98] Instead, he asserted, it was Ferdinand Meyer who told him, when he became chief, that "he [Meyer] would attend to the policing of gambling houses."[99] There were several reasons that he first resigned on September 14, 1867, one of which was the board's statement to the owner of an illegal billiard saloon that he would not be troubled by the police "if he managed his affairs a little more quietly."[100] Fenn's resignation was accepted three weeks later, effective, as he had requested, on October 22, 1867. However, many citizens of both political parties called upon him, some who were friends of the board, said Fenn, and urged him to remain as chief of police. He yielded and requested the board to withdraw his resignation, which it did. The board, however, reappointed Fenn "till further orders."[101]

Fenn levied his own charges against Vice President Meyer, various ranking police officers, and the legislative committee that had investigated the police department. In February, Fenn went to the state capitol building in Jefferson City and distributed copies of his booklet to state legislators.[102] Soon after, Fenn vanished from public life.

✳   ✳   ✳

In July, the recommendation of the committee that visited the eastern cities in April 1865 came to fruition with the inauguration of a police telegraph system. The system, installed by the New York firm of Gamewell and Company, used the "dial telegraph" method. Instead of having to hire operators who were qualified in the Morse code, the dial telegraph incorporated a round dial with letters and numbers. "All that is required is to spell out the words by simply placing the finger upon the stops at each letter round the dial."[103] In St. Louis, the police telegraph had two loops. The first was a police line that connected the mayor's office, the four district station houses, and the three district substations. The second loop connected police headquarters (at the Second Police District station house); the mayor's office; the City Workhouse; the House of Refuge; the Thornton and Veto engine houses; and the Iron Mountain, Pacific, and North Missouri railroad depots.

The general election of 1868 had been preceded by mass meetings and processions of a variety of political organizations that had, on occasion, become unruly. Both the mayor and the police commissioners were determined that this first general election since the Civil War would be an honest and quiet election. On October 28, Mayor Thomas issued a proclamation that, among other things, ordered "all shops, bars, and other places where intoxicating liquors or drinks are customarily sold, given or dispensed, to be closed before 6 o'clock Monday evening until Tuesday night at 12 o'clock."[104] The board asked the mayor to expand the proclamation to forbid all persons from selling, giving, lending, bartering or otherwise dispensing or distributing intoxicating liquors during this period. Mayor Thomas, demurred, stating that

> since the 1st of May of this year, I have sent to you twenty-one communications, most of which were relative to violations of city ordinances, none of which have been answered by your Board . . . and before I can consent to take into consideration your amendments to my proclamation, I must insist upon your Board enforcing the ordinances of the city which I have already referred to, and also that you will carry out the instructions of the Governor to enforce my proclamation. . . .[105]

The matter ended there.

In preparation for the general election, the board issued general election orders to the police about keeping the peace at the polling places and so forth; their only specific orders concerned Mayor Thomas's proclamation. Since the mayor would not include the request of the board that no liquor be given away or bartered, the board specifically ordered the police to make certain that all places that dispensed alcoholic beverages were closed on election day. The board referred to another part of the mayor's proclamation, that minors be kept indoors on election day, as having no basis in law or authority during the daylight hours, and the police need not enforce that part of the proclamation.[106]

Chief Lee issued more specific orders, known as General Orders, to the officers. Each precinct voting place would be staffed by a regular police officer or special officer. A sergeant "or other prudent and intelligent officer" would be in command of the officers. The mounted patrol would be detailed so that the officers in each voting place could communicate with each other every half hour. For the first time in St. Louis, the officers in the voting places would remain after the closing of the polls and, on a blank form provided, record the returns as counted by the election judges. The forms would then be taken to the captain of the appropriate police district and then to police headquarters by mounted officers, for the convenience of the press. Chief Lee read the incoming election returns to the reporters gathered at police headquarters. Those reporters were so impressed that they unanimously voted a preamble and resolution to the Board of Police Commissioners, the chief of police, and the police force: "Whereas, The Board of Police Commissioners, the Chief of Police, and members of the force generally, have given every aid, consistent with duty, to the city press in acquiring prompt and correct returns of the elections: therefore, Resolved, That the thanks of reporters of the press of the city are hereby tendered to them, individually and collectively, for this courtesy, saving, as it does, a vast amount of labor, perplexity and *shoe-leather*."[107] In a letter dated November 4, 1868, Mayor Thomas thanked the officers and patrolmen of the police department, as well as the voters and all citizens, for a quiet and orderly election day.

The year ended with the reappointment of police officers for a four-year term (as required by the original 1861 police act) effective January 1, 1869.

1869

Even though his term would end in April (and he hadn't yet said anything about running for another two-year term), Mayor Thomas was not finished with the Board of Police Commissioners. In a January 16, 1869, cover letter for another memorial to the members of the General Assembly, addressed to Lieutenant Governor E. O. Stanard, the president of the Missouri Senate, Thomas again complained about the method of appointing the Board of Police Commissioners. He asked the legislature to change the law to give the mayor of St. Louis and the city council the power to select commissioners for the police board.[108] Thomas also asked for authorization allowing the mayor to appoint accountants to audit the board's books.

In his memorial, Thomas used various pieces of published testimony of the investigation by the Joint Committee of the General Assembly to demonstrate two things. First, the members of the committee could not possibly, as they stated in their report, have read all the books, vouchers, and so forth of the Board of Police Commissioners in the time they had listed. That is why the mayor called for a separate audit. Second, Thomas asserted about his charges of corrupt and improper acts on the part of the board, "I think the testimony, to any other three persons, except the committee, shows that they were fully sustained."[109]

The General Assembly did not authorize an outside audit. In February, however, a politically sensitive bill was crafted by the St. Louis members of the legislature that would change the manner of appointment of the police commissioners. This proposal was similar to those that Mayor Thomas had suggested in the past but, from a political standpoint, it left no one out of the process. The bill provided that one commissioner would be nominated by the mayor and confirmed by the city council; one would be nominated by the governor and confirmed by the Senate; one would be appointed by the county court; and the fourth would be elected by the people of the city. The mayor would continue as ex officio president of the board. If passed, the bill would become effective in April; it would oust the present board at that time. The proposed bill did not pass.

In February, Joseph McClurg, who had been elected governor of Missouri in November 1868 and inaugurated in January 1869, appointed Samuel Bonner to replace John Codding[110] and reappointed Ferdinand Meyer to a new four-year term on the Board of Police Commissioners. Bonner had retired from the iron-works firm Samuel Bonner and Company, where he had been a partner with former police commissioner James Corbitt. He was also a former state senator. Otto Lademann and William Hequembourg, whose terms would expire in 1870 and 1871, respectively, were retained on the board.

Meanwhile, the *Missouri Democrat* published a letter from Mayor Thomas in which he stated that he was "positively declining to be a candidate of any party for the office of Mayor. . . ."[111] Nonetheless, Thomas, who had been elected and twice reelected as a Radical Republican, accepted the nomination of Anti-Radicals. He was decisively beaten by Radical Republican candidate Nathan Cole.

Mayor Thomas addressed the city council on his last day in office, April 12. He proceeded to review all the improvements in the city that had taken place under his administration. Midway through his address, Thomas attacked the Board of Police Commissioners, stating that he believed that he had proven all of the charges against the board before the Joint Committee the previous year, including those against Chief William Lee. Thomas accused the police department of failing to enforce the ordinances against beer-jerking saloons and gambling houses until the past eighteen months. "As for houses of assignation, I am not aware that even an attempt is made to suppress them, or to do more than occasionally arrest some of the poorer class of 'demoralized females' on a charge of vagrancy."[112]

Thus did James S. Thomas end his mayoral life. And, while he saw the work begun, he would not be the mayor when the county jail, police headquarters, county court, and police courts would be combined in a newly constructed quarters.[113] The plans and cost estimates for the new county courthouse, by architect Thomas W. Walsh, were approved by the county court in February. It would face Clark Avenue and cover the entire block between Clark and Spruce, Eleventh and Twelfth streets. There was to be a basement, and the building would be three and four stories high, in a modified Renaissance style. Walsh was also appointed superintendent of the construction of the new building.[114] The first order of business would be to demolish the old Chouteau mansion standing on the site.

The project would take over two years to build. It was completed and occupied in autumn 1871 by the criminal court (felonies), the Court of Criminal Correction (misdemeanors), the police court of the First District (city ordinances), the police department, and the city jail. While there were only three courts in the building, it would be designated the Four Courts building. That name was supposedly bestowed by one of the judges who was a native of Ireland; he thought it resembled the Four Courts in Dublin.[115]

In June 1869, the board adopted a revision of the police department's rules and regulations that were printed in 1861.[116] The revision was a bound, pocket-size manual containing over one hundred printed pages and several blank pages for notes and for pasting revisions and supplements. One thousand copies of the *Manual of the Board of Police Commissioners of the City of St. Louis, State of Missouri* were

Four Courts building at Twelfth and Clark streets. Photograph by Emil Boehl, ca. 1870. Missouri History Museum.

printed by Missouri Democrat Print in St. Louis. The manual covered such things as the duties and responsibilities of each rank, a description of the uniforms of the various ranks, the laws of arrest, first aid for various injuries, forty-five general rules governing all officers, and even "Advice to a Young Policeman." The latter contained such things as responsibilities when walking a beat, how to handle an arrest, police ethics, and how to testify in court. Each member of the police department received a copy of the manual, as did all new policemen.

Virtually hidden among the many rules and regulations (below the "Uniform" segment of the manual) was a section titled "School of Instruction." First brought up after a committee toured some eastern cities in 1865, and then formally proposed by former chief of police Fenn in 1868, the School of Instruction would be attended by all newly appointed patrolmen. One of the captains of police would conduct the school, at the Second (Central) District police station, for one hour each day for thirty days. The remaining eleven hours of a new patrolman's daily shift would be assigned to a beat accompanied by a patrolman "so as to learn the practical mode of discharging patrol duty."[117] During the thirty hours of training, the new policemen would receive "full and systematic instruction and explanation in respect to the police law, the laws of the State, and the laws and ordinances of the city so far as they concern police duties, and also in the rules and regulations of the Police Department."[118]

The first class of the School of Instruction met on Tuesday, August 31, 1869. Seven applicants were accepted by the board and assigned to the school "in accordance with the recently revised & adopted Police Rules and Regulations."[119] The School of Instruction training period served as a probationary period. The applicants were evaluated by the captain after the thirty hours of instruction and the results were forwarded to the board, which rejected the applicant if it determined that he was not competent. Those who received favorable evaluations were then given a physical examination by a surgeon and, if the doctor's report was favorable, given a commission and assigned to full police duty.[120]

On September 29, in preparation for ordering the material for the winter police uniforms, the board requested that the New York City Board of Police Commissioners send by express "samples of pantaloons, coats and overcoats worn by their force, with the name and address of the manufacturers, and price."[121] The police department continued to model its uniforms after those of the New York City Police Department.

At that same meeting, board vice president Ferdinand Meyer proposed a radical change in the hours of police duty: an eight-hour shift. The police, who worked twelve hours a day, 365 days a year, would not now, however, work eight hours a day. Rather, Meyer proposed that, in a twenty-four-hour period, the police would work eight hours, have eight hours off, and then would return for eight hours of duty. The board approved such a change to go into effect whenever Vice President Meyer and Chief Lee deemed the change expedient.

Three weeks later, Vice President Meyer reported that he had consulted two doctors from the St. Louis Board of Health concerning the change, and they gave the proposal their approval. Meyer's report was approved by the board, and the change was ordered into effect on October 15. On October 19, all police sergeants were called before the board and "questioned relative to the working of the eight hour system. . . ."[122] Five sergeants spoke against the system, while the remainder (perhaps fifteen sergeants) spoke in favor. The eight-hour system remained in effect.

The police department's examining physician appeared at the November 16 board meeting. He stated that he believed the eight-hour on, eight-hour off schedule was not working; it was detrimental to the health of the men. The board apparently had a great deal of confidence in the physician; it ordered the immediate return to twelve-hour shifts. The first platoon would work 11:00 p.m. to 11:00 a.m. The second platoon would work 11:00 a.m. to 11:00 p.m. Each officer would be allowed a one-hour meal.

The board ended the year by authorizing an increase in size of the police substation in Lafayette Park. The Lafayette Park commissioners had requested the additional room, agreeing to split the cost with the board.

Restored Lafayette Park substation, 2004. Courtesy of the author.

The period after the Civil War had been marked by continuous confrontations with the mayor; an investigation of the department; and a high turnover rate of police commissioners, chiefs, and, especially, policemen. It was a formula for disarray and disaster. Yet, there was innovation and accomplishment. The police telegraph system, which connected headquarters, the district station houses, the board, chief of police, and the mayor, was inaugurated. A mounted patrol was established to patrol both within and beyond the city limits, and various boards worked to amend the state law that created the metropolitan police in order to reflect a changing mission.

Chapter Four

Politics, Revolution, and the "Social Evil"

THE UPCOMING YEAR WOULD BE most unusual. During 1870, (1) the entire composition of the Board of Police Commissioners would change, with three of the commissioners being forced out of office; (2) all of those in the command structure of the department (chief of police and captains) would resign from the police force; (3) the police department would, temporarily, be commanded by a police sergeant; and (4) a former chief of police would become the new chief.

1870

A letter from Commissioner Otto Lademann was read at the meeting of February 22. Lademann explained in the letter that his business affairs took him out of the city on Tuesdays, the day of board meetings, and Governor Joseph McClurg had accepted his resignation from the board. Appearing at the meeting was Lademann's replacement, Julius Hunicke, who was to serve out the remaining fifteen months of Lademann's term. The new commissioner was the owner of Julius Hunicke and Company, a supplier to breweries of malt, hops, and other brewing sundries.

In April, the city of Carondelet, south of the St. Louis city limits, was annexed. The annexation increased the geographical area of the city by approximately four square miles, to approximately twenty-two square miles. The board decided to make the Carondelet addition a part of the First Police District. A substation would be established to serve that area, which would be patrolled by mounted police. Caron-delet was almost as old as St. Louis and was named after the Spanish governor of the late 1790s, Baron de Carondelet. It was the home of foundries and ironworks, and was the city where engineer James B. Eads produced seven ironclad gunboats for the Union army in sixty-five days in 1862.[1]

The 1870, the U.S. Census reported that the addition of the property south of Keokuk Street and the city of Carondelet assisted the city of St. Louis in nearly doubling its 1860 population of 160,733. That population increase made St. Louis the fourth-largest metropolitan area in the country behind New York City, Philadelphia, and Brooklyn. While there were accusations, especially from Chicago newspapers, that the census takers in St. Louis had inflated the numbers (they *did* wait until the Chicago figures were in before reporting the St. Louis numbers), the Census Bureau officially listed the St. Louis population as 310,869.

The board successfully lobbied the city council for additional men.[2] City Ordinance 7260, approved May 25, 1870, authorized an increase in the force of 6 sergeants and 44 patrolmen, bringing the authorized strength to 30 sergeants, 304 patrolmen, and 5 detectives.[a]

Approximately fifteen mounted police officers patrolled where needed throughout the city, but they also patrolled the main roads up to three miles outside the city limits, an additional thirty-five square miles.[3] Each officer and his mount were officially assigned to one of the four districts until a special board meeting was called on June 30. At that meeting, the board established a fifth police district, which was designated the Mounted Police District. The mounted officers would be commanded by a sergeant headquartered at the Second District substation on Laclede Avenue near the Wedge House hotel.[4] The mounted officers would continue to ride throughout the city and within the three-mile area surrounding the city limits. Since the mounted officers had five designated beats, a mounted officer on each watch was responsible for an area of eight to nine square miles.

---

[a] Detectives were selected from the patrolman ranks and received the same pay as patrolmen, $75 a month.

Mounted officers who made an arrest would take the arrested person to the nearest police station for processing.

Meanwhile, at a special meeting of the board on September 22, the widow and children of Sergeant John Sturdy, who was murdered on duty in 1863, were, upon the recommendation of a committee from the Police Relief Fund, awarded $150. The sensitivity of the board toward this family of a police officer killed while performing police duty was not an isolated incident. The Board of Police Commissioners had, in the past, assisted these families and the families of those who died and were injured in the line of duty, and it would do so in the future.

The Ferdinand Meyer board would not, however, have another opportunity to assist such families; word had gotten out that Governor McClurg was preparing to remove the board members. It was probably for this reason that the board held the special meeting to complete two items of business: award the money to the Sturdy family and appoint two new members to the force.

The next regular meeting of the board was scheduled for Tuesday, September 27, but on Saturday afternoon, September 24, Governor McClurg informed Commissioners Meyer, Hequembourg, and Hunicke, by telegraph, that they were being removed from office that day. The *Missouri Republican* stated in an editorial that "partisan friends of Governor McClurg have been exceedingly active for some time in gathering bits and shreds of testimony—not always from the most reliable or trustworthy sources—upon which to base charges against some of the Police Board." Board vice president Meyer had, said the *Republican*, "thought fit as a citizen to prefer Mr. [B. Gratz] Brown to Mr. McClurg as a candidate for governor. It is charged that he has employed the police force to distribute cards announcing his own candidacy for sheriff. If this is a fact, the method of electioneering is probably not new, though it has not been complained of before, except by Democrats."[5] The editorial further noted that, while not necessarily in B. Gratz Brown's camp, neither Hunicke nor Hequembourg supported McClurg's reelection.[6]

And, while the newspapers expressed regret at the politics that caused the removal of the three commissioners, the timing of the removals was also of great concern. The biggest annual event of the year, the Agricultural and Mechanical Fair, would be held at the Fairgrounds, at Grand Avenue and Natural Bridge Road, in October. The fair always required extra police protection and coordination with the organizers. The fair had an international reputation and attracted thousands of visitors to the city.[7] There was concern that the new members of the board would not be prepared to deal with the protection of the fair, and the fairgoers, in such a short period of time.

Since the new board members had decided to begin their tenure with a three o'clock meeting on Monday afternoon, September 26, the old board met for its final meeting at nine o'clock that morning. Mayor Cole and Commissioners Meyer, Hequembourg, and Hunicke were present. Commissioner Samuel Bonner was still out of town. The only order of business was to place on the minutes the numerous resignations received by the board. The first resignation was that of the chief of police, William Lee. That letter was followed by letters of resignation from Captain Dan O'Connor, commander, Third Police District, and Captain Christian Kohlhund, commander, Second Police District. Both stated that they could not serve under a board that was appointed for purely partisan reasons. O'Connor and Kohlhund were the only captains in the police department at that time. One of the four captains authorized for the department had been given the opportunity to resign earlier, and another had been dismissed from the force. Neither had been replaced before Governor McClurg's action. Also resigning was the board's attorney, former commissioner Lucien Eaton; Sergeant of Detectives Laurence Harrigan; and six sergeants assigned to the districts, including the commander of the Mounted Police District. Two clerks in the chief's office also resigned.[8] A seventh sergeant would resign the next day. The old board then adjourned.

The newly appointed members of the board, William B. Baker, William Moran, and S. Martin Randolph, met with the ex officio board president Mayor Nathan Cole, at three o'clock. The first item of business was the election of officers. Randolph was elected vice president. Baker was nominated for the office of treasurer but, after learning from Mayor Cole that the position required a $50,000 bond, he declined. After Moran also declined the position, the board elected Samuel Bonner, who was still out of town, as treasurer.

It immediately became apparent that the new members of the board had no knowledge of board or police department operations. Randolph asked Mayor Cole if one of the board members served as secretary. Cole replied that the secretary was appointed by the board, and he recommended the reappointment of George Gavin. When it was learned that Gavin had not resigned, he was unanimously reappointed as secretary of the board.[b]

Since there were no clerks left in the department, Secretary Gavin was authorized to detail patrolmen to fill the clerical slots. Since all the captains had resigned, Randolph asked Mayor Cole who was in charge of the police districts. Cole replied that he didn't know, but the former chief of police, William Lee, could inform the board. Lee was summoned, gave the required information, and left the meeting.[9]

William Baker asked the mayor how he usually found a chief of police. Vice President Randolph said that the chief must be appointed from the rank of captain. Mayor Cole reminded the board that the police department had no captains; they had all resigned. It was finally decided that Fourth District Sergeant Henry A. Burgess could best serve as chief of police. He was summoned and, after initially declining the job because he didn't feel qualified, accepted the position of chief of police pro tem. (At the regular board meeting the next day, Sergeant Burgess was promoted to captain.) Four sergeants were assigned to command the four regular districts, and a patrolman was given the command of the Mounted Police District.[10]

The new board would meet every day, including Saturday, for the first week of its tenure. After an executive session on Friday, September 30, the board announced the appointment of James McDonough as the new chief of police. This was the second time that McDonough

---

[b]George Gavin's first appearance in the board minutes was May 22, 1865, where it was noted that he was the clerk of the Board of Police Commissioners. On August 1, 1865, he was appointed to the new position of secretary of the board. He served in that capacity until April 10, 1883. Gavin later served as a clerk and a special patrolman. He was appointed a turnkey in 1885 and served as such until he left the police department on August 11, 1896.

had been appointed chief of police; he had served as chief under the first Board of Police Commissioners in 1861.[11] He was about fifty-three years of age at the time of his second appointment.

Samuel Bonner first met with the new members of the board at the Saturday meeting. He declined the position of board treasurer, to which he had been elected in his absence. William Baker was then elected to the position. On the recommendation of Chief McDonough, Thomas O'Neill was promoted to sergeant and temporarily placed in charge of the detective force. Captain Burgess was assigned the command of the Second District. As was usually the case, the three new police commissioners had varied backgrounds. Randolph was a member of the firm of Randolph Brothers, architects. Moran was the proprietor of the City Screw and Bolt Works. Baker was characterized by the *Missouri Republican* as "well known in business circles and was recently secretary of the Merchants' Exchange and board of trade."[12] (The Merchants' Exchange was formed when the Millers' Exchange and the Chamber of Commerce merged in 1850. "Here millers, merchants, steamboat owners, and speculators exchanged information and ideas and bought and sold commodities and commodity futures.")[13]

Bonner's attendance at the meeting of October 1 was to be his first and last with the new board. He resigned on October 31. A new police commissioner, M. A. Rosenblatt, appeared at the regular board meeting on November 1 as Bonner's replacement. Rosenblatt was a partner in the firm of Rosenblatt and Strasburger, importers of watches and chains, and the secretary of the State Republican Committee.[c] The *Missouri Democrat* editorialized that Rosenblatt "is an active partisan, and may expect to attempt to use the police force of this city in the interest of McClurg." The editorial continued that, if this was the case, Rosenblatt would be opposed by Randolph, the vice president of the board who, said the *Democrat*, "declares that in his official business he will have nothing to do with politics. A conflict

---

[c] Rosenblatt resigned his Republican committee post the day before being appointed a police commissioner.

may therefore be expected between Randolph and Rosenblatt, and the Governor may find it necessary to turn the former gentleman out to make way for some tool who is willing to prostitute the police force to a partisan machine."[14]

The regular board meeting of November 8 was canceled because of the state and county elections. Radical Republican governor McClurg was defeated by Liberal Republican B. Gratz Brown, the former U.S. senator from Missouri. Governor-elect Brown would have the opportunity to change the face of the board after his January 1871 inauguration.

In October, Chief McDonough went public with a plan to aid the homeless. As a former captain in the old city guard and the chief of police in 1861, McDonough was well aware of the number of persons who sought shelter in police stations in the sometimes-bitter St. Louis winters. Additional relief, in the form of food, clothing, and other necessities, was the sole province of private agencies. As the *Missouri Democrat* pointed out, "There is, we regret to say, no place provided by the city authorities in which these homeless creatures may seek warmth and repose, and they have been allowed to lodge at the [police] stations only to save them by death to exposure in the streets."[15] McDonough was also a realist. As he noted in his letter to the board, reprinted in the local newspapers, "Neither are we by any means certain that the prisoners may not invoke their [the homeless persons in the station] aid to assist them in putting out of the way any outside evidence of guilt."[16] McDonough, while aware of the plight of the homeless in the winter, was alerting the board that there were real dangers in allowing so many people to be lodged in the station houses with prisoners present.

McDonough presented his plan at the board meeting of October 25. The Board agreed that something must be done and suggested that the assistance of the city council be sought. Mayor Cole, however, discouraged the idea, stating, in effect, that there was simply no money to appropriate. Cole added that, while the Provident Association aided the kinds of people who were being discussed, it would be unable to handle the additional number of people that would nightly come to the police stations for lodging. Commissioner Baker proposed that influential citizens be approached and asked for private subscriptions to aid the poor and homeless.[17]

A letter from the superintendent and the matron of the St. Louis Relief Association, Mr. and Mrs. C. W. Harding, to both the police board and the Board of Health, provided the solution. The Hardings petitioned for a city poorhouse and offered to run it for two months for a sum not to exceed $200. That amount would be acquired through private donations; beds could be borrowed from City Hospital and Quarantine Hospital. Once established, police officers who came upon the homeless could bring them to the poorhouse. The board accepted the Hardings' offer and stated that the board would contribute the difference if the $200 objective was not met.

Chief McDonough formed a committee composed of eminent citizens and petitioned the county court for $1,000 to establish such a facility. The court contributed that sum to the committee, which not only selected McDonough as treasurer, but also made him responsible for the project. With the guidance of the board and the citizens' committee, McDonough established the Institution for the Houseless and Homeless at 213 Green Street.[18] The institution would, in the future, come under the direct control and direction of the police department. As McDonough would later state, "The Police force of this city are now made the providers and dispensers of public charity. . . ."[19] McDonough saw the establishment and operation of the facility as a crime prevention effort:

> An institution of this kind will prevent crime of every grade, by furnishing relief to those who are forced to commit crimes, only through necessity. The great majority of those who are driven to seek this species of aid, would work for a support if they could obtain it, and if there be any defence for guilt, it offers itself in behalf of a man who is homeless and without a friend in a large city upon a winter's night.[20]

From November 1870 through March 1871, the Institution for the Houseless and Homeless would admit 11,780 persons. Most of the admissions would come from police referrals in the four police districts, but 117 were referred by the mayor's office and 445 from the city dispensary. In addition to providing food, clothing, and shelter, the institution was able to find jobs for 807 males and 19 females.[21]

There were others in the city who had a place to live, but were living in poverty, kept alive by the charity of neighbors who had barely enough to provide for themselves. Before the winter of 1870–1871 was over, the board had assigned Officer John C. Chapman to make visits, with a horse and wagon, to destitute families. From December 1870 through February 1871, the poor in St. Louis received over six tons of food, meat, coffee, and soap, plus coal, wood, clothing, blankets, shoes, and boots. Chapman personally made almost two thousand visits to homes and delivered over three thousand rations.

Meanwhile, laws were being passed, and plans made, that would involve the police in a far different and innovative role, one that was not performed by police in any urban area. It was a unique response to the "social evil" of prostitution. While the act of March 13, 1867, had given the vice president of the Board of Police Commissioners the power to issue search warrants to enter named establishments and seize gambling devices, no such power was extended to the board to deal with the problem of prostitution.

Prostitution in St. Louis was similar to that in other cities. St. Louis had "a few first class brothels patronized by respected gentlemen of means."[22] As elsewhere, bawdy houses ranged from first rate to the worst. There were also "houses of assignation," hotels or other establishments where prostitutes took their clients. Houses of assignation in St. Louis ranged from "outwardly respectable houses and hotels . . . to flea bags catering to common streetwalkers."[23] The report issued by the 1868 Joint Committee of the General Assembly to investigate the police department contained several references to prostitution. One bawdy house, known as Madame Callahan's, was described by a witness as "a very elegant mansion."[24] A policeman described the less-than-first-rate City Hotel as "an assignation house" where he had seen prostitutes and thieves.[25]

In 1869, police board vice president Ferdinand Meyer "and other officials and citizens" spearheaded a drive to get social evil legislation through the state legislature.[26] In 1870, State Senator Louis Gottschalk of St. Louis introduced Senate Bill 362 to revise the charter of the city of St. Louis and extend the geographical limits of the city. The bill also provided that the bicameral form of city government would be changed to a unicameral city council. In the latter section, a clause was inserted granting the city the power "to regulate or suppress bawdy and disorderly houses, houses of ill-fame or assignation."[27] There was little opposition to the bill, and it was passed and sent to the governor, who signed it into law on March 14, 1870.

The word "regulate" gave the city the enabling legislation needed to write a social evil ordinance. In addition, the new city charter reorganized the Board of Health in St. Louis to include representatives from the Board of Police Commissioners and the city council. The newly constituted Board of Health "consisted of the mayor as ex officio chairman, two physicians appointed by the mayor, one of the police commissioners, and an alderman."[28] Ferdinand Meyer, who had left the police board upon expiration of his term of office in 1870, was appointed to the Board of Health, but a current member of the police board was also assigned to the Board of Health. The city ordinance, known as the "social evil ordinance," was passed by the city council on July 5, 1870, and became law on July 9.

Under the new Ordinance to Regulate and Suppress Houses of Ill-Fame, the police were required to prepare a record of all bawdy houses, houses of ill fame and assignation, and prostitutes within the city of St. Louis for the Board of Health. This was probably not as difficult a task as might be imagined since, according to the *Missouri Democrat*: "The police have always kept a registry of this kind, and the number of vile women for the past year was about 1,000."[29] If a register of prostitutes did exist, it was completely updated; police officers worked on the register for about two weeks before declaring the work completed. Then the two boards were given the power to make regulations and to attempt to reform the prostitutes. Fees were to be paid by both the prostitutes and the bawdy-house keepers. These fees were collected to pay for the entire system.

The joint boards met to draft regulations and, on July 21, approved the regulations. Most of the rules regulated prostitutes and their presence in public: Prostitutes could not stand in windows, ride in open carriages in the daytime, or visit saloons. They could not rent or inhabit a room without first obtaining permission of the Board of Police Commissioners. Neither they nor the keepers of bawdy houses could move to another location within the city without first making application to, and receiving permission from, the board. In addition, each keeper of a bawdy house or house of assignation had to pay $10 a month, payable the first week of each month, for "hospital dues." Each prostitute had to pay fifty cents a week. Any person violating the rules was deemed guilty of a misdemeanor and, if convicted, was to be fined not less than $5 or more than $50 for each offense.[30] The Board of Health divided the city into six districts. All of the districts extended from the western city limits to the Mississippi River.[31] After the members voted by secret ballot, the board appointed a physician to attend each district. The social evil experiment was ready to commence.

Once the experiment got under way, the police would be called upon to enforce the ordinance and the regulations of the Board of Health, continually update the registry, and keep statistical information about prostitutes and keepers of bawdy houses and houses of assignation, their location, and the number of arrests and charges filed. While there were believed to be one thousand prostitutes in the city, the police felt that the number registered might be between seven hundred and eight hundred. Said the *Missouri Democrat*, "Many women have left the city rather than be subjected to the rigid surveillance required, and more have reformed and abandoned their odious traffic."[32]

Problems developed early. First, one of the medical inspectors reported that some of the prostitutes were refusing to pay the fees established by the Board of Health. Seven infected prostitutes, admitted to City Hospital for treatment, escaped within a month of the start of the program. A running feud between one of the medical inspectors and a Catholic priest who opposed the ordinance was printed in one of the local newspapers. The medical inspector resigned after it was charged that he was promoting the system for his own profit. Finally, a court ruled that the social evil regulations, since they were not included in any city ordinance, did not have the force of law and the police were prohibited from arresting anyone for violating the regulations. The police responded by arresting violators under the vagrancy ordinance.[33]

The city council began working on the problems at the start of the new session in December 1870. The council concluded its work with approval of Chapter XIV of the city ordinances, "Houses of Ill-Fame," on July 10, 1871. The Board of Health regulations were included in the ordinance as was the authorization to "erect, purchase, or rent suitable buildings to be used as a hospital and House of Industry for the exclusive care, medical treatment and industrial employment of diseased bawds and prostitutes."[34] The ordinance also forbade use of City Hospital for the treatment of diseased prostitutes. As problems arose over time, the ordinance was amended to address the situation.

On March 31, 1871, the end of the fiscal year in St. Louis, the police department would release the statistical information for eight months of the experiment. The number of registered prostitutes was 1,284. There were 136 bawdy houses and 9 houses of assignation registered, while 252 prostitutes lived in single rooms. Surprisingly, there were 821 permits issued for a change of residence. The actual number of prostitutes reflected in this number is not known since some might have requested a move two or more times. In addition to the registered houses and prostitutes, police in fiscal year 1870–1871 arrested fifty-three persons for keeping a bawdy house. Many of these arrests, however, could have occurred before the inception of the experiment.[35]

1871

On January 9, 1871, B. Gratz Brown was inaugurated the twentieth governor of Missouri. Three weeks later, Governor Brown appointed a new police commissioner, William Patrick. Patrick attended the board meeting of February 3, but his commission did not indicate which commissioner he was replacing. A special board meeting was called for February 10, and Patrick appeared to take the place of William B. Baker. He was unanimously elected treasurer of the board. Patrick had also been treasurer of the second Board of Police Commissioners, appointed by Provisional Governor Hamilton Gamble in September 1861. He served until February 1865.

At the regular meeting on February 21, two commissioners appointed by Governor Brown, Julius Hunicke and Oliver Filley, replaced M. A. Rosenblatt and William Moran. Hunicke had been one of the members of the board ousted by Governor McClurg the previous September. Filley and a partner, Gerard B. Allen, owned the Fulton Iron Works. At a special meeting two days later, William F. Ferguson was seated as S. Martin Randolph's replacement. Ferguson had been a probate court judge in St. Louis.

With the board now at full strength, officers were elected. William Ferguson was elected vice president. William Patrick resigned as treasurer of the Randolph board and was elected treasurer of the new board. George Gavin was retained as secretary of the board. Mayor Cole selected Julius Hunicke as the board's representative on the Board of Health. Primarily because he was a member of the Merchants' Exchange and familiar with purchasing procedures, Hunicke was selected to be in charge of purchasing all supplies for the police department.[36] He became, in effect, the first holder of a new board position that would be referred to as purchasing member of the board. The April 1872 annual report of the board would list Hunicke as the holder of that office.

At the first board meeting in March, Chief McDonough recommended that Sergeant Thomas O'Neill, who was in charge of the detective force, be promoted to the rank of captain. To fill the position that would be vacated by O'Neill, McDonough recommended that former Sergeant Laurence Harrigan be reinstated as a sergeant and placed in charge of the detectives.[37] The board approved Chief McDonough's recommendations. Also upon the recommendation of McDonough, one captain, three sergeants, and five patrolmen were dropped from the rolls of the force for inefficiency.[38]

In May, Chief McDonough proposed to the board that a police convention be held in St. Louis in the fall. The city council passed a resolution the next month establishing committees for the National Police Convention. Members of the Board of Police Commissioners and the members of the police committee of the city council met as a committee. It resolved that the expenses of hosting the convention should not exceed $4,000. Half of that amount would be contributed by the board, and the remainder would come from the City Contingent Fund. Planning for the convention would be handled by an executive committee. Three councilmen were appointed to the executive committee, as were Commissioners Ferguson and Patrick and Chief McDonough. The dates chosen for the convention were Friday, October 20, through Monday, October 23, 1871. No program was planned for Sunday, October 22.

In June, the city Board of Health asked the police department to take on yet another task. The city council had passed an ordinance requiring the registration of all marriages and births in the city. The Board of Health asked that the Board of Police Commissioners take any steps, "as in its judgment seems advisable," to enforce the ordinance.[39] While the board minutes do not indicate what steps were taken, the board had always done what was deemed necessary to cooperate with the Board of Health. The ultimate burden was on the individual beat officers.

Also in June, the city council passed an ordinance authorizing an increase in the size of the police force by fifty patrolmen and four sergeants. On June 30, the board began appointing applicants to the force. For the first time, however, the board sent the names of the appointees to the appropriate police districts "for the purpose of inquiring as to whether they are of good moral character."[40] Although limited in nature, the board now required background investigations of the appointees before they were sworn in as commissioned officers.

Chief McDonough was granted a leave of absence of one month, beginning July 5, "for the purpose of visiting various cities in the country on police business."[41] While the "police business" was not specified, it likely included the usual visits to determine what advancements had been made by other police departments. In addition, McDonough was drumming up support for the October police convention in St. Louis. The police convention was held at the Temple Building, diagonally across the street from the Southern Hotel. Conference members were housed at the Southern Hotel, which occupied the entire city block from Walnut to Elm streets, and Fourth to Broadway.[42] Completed just six years earlier, it was one of St. Louis's finest hotels. The attendees were mostly chiefs of police and city marshals, but included mayors, city attorneys, police commissioners, sheriffs, prosecutors, prison officials, detectives, police captains and lieutenants, and even a few police clerks. The largest contingent, 16, came from Ohio. The *Official Proceedings* booklet printed after the convention listed 112 delegates from twenty-one states and the District of Columbia.[43]

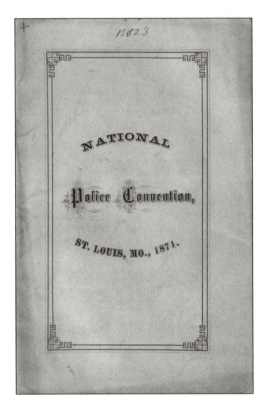

Official Proceedings publication, 1871 National Police Convention.
Courtesy of the author.

Six topics were proposed, and agreed upon, for discussion at the convention: (1) improvement of the condition of neglected and abandoned youth of the country; (2) provision of a systematic plan of transmitting detective information throughout the states for the better prevention and detection of crime; (3) consideration of the social evil question; (4) ways to perfect the police telegraph system throughout the country; (5) the use of photography in police work; and (6) the question of rewards for extraordinary services by police.[44] The convention voted to meet again on the first Monday in June 1872, in Washington, D.C. With the assistance of the Board of Police Commissioners and city officials, Chief McDonough had organized the first national meeting of police officials in the country.

* * *

At approximately 9:00 p.m. on Sunday, October 8, 1871, a fire began in Chicago, Illinois, that would burn for almost thirty-six hours and virtually destroy downtown Chicago. In a gesture that would regularly be repeated, the district captains reported that all the men under their commands had volunteered to contribute one day's pay toward "relieving the sufferers from the Chicago fire."[45] Obviously, there were officers who remembered what the fire of 1849 had done to downtown St. Louis.

As 1872 approached, the board prepared to move its offices and police headquarters to the new Four Courts building.

1872

In mid-January, Commissioner Filley resigned from the board for medical reasons. His replacement would attend the meeting of January 30. Governor Brown appointed Joseph Pulitzer to fill the remaining thirteen months of Filley's term. Pulitzer was a relative newcomer to St. Louis. He emigrated from Hungary in 1864 and joined the First New York Lincoln Cavalry. He was discharged from duty in July 1865. Because there were so many discharged soldiers in New York City, jobs were few. He decided to go west, and arrived in St. Louis in October 1865. He worked at many odd jobs, including that of warden of Arsenal Island, where many of those who died from the 1866 cholera epidemic were brought to be buried. In March 1867, he became an American citizen. In 1868, he landed a job as a reporter for the Republican *Westliche Post*, a German-language newspaper.[46]

Joseph Pulitzer. Photograph, 1870. Missouri History Museum.

Pulitzer was only twenty-four years old when he joined the board. He was only twenty-five years old, later that same year, when some of the proprietors of the *Westliche Post* sold him "a proprietary interest in that paper on very liberal terms."

On February 3, the offices of the Board of Police Commissioners and chief of police were moved to the new Four Courts building.[d] Since the lease had not expired, the board did not vacate the building at 220 Chestnut Street. It would later be used as a substation for the Second Police District. That same day, the board voted to decentralize the School of Instruction. "On motion it was ordered that Captains

---

[d] A month later, the board would receive approval from the county court to move the calaboose to the basement of the Four Courts building.

of Police establish at their respective district main stations a 'School of Instruction' for new policemen, in lieu of the general school heretofore in use at Police Head Quarters."[47] The board also received a sample of flannel used in the summer uniforms of the New York City Police Department and approved the purchase of a sufficient amount for summer uniforms.

On April 15, the board forwarded the *Eleventh Annual Report of the Board of Police Commissioners* to the city council. This report was unlike its predecessors; it was independently published by the board and not included in the annual city report. Over the following years, the annual reports of the Board of Police Commissioners alternated between independent publications and part of the *Mayor's Message with Accompanying Documents.*

As was the practice, the 1872 annual report of the board also contained the annual report of the chief of police. Chief McDonough's report to the board included the second annual report of the social evil experiment. At the end of March 1872, the report indicated, there was little change in some areas. The number of registered bawdy houses remained the same, and houses of assignation dropped from nine to six. The number of registered prostitutes declined to 703. The report notes that a large number of previously registered prostitutes living in single rooms worked in houses of assignation and were thus checked by medical inspectors. In his report to the board, McDonough made several comments about the moral issues involved in the social evil experiment. The prostitutes were more "decorous" in their manner; prostitutes plying their trade on the streets "have been almost entirely discontinued"; a considerable number of abandoned women had been reclaimed and restored to respectable life; and juvenile prostitution "has been greatly diminished, if not wholly removed." There were only three arrests for keeping a bawdy house.[48]

As treasurer of the Institution for the Houseless and Homeless, Chief McDonough also presented that annual report to the board. That institution, run by the police department with donations of money and goods from businesses and private citizens, had now become a year-round effort. From March 1871 through February 1872, the institution at 213 Green Street logged over 23,000 admissions. This number was listed as "admissions," not "persons." There were, no doubt, many persons who were admitted on several different occasions. No one was excluded. In addition to whites and blacks who were U.S. citizens, McDonough's statistical record listed American Indians and citizens from twelve foreign countries. Two patrolmen were each provided with a horse and wagon and visited the homes of the "destitute poor." Yet, said McDonough, the entire effort had been achieved "without the slightest interference with the police duties proper of the force."[49]

In December, all but eleven members of the force signed a letter to the board that they had formed the Mutual Life Association. Upon the death of a member of the association, all other members would be assessed $2. If the board approved, the assessment would be deducted from each member's pay for that month. The board approved the organization of the Mutual Life Association, the assessment, and the deduction of the assessment from each member's pay.

1873

In March, the recently inaugurated governor of Missouri, Silas Woodson, decided that he wanted to replace the entire Board of Police Commissioners in St. Louis. It was not to be an easy task; both Julius Hunicke and William Patrick had two years remaining in their terms. Hunicke, however, sent Governor Woodson his resignation; he would remain on the board until a replacement was named. Patrick, on the other hand, wished to complete his term on the board.

On March 3, Governor Woodson sent the names of Charles C. Rainwater, David H. Armstrong, Charles Green, and James Sweeney to the Senate executive session for confirmation. On March 6, Rainwater and Armstrong were confirmed, but Sweeney and Green were rejected. Woodson forwarded the name of Lewis Dorsheimer to the executive session of the Senate; he was confirmed on March 14. The governor still needed a replacement for William Patrick, and he asked Patrick to resign. Patrick declined.[50] Woodson again sent in the name of James Sweeney. Sweeney was never confirmed, and Patrick remained on the board with new appointees Armstrong, Rainwater, and Dorsheimer.[51]

Armstrong's appointment was for two years, replacing Hunicke. Rainwater was appointed to a four-year term to replace Pulitzer, whose term had expired. Dorsheimer, who replaced William F. Ferguson, whose term expired, was also given a four-year appointment. Patrick had two more years remaining in his term of office.

Armstrong was well known in St. Louis. He had been the city comptroller, the aide-de-camp to Governor Sterling Price, and the Postmaster of St. Louis from 1854 to 1858. He had also been the

David H. Armstrong. Photograph by Falk, New York, mid- to late nineteenth century. Missouri History Museum.

principal of the Benton School, one of the earliest of the St. Louis Public Schools. Armstrong was the chairman of the State Democratic Committee in 1870. He would later serve on the City Charter Committee and, in 1877, become a United States senator. Rainwater was a partner in the firm of Bradford, Rainwater and Company, wholesalers of hats, caps, straw goods, furs, and gloves, and the president and treasurer of a manufacturing firm, the Missouri Metal Blind Company. At the time of his appointment to the board, Dorsheimer was in the process of retiring from the wholesale saddlery business. He had also recently resigned as a trustee of the St. Louis Blind Asylum.

Charles C. Rainwater. Photograph by F. W. Guerin, 1884.
Missouri History Museum.

The Mutual Life Association, the police life insurance policy approved by the board in December 1872, made its first payment in March. All members were assessed $2, giving $748 to the family of the late patrolman Nathan Pepper.

The month of March was highlighted by a strike of the St. Louis, Kansas City and Northern Railroad by the Brotherhood of Locomotive Engineers. Trouble began when the railroad hired a locomotive engineer who did not join the brotherhood. The brotherhood in Moberly, Missouri (about 150 miles from St. Louis, 100 miles from Kansas City), sent a letter to the superintendent of machinery of the railroad in late February asking that the "scab" be removed from "Engine No. 10."[52] When no reply was received, a committee met with the general superintendent of the railroad, W. C. Van Horne, in St. Louis the first week of March. Van Horne gave the committee no assurances that the engineer would be retained or dismissed and, the following day, was met by another, larger committee. On Sunday, March 9, Van Horne sent a telegram to the superintendent of machinery stating that, if the engineer in question was "a competent and sober man," he would be "fully sustained" in retaining him. The brotherhood found this reply unsatisfactory, and the railroad prepared for a strike.

As was customary, railroad officials hired some new engineers who were sent over the road to learn the route. On Friday, March 14, one of the old engineers was instructed to "take over the line." He took the new man about forty or fifty miles east of Moberly, put him off the engine, and continued to St. Charles. A large number of strikers gathered at St. Charles and began to stop passenger trains, refusing to allow them to be removed to sidetracks. About 1:00 a.m. on Sunday morning, a force of ten St. Louis policemen, under the command of Sergeant Henry Frangel of the Second District, were dispatched to St. Charles. In the meantime, strikers stopped an express train from Kansas City at Harlem, just outside Kansas City. After first being overpowered, Kansas City police regained control of the scene, arresting several strikers.

Strikers began seizing trains, running one off the track, and they obstructed the rails by overturning other engines as trains arrived. The superintendent of the railroad requested additional police assistance, and thirty-eight St. Louis police, under the command of Captain Thomas O'Neill of the Fourth District, were sent to Moberly. An eastbound mail train from Kansas City was seized at Lexington, about forty miles from Kansas City; the sheriff of Ray County and his posse arrested all of those involved. Governor Woodson placed Companies A and B of the St. Louis National Guard on alert and they assembled at their armory. They would not be needed.

Captain O'Neill telegraphed Chief McDonough for additional officers, rifles, and ammunition. The rifles and ammunition were sent on the next train west. Ten officers then boarded a train for Moberly. While pulling up a grade just west of St. Charles, with the ten officers riding on the front, the engine struck a pile of railroad ties placed on the tracks and derailed. The officers were uninjured and assisted in placing the engine back on the tracks. They proceeded to Moberly.

"About forty of the worst characters" got on two eastbound trains at Moberly. When the second train arrived in St. Charles, all but seven of the officers and Sergeant Frangel boarded the train to protect it on the trip to St. Louis.[e] The strikers got off the train and, after it had departed, derailed an engine that blocked the main line. On Wednesday, March 19, Frangel requested assistance. Captain Anton Huebler of the Second District, along with eight policemen and additional arms and ammunition, was dispatched to St. Charles. Another squad of officers went to St. Charles later that day.

That same day, Captain O'Neill reported to Chief McDonough that Moberly was quiet, but he felt that a complete withdrawal of police would be the signal for more outbreaks of violence. The following day, McDonough telegraphed O'Neill to return to St. Louis, leaving a sergeant and ten men. That night, the superintendent of the St. Louis, Kansas City and Northern Railroad declared that the strike had ended and that trains would be running on schedule on Friday. The strike had lasted less than a week. The experience the police force gained by handling the railroad strike would become useful in four years, when St. Louis would find itself in the throes of a railway strike.

The state legislature passed a new law, effective March 24, granting St. Louis officials some budgetary control over the police. The act gave the city council the power to set salaries for each rank, but set a maximum salary for each. The cap for each rank was higher than that currently paid the members of those ranks.

In addition to licensing all private watchmen, the Board of Police Commissioners was responsible, by ordinance, for determining the locations of stands for hacks, baggage wagons, furniture cars, wood and coal wagons, and hand expresses. Under city ordinances, the city collector was required to refer all applications for certain licenses to

---

[e] An undetermined number of additional officers had been sent to St. Charles after the arrival of the initial contingent.

the board. The board had to conduct investigations (which would be done by the sergeants and patrolmen) "and report as to whether the applicant is of good moral character and worthy of a license." The board indicated whether it approved or disapproved of the applicant; the collector abided by the decision of the board. Those required to get board approval before licenses were issued included pawnbrokers, intelligence offices (employment agencies), museums, junk shops, and shows and exhibitions of all kinds.[53]

The board elected officers in April. Charles Rainwater was elected vice president; William Patrick continued as treasurer. George Gavin was retained as secretary to the board. The board deferred the election of a purchasing member. (Lewis Dorsheimer would be elected to that position in May.) That same month, the board requested Chief McDonough to provide a list of all gambling houses known to the police. After obtaining the list, the board put the gambling houses on notice by passing a resolution that it "is the unqualified determination of this Board to suppress gambling in all such houses, and that every means in their power will be brought to bear to accomplish the same." Chief McDonough was instructed to furnish a copy of the resolution to each person keeping, or suspected of keeping, a gambling house.[54]

The Police Relief Fund began to aid working police officers. A patrolman requested a $60 loan for eight months. The board approved the loan, at an 8 percent annual interest rate, provided that he and a sergeant signed a note in that amount and presented it to the treasurer of the board. It was likely that the sergeant was asked to co-sign the loan as surety.

The police uniforms continued to evolve. In May, the sergeants' shields were redistributed by seniority, and their silver-colored uniform buttons were changed to gilt buttons to distinguish them from patrolmen. The board also established a *Roll of Honor* book, in which the names of members of the force "who for gallantry, efficiency, zeal, and distinguished and meritorious conduct, shall be adjudged to merit it."[55]

In July, Rainwater and Patrick were assigned the task of revising the police manual of 1869 and having it printed. And, in what was an unusual decision, the board turned down a pay raise for the police force.

Mayor Brown informed the board that the city council had passed an ordinance increasing the pay of the police to the maximum amounts cited in the March 24 state law, but he wanted the board's input before he signed the ordinance into law. The board replied that they were able to get the very best applicants under the current pay scale.[56]

Chief McDonough, meanwhile, had run into some problems. Based upon the complaints of two citizens, McDonough was brought before the board on August 29 to answer to two separate charges. The first complaint charged that McDonough was guilty of willful and malicious oppression, misconduct, and abuse of his authority as chief of police in the arrest of a man, his wife, and female servant without just cause or provocation. Two patrolmen the chief had commanded to accompany him were not charged. Four specifications, describing the acts that McDonough was alleged to have committed, were attached.[57] The second charge was based upon the complaint of a different citizen. McDonough was accused by the citizen of being "so under the influence of liquor in the vicinity of the Olympic Theatre" on July 17, 1873, that he "acted in such a manner, that he then and there became the laughing stock of by standers [sic] and citizens."[58]

After two days of testimony, McDonough made a statement in his defense. The board then took the decision under advisement and adjourned. On Monday, September 1, a transcript of the testimony was received; the members of the board reviewed the testimony and then ordered the entire transcript be given to the press. It then discussed the evidence. The second charge, being under the influence of liquor, was dismissed. The board also struck the words "willful and malicious" from the first charge, that charge now reading "oppression, misconduct, and abuse of his authority. . . ." After further deliberation of the first charge and the four specifications, the board found McDonough guilty on all counts and assessed a thirty-day suspension effective the next day. Captain Anton Huebler was appointed acting chief of police during McDonough's suspension.[59]

At the board meeting of September 23, the board read a petition from "a large number of citizens," including members of the county court and the recent grand jury, requesting that Chief McDonough be reinstated before the expiration of his term of suspension. The board restored McDonough to duty effective October 1, twenty-nine days after being suspended.

On October 28, the board approved Chief McDonough's recommendation that the two platoons rotate quarterly. Until this time, an officer remained on either the first (11:00 p.m. to 11:00 a.m.) or second platoon. The first rotation would begin on November 1, 1873. The platoons would again rotate on February 1, 1874.

At that same meeting, the board approved an appropriation of $500 from the Police Relief Fund for the benefit of the Memphis police. At a later meeting, the donation was listed as paid for "the Memphis sufferers." A Memphis Relief Committee had been established in St. Louis to accept donations for those who were victims of yellow fever in that Tennessee city. This was the second time that the police in St. Louis demonstrated their generosity, the first being for the sufferers of the Chicago fire two years earlier.

In November, Dr. William R. Faulkner was appointed as "Superintendent of the Mounted District Police Stables at $75 per month." Horses and all horse equipment and supplies were placed under his

Dr. William R. Faulkner. Halftone, 1902. Missouri History Museum.

control. Faulkner was a well-known veterinarian; his pay was that of a patrolman.

1874

On March 6 and 7, 1874, the board held special meetings to determine whether the social evil ordinance had been properly enforced by the police. Chief McDonough and the three district captains "were examined & testimony taken."[60] Members of the press also noted that all the sergeants were also called before the board.[61] And, while the press was not permitted at the meetings, "news soon leaked that two police captains had told the board that half of the prostitutes in the city were not registered, and that all of the officers and sergeants were opposed to the ordinance."[62]

Chief of Police McDonough gave the board his resignation on March 10. The board accepted it and appointed Captain Henry Burgess, Third District, as acting chief of police.

In fiscal year 1873–1874, ending on March 31, the social evil experiment was mentioned only once, where the arrest of one female was attributed to "escaping from social evil hospital."[63] The reason for the sparse information about the social evil experiment in the police board's annual report was that the experiment ended in April 1874. A variety of people and institutions had contributed to the demise of the experiment. Many clergymen, led by William Greenleaf Eliot, a Unitarian minister and chancellor of Washington University in St. Louis, had opposed the experiment from the beginning. In 1873, Eliot and others began to see the possibility of defeating the ordinance. A group of women opposed to the experiment aligned themselves with the feminist movement in Missouri to have the "regulation" portion of the state law repealed. A bill was introduced in the state legislature to remove that section, but it failed. It would be revisited.[64] Other women petitioned the city council to overturn the social evil ordinance, and petitions were continually sent to the state legislature. One of the leaders of the women's opposition was the wife of police commissioner William Patrick. Two St. Louis newspapers, the *Globe* and the *Democrat*, joined in the chorus of opposition.

Lawsuits were filed, and the finding in one suit sounded the death knell for the experiment. In a December 1873 city court case, the court found that the social evil ordinance and the ninth clause in the vagrancy ordinance contradicted each other and both could not stand. The court struck down the portion of the vagrancy ordinance that police used to make a case that associating with prostitutes was a misdemeanor; the social evil ordinance was permitted to stand. With the loss of the vagrancy ordinance, a useful tool to the police, police began to reconsider their support of the social evil ordinance. The vice president of the police board, Charles Rainwater, also came out against the social evil experiment.

In February 1874, Senator James C. McGinnis of St. Louis reintroduced a bill to take away the power given to the city of St. Louis to regulate prostitution. The bill, which passed on March 18, also included a section that prevented the police from making raids on bawdy houses. It was feared that the police would use the lists of prostitutes, who had registered in good faith during the social evil experiment, in their raids. Under the law, the police were not permitted to enter bawdy houses except on official business. "Official business" was limited to (1) arresting a prostitute or the keeper of the bawdy house on a warrant of the Board of Health for being diseased and (2) executing a warrant, based upon an affidavit of some reliable person, that the structure was a bawdy house. Another bill, passed the next day, prohibited the police from raiding "suspected" bawdy houses.[65]

The social evil experiment was the first such effort in the United States. Whether it was a success or a failure was overshadowed by the uniqueness of the social experiment. Representatives from several cities in the country visited St. Louis to observe the program and report their findings. Social evil laws were debated in Chicago, Cincinnati, and San Francisco, but none was ever enacted. Discussions of social evil laws continued well into the next century.[66]

*   *   *

At the meeting of May 19, 1874, the board approved the police manual revised by Commissioners Rainwater and Patrick and ordered one thousand copies of the 1874 police manual printed by the lowest bidder, the St. Louis Times Company.

At a special meeting on May 27, with all board members and Mayor Brown present, a vote was taken to select a new chief of police. The sergeant of detectives, Laurence Harrigan, received the most votes. He was promoted to chief of police effective June 1. Harrigan had resigned from the force during the mass resignations of September 1870. At Chief McDonough's request, the board reinstated Harrigan to the force at the rank of sergeant in March 1871, and returned him to his old position of sergeant of detectives, which he held until his promotion to chief of police. Sergeant Daniel O'Connor was appointed to take Harrigan's former position of sergeant of detectives. Harrigan was a shoemaker when he left New York City for St. Louis in 1853. He continued that trade in St. Louis until he was appointed to the police department as a private on June 15, 1857. He was promoted to sergeant in 1859 and retained that rank when the police department became the metropolitan police department in 1861. He was promoted to lieutenant in 1866, but returned to the rank of sergeant when the lieutenant rank was abolished in March 1867. Harrigan was the second chief of police to be promoted from the ranks—Captain William Lee being the first—and the first officer below the rank of captain to be selected as chief.

In June, former chief William Lee, who had resigned in protest of political interference by Governor McClurg in September 1870, was reinstated on the force as a patrolman.

In July, the Board of Police Commissioners made a major change in the uniforms of the chief of police, captains, and sergeants. Effective September 1, they would be required to wear white shirts and collars. While the board minutes failed to explain this change, it was probably meant to further distinguish the upper ranks from the lower. It was also likely to have been a reaction to a similar change by one or more of the large eastern police departments; St. Louis police officers were wearing uniforms based on those of the New York City Police Department.

In September, the board adopted a resolution to direct Chief Harrigan "to inform Lonergan and Thiele that their 'Detective Force' or any other detective force in the city is a violation of law and they must at once cease detective operations."[67] The firm of Lonergan and Thiele was one of the private detective agencies that had begun springing up at that time. The board believed that the detectives in the police department were the only detectives permitted by law. Six months after this decision, and after obtaining legal opinions, the board would license private detective firms under the private watchman section of the 1861 state law establishing the metropolitan police department.

Also in September, with no fanfare, Patrolman (and former chief of police) William Lee was promoted to sergeant. He would rise to his former rank of captain early in 1875.

As 1874 came to a close, board minutes indicate that many, if not all, of the districts were running "soup houses." There was a reference to the "Lodging and Soup House" in the Third District; Turnkey Matthew Little was placed in charge.[68] The board also required that all men who went to the soup houses and received accommodations, and who were physically able to perform manual labor, were required to clean streets "or such other city work as the Mayor or Street Superintendent may designate."[69]

1875

Commissioner William Patrick's term of office expired on February 2, 1875, and the newly elected governor, Charles Hardin, appointed Dr. James C. Nidelet as his replacement. As it happened, the regular meeting of the board occurred that same day. Dr. Nidelet was introduced by William Patrick, who then left the meeting. Lewis Dorsheimer was elected to serve as treasurer of the board until they could formally organize.

At the board meeting two weeks later, Commissioner David Armstrong introduced his successor, John G. Priest. Armstrong's term officially expired the next day, but he stepped down so that the board would be composed of those commissioners who would serve for at least the next two years.

Dr. James C. Nidelet. Steel engraving by A. H. Ritchie, 1883.
Missouri History Museum.

John G. Priest. Photograph by J. A. Scholten, 1883.
Missouri History Museum.

Nidelet was a physician with a private practice at 927 North Broadway. Priest was a successful real estate and financial agent. He was also a former Missouri representative to the National Democratic Executive Committee, a member of the board of managers of the House of Refuge, a member of the Mullanphy Emigrant Relief Fund, a director of the St. Louis National Bank, and a member of the St. Louis Mutual Life Insurance Company.

In February 1875, the board was informed that the Missouri House of Representatives had passed a bill that would permit the board to supply officers with summer and winter uniforms paid out of the funds within the board's control. The board noted that the city wasn't in a financial condition to allow that. It was the feeling of the board members that any future increase in revenue should be used to increase the size of the force—which the board was authorized to increase by fifty more men—rather than supply uniforms. (Officers still purchased their own uniforms.) The board asked that the bill not be passed: "we are of the opinion that if the bill shall pass, it will impose an additional unnecessary burden upon the tax payers of Saint Louis, that it will in no wise contribute to the efficiency of the police force, and will be in all respects unnecessary and inexpedient."[70]

Priest and Rainwater, meanwhile, were appointed to meet with a lawyer and then draw up a suitable form of license for private detectives. The board would also be responsible for establishing rules and regulations for private detectives.

March was an extremely busy month, beginning with the election of officers. Nidelet was elected vice (and acting) president, and Rainwater was elected treasurer. Dorsheimer would continue to hold the position of purchasing member. Priest would be the board's representative on the Board of Health. The board also agreed to take control of the county jail in the Four Courts building. Said the board, "the members of the Board and the officers of the Police Dept. believe that all prisoners in our city should properly be under the control and management of the Police Department."[71]

On March 23, the board called for Chief Harrigan and the district commanders and, upon consultation with them, redistricted the city into six districts (including the mounted district). A few days after the redistricting went into effect, Harrigan recommended that the police districts be named First, Second, Central, Third, Fourth, and Fifth (Mounted) districts, and that the mounted district be reduced to one platoon of sixteen men. The recently renamed Third District, which encompassed the central business district of St. Louis, would be called the Central District. In that way, the number designations of Districts Three, Four, and Five (Mounted) would remain the same. The board approved Harrigan's recommendation, effective April 20.[72]

Also in March, the names of eight sergeants were placed in nomination for two captain vacancies. Each came before the board to be examined. Harrigan recommended that two sergeants, one of them being William Lee, be promoted to the rank of captain. After a vote, both were promoted to captain, effective the same day that the redistricting plan went into effect. Former chief Lee had quickly risen to his old rank of captain. Except for his time as chief of police (and some time off after he resigned), and his most recent ten months as a patrolman and a sergeant, Lee had been a captain of police since 1855.

The board approved the rules and regulations for private detectives composed by Rainwater and Priest. The rules required applicants to be licensed by the board, to work for only one private detective agency, to keep a book of daily activities open to the board or any officer designated by the board, to report all those acting as private detectives without a license, and to report the presence of all known thieves and any information "they may obtain relative to the commission of crime or that may lead to the arrest of criminals."[73] Private detectives had to wear a badge of office designated by the board and display it to any police officer when requested. The board could revoke the license of any private detective failing to comply with the rules and regulations or found guilty of "any immoral or questionable practices, or who shall be found negligent in the performance of his duties to his employers...."[74]

On April 13, Mayor Arthur B. Barret was inaugurated as mayor of the city of St. Louis and later attended his first (and only) board meeting. Mayor Barret missed the meeting of April 20 and died on April 24. The board called a special meeting on April 24 to make the necessary police arrangements regarding the death of the mayor. Police head-quarters, the boardrooms, and all police stations would be draped in black. A battalion of patrol officers and sixteen mounted officers (the entire complement) would be detailed to attend the mayor's funeral on Tuesday, April 27. The police department would also engage the Arsenal band for the occasion.

In an election to choose Barret's successor, Democrat James H. Britton, a banker and the treasurer of the St. Louis and Illinois Bridge Company, won over Independent Henry Overstolz, who had been a banker, wholesale grocer, and president of an insurance company.[75] Overstolz claimed fraud had been committed and demanded a recount of the ballots. Later testimony "revealed fraudulent voting in ten of the twelve wards, including repeating and ballot box stuffing by election judges."[76] It would be several months before the issue was decided. In the meantime, Britton took his seat as mayor of St. Louis.

In April, the board approved Chief Harrigan's recommendation for the institution of a so-called Ladies' Platoon (or Broadway Squad). The platoon would patrol Fourth and Broadway streets, between Elm Street and Franklin Avenue, from 9:00 a.m. to 9:00 p.m. Each officer would patrol one block. The officers were to "stop fast driving, keep the sidewalks clear of loafers, assist ladies in crossing the streets, get-ting on and off the street cars, and to impart information to those asking for it."[77] The officers selected were all at least six feet tall and "very gallant and well versed in etiquette."[78] They wore white gloves and had tassels attached to their police clubs. The sixteen officers and their sergeant began patrolling on April 22.[79]

On July 1, the city council passed Ordinance 9579, referred to as the (new) Social Evil Ordinance. The ordinance outlawed houses of prostitution, and such houses were given a variety of names in the ordinance. It prohibited prostitutes from "wandering around the streets in the night time"; frequenting beer houses or "places of pub-lic resort"; and being employed as a singer, dancer, or "beer-carrier or waiter-girl" in such places. All violations were misdemeanors, punish-able by a variety of fines up to $100. Anyone who frequented or lived in such houses was also guilty of a misdemeanor.

Other than enforcement, however, most germane to the police department was "Clause Third": "Any person who shall permit any house, rooms or tenements in his or her possession, or under his or her charge and control, to be used for the purpose of prostitution, or house of bad repute, after ten days' notice from the Police Commissioners of such use of such house, rooms, or tenements, shall be deemed guilty of a misdemeanor, and upon conviction thereof, shall be fined no less than fifty dollars."[80]

Chief Harrigan provided the board with a copy of the recently enacted ordinance, along with a list of the houses of prostitution in the city. The board's attorney defined the powers of the police under the new ordinance, and the board instructed the attorney to draw up a notice to be served on houses of prostitution and upon agents or owners of such houses. The first complaint of a house of prostitution under the new Social Evil Ordinance was made to the board within the month. The board requested that future complaints concerning houses of prostitution be referred to the chief of police for inquiry and report to the board, before any action would be taken. The decision was a sound one, as the complaints continued.

Gambling continued to be a problem. During fiscal year 1875–1876, 305 faro houses and 97 keno houses were raided, resulting in numerous arrests and the seizure and ultimate destruction of numerous pieces of gambling apparatus. Twenty-five raids were made on a new gambling venture referred to as the Missouri State Lottery, which involved the sale of lottery and policy tickets. The lottery wheels and other gambling paraphernalia were not destroyed in these instances because of a pending case in the Missouri Supreme Court.

✻   ✻   ✻

On July 20, 1875, the board received a unique request, a petition signed by numerous residents of the town of Kirkwood, Missouri, and vicinity asking that a police station and a detail of police be established in Kirkwood. A delegation presented the petition. On motion, the request was referred to Commissioners Priest and Rainwater for an inquiry and report. Rainwater went to Kirkwood to discuss the idea. As a result, Rainwater recommended that the petition be granted and, to that end, submitted a resolution: "Resolved, That the Chief of Police be, and is hereby instructed to detail (1) one sergeant of police and (5) five men (Mounted) to serve on detached duty in the central and western portion of the county, with official Head Quarters at Kirkwood. Resolved, That the proposition of the city council and Trustees at Kirkwood to furnish an office, station and stables, for the use of this department, free of cost, be accepted, and that a station be and is hereby established at Kirkwood."[81]

The board adopted the resolution, but Commissioner Priest introduced a proviso: "Provided, That within twelve months from August 1st, 1875 the authorities of Kirkwood shall erect a building suitable for police purposes, to be determined by this Board, for the use of the force assigned to that locality."[82] The proviso was also adopted, and Rainwater was authorized to connect the police station at Kirkwood, when opened, by police telegraph to police headquarters in the Four Courts building.

At the first board meeting in August, a committee from the Kirkwood delegation came before the board and said that it was without authority to promise a police building within a year. However, it would take measures to submit the board's proposition to the people. The board then modified its provision of July 27 to accept "good individual security in the premises."[83] A week later, an agreement signed by fifteen residents of Kirkwood was received by the board. A dollar amount was listed opposite each name on the list, that amount being contributed to guarantee the building of a suitable police station, "not to cost less than $10,000," in Kirkwood before August 1, 1876.[84]

The board then passed a resolution instructing Chief Harrigan to detail one sergeant and five mounted patrolmen in Kirkwood "under an agreement made by this Board with citizens of Kirkwood this day submitted. . . ." The officers detailed were to be instructed that they were to report to, and receive orders only from, the officer in command. The board also reserved the right to abandon the plan, or change the assignment of any portion of the police force, anytime before the work on the facility in Kirkwood was begun or because of "a non-compliance of the agreement made with the citizens of Kirkwood."[85]

The sergeant and mounted patrolmen were dispatched to Kirkwood. Kirkwood is approximately thirteen miles from St. Louis, and it was served by two railroad lines. It is not known whether the men rode their horses to Kirkwood that first day or took a train; the train ride from St. Louis to Kirkwood took forty to forty-five minutes.

The horses were stabled in Kirkwood, but there is no official notation whether the officers resided in Kirkwood or returned each day to St. Louis. The minutes of the board made no reference to travel by the detailed officers, or to the hours that they were to serve. An unrelated newspaper article about one of the officers in Kirkwood, however, noted that he and his family lived in Kirkwood.[86] The mounted officers patrolled Kirkwood and areas of the county south and west of that town.

Since 1874, the trustees of Kirkwood had rented two rooms for $12 a month. One of the rooms was used for board meetings, the

First Kirkwood City Hall. Courtesy of City of Kirkwood, Missouri.

other as a city jail. On October 5, 1875, they submitted a proposition to the voters to build or buy a building "for a Police Station and Calaboose."[87] The proposition obviously passed, for the trustees bought a parcel of land on the north side of Madison, just west of Webster (now Kirkwood) Road, a block from the railroad station. Kirkwood built a two-story city hall and jail and a stable for the police horses.[88] That location is now a part of the site of the present Kirkwood City Hall

It is apparent that the board also sent a hostler to care for the horses in Kirkwood. When necessary, one of the officers looked after prisoners. At the board meeting of August 17, the hostler at Kirkwood was promoted to the rank of turnkey, to act as turnkey and hostler. One patrolman was returned to city service. Another patrolman returned to the city the next month. Until they were removed, shortly after the city and county of St. Louis became separate entities, the police presence in Kirkwood would consist of a sergeant, three mounted patrolmen, and a turnkey-hostler.

✳   ✳   ✳

About seven o'clock on Thursday evening, September 9, 1875, two men about nineteen years of age, George Mitchell (alias George Gassert) and William Salisbury, went to Fred Fisher's grocery store on the southwest corner of Jefferson and Morgan. Both men had reportedly been drinking before they entered the store. They went to the cubbyhole that served as a saloon in the rear of the grocery and ordered beer. The two were served the beer and started to walk out without paying. Fisher stopped them and demanded payment, and they threatened to "lick him on the spot."[89] Fisher then called Third District patrolman John Cummings, who was on Jefferson walking his beat. Cummings was informed of the situation and told Mitchell and Salisbury that they were to accompany him to the station house. They paid no attention and continued walking. Cummings caught up with Salisbury and attempted to arrest him, but Mitchell came from behind and struck the officer on the right side of his head with a hickory club. Cummings fell to the sidewalk, where he was kicked in the head several times. The street lamps had not yet been lighted, and Mitchell and Salisbury ran off into the darkness.

With the assistance of two friends, Cummings then walked to the home of a fellow police officer, and later moved to his home at 1508 O'Fallon Street. That evening, the officer was examined by a physician who apparently felt that the injuries were minor. A second physician was called about four o'clock on Friday morning. He determined that Cummings's skull had been fractured; Cummings died about five o'clock, while being treated by the second physician.[90]

Both Mitchell and Salisbury were arrested the next day. At a coroner's inquest on Saturday, the cause of death was determined to be murder at the hands of George Mitchell. Salisbury was held as an accessory to the murder of Patrolman Cummings.

Cummings was thirty-seven years old and had been on the force a little more than a year. He had served in the Confederate army under the present treasurer of the Board of Police Commissioners, Charles Rainwater. Cummings was survived by his wife, and was buried on Monday, September 13, with full military honors.

At the board meeting the day after the funeral, the board offered Circuit Attorney Cole Normello the assistance of the board's attorney, G. P. Ellerbee, in the prosecution of the murderers of Patrolman Cummings. The board also authorized a $25 award to a citizen, Levi Williams, "for assistance in arresting the murderer of Officer Cummings."[91]

Finally, at the September 14 meeting, the board selected Commissioners Nidelet and Rainwater to form a committee to inquire into arming the members of the department with a standard service revolver. Under the provisions of the 1861 law establishing the board and the metropolitan police, all officers were to be armed. Each officer, however, had to provide his own revolver, with no standard to guide him. The committee was advised to select "the cheapest and best pistol. . . ."[92] The reason for the "cheapest and best" prerequisite was that, for the first time, the police department would pay for and supply the force with the selected weapon.

At the meeting of August 31, the board read the affidavit of one George C. Miller, of the Missouri State Lottery, in which he swore that on August 17 he had a conversation with Detective Albert J. Stiles, who "insinuated imputations upon the Chief and one of the members of the board."[93] Stiles was ordered to appear at the next board meeting, where the case was continued until the meeting of October 27. Before that meeting, however, the board received additional information from an outside source and instructed Chief Harrigan to have charges preferred against Stiles for presentation at the meeting. Stiles was to be charged with one count of "insubordination" and two counts of "conduct unbecoming an officer and a gentleman."[94] Stiles, however, did not appear at the meeting.

Another meeting was called for October 30, and the officer was notified to appear. Detective Stiles also failed to attend that meeting. Instead, he sent a notarized letter to the board, which was read at the October 30 meeting. In the letter, Stiles acknowledged receiving the charges and specifications but denounced the timeliness of serving him with them two days before he was to appear. He also responded to the charges. Stiles then, in his letter, proceeded to list specific charges against Chief Harrigan and listed various witnesses who he claimed would support his charges. With his notarized letter, Detective Stiles included a letter of resignation from the force. The board, however, would not accept his letter of resignation.

The next day, Harrigan specifically noted each charge made by Stiles and not only denied each one, but specifically demonstrated how each could not have occurred as claimed. Harrigan thought that the source of the problem between him and Stiles was his refusal, about a month previous, to consider Stiles for the rank of chief of detectives.[f] Harrigan told Stiles that "as long as he was Chief of Police, Stiles could not be Chief of Detectives." It was after Harrigan's statement to Stiles that, said Harrigan, "his [Stiles's] subordinates went to work and informed certain parties that, as Harrigan was against him, he would have him removed, that he was backed by men who made governors and that the Chief and several captains would have to go."[95]

---

[f] "Chief of detectives" was another name for "sergeant of detectives" and was only an honorary title. The 1874 police manual did not include such a position.

The board met on November 3 and, afterward, issued a subpoena for the appearance of Detective Stiles before a special meeting of the board on Saturday, November 6. The special meeting was called so that Stiles would testify to the charges he had made against Chief Harrigan. The meeting would be open to the public.

The meeting of November 6 was opened, and Stiles was called to testify. He refused, stating that his attorney would answer for him. He then left the boardroom. Upon order of the board, Captain Lee left the boardroom and returned with Stiles, who was placed on the stand and questioned by Vice President Priest. Stiles repeated the charge that Chief Harrigan had George C. Miller file a false affidavit against him. And, said Stiles, if Harrigan had been friendly to him he would never have sent the October 30 affidavit to the board. The questioning continued, but Stiles would often decline to answer a question or attorney Frank J. Bowman would object, then be ordered by Mayor Britton to sit down.[96] "The witness persistently refused to answer a question propounded by the Board and was ordered under arrest for contempt, but finally relenting and answering the question, was liberated and allowed to proceed."[97] The board asked Chief Harrigan if he wanted counsel; he stated that, since the other side had no counsel, he would also proceed without a lawyer. But, "when attorney Bowman persisted in prompting Stiles and acting as his attorney, the Chief was authorized to employ counsel. He employed Col. A.W. Slayback."[98] The case was then continued to November 11.

On November 10, Stiles applied to the circuit court for a writ of mandamus to allow him the benefit of counsel at the meeting scheduled for the next evening. Stiles claimed that he was subpoenaed as a witness as a pretense, that he was the real defendant in the matter.[99] The following day, the circuit court declined to issue a writ of mandamus, stating that "nothing had yet occurred affecting Mr. Stiles that would entitle him to counsel."[100]

On November 11, thirteen witnesses were called by the board, and ten by Albert Stiles. The board then went into executive session to render a finding. The board returned to the boardroom and announced that "[Stiles's statements have] entirely failed to be substantiated by testimony, which had failed to prove any one of said specific charges. Therefore, Resolved, that this Board dismiss said statements from further consideration, and find no cause after the fullest investigation to lose confidence in the honesty and integrity of the Chief of Police."[101]

On November 18, Chief Harrigan abruptly resigned. Said Harrigan in his letter of resignation to the board, "Owing to recent unpleasant events, I feel that it is best that I should sever my connection with this department as I have made arrangements to engage in other business that I may be able to devote more of my time to my family."[102] He thanked the board for "the many acts of kindness" to him and asked that the board accept his resignation "without delay."[103] The board accepted Harrigan's resignation and then unanimously adopted a resolution dismissing Albert Stiles from the police force. The police department, however, had not heard the last from Stiles.

At a special meeting on November 27, the board went into executive session to select a chief of police. Two persons were nominated: Captain Anton Huebler and former chief of police James McDonough. McDonough received the majority of the votes and was named chief of police effective December 1, 1875. It was McDonough's third turn as chief, having previously served as the first chief of the new metropolitan department in 1861 and, again, from 1870 to 1874. Harrigan had succeeded McDonough upon the latter's resignation in 1874; McDonough was now succeeding his successor.

Meanwhile, the board established rules for recommissioning officers. The 1861 law establishing the board and the police department required the recommissioning of officers every four years.[g] No rules had ever been put in place; previous boards made their own determinations as to who qualified for another four-year stint. The rules applied to all commissioned officers from patrolmen to the chief of police. The next recommissioning was scheduled for January 1, 1876.

The board required all captains to rate their sergeants and patrolmen as first class, second class, or third class and to submit a written

---

[g]Before 1861, police officers were given one-year appointments.

recommendation for each. The board would interview all sergeants and patrolmen over a six-week period beginning October 13. Those who were rated low and failed to pass the board interview were allowed to continue on the force, unless otherwise removed for cause, until January 1, 1876.[104]

In the midst of the Stiles controversy, the board also made another significant decision. Effective January 1, 1876, Rule 108 of the police manual was amended to increase the time a new officer would spend in the School of Instruction from one month to ninety days. This amendment automatically extended the probationary period to ninety days.[105]

In October, the board declared that, on January 1, 1876, officers would begin wearing metal numbers on their caps, the numbers to correspond with the numbers on the officers' stars.[106] The practice continues to this day.

Other events were taking place at the same time. The board was meeting several times a week to personally interview each police officer in the department to determine his eligibility for a new four-year commission beginning on January 1, 1876. The board also discussed the possibility of the police department hosting a charity ball for the benefit of the poor. The department still had soup houses in various districts and had, in November, opened yet another. Turnkey Matthew Little, who had supervised the operation of other soup houses for the department, was again transferred to open the newest one. The board decided to sponsor such a ball, on December 15, at the Masonic Hall at Seventh and Market streets.

After the charity ball, the board formally established the Police Poor Fund. The proceeds of the ball, and any other funds coming into the hands of officers for charitable purposes, would be placed in the Poor Fund. Such funds would go to the board treasurer and could be distributed only upon the authority of the board.

1876

The first month of the new year was a very busy one for the board. It began with the establishment of rules for management and distribution of the Police Poor Fund. The Police Poor Fund would be under the exclusive control of the board, "to be used exclusively for the immediate relief of the destitute deserving poor of the city of Saint Louis, for the purchase of food and fuel necessary for the maintenance of the police lodging house or soup house and the payment of any officer or employee that may be required in conducting the relief, and any other expenditures . . . in furnishing aid to the destitute class."[107]

The captains of the various police districts would have their districts searched for the "deserving poor" and report what assistance was required. The chief would then furnish what was necessary and make a report at the next meeting of the board. The chief of police and the treasurer of the board would be required to keep a full record of their accounts, with receipts. Such records would be open to the inspection of the board "or any reputable citizen."[108] Commissioner Lewis Dorsheimer, the purchasing member of the board, received $300, and Chief McDonough $100, for the first week of operation of the Police Poor Fund. Weekly reports of expenditures would be a continuing feature of the board minutes.

The establishment of the rules for the Poor Fund was followed by a communication from Charles P. Chouteau, president of the Carondelet Relief Association (in the southernmost part of the city) asking for aid from the Poor Fund for the destitute of his district. The board authorized Chouteau to draw upon the House of Refuge for $250 worth of bread. Captain William Lee, the First District commander, was asked to cooperate with Chouteau in determining who was in need of charity in his district.

Commissioner John Priest introduced a resolution that would abolish the position of sergeant of detectives and have all detectives report directly to the chief of police. The board adopted Priest's resolution. The resolution was passed and took effect on January 4, 1876.[109]

On February 9, 1876, the board lost a member. On that day, the city council adopted a resolution declaring that Henry Overstolz had been elected mayor on May 15, 1875, not James H. Britton, and asking the board to recognize Overstolz as such. Mayor Overstolz would take his seat as the ex officio president of the board at the meeting of February 15.

Chief McDonough, meanwhile, tried a new strategy to deal with the gambling situation. He asked the board to permit him to place an officer at the door of each faro house with instructions to take down the name of every person entering the house. The board gave its approval.[110]

On payday, April 3, all commissioned officers were presented with their commissions; they expired on January 1, 1880.[111] The board informed the force that any officer who resigned voluntarily or otherwise honorably severed his connection with the department could keep the commission, and the honorable discharge would be noted on it. Anyone dismissed from the force would be required to return the commission to the board.

In an effort to reduce costs, the board, effective May 1, began a new pay schedule. Officers would be classified as first- or second-class officers. Those presently on the force were classified as first class and would continue to receive $75 per month. Officers hired after May 1 were to be classified as second class, receiving $60 per month for the first six months of duty. Special officers, those sworn in for a specific event or for a specified duration, would also be listed in the second class.

One of the specific events requiring the hiring of special officers began on June 27. That date signaled the beginning of the Democratic National Convention in the auditorium of the new Merchants' Exchange Building on Third Street, between Chestnut and Pine. The police and fire departments staged a combined full-dress parade that evening. As the fire and police parade continued past the east side of the courthouse (on Fourth Street), it was reviewed by Governor Hardin, Mayor Overstolz, and other city officials.[112]

In September, the board announced the first firearms policy. While the metropolitan police force in St. Louis had been armed since its inception, the various manuals of rules and regulations published by the board over the years never addressed the use of firearms. On September 5, the board instructed Chief McDonough to "verbally order" the captains to notify their officers "that the free use of fire arms is expressly prohibited by this Board, except in extreme cases, to be determined by the good sound judgment of the officer."[113]

That same month, the board decided that no more money would be expended on the Poor Fund without a special order from the board. Apparently short of money in the fund, primarily financed by the December 1875 charity ball, the board began to directly handle requests. A month after announcing the new policy, the board approved the expenditure of $5 from the Poor Fund for each of an unspecified number of families reported to the board as destitute. The board also requested a physician, Dr. A. C. Robinson, to visit one of the families.[114] The board would continue the practice of giving either $3 or $5 to each family reported to be destitute (and sometimes sending a physician) until the next charity ball on December 20.

On October 31, the board issued an order outlining the conduct of police stationed at polling places for the November 7 general election. In addition, Mayor Overstolz ordered the closing of all saloons and other places where liquor was sold on election day. The board allotted fifty cents to each officer assigned to a polling place so that the officer would eat lunch at a restaurant rather than going home for lunch. The November election was a general election complete with national, state, and local candidates and issues. There was no comparison, however, with the special election held in August.

Chapter Five

A New City Charter and Old Problems

WHILE THE MINUTES OF THE October 1876 board meetings referred to the elaborate plans for the November general election, earlier minutes contained no such reference to the special election of August 22, 1876. On that day, the voters had been asked to consider the "Scheme for the Separation and Reorganization of the Governments of the City and County of St. Louis and the Adjustment of Their Relations." The unwieldy name had been preceded by years of equally unwieldy political maneuvering. The desire for separation of city and county could be traced back to the Missouri Constitution of 1865. Two years after the passage of that constitution, one had to look through more than one hundred state statutes to put together a "charter" of St. Louis. In addition, city taxpayers felt that they were unfairly taxed. The county collected almost $2 million from city residents in 1869, for example, but the city was only able to collect $302,000 from licenses and fees.[1] Out of the $302,000, and in addition to the ordinary expenses of a big city, the city had to pay the operational costs of organizations under the control of state-appointed departmental boards. The metropolitan police department was one of these. By 1870, the concept of "home rule" for St. Louis was being bandied about.

In 1875, a constitutional convention had convened in Missouri. There were twelve delegates from the city of St. Louis and two from St. Louis County. The St. Louis committee unanimously recommended municipal home rule for St. Louis. In November 1875, Missouri voters approved the constitution. Article IX, Section 20, authorized the election of a thirteen-member Board of Freeholders from the city and county. They were "to write a city charter, separate the two governments, define the new boundaries, reorganize the county government, and settle outstanding financial differences."[2]

The freeholders met fifty-two times between April 8 and July 3, obtaining information from citizens and city officials and studying the charters of New York, Philadelphia, and Chicago.[3] While the scheme addressed the elections of a city sheriff, coroner, and public administrator, and established the offices of city marshal, city assessor, and other offices, the proposed city boundaries were a central source of contention. A majority of the city members of the Board of Freeholders wanted limits that would include the new city parks. This included Tower Grove Park on the south side, Forest Park (which had just been purchased by the city) in the west, and O'Fallon Park on the north side. The city also wanted a strip of land running along the Mississippi River, on the north side, to the Mississippi River's Chain of Rocks, where the city planned to build a new waterworks. The county and a minority of the city representatives opposed such generous boundaries, but the majority won the point.[4] The St. Louis city limits that were established exist today.

Section 14 addressed the police department:

> The metropolitan police force of the City of St. Louis as now established by law shall be maintained at the cost of the City of St. Louis; provided, however, that the metropolitan police of the City of St. Louis shall have the same power and jurisdiction in the County of St. Louis as constituted by this scheme as now provided by law; provided, that upon a petition of the county court of St. Louis County the board of police commissioners shall appoint and equip not more than twenty policemen as provided in the act approved March 13, 1867, for duty in said county. The cost of equipping and maintaining said police shall be paid by the county as herein established.[5]

A favorable vote would, in the future, create more problems for the police than the possibility of fielding a mounted unit for the county. While most of the land west of Grand Avenue was farmland, the city would increase in size from 17.98 square miles to 61.37 square miles.[6] As unlikely as it might have seemed at the time, new residential subdivisions would be built west of Grand, the population of the city would continue to grow and, less than thirty years later, the number of police districts in the city would double and the number of police officers would triple.

The returns of the special election of August 22, 1876, showed that both the charter and the scheme were defeated. Both had passed by narrow margins in the city, but county residents voted against separation. Those in the area to be annexed by the city under the scheme (those in the area generally west of Grand Avenue) voted four to one against the charter. The results were contested in court, and a five-man investigatory commission was appointed by Judge Louis Gottschalk. The commission found that election officials had destroyed hundreds of ballots that had been replaced by fraudulent ballots, they had sworn to false returns and, in general, they tried to turn the election "into a shameless farce."[7] The commission ultimately ruled that the scheme had carried by 1,253 votes, and the charter by 3,221. These results were certified and sent to the secretary of state, but they were also challenged in court. In April 1877, almost nine months after the election, the county court was ordered to vacate its St. Louis offices. Henry Overstolz was reelected mayor under the new charter.

During the nine months of court challenges, the Board of Police Commissioners carried out business as usual. At the meeting of November 21, 1876, the board entertained the application of the first minority applicant for a police position, believed to be William H. Berzey.[a] Berzey, who applied for the position of detective, was parenthetically listed in the minutes as "colored."[8] His application was "filed," a notation that meant that no action was taken. At the next meeting, November 28, Berzey's application, signed by a number of citizens recommending his appointment to the police force as a detective, was "laid over" pending further action.

---

[a] No other name remotely like "Berzey" appears in the city directories of the time. William Berzey was of French Creole extraction.

A motion was made and adopted at the December 12 meeting that William Berzey "be employed temporarily on special duty at a salary of $60.00 per month and be assigned to Chief [of] Police for orders."[9] There is no indication how Chief McDonough used the first "colored" officer, but it is likely that he was used to infiltrate black gambling houses and houses of prostitution to gather evidence for the issuance of warrants. At any rate, upon the recommendation of McDonough, Berzey was "dropped from the rolls" of the department effective December 31, 1876.[10] While black aspirants for the police department would continue to file applications, it would be almost twenty-five years before the hiring of the next black police applicant.

The police department continued to help the poor. The second charity ball was scheduled for December 20. It would raise over $8,000 for aiding the poor over the next year. The Institution for the House-less and Homeless, which Chief McDonough had helped establish in his last term as chief of police, had moved. It was now located in an old tobacco warehouse on the western portion of city hall property (which was on Eleventh Street between Market and Chestnut) and was called the Soup House.[b] The Soup House lodged both men and women, and served one meal a day. Over five hundred people a day were fed at a cost of less than five cents a person. Women and children were permitted to obtain soup, bread, and meat to take home to their families. The latter had to make application to the officer on whose beat they resided.

The beat officer would determine if they were "worthy objects of charity"; he would write an order naming the number of persons in the family. The order was then taken to the mayor's secretary and coun-tersigned. The bearer was then permitted the appropriate amount of food each day. Used clothing was also accepted by the Soup House for those who were unable to procure warm clothing. Lewis Dorsheimer, the purchasing member of the board, oversaw the operation of the Soup House.[11] The Police Poor Fund was the recipient of the annual charity ball. The proceeds of the charity ball were used to run the

[b] The Civil Courts Building, completed in 1930, now occupies the site of the Soup House.

Soup House and provide for other destitute persons throughout the city. At its last meeting of 1876, the board approved the continuation of the Poor Fund.

Residents of Bridgeton, a town in north St. Louis County, requested that one Joseph D. Porter of Bridgeton be appointed a special police officer "to preserve the peace and keep order there, especially on Sundays." Instead, the board ordered that a member of the regular police force be detailed there "until further notice."[12] While the board was aware that it could order police into the county, it was obviously not so certain that it could, in effect, "deputize" citizens exclusively for service in the county.

1877

At its meeting of January 23, 1877, the board received a request from the newly formed St. Louis County Court that the metropolitan police continue to patrol those parts of the county that they patrolled before the charter and separation scheme election. The board agreed to do so. About that same time, the board purchased a "copying machine" for Chief McDonough. The board paid the Papyrograph Company $62.50.[13]

On February 13, the board learned that two new board members had been appointed by Governor John S. Phelps to replace Lewis Dorsheimer and Charles Rainwater, whose terms had expired. The new commissioners were Basil Duke and David Armstrong. The board notified them that the next meeting of the board would be Tuesday, February 20, at 7:30 p.m. The board also extended special thanks to outgoing purchasing member Dorsheimer, who was the manager of the Poor Fund and supervisor of the Soup House. The board asked Dorsheimer to remain in his position at the Soup House.

This was the second time that David Armstrong had served as a police commissioner. Current board member John G. Priest had replaced Armstrong after his term of office expired in 1875. While he had a four-year appointment to the board, Armstrong would remain on the board only until October, when he would be appointed to fill the unexpired term of recently deceased U.S. senator Louis V. Bogy. Basil Duke, a lawyer in St. Louis for thirty years, was a cousin of Basil Wilson Duke, a member of the first Board of Police Commissioners. Duke also was appointed for four years.

The board soon began to feel the effects of the new city charter. Since the charter required the board to use the legal services of the city, the board was no longer permitted to have its own attorney. The charter also prohibited police from riding free on the streetcars. Captains from the Second, Third, Fourth, and Central districts were provided with horses. Because of the great distance, the captain of the First District had previously been the only captain provided with a horse.

On March 27, the board sent a letter to the Honorable H. L. Sutton, presiding justice of the St. Louis County Court, stating that since January 27 the board had continued policing in the county at his request. However, as the fiscal year was about to close, and there were no longer any funds, the county policing must be discontinued. The letter concluded that "any ideas the Judge might have should be laid before the board between the first and tenth of April."[14]

Justice Sutton replied, on April 5, that the court had no funds to pay the metropolitan police for patrolling in the county of St. Louis. Accordingly, Captain Warren Fox, commander of the Mounted Patrol, was instructed to withdraw his men and all police property from Kirkwood and return to the Mounted Police station in the city on April 10. The mounted unit had patrolled Kirkwood, and areas south and west of Kirkwood, since August 1875, approximately twenty months.

Disaster struck in the early morning hours the day after the mounted force returned from Kirkwood. At approximately 1:30 a.m. the morning of April 11, the upper portion of the seven-story Southern Hotel was discovered on fire, and flames were seen coming through the roof. Numerous alarms were turned in and the entire force of engine companies responded, as did ladder companies.[15]

Female employees were at the windows of the upper floors of the building yelling for help and throwing down sheets and pulling them up again. Flames could be seen behind them. A Skinner Hook and Ladder Company truck was placed in position against the curb, but the ladder did not touch the building or reach the seventh floor. Mattresses were brought out and piled on one another for anyone who jumped. Said the reporter for the *St. Louis Globe-Democrat*, however, "Such a leap would have been certain death. . . ."[16] One woman

Southern Hotel. Photograph by Robert Benecke, 1863.
Missouri History Museum.

jumped from a sixth-floor window onto the roof of Tony Faust's one-story building. Another woman, scaling down a makeshift rope of bed linens from the same floor, also fell onto Faust's roof when the sheets ripped. Both were killed.[17] Two other female employees also jumped from windows. One survived, but the other did not.[18] Firemen, most notably Phelim O'Toole, Mike Hester, Andy Kirk, Barney McKernan, and Ed Thorne, were credited with saving more than two dozen people.[19] By 4:00 a.m., only one section of wall in the southeast corner of the hotel remained standing. The other walls had fallen, crashing into nearby buildings. Firemen and spectators assisted in raising ladders and rescuing those persons they could.[20]

The board immediately volunteered to the city coroner the services of police officers to conduct "a full and thorough investigation as to the cause of and incidents connected with the deplorable calamity befallen this community in the loss of life. . . ."[21] The board also asked all of the Southern Hotel servant girls to be present at a special board meeting on Saturday, May 5, for the distribution of donations from benefits given by Ben De Bar, proprietor of De Bar's Opera House. At that meeting, the board, assisted by one of the proprietors, the housekeeper, and the chief laundress, distributed the donations and arranged to pay the funeral expenses of one servant girl who died in the fire.[22]

In the meantime, the board elected its officers. The vice (and acting) president was David Armstrong; treasurer, Basil Duke; and purchasing member, Dr. James Nidelet. Board Secretary George Gavin was reappointed. On May 8, the board changed the working hours of the two platoons. Instead of one platoon working 11:00 a.m. to 11:00 p.m. and the second working 11:00 p.m. to 11:00 a.m., the shifts were changed to 7:00 a.m. to 7:00 p.m. and 7:00 p.m. to 7:00 a.m. The two platoons were still being rotated on a quarterly basis that had begun on November 1, 1873.

Meanwhile, a railroad strike was looming in St. Louis, one that would be a far greater test of the police department than the St. Louis, Kansas City and Northern strike of 1873. The railroads, which had overbuilt since the panic of 1873, began to cut costs. The physical assets of the railroads were allowed to deteriorate, train crews were cut to dangerous levels, wages were cut twice before 1877, and workers were forced to work overtime without pay. Protestors were fired and local strikes crushed. An additional 10 percent wage cut by eastern railroads "led to massive uprisings, total stoppage of freight traffic, extensive property destruction, and pitched battles between police, militia, and strikers in Pittsburgh, Baltimore, and elsewhere. By Sunday, July 22, one million men were on strike, not called out by the Railway Brotherhoods, but by local workers' committees and *ad hoc* unions."[23]

It was not thought that St. Louis was in any danger from the eastern strikes but, on the same day that violence was occurring in Pittsburgh,

railroad and bridge transit company workers elected a strike committee in East St. Louis, Illinois. The workers stopped all freight traffic
and took over the depots, yards, and streets of East St. Louis without
any property damage or personal injury.[24] The strike then spread to
a car works, the stockyards, and other industries in East St. Louis.[25]
Strikers took over the St. Louis Union Depot and yards the next day.
The St. Louis strike, however, was different; it had been taken over
by the Workingmen's Party. The party, a small socialist organization,
was composed of German-, English-, and Bohemian-speaking men.
While a few craft unions joined the strike, the major resource of the
Workingmen's Party was the "thousands of unemployed, and ordinary
workers, organized and unorganized."[26] On Monday evening, July
23, five thousand people had rallied at the Lucas Market, which was
located between Chestnut and Olive streets in the area now occupied
by Tucker Boulevard. The next day, committees from the party began
visiting shops and foundries with the result that workers began walking out.[27] A Workingmen's Party rally at the market that evening drew
an estimated ten thousand people or more.

The next afternoon thousands of men gathered on Locust
Street and, marching behind a band playing the French *Marseillaise*,
marched past the shops, factories, and mills. Employees left their jobs
and joined the parade. "By nightfall nearly every manufacturing plant,
large or small, was shut down; the downtown saloons were closed
[ordered by the mayor *and* the strike committee], and the city's food
supplies were diminishing. The horse cars and waterworks were not
disturbed, however."[28]

On Thursday, the fourth day of strike activities in St. Louis, "an
impromptu force seized the giant Belcher Sugar Refinery; the barbers
all walked out, demanding fifteen cents for haircuts, and on the levee
a number of barge and packet companies agreed to wage demands."[29]
At a meeting at the Lucas Market that evening, the strike committee
did not attend. "They had nothing new to offer, and the demand for
guns was growing more insistent. They had no guns, and they did
not want any."[30] The crowd wanted to seize the Four Courts, but
slowly broke up and walked to Broadway and Biddle, the new strike
headquarters at Schuler's Hall. There, they learned that the strike

committee had nothing to tell them. The strike would be over the next day, Friday, July 27.

The Board of Police Commissioners met on Tuesday, Wednesday, and Friday of the strike week. Minutes of those meetings provide some background information about preparations by the police. At the first meeting, on Tuesday, the superintendent of St. Louis's Union Depot and two railroad officials met with the board to discuss the railroad strike and its effect in the St. Louis area. Captain Warren Fox was then ordered to bring his entire mounted force to police headquarters at the Four Courts. The district commanders were ordered to hold their men in readiness at the district stations, subject to the orders of the board.

At the Wednesday meeting, the board ordered the sheriff of the city of St. Louis to form a posse comitatus. The sheriff was ordered to include in the posse those who had responded to a proclamation issued by Mayor Overstolz and to recruit additional citizens until there were five thousand men. The men were to encamp at Lafayette Park. At the Friday meeting, the board ordered Chief McDonough to send "as many policemen as he can concentrate" to Schuler's Hall "to arrest all violators of the law found there and bring them to police HQ" (the police may have had plainclothes officers attending the various meetings for the purpose of identifying the strike leaders).[31] General A. J. Smith, one of the joint commanders of the citizens' militia, was requested to furnish the necessary military assistance. Because of General Smith's opposition to the plan, the citizens' militia would actually be led by General John D. Stevenson, also a member of the Committee of Public Safety.[32]

The Friday march to Schuler's Hall began at the Four Courts, on Twelfth Street, made its way to Broadway, and then north to Biddle, a distance of approximately one mile. The march resembled a parade. Board vice president David Armstrong and Chief McDonough led the group. They were followed by the mounted police "occupying nearly the full width of the street."[33] The mounted officers were followed by two lines of foot police armed, in addition to their sidearms, with bayoneted muskets. Mayor Overstolz walked behind the police with three other city officials.[34] General Stevenson led about six hundred members of the citizens' militia, including an artillery battery.[35] Also included were members of the St. Louis National Guard, who were either marching with, or behind, the citizens' militia.

Upon reaching Schuler's Hall, the National Guard set up a line on Broadway, facing the building. David T. Burbank described the action:

> The two cannon were placed in the streets so as to cover diagonally the front of the Hall, from whose upper floors, the strikers, still unintimidated, were jeering the troops and the police. When within about fifty yards of the Hall, the mounted police spurred their horses to a brisk trot, charging directly into the crowd. The crowd opened and retreated before the police, shouting and cursing, but soon began to press forward again; and the police charged again and again, driving the crowd before them in every direction in the utmost confusion.[36]

Burbank added that the attack by the mounted police apparently demoralized the strikers in Schuler's Hall. "Some jumped from the third-story porch to the roof of an adjoining building, and running over a couple of roofs, made a descent. Others shinned down the pillars on the porches. Still others simply dropped from the second-floor balcony on to the sidewalk, and several suffered serious sprains."[37]

The foot police, led by Captain Lee, entered the building and arrested those who remained. Detective Hugh O'Neil reportedly stopped those dashing for the door by facing them with two cocked revolvers. Those arrested were marched to the Four Courts between two files of police. The militia was not involved in the action, and no shots were fired by either the police or the militia.[38] Unlike the strikes in the eastern cities, there was little violence. While individual arrests would continue for several more days, and court appearances were scheduled, the storming of Schuler's Hall essentially marked the end of the strike in St. Louis.

The poor economic times continued. The profits of the charity ball in December 1876 were still being used by the police to provide food and shelter. In August, after the board advertised that the police department would hire one hundred new officers, there were plenty of applicants. The board, however, had tightened the qualifications of applicants. Rule 96 of the 1874 police manual stated that, in order to be appointed a police officer, an applicant must be "of good moral character and habits." The board included the phrase "of strictly temperate habits," an allusion to the disciplinary problems of some members of the present force.[39] The board also added that "before being accepted he must undergo a thorough medical examination as to his physical condition."[40] Those selected would be appointed special officers at the rate of $60 per month until they had completed the police department's School of Instruction. Finally, the board added that "the application of no ex officer, dropped or dismissed from the force for cause will be entertained."[41]

The board personally interviewed applicants over a two-day period. Of those interviewed, 103 were accepted pending the results of the physician's examination of their physical health. The minutes of the August 21 board meeting indicate that 19 of the selected applicants had failed the physical exam. On Monday, August 27, the remainder began attending the School of Instruction in the districts to which they had been assigned.

Along with the general population, police officers also struggled with the poor economic situation. As August came to a close, the board, responding to an increasing amount of citizens' complaints about officers not paying their debts, ordered that Rule 152 of the police manual be "rigidly enforced."[42] The rule was one sentence long: "Non-payment of indebtedness for clothing and subsistence incurred by an officer while a member of the force shall be cause for ignominious dismissal." In spite of Rule 152 and the promise of rigid enforcement, the board continued to receive complaints from creditors. Another warning was issued the first week of September, followed by a resolution that "any member of the Police Force against whom complaint is made for neglecting or failing to settle any indebtedness contracted by him since his appointment to the force—no matter of what nature or character—shall be immediately dismissed from the Department."[43] This resolution obviously had some effect; it would be many months before another officer was brought before the board for failing to settle any indebtedness. In any event, the board had other issues with which to deal.

At a special meeting of the board on Monday, September 3, a "committee of citizen tax payers," composed of Captain Silas Bent Jr., Thomas Fult, and Adolphus Meier, appeared and presented a memorial for the creation and maintenance of an armed force in the city, to be an auxiliary to the police force, "in preserving order and protecting property in times of riot or mob violence." Recalling the labor strike earlier in the year and, in the words of the board, "how poorly the authorities were prepared to meet the emergency,"[44] the board approved the memorial and ordered that it be sent to the Municipal Assembly for its information.[45]

At another special meeting, on October 17, Silas Bent Jr. was seated as a police commissioner, replacing David Armstrong. Governor John Phelps had accepted Armstrong's resignation from the board in order to appoint Armstrong to complete the term of the late U.S. senator Louis V. Bogy. Bent, the son of Judge Silas Bent, received an appointment in the U.S. Navy in 1836. He rose to the rank of captain and served with the Navy until the eve of the Civil War, when he returned to St. Louis. He was involved in many different business enterprises and was a member of the board of trustees of the Missouri Institution for the Education of the Blind.[46] Since Armstrong had been the vice and acting president of the board, the board elected John G. Priest to that office. Basil Duke remained as treasurer, Dr. James Nidelet as purchasing member.

Tragedy struck the police force during the morning of Friday, November 16, 1877. Frank Rand (or Rande) entered Ed Wright's pawnshop on Vine Street, between Third and Fourth streets, to redeem a valise he had pawned in July. He was accompanied by a young man known as James Morrison. Rand was a suspect in several murders committed in Illinois, and Wright had been warned to be aware that Rand might show up to get the valise. Following the earlier instructions of Chief James McDonough, Wright alerted his clerk, with a prearranged signal, to leave the shop and inform the nearest policeman. Clerk George Hess did so, finding Patrolmen John S.

White and Tom Heffernan. Hess warned the officers that Rand was in the shop.[47]

The officers quickly entered the pawnshop and caught Rand by surprise. As the officers grabbed him, Rand pulled out a revolver, cocked it, and pointed it at Patrolman White. Patrolman Heffernan grabbed the revolver with both hands and, during the struggle, it discharged, striking White in the right leg. Rand was subdued after being shot once in the chest by the pawnshop clerk, and once in the knee by Heffernan. While Rand was being subdued, pawnbroker Wright had pulled a pistol and used it to hold Rand's companion, Morrison, at bay.

A half dozen police officers arrived and took Rand and Morrison into custody. A doctor was called for White. The bullet had severed the femoral artery in his right leg, and the doctor applied a tourniquet to stop the flow of blood. An ambulance arrived and took White to his home, where he was attended to by four additional physicians. Officer White was expected to recover from his wound.

Frank Rand was taken in a wagon to the Chestnut Street substation, where Sergeant Peletiah Jenks ordered Rand taken to the city dispensary.[48] Rand was treated for his injuries and placed under police guard in the city dispensary. He was later extradited to Illinois, where he had been indicted for first-degree murder. While being held in Galesburg, Illinois, Rand admitted that his real name was Charles C. Scott, and he lived in Fairfield, Iowa. He was later sentenced to the state penitentiary in Joliet, Illinois where, on March 7, 1884, he committed suicide by hanging himself in his cell.[49]

In the meantime, in order to save Patrolman White's life, his leg was amputated the next day. White died, however, that evening, November 18, 1877. On Tuesday, November 20, after a funeral with full police honors, John S. White was laid to rest in Calvary Cemetery. The board approved collections for White's wife and children. Members of the police department donated $1,008, and money was donated by citizens and businesses in Missouri and Illinois.

With the recent railroad strike in mind (and the more violent situations that occurred in some cities in the east), the police department went into a defensive, military mode. At the meeting of December 11, Silas Bent Jr. introduced a resolution that stated that, in the judgment of the board, "there exists an exigency in the peace and good order of this city that warrants and demands an increase in the metropolitan police of the city of St. Louis. Be it therefore Resolved that a force of not more than one thousand men be enrolled as a Special Police, subject to the requirements and orders of this Board."[50] The resolution was adopted and Bent, Priest, and Nidelet were appointed to a committee to confer with the heads of military companies in the city who had petitioned to be enrolled as special police. The men were to take the same oath as regular police officers, but would be known as the Police Reserves.[51]

Over the next four months, the various police commissioners swore in 455 members of nine companies (A through I), which became the First Regiment, Police Reserves.[52] The nine companies were supplied by the board with arms and ammunition and with places to drill. The members supplied their own uniforms. While the number of police reserves never reached one thousand, the board had enrolled 535 by April 1879.[c]

1878

The new year began on a cataclysmic note. On Thursday, January 3, 1878, Patrolman Benjamin Ayers and Sergeant William Blodgett, both of the Mounted District, met on the street and Patrolman Ayers gave Sergeant Blodgett a pistol he had borrowed so that it could be returned to the owner. The sergeant put the pistol in the inside pocket of his coat. At Garrison Avenue and Pine Street, the pistol fell out of the sergeant's inside coat pocket, slid down the inside of his

---

[c] In addition to preparing to supplement the police force when needed, the Police Reserves, in March 1878, performed a public drill and gave a vocal concert, raising $1,950.65 for the poor of the city. This would to be added to the over $7,000 raised at the police charity ball of December 1877.

coat, and struck the pavement. Upon hitting the pavement, the pistol discharged and the ball struck Ayers on the inside of his left leg and traveled upward. Doctor (and police commissioner) James Nidelet was summoned to tend to Ayers. Although Dr. Nidelet tended to Ayers most of that day and evening, he was unable to locate the ball.[53] Ayers, who was appointed to the police department on May 20, 1876, died the next morning, leaving a wife and three children.[54] On Sunday afternoon, January 6, funeral services were held for Ayers and his body was taken to Bellefontaine Cemetery for burial, accompanied by the entire Mounted District Platoon.[55]

In May, the board adopted a standard revolver. The make and caliber of the revolver were not indicated, but one hundred were purchased from William Read and Sons in Boston. The minutes of the board meeting noted that officers could purchase a revolver from the police department for $9, payable in four monthly payments of $2.25. It became the officer's private property upon leaving the force.[56] In August, the board would purchase two hundred more of the revolvers, with ammunition, from the Boston company.

Another kind of technology became available to the police department in March. The manager of the Telephone Exchange offered to place a telephone at police headquarters, connecting it with other institutions installing telephones. The proposal was referred to Silas Bent Jr. for an inquiry and report. Bent reported favorably at the next meeting, noting that there would be no charge to the police department. The board approved the proposal, and the Telephone Exchange installed a telephone at police headquarters in the Four Courts. Since this was the first telephone installed in the police department, there was no telephone contact with the district stations and substations, but headquarters would be in telephone contact with all other city institutions having a telephone.[57] In May, a telephone was installed in Chief McDonough's home so that he could keep in touch with headquarters.

In June, McDonough brought to the attention of the board that there were several unlicensed private detective agencies in the city. The board had, by an 1875 state statute, sole authority to license private detectives. Board vice president John Priest and Commissioner Bent were appointed to a committee to investigate the chief's report. Priest and Bent found three unlicensed private detective agencies. One of these belonged to former detective Albert J. Stiles, who had been dismissed from the police department in 1875. Stiles had an agency at Broadway and Olive streets.[58] Summonses to appear before the board were issued, and representatives of the three agencies responded. All asked the board to be licensed. The board took no action on the three cases before them, but instructed the secretary of the board to send a letter to all of the private detective agencies in the city to have all of their employees obtain an application form for a private detective license so that the board could rule on each.[59]

A monumental event in the seventeen-year history of the metropolitan police department was reported at the July 30 meeting. Vice President Priest reported that he had met with Chief McDonough and the captains with regard to a "one-day furlough every two weeks." As a result, the board, at the July 30 meeting, resolved:

> That for the month of August, 1878 and every month thereafter, the Sergeants, patrolman [*sic*] and Special Officers on duty as patrolmen or other special service, shall be allowed one day in each month off duty without deduction of pay, and that the Captains shall on the first day of each month announce to their respective commands, the name of the officer and the day on which he is relieved of duty; and that officers when off duty under this resolution shall have the privilege of wearing citizens dress.[60]

The board further resolved that it reserved the right to suspend or change the resolution when, in the board's judgment, it was desirable to do so. Captains were given the discretion to withhold the day off for any man under their command "for good cause." Such a change, however, had to be reported to the chief of police who, in turn, was required to report it to the vice president of the board.[61]

In late August, the St. Louis Agricultural and Mechanical Association (A & M) asked the board to authorize a police station on the fairgrounds on Grand Avenue and Natural Bridge Road. The A & M association would erect the building. The board accepted the offer, resolving that it would become the Fairgrounds substation of the

Fifth (Mounted) District. The new substation would be completed before the beginning of the annual Agricultural and Mechanical Fair in the park. Priest and Nidelet were selected to supervise construction of the station.[62]

Before the October fair, however, yellow fever struck the southern United States. The fever struck in Alabama, Arkansas, Louisiana, Mississippi, and Tennessee, eventually killing thousands of people. Doctors, nurses, and midwives from Memphis, Tennessee, volunteered to assist throughout the various states. Ten horses and buggies for the use of physicians were dispatched from Louisville, Kentucky.[63] In St. Louis, the Merchants' Exchange began a relief fund for the victims of yellow fever in the south. On September 10, the board announced that the police had raised $922.55 by selling tickets to the Jockey Club "for the benefit of yellow fever sufferers." The board also ordered that two thousand tickets for a chamber of commerce benefit concert be distributed to, and sold by, police officers.[64] In October, the board reported that police officers had received over $1,700 in donations for the yellow fever sufferers.[65]

The Police Poor Fund was still in operation. In February, the board had ordered that "all fines assessed against police officers shall be collected at end of each month, and handed to the Treasurer to be added to the poor fund of the department."[66] In October, the police captains asked that the board rescind the order that all fines against officers would go to the Poor Fund. Because the Police Relief Fund was in dire circumstances, the captains asked the board to order that all fines, and the proceeds of all unclaimed property, be placed to the credit of the Police Relief Fund. The board accepted the recommendations of the captains.

The annual Agricultural and Mechanical Fair started its week-long run at the fairgrounds on Monday, October 7. Something new, a downtown parade, was scheduled for Tuesday evening. Two hundred men, described as "prominent gentlemen," had formed an organization in March to substitute the trade procession with a "New Orleans–style pageant."[67] It was scheduled during the Agricultural and Mechanical Fair to "boost farmers' attendance at the fair, the popularity of which had waned after the Civil War."[68] An elaborate parade was staged, with numerous floats, each pulled by six horses.[69] It was led by Captain Warren Fox, commander of the mounted police, and twenty foot officers who cleared the parade route ahead of the marchers and floats. The foot officers were followed by two platoons of mounted police in full dress uniform. The parade was apparently well received by the citizens. As the *Globe-Democrat* noted, "the demonstration last evening was the first appearance in public of the Veiled Prophets, and the public can judge of the wisdom of the movement. It was the biggest show ever seen in the city, . . ."[70] It was the first Veiled Prophet Parade in St. Louis, a tradition that continues to this day. The leader of the Veiled Prophets that first year, referred to in the *Globe-Democrat* as the "Grand Mogul" (the Veiled Prophet of Khorassan in later years), was identified as John Priest, the vice and acting president of the Board of Police Commissioners.[71]

The year closed with the fourth annual charity ball (which brought in just over $8,000 for the Police Poor Fund) and the beginning of a donnybrook that would ultimately include some present members of the board, a former police commissioner, the chief of police, the St. Louis delegation to the Missouri General Assembly, and Governor Phelps. The result of this public brawl would be a Senate investigation of the governor's proposed police commission appointments, a St. Louis grand jury investigation, and yet another outcry to return at least partial control of the police department to the city. It would be the first scandal within the police department since the Civil War.

On December 28, the *St. Louis Post and Dispatch* reported a conversation between a reporter for the paper and Dr. James Nidelet, the purchasing member of the board. According to the reporter, Nidelet claimed that he was being followed by two police detectives who were attempting to find out "anything against me."[72]

The article led to interviews with Vice President Priest and Chief McDonough. Both denied that they had ordered any detectives to follow Nidelet. One of the two detectives named by Nidelet was also interviewed and denied the allegations.[73]

1879

The verbal sparring continued when the *Globe-Democrat* joined the fray, stating that both Priest and Nidelet were posturing. The newspaper said that "it is certain that both men are moving heaven and earth to obtain a renomination at the hands of the Governor, and that, in the same way, their interests are so antagonistic that each is strenuously opposed to the reappointment of the other."[74]

The matter appeared to have been laid to rest when, on February 11, Governor Phelps nominated Nidelet, David Armstrong, and William Ladd for the Board of Police Commissioners in St. Louis. The names were sent to the Senate for confirmation.[75] Instead of confirming the nominees, the Senate adopted a motion to appoint a committee composed of two members of the Senate from St. Louis and three from outside it to gather information about the nominees. They would begin hearings on February 17.

The five members of the Senate committee checked into the Laclede Hotel, on the southwest corner of Broadway and Chestnut streets, across from the courthouse.[d] On Monday, they began taking testimony from witnesses, behind closed doors, in a parlor of the hotel. Witnesses would be sworn not to reveal what they had heard or testified to during the examination. Two police officers were stationed outside of the parlor doors to prevent anyone from listening through them.[76]

The next day, the *Post and Dispatch* published a detailed account of the secret testimony of all of Monday's witnesses, stating, "whether it was through Edison's microphone, by the leakiness of a member of the committee, or by a pumping process applied to all the witnesses examined, must remain a mystery."[77] After the Tuesday afternoon edition of the *Post and Dispatch* had hit the streets, the Senate committee read the accounts and then began investigating how the information

---

[d] Today, the southwest corner of Broadway and Chestnut (across from what is now called the Old Courthouse) is the site of Kiener Plaza, the first block of a six-block mall that extends west from the courthouse.

could have been collected. After several hours, it found that conversation in the committee's parlor could easily be overheard in an adjoining parlor. The wall separating the two parlors had only the wall boards in each parlor; there was no insulation between the two boards. By then, however, all of Monday's testimony had been overheard and published, and the testimony heard before the Tuesday edition was distributed and the method of disclosure discovered.[78]

Those testifying, according to the account published in the *Post and Dispatch*, consisted of a wide range of people from a hotel clerk, to local politicians, to bankers, to the operator of an illegal gambling house, to a former Union army general. There were those who testified on behalf of Nidelet and Ladd, those who said that they had nothing to contribute to the investigation, and those who testified against Nidelet and Ladd. There was testimony of a gambling ring in St. Louis that allegedly included Nidelet when he was vice and acting president of the board.

One of the duties of the vice president of the board was to issue warrants against gambling houses. According to one witness, R. C. Pate, a lawyer named A. B. Wakefield offered him immunity from police interference for 25 percent of the profits from Pate's keno operation. The money allegedly went to Nidelet for warning Wakefield when a gambling warrant had been issued for Pate's gambling house.[79] At least one witness implicated William Ladd with the gamblers. On the other side, dozens of members of the Tobacco Merchants, the Cotton Exchange, and the Merchants' Exchange supported Ladd, signing petitions attesting to his integrity and honor. The testimony of Nidelet and Ladd before the Senate committee occurred after the discovery of the manner in which reporters of the *Post and Dispatch* had listened in on the testimony. Their testimony was not overheard.

The committee returned to Jefferson City on Wednesday night. In the end, however, and regardless of the veracity of the testimony of the many witnesses who testified against Nidelet and, to a lesser extent, Ladd, the investigation had tarnished them. The March term of the grand jury would begin an investigation into the so-called gambling ring in St. Louis and any connection to the police department. It would present its final report on May 1.

On Monday, February 24, the Missouri Senate met to hear the report of the investigating committee. David Armstrong was first confirmed, and then the discussion turned to Nidelet and Ladd. Both were rejected by the Senate.[80] Governor Phelps would have to nominate two different candidates.

At the board meeting following the rejection of Nidelet and Ladd, acting vice president Bent called a special meeting of the board. Vice President Priest was out of town, and purchasing member Nidelet was marked "absent."[81] Besides Bent, Mayor Overstolz and Basil Duke were in attendance. The minutes referred to the interview with Governor Phelps published in the February 17 edition of the *Post and Dispatch* in which the governor stated that he had heard that the police department had been used to follow people to make them victims of blackmail.[82]

The minutes note that the reporter, J. E. Waters, made an affidavit under oath on February 21 that not only had Governor Phelps made the statements attributed to him, but also stated that "he while Governor, had never entered the city of Saint Louis without being watched and dogged in every step he had taken and every house he had visited by parties trying to get a hold on him, and find out if he did not visit disreputable houses."[83] Bent introduced a preamble and resolution that "the fact should be proven and fixed upon those who were guilty of the outrage, and if not true, then it is equally due to the efficiency of the Police Dept and the vindication of its character, as well as, that of the Commissioners, who have administered its affairs for the last two years, that they should be relieved from such scandalous imputations."[84] It was further resolved that a copy of the resolutions be sent to Governor Phelps and to the press.

A copy of the preamble and resolutions were sent to Phelps along with a letter from the board. In the letter, the board threw down the gauntlet:

> The commissioners would be rejoiced to know that you have been misrepresented in these reports. But if the facts in the case are such as to deny them that gratification then it becomes my duty to inform you that not only the Police Commissioners, but also

the people of St. Louis, whom they serve, will expect you to take the necessary steps to substantiate your charges. And in view of the fact that a majority of the Commissioners are about to retire from the Board, it is but just to them that such action as you may deem proper to take in the premises shall be instituted with as little delay as practicable.[85]

The letter was signed by Silas Bent, acting vice president.

Governor Phelps responded the following Monday. The governor acknowledged that he had said that the information "had been reported to me." He also said in the interview that "if the force was used in that manner [as reported to him], it might be used to follow me, or anyone else." Said the governor, "I do not profess to give the language used, but the idea expressed. I did not state the police had followed me, nor had I reason to entertain such an opinion."[86] Board vice president John Priest, who was not present when the preamble and resolutions were read and adopted, but who was present at the meeting at which the response of Governor Phelps was read, added that if he were present when a vote was taken to adopt them, "he would have cheerfully voted for them."[87]

Even though David Armstrong was confirmed by the Senate on February 24, he elected not to take his seat on the board until the other two members had been nominated by Governor Phelps and confirmed.[88] It wasn't until April 16 that Governor Phelps sent the names of two nominees to the Senate. The two, John D. Finney and Leslie A. Moffett, had been among the fifteen possible nominees who had emerged during the first week of February. The Senate confirmed both men the same day it received the names of the two nominees.

Armstrong, Finney, and Moffett appeared at the next meeting of the Board of Police Commissioners, April 22. Armstrong was given the two-year term (ending January 1, 1881); Finney and Moffett received four-year terms that ended on January 1, 1883. John Finney had formerly been connected with the carpet company of Finney and McGrath. He served two terms as a county court judge and, at the time he was appointed to the board, was chief deputy sheriff of the city of St. Louis. Leslie Moffett was a principal in the real estate firm of January and Moffett. His appointment to the board was his first public office. Armstrong was elected vice president, Duke was reelected treasurer, and Moffett was elected purchasing member. George Gavin was, for the fourteenth consecutive year, elected secretary of the board.[89]

The board called a special meeting for April 30 to hear a request from the St. Louis school board. At the special meeting, a committee from the school board asked the board for police assistance in taking the census of all children of school age in the city. The information was now required, by state law, to be reported to the Missouri superintendent of public schools. The board postponed acting on the request until a special meeting called for the next day, when the school board committee could make its presentation before Chief McDonough and all of the captains. The committee from the school board assured the board that "a handsome donation would be made from the school funds to the Police Relief Fund upon completion of the work. . . ."[90] The board, chief, and captains discussed the situation in private and agreed to take on this added responsibility. Even in the face of a reduction in the force, there was apparently no other organization in the city equipped to conduct such a census. The census would begin on May 12. The school board would later donate $2,000 to the Police Relief Fund.[91]

On May 1, the March term of the grand jury presented its final report to Judge Henry D. Laughlin of the criminal court. At its formation in March, the grand jury was charged with determining if board member Dr. James Nidelet was guilty of corruption in office by taking money from owners of gambling operations "in return for protection illegally extended by him, and information illegally given by him to the persons interested in the business of gambling. . . ."[92] The panel was also charged with determining whether Nidelet was guilty "of oppression and corruption in office toward certain persons engaged in the business of lottery dealing in this city."[93]

On the first charge, the grand jury found that a lawyer, A. B. Wakefield, collected money from gambling operators "upon representations that he [Wakefield] could procure such information from J. C. Nidelet, with respect to intended raids upon their establishments, as would be of great pecuniary value to them."[94] The grand jury, however, could find no evidence that Nidelet ever received such money. Wakefield testified that the money he collected was not for information furnished by the board, but for legal services rendered by him. However, the report stated, "he is not very well able to define it."[95] When further questioned as to his qualifications to practice law, "he displays a degree of ignorance which would be very comical if it did not suggest that he makes use of the license of a lawyer to cover the sinister acts of a citizen."[96] Wakefield's examination by the grand jury resulted in him being indicted for perjury.

As for Nidelet, the grand jury could find no evidence that he had taken any money from gambling interests. On the second charge, oppression and corruption in office toward those in the lottery business, the grand jury found "a strong chain of circumstantial evidence against him. . . . So we are compelled to leave the public in the same dilemma which we find ourselves—that of deciding, with the circumstantial evidence clearly against him, whether Police Commissioner Nidelet was more than zealous or less than honest in the prosecution of what is known as the lottery war."[97] Nidelet had lost his bid for reappointment to the Board of Police Commissioners, but escaped a grand jury indictment.

That did not end the grand jury's report. It also took the Board of Police Commissioners to task on its position toward gambling in St. Louis: "On the general subject of gambling, we find that what may be called 'the gambling interest' has for many years been a source of corruption to the Police Department. . . . Through its representatives, it has boasted of its power to control the police, and more than once it has exercised that power."[98]

The report blamed the Board of Police Commissioners for misconstruing the gambling laws. The board, said the jurors, "assumed to regulate a crime which it is their duty to suppress. The Commissioners have assumed and exercised a power 'to bind and to loose' which the law never delegated to them."[99] To illustrate the point, the grand jury noted that a daily report was given to the vice president of the board indicating which gambling houses were open and which were closed:

With this report before him the vice president of the board allows or interdicts gambling as may seem best to his judgment or caprice. Gambling cannot be lawful on Monday and unlawful on Tuesday, and it is the business of the Police Commissioners to enforce laws and not to interpret them. If gambling is lawful, it should not be molested; if unlawful, it should not be tolerated. The statutes declare gambling to be unlawful, and make it the business of the police to deal with it as they would deal with any other crime.[100]

The newly constituted board took notice of the grand jury report. In June, it would take a new approach to the suppression of gambling in the city.

On Sunday, June 1, Patrolman Charles Printz was killed while attempting to arrest Charles Sanders. Sanders was twenty-two years old and had no steady job. He frequented the area of the slums at Second and Poplar streets and was later described by Chief of Police McDonough as "a frequenter of low saloons and bawdy houses."[101] Sanders had, just nine weeks earlier, been released from jail after serving eight or nine months for cutting a piano player in a saloon. He had three sisters, all living in St. Louis. One of them lived with her husband and father-in-law at 505 Marion Street, on the south side of the city. Her husband, Leon Martin, had previously told Sanders not to come to their house again.[102]

About 7:15 p.m. on June 1, Charles Sanders came to the Martin residence. Leon Martin was tending his garden in the rear yard. His father, Antoine Martin, was sitting on the front porch when he saw Sanders approaching. Sanders went to the rear of the house, spoke with Leon Martin, and then began flourishing a revolver. Sanders's sister came out of the house and argued with her brother. Sanders put his gun in his hip pocket and appeared to calm down.[103] Several times during the encounter, Sanders was reported to have said that he was not going to be arrested, especially by Officer Printz.[104]

Meanwhile, Antoine Martin had left the front porch to find a policeman. He found Officer Printz on Carondelet Avenue (now South Broadway), and they went to the Martin house. On the way to the house, Printz asked Antoine Martin the name of the person who was causing the disturbance. Martin replied that it was Charles

Sanders. Printz remarked that this would not be the first time he had arrested Sanders.[105]

When they reached the Martin house, Officer Printz greeted Charles Sanders by name. After some banter, according to Leon Martin:

> Printz made a quick movement to get the pistol that he knew Sanders had. There was a scuffle immediately, and the two men struggled out into the street. Printz struck Sanders on the head with his club. Sanders seemed stunned, but did not fall. He let go his hold of the officer and retreated several feet, and having got his pistol out he fired a shot which missed its mark. They then clinched again and struggled out into the street when Sanders broke loose again, and fired the second and fatal shot.[106]

The officer struck Sanders on the shoulder with his club. He stepped back and raised the club again, swung weakly, missing Sanders, and fell to the street dead. The officer's revolver was under what was described as his "heavy rubber overcoat."[107] Sanders made good his escape.

In the meantime, four men had picked up Printz and carried him to the drugstore at Carondelet and Marion, where a medical student was on duty. The medical student was quickly joined by three medical doctors, but Printz was already dead.[108] Chief McDonough went to the funeral home where Printz was taken and gathered sufficient information about Charles Sanders to telegraph a description throughout the city and, later, beyond the city limits. As a result of tips, officers scoured various locations in Illinois to no avail.

The funeral of Patrolman Charles Printz was held on Wednesday, June 4, 1879. After a brief ceremony at the deceased officer's home, the procession began to the new Picker Cemetery on Gravois Road. At the request of various officers, and upon the recommendation of Chief McDonough, the board permitted all police in the city to wear "crape on their stars for the next thirty days."[109] This was the first time that police officers in St. Louis were permitted to so honor a fallen comrade. Police officers continue that tradition today. Patrolman Charles Printz was thirty-seven years old. He left behind a wife and four children; Mrs. Printz was pregnant at the time of the officer's death.[110]

Over the next two years, the Board of Police Commissioners spent almost $700 and countless man-hours pursuing leads to the whereabouts of Charles Sanders.[111] He was arrested by members of the Chicago Police Department in 1893. A collection was taken and $226 was collected for a reward for the Chicago police. The board sent $200 to the superintendent of the Chicago Police Department, Austin J. Doyle, and placed the remaining $26 in the coffers of the Police Relief Fund. Superintendent Doyle declined the reward, returning it to the board with some kind remarks. The board returned the money to the officers who had donated it.[112] The disposition of Sanders's case is unknown.

In the meantime, the usual $2 was collected from each member of the force (the police Mutual Life Association) to be presented to Mrs. Printz. The community also became involved. The H.M.S. Pinafore Company, performing at Uhrig's Cave, presented a benefit performance for the Printz family on June 7, 1879.[113] The performance raised $2,119.70. A bigger surprise came in October, when a citizen reported to the board that he had purchased a house for the Printz family at 2418 McNair and requested the approval of the board. A committee of the board looked into the situation. The board later approved the donation provided that all taxes were paid on the property through the following January.[114] In January, the board spent $70 for connecting Mrs. Printz's home to the water system, and another $30.45 for necessary carpentry work.[115]

The board had several major issues that would occupy much of its time in the latter half of 1879. First, the board made preparations to comply with a new state law, effective July 18, that established a state militia. The Police Reserves, while essentially retaining the same status, would begin the transition to become a part of the state militia. There were now six companies.

The second item was to deal with the findings of the May report of the St. Louis grand jury that the earlier board had tolerated gambling in the city. In June, the board began an effort to suppress gambling in the city, especially the lotteries. Mayor Overstolz called a special meeting of the board to discuss the best way to prosecute those in the gambling and lottery operations. The meeting was attended by four

Uhrig's Cave. Photograph by Robert Benecke, ca. 1870.
Missouri History Museum.

attorneys, including the city counselor. As a result, the board ordered
Vice President Armstrong to detail at least five policemen to secure
evidence sufficient to convict gamblers. Armstrong was also authorized "to employ outside of the force such men as in his judgment will
aid in the procuring of the evidence. . . ."[116]

At its meeting of July 15, the board made it perfectly clear that
gambling would no longer be tolerated. The board adopted a resolution that Armstrong should "notify the various persons interested;
either by circular or by publication in the City Press; that on the 21st
day of July 1879, the sale of lottery tickets and the practice of gambling under its various forms, will not be further tolerated in this city;
and that to effect these objects the full power of the Board will be
exercised." The resolution directed the vice president to instruct the

police force to visit every lottery station and gambling house on their respective beats (at a prearranged time throughout the city) and shut down the operations. The crackdown began in late August.[117]

A week later, Chief McDonough reported that keno and faro banks and the St. Louis Lottery had been shut down. Because of pending legal actions concerning the state lottery law in the Missouri Supreme Court, the Missouri State Lottery remained open. The board, however, ordered that Court of Criminal Correction cases arising out of the arrests of Missouri Lottery employees go forward. The board even asked Mayor Overstolz to instruct the city counselor to assist the prosecuting attorney's office in prosecuting the Missouri Lottery cases.[118] At a later board meeting, Vice President Armstrong would remark that there were enough lottery and gambling cases before the Court of Criminal Correction "to occupy it for the next six months."[119] In its annual report for fiscal year 1879–1880, the board reported 250 arrests for gambling. There were 68 gambling arrests in the previous fiscal year.[120]

❊   ❊   ❊

Because of the failure of the Municipal Assembly to pass an appropriations bill, the board ran out of funds early in the 1879–1880 fiscal year. Contingency plans were formulated at the board meeting of April 29. The board determined that (1) the force would have to be reduced in size and (2) the resolution of July 30, 1878, allowing each member of the force one day off a month, would be rescinded.[121] To meet the June payroll, the board invoked Section 15 of the 1861 Metropolitan Police Act and issued a certificate of indebtedness for $5,000, payable twenty days after the payroll date.[122] The board ordered sergeants on duty at district stations to be replaced by patrolmen. Sergeants were returned to "active precinct duty."[123]

The police appropriations bill, meanwhile, was apparently being held hostage to gain concessions from the board. On June 24, the House of Delegates (the lower body) sent a letter to the board asking that it restore the one-day leave of absence each month for the members of the force.[124]

At the same time, the House of Delegates passed a second resolution requesting that the police be instructed to enforce the city
ordinance prohibiting the driving of stock on streets within one
hundred feet of any public park or other public place. The flavor of
the dispute was evident in the reply of the board. The resolution was
referred to Vice President David Armstrong with instructions "to
procure the number of the ordinance from the clerk of the House of
Delegates; if such ordinance exists."[125] The appropriations bill finally
was passed, but the board was already $41,000 in debt from the previ-
ous fiscal year. The city and the board were beginning to feel the pinch
resulting from the 1876 separation of the city from the county of St.
Louis. By state law, the county had been supplying 25 percent of the
police budget before the separation.

On July 22, the board informed the captains that they were to prepare lists of all the men in their districts, grading them first, second,
or third class, "according to their merit and efficiency," and have the
lists ready for an upcoming special board meeting. Through the use
of these lists, the board, on August 12, laid off eleven patrolmen and
one turnkey. They were dropped from the rolls "for want of means to
pay them." Another patrolman was reduced to turnkey and another
to a "special." In addition, the board ordered that no one would be
paid during an absence of duty unless approved by the board. The
appropriations bill was eventually passed, but was $4,000 less than the
previous fiscal year.[126]

Finally, the board had to face continuing complaints from citizens who lived between the pre-1876 city limits (approximately
Grand Avenue) and the post-1876 boundaries (the present city limits) resulting from the 1876 charter and scheme. The areas between
Grand Avenue and the new city limits (referred to as "the suburbs")
were being patrolled by officers from the Mounted (Fifth) District.
The 1876 charter and scheme had almost tripled the geographical
size of the city. The population had also increased over time and with
the additional geographical area.[127] Yet the force had been limited,
since 1872, to 6 captains, 46 sergeants, and 401 patrolmen.[128] Most
of the patrol force was deployed in the central portion of the city.
Each patrolman walked a beat of approximately four blocks. The

beats grew larger as they extended from the central city. The amount of time to walk these beats was as little as once an hour to as much as once every six hours.[129]

At the meeting of November 25, the board discussed the feasibility of creating the position of chief of detectives to replace the sergeant of detectives.[130] While the board did not note what police rank the chief of detectives would hold, he would receive the pay of a captain, $150 per month. The board agreed to create the position, and the names of three candidates were put forward for a vote. None of the candidates received a majority vote of the board and the issue was "laid over" to the next meeting.[131] A vote was not noted on any subsequent meetings of the board. The matter was probably dropped, for no mention of a chief of detectives was made in the annual report of the board for the fiscal year ending April 12, 1880.[132]

The year ended with the fifth annual charity ball to benefit the Police Poor Fund. The ball had gross receipts of over $10,000.[133]

1880

The board reaffirmed an old order in January 1880. A patrolman appeared before the board charged with "wearing citizen's dress without proper authority." The rule that officers must wear their police uniform when off duty and away from their home was instituted in October 1867. Rather than face disciplinary action, the patrolman's resignation was accepted "while under charges."[134]

The less fortunate were also a source of discussion in early 1880. At the meeting of January 24, Vice President Armstrong requested permission from the board to allow policemen to sell tickets to citizens on their beats for dramatic performances at Pope's Theatre in aid of those starving in Ireland. The board approved the request. The police department later forwarded the sum of $1,153 to the citizen's committee sponsoring the appeal.

A unique event in the history of the police department began with a citizen's complaint on April 13. The board minutes of that meeting note that "the Pastor of the Italian church at 6th & Spruce [with a few prominent members of his church] appeared before the Board & remonstrated against the notorious immoral conduct of persons and places in that vicinity to the great detriment of the interests of said church."

After hearing the complaint, the board ordered "that proper steps be taken to abate the situation complained of as far as possible." The "Italian church" was St. Bonaventura. The pastor was the Reverend Nazaren Orfei. While complaints of prostitution were not unusual, the "proper steps" taken to "abate the situation" were unique. In the month following the complaint, Father Orfei was commissioned a sergeant of police.[135]

At the board meeting of July 30, the board passed a resolution giving thanks to "the Rev. N. Orfei, pastor of the Italian Church at 6th and Spruce, for the great reformation he has effected in the morals of that locality since he was invested with police powers in May last." Father Orfei resigned his appointment as sergeant of police on April 27, 1881.

The board continued to receive complaints from citizens regarding police protection. For instance, those living in the "southern suburbs" around South Grand and Chippewa, and those in the northern portion of the city around the Water Tower on North Grand, requested additional police protection. These requests were forwarded to Captain Warren Fox, commander of the mounted police.[136] However, as noted earlier, the mounted force had to patrol an extremely large geographical area with a force that was meant to patrol the pre-1876 split from the county of St. Louis. Residents near Taylor and St. Charles Road (now Martin Luther King Drive) took their concerns before the board in a different manner. At the meeting of March 30, "citizens and property owners" in that area presented the board with a deed to a lot on the southeast corner of that intersection for the erection of a police station.[137] It is likely that the lot was on the southeast corner of Deer and St. Charles Road, the location of police facilities for the next one hundred years. The board accepted the deed and, later, purchased an additional seventy feet.[138]

At the meeting of May 18, the board restored the one day off per month policy: "Resolved That the officers of the police force be allowed one day off during each month; the day to be arranged by the captains of the different districts."[139] In September, Captains William Lee and Warren Fox and a Sergeant Price asked for an additional six days' pay while they were absent with leave in Chicago in August as they had not taken the days allowed under the resolution of the board of May 1880. They were to be disappointed. The board then adopted a resolution clarifying the policy; the board intended the one day off each month in the resolution of May 1880 to apply only to patrolmen.[140]

Beginning early the next year, however, sergeants would be allowed one day off each month.[141] In March 1882, turnkeys, commissioned officers below the rank of patrolman who worked as police jailers, would also request one day off.[142] The request was denied, but a similar petition was approved one year later.[143]

Meanwhile, the lottery case was being determined in the courts. In April, the Missouri Supreme Court handed down its decision in the Missouri Lottery situation that had been given the attention of the police department for the past five years. The court was asked to rule, in *The State ex rel. The Attorney General v. France* (1880), on an 1849 contract with the town of New Franklin, Missouri. In 1833, the Missouri legislature had passed a statute authorizing a state lottery to enable the town of New Franklin to build a railroad to the Missouri River. It was this statute, with subsequent amendments, that Missouri Lottery ticket vendors had relied upon to legitimize lottery sales. The court ruled in *France* that the contract of 1849 had been fully executed and there was no longer a legal basis for a state lottery.[144]

In June, two attorneys representing the Missouri State Lottery and two representing the St. Louis Academy of Music and Art Lottery appeared before the board. They asked that, inasmuch as the recent Missouri Supreme Court decision abolished said lotteries, all further court proceedings be suspended and that all convictions now pending be dealt with as leniently as the board could afford to recommend to the courts. The board told them to put it in writing for a special board meeting of Saturday, June 19. The city attorney was called and requested to suspend, for ten days, all further prosecution of any lottery cases in his hands. The board also requested that the city counselor (the prosecutor of city ordinance violations) be consulted for his legal opinion in the matter.[145]

The attorneys' petitions were read at the special board meeting on June 19. Upon consultation with the city counselor and the city attorney, the question was laid over for two weeks, and the city attorney was asked to continue such cases now in his hands.

In July, the board resolved that, upon payment of a fine of $50 and costs and a pledge not to again engage in the selling of lottery tickets, the board would recommend that all cases against lottery vendors be settled.[146] That would have been the end of the lottery issue, but plaintiffs in the *France* decision appealed to the U.S. Supreme Court, arguing that the lottery contract had not yet expired and that the Missouri Supreme Court had erred in ruling that it had expired.

In the meantime, the owners of the Missouri State Lottery also applied for an injunction in the federal court, then known as the circuit court for the Eastern District of Missouri. In that case, *Murray and Another v. Overstoltz* [*sic*] *and Others* (1880), the owners argued that they should be able to operate the lottery while awaiting the decision of the U.S. Supreme Court. The federal circuit court ruled that, since the owners had appealed the Missouri Supreme Court decision to the U.S. Supreme Court, the circuit court was prohibited from issuing an injunction; an injunction was now the purview of the U.S. Supreme Court.[147] Slightly more than a month after the unsuccessful attempt to obtain an injunction in the circuit court, the U.S. Supreme Court (in *France v. Missouri*, 1880) dismissed the case because no federal question had been raised.[148]

With the Missouri State Lottery no longer being an issue, the board redoubled its efforts to crack down on other games of chance. In June, the board began what might today be referred to as a "gambling squad." To do so, the board adopted a resolution that:

> a detail of police officers, of three or more, be put in citizen's dress, with orders to devote their whole time to getting evidence to suppress Keno, bunko, faro, or any game of gambling that is carried on,

contrary to law; and that the Vice President is authorized to use any money that he may require to allow the officers to play in any game of chance, that may enable them to obtain evidence to convict the gamblers.[149]

In July, the board expanded the role of plainclothes officers by giving the captains authority to detail any number of patrolmen "in citizen's dress" when the captains felt it necessary.[150]

At the meeting of July 3, the board redistricting committee, composed of commissioners Leslie Moffett and David Armstrong, presented its recommendations. The committee, appointed in May, recommended new boundaries based upon the tradition that all of the districts have the Mississippi River as an eastern boundary. The boundaries were only slightly changed.

The Mounted District, with approximately thirty mounted officers on each twelve-hour platoon, patrolled forty-five (73 percent) of the sixty-two square miles within the city limits. The city west of Grand Avenue was mostly meadows and farmland, but did contain some country homes.[151] The board obviously saw no need to expand police districts beyond the city limits that existed in 1855.

At the meeting of August 19, a police sergeant's application for a thirty-day furlough unknowingly set into motion a series of events that would rock the board early the next year. Sergeant Morgan Boland of the Second District had applied to the board for a thirty-day furlough, effective August 17, to run in the November election for the office of sheriff of the city of St. Louis. All requests for furloughs had to be approved by the board. A vote was called for, and Boland's application was rejected. His resignation was tendered, and accepted, at the next board meeting. Morgan Boland would lose his bid for sheriff, but the board had not heard the last of him.

In November, the board announced that the police department would again sponsor the annual charity ball (the sixth) to be held for the benefit of the poor in St. Louis. Former commissioner Charles Rainwater would chair the event.[152] (As a result of the charity ball, the Police Poor Fund would be the recipient of approximately $12,000 for distribution to the poor.)[153]

About two o'clock on the bitterly cold morning of Sunday, December 5, Patrolman Michael Walsh of the Central District was shot to death.[154] Walsh was the eighth officer killed in the twenty-year history of the St. Louis Metropolitan Police Department.[155] He was walking his beat when he heard the rapping of a nightstick from the beat just north of his.[156] Walsh responded and met Patrolman Sheehan, who explained that he had found the front door open at the residence on the corner of Sixteenth and Olive streets and thought that burglars might be inside. The officers decided that Walsh would remain in the front of the residence while Sheehan went to the stable in the rear to awaken the stableman. While the stableman got dressed, Patrolman Sheehan returned to the front of the house to rejoin Patrolman Walsh. A rap for assistance was then heard coming from their west. That call was soon followed by other raps from various beats to the west. (Burglars had broken into three stores on Market Street.)

Walsh and Sheehan decided that the possible burglary was important enough for them to remain at their location and, since whatever was occurring was west of them, they would stop anyone coming from the west. They did stop four men, who identified themselves as musicians returning from a job at Uhrig's Cave. Sheehan stopped another man, who also proved to be a musician, and then returned to the stable at the rear of the residence to get the stableman.

As Sheehan stood by the carriage house, he could see Officer Walsh standing on the corner with two men. One of the men pointed a revolver at Walsh's head and fired. One of the men then ran south on Sixteenth Street; the man who shot Patrolman Walsh ran west on Olive Street. Patrolman Sheehan ran after the latter and fired two shots at him. The assailant then returned fire, firing one time in Sheehan's direction. At Seventeenth and Olive streets, the man turned the corner and ran south on Seventeenth. Sheehan turned the same corner but the assailant was gone, so he returned to the scene to assist Patrolman Walsh. Walsh was taken to the city dispensary in a carriage that had been passing the scene, but dispensary personnel sent him to the City Hospital. Walsh died en route to the hospital; he was thirty-six years old and had been on the police force for ten years. Because of his athletic build and height (six feet, two inches) Walsh had spent some time on the Broadway squad, the so-called Ladies Platoon. He left a wife and two children.

Patrolman Walsh's funeral was held on Wednesday, December 8, beginning with a Mass at St. Lawrence O'Toole Catholic Church at Fourteenth and O'Fallon streets. A "great crowd" attended the funeral and, in spite of the extremely cold weather, many followed the cortege to Calvary Cemetery.[157]

The following day, Chief James McDonough offered a $500 reward "for information that will lead to the arrest and conviction of the party who shot and killed Officer Walsh on Sunday morning last."[158] The suspected murderer of Walsh would be identified in April 1881. He was arrested in Louisville, Kentucky, based upon information supplied by a member of the burglary ring that the suspect headed.

1881

While 1881 would be a year that would not easily be forgotten in the history of the police department, the first three months were particularly complicated, controversial, and politically charged. At the first meeting of the year, J. Milton Turner and P. H. Murray, chairman and vice chairman of the Executive Committee of the Republican Union of Negro Citizens, respectively, "appeared before the Board and presented a petition asking for the appointment of some negro citizens on the police force of this city. It was ordered that the petition be taken under consideration."[159] Turner, who had been born a slave, was a self-taught lawyer. In 1871, President Ulysses S. Grant appointed him minister resident and consul general to Liberia.[160] He served in that position until 1878, when he returned to Missouri.[161]

A newspaper account of the board meeting quoted Vice President Armstrong as stating that "in 1877 Overstolz formed an alliance with Chauncey I. Filley by which the negro vote was to be thrown to his [undecipherable] consideration being that he should confirm the appointment of a [undecipherable] number of negroes on the police force on Filley's recommendation. He [Armstrong] objected to this because it mixed police matters and politics. The men who came recommended by Filley were all rejected because they did not come up to the standard."[162]

Turner and Murray, accompanied by the secretary of the Executive Committee, Albert Burgess, had visited Mayor Overstolz in December 1880. They had presented him with a petition asking that the mayor nominate for positions in the city administration "such negroes as may possess merit and ability."[163] In his conversation with the three, Mayor Overstolz noted that he was in favor of employing "colored men" on the force. When he brought this conviction to the board, said the mayor, "the board had laughed at him."[164] He further mentioned that "at one time he had a colored detective appointed, and after the detective had served about three days he was discharged by the board."[165] Regardless of whose recollection was closer to the truth, the reality was that no black citizen would be appointed to the police force for another twenty years.

On the same day of the board's first meeting, the *St. Louis Post-Dispatch* (formerly the *Post and Dispatch*) ran a front-page article calling St. Louis "a Gambler's Paradise."[166] The newspaper had, on New Year's Eve, sent its entire contingent of reporters to find gambling houses. *Post-Dispatch* reporters found seventeen gambling houses operating, seven keno, and ten faro. "The Police Board knows of the existence of these places. If it does not know, it can inform itself by reading this article."[167] The *Post-Dispatch* then listed the seventeen gambling houses by name and address, indicating what game was being played at each address. The grand jury would be charged with looking into the police department and enforcement of gambling laws.

At that same meeting, purchasing member Leslie Moffett made a motion that would signal the beginning of a new technology in St. Louis police communications. Moffett moved that a committee be appointed to visit Chicago to learn of the "recently improved system of police telephoning, with a view of having the same introduced here."[168] The motion was adopted, and Moffett and David Armstrong were selected to go to Chicago. The "system of police telephoning" was the institution of the police call box. Upcoming events, however, would postpone the call box program.

Chapter Six

The Crittenden Years

THE FOUR-YEAR TERM of Democratic governor Thomas T. Crittenden, which began in January 1881, cannot be considered dull. Among other things, Governor Crittenden would have a continuous problem with his appointments to the St. Louis Board of Police Commissioners. The commissions of David Armstrong and Basil Duke were due to expire on January 25, 1881. Governor Crittenden moved quickly to name their replacements. The *St. Louis Post-Dispatch* reported that Crittenden had sent to the Senate for confirmation the names of Morgan Boland and Alexander Kinkead.[1] Many people likely knew the name of Morgan Boland. He was the ex-police sergeant who had resigned from the police force in an unsuccessful bid for the office of sheriff. Alexander Kinkead was not known to the general public or to the state senators from St. Louis. The senators learned that he formerly owned and operated a grocery at Twenty-second Street and Clark Avenue, but was, at the time of his nomination, "in the produce and chicken line" at a downtown location.[2] The *Globe-Democrat* reported that many businessmen signed a petition to Governor Crittenden in Kinkead's behalf, and that he had the support of the pastor of his church, a longtime personal friend of the governor's.[3]

Two principal English-language newspapers, the *Post-Dispatch* and the *Globe-Democrat*, kept the names of Boland and Kinkead before the public on virtually a daily basis for the week before their confirmation on Thursday, January 20. The *Globe-Democrat* (the morning newspaper) reported that, on January 20, "several St. Louisans stood shivering in the rotunda, and Boland and Kinkead were on the ragged

Thomas T. Crittenden. Photograph by D. P. Thomson, ca. 1870.
Missouri History Museum.

edge of the crowd for a time."[4] Both would make their first appearance
as police commissioners at the board meeting the following Tuesday.
Morgan Boland would become the first former police officer to
become a member of the Board of Police Commissioners. While
some good was accomplished, the board that now included Boland
and Kinkead would become at the least an embarrassment, and at the
worst a political disaster.

At the meeting of January 25, the newly formed board elected
officers. The former police sergeant, Morgan Boland, was elected
vice (and acting) president; John Finney, treasurer; and Alexander
Kinkead, purchasing member. Leslie Moffett was the fourth member. George Gavin would continue as secretary of the board. The only
other business conducted that day was the adoption of a resolution,
introduced by Boland, expressing appreciation and best wishes to former commissioners David Armstrong and Basil Duke.

Two important points framed the next meeting. First, the board
resolved to endorse a bill, proposed by Representative Charles P.
Johnson of St. Louis, that would establish the Mutual Police Relief
Association. The board noted that there was no provision in Missouri

law "for the relief of superanuated police officers, or officers who may become physically disabled by diseases contracted or wounds received while in the service of the Board."[5] The proposed association would "be under the exclusive control of a Board of Directors, elected annually by the members of said Relief Association, whose rules & by laws shall conform to, and be consistent with the manual of the Police Dep't and subject to the approval of the Board of Police Commissrs."[6]

The second point contained two related items of business that would begin a period of dissension and power struggles among members of the board. As was the practice, Chief James McDonough informed the board of the transfers that he had made since the last board meeting. Chief McDonough's list included the transfers of two captains, Joseph Hercules and William Lee, who were transferred upon the instructions of Vice President Boland. Boland then informed the board that he had removed Dr. William Faulkner as superintendent of the police stables and appointed one Samuel S. Stanton as his replacement. Faulkner had been superintendent for the past eight years.

Mayor Overstolz opposed the vice president assuming any important transactions without the prior concurrence of the board. Treasurer Finney added that previous vice presidents had made changes of officers below the rank of captain without prior approval of the board, and he moved that all of the transfers reported by Chief McDonough, except those of Captains Hercules and Lee, be approved. Finney's motion was approved. He then moved that the transfers of Hercules and Lee be approved "with the understanding that the Vice President transcended his authority in making the change."[7] The transfer of Captain (and former chief of police) William Lee from the Central District to the Second District, which was seen as a demotion in status, would have a profound and lasting effect on Lee.

The board then proceeded to vote on the issue of the removal of Dr. Faulkner. Three votes were cast for Faulkner's retention, two for his removal. Faulkner was reinstated as superintendent of police stables. As would be the case for some time, the three to two votes had Mayor Overstolz and Commissioners Finney and Moffett voting in the majority against Boland and Kinkead. Although it is not known whether Kinkead even knew Morgan Boland before their appointments to the board, he would continue to join Boland in upcoming issues requiring a vote.

At the next meeting, February 8, Vice President Boland notified the board that he had "suspended" Faulkner and, again, appointed Samuel Stanton as superintendent of stables pro tem, subject to the approval of the board. (According to the *Globe-Democrat*, Boland had suspended Faulkner on February 2, the day after the board had voted to reinstate him.)[8] The board again voted three votes for retention, two for removal. Faulkner was again reinstated.[9]

At the following meeting, February 15, on a motion by Morgan Boland and a unanimous vote, James McDonough was reappointed chief of police for four years "commencing on Jan 1, 1881."[10] Boland then informed the board that he had—for the third time—suspended William Faulkner and appointed Samuel Stanton as superintendent pro tem. Another vote by the board produced the same three to two vote against removing Faulkner.

This last attempt by Boland to remove Faulkner resulted in Mayor Overstolz introducing a resolution: "Whereas Police Commissioner Morgan Boland Vice & Acting president of this Board, refuses to conform his official action to the lawful orders of the Board, therefore be it Resolved by the Board of Police Commissioners of the City of St. Louis that the said Morgan Boland be, and he is hereby removed from the position of Vice and Acting President of said Board."[11]

Boland asked that, before the board acted upon the resolution, he be permitted to submit (and the board read) a number of affidavits charging William Faulkner with dishonesty in his official capacity as superintendent of the police stables. Secretary Gavin then read the affidavits to the board. The board called a special meeting for March 2 to hear any charges brought by Boland against Faulkner. (Boland subsequently failed to file formal charges against Faulkner, and the board didn't meet on March 2.)

The board then proceeded to vote on Mayor Overstolz's resolution to remove Boland as vice and acting president of the board. With Boland and Alexander Kinkead voting against the resolution, and the other three members voting for it, Boland was removed from that position. Boland then moved that a vice president be elected to fill the opening, and he nominated Kinkead. The motion lost, and the board voted to table the election of a vice president until the next meeting.

After William Faulkner was first removed from his position, the *Globe-Democrat* began to investigate the situation on the board. The newspaper quoted an anonymous source, "well posted on political matters, and who enjoys the confidence of the powers that be," that Samuel Stanton was given the position when he presented Boland with a letter from Governor Crittenden and a recommendation signed by a number of senators and representatives.[12]

The *Globe-Democrat* learned that Stanton was from Ste. Genevieve, Missouri, and had no legal claim on a city office as he had not been a resident of St. Louis for the previous two years. The newspaper also interviewed Crittenden. The governor first denied that he had ever seen Stanton, but later recalled that Stanton had come to his office a few days earlier, showed the governor some letters (which the governor said he did not read), and said that he was going to be appointed to the position the following Monday. Governor Crittenden denied that he had recommended Stanton and stated, "I am not controlling or endeavoring to control the Police Board of St. Louis, nor any member of it, and no man has got a scratch of a pen or word from me in the shape of a recommendation."[13]

On February 19, attorneys for Morgan Boland filed a petition in the circuit court asking the court to issue a writ of mandamus compelling the members of the board to reinstate him as vice president. In the petition, filed against the board collectively and against each member of the board, Boland contended that he was duly elected to the office of vice president and that the board had no legal right to pass the resolution of February 15 removing him from that office.[14] The arguments in the case were heard one week later. At the conclusion of the hearing, the case was taken under advisement.[15] Boland lost his bid for a writ of mandamus on February 28.

In the meantime, Captain William Lee, whom Morgan Boland had transferred from the Central to the Second District at the first meeting of the Boland board on January 25, was committed to the city asylum for the insane on February 9.[16] The *St. Louis Globe-Democrat* reported that "for some days past he has given signs of a failing mind, and two or three nights ago he said to his men, who were drawn up at relief time, that it was needless for them to wear uniforms, as the Chief of Police went in citizen's dress."[17] This statement was reported to the board, and a leave of absence was granted to Captain Lee, at his request, so that he might rest. The next morning, Lee registered at the Laclede Hotel, where he was found by Captains Kennett and Fox, speaking incoherently. They took him to the Chestnut Street substation, where he was examined by two physicians who recommended, after consulting with Lee's wife, Mary, that he be transferred to the city asylum. The superintendent of the asylum was instructed to provide Captain Lee with "every comfort."[18]

One week later, Chief McDonough reported to the board that Captain Lee "is almost if not entirely well," but would remain at the insane asylum for a few more days, on the advice of his physician.[19] (Chief McDonough's report was optimistic, for Lee was soon sent to Hot Springs, Arkansas, apparently in the hope that the hot spring waters would assist in his rehabilitation.) However, in April, Chief McDonough sent Captain Warren Fox to Hot Springs to bring Captain Lee back to St. Louis. In reporting his actions to the board, McDonough said that he had received dispatches from Lee "showing that his brain malady has returned."[20] He was continued on sick leave but, on May 2, 1882, demoted to the rank of patrolman. A sergeant was promoted to captain to take his place.[21] In February 1883, William Lee, after being on sick leave for over two years, would be dropped from the rolls of the police department.[22]

Meanwhile, the *St. Louis Post-Dispatch* continued its series of articles, begun in January, listing the gambling houses in the city that were closed and those that were running. The lists, under the headline, "Where's the Police?," included the names of the operator, the address, and the type of gambling at each location. The newspaper noted that those that were operating were doing so "in direct violation of both the statute of the State and the ordinance of the city."[23]

The *Post-Dispatch* would follow, on March 1, with a three-column list of houses of ill repute. Like the gambling houses, the listings included names, addresses and, in most cases, whether the houses could be considered "orderly" or "disorderly" in nature. The newspaper had gotten the list from a recent report of the Criminal Court grand jury and claimed that police department compiled the list.[24] The article also reprinted Clauses 3 and 7 of City Ordinance 9579, adopted in July 1875 and still in force:

> Clause 3. Any person who shall permit any house, rooms or tenements in his or her possession, or under his or her charge and control, to be used for the purposes of prostitution or house of bad repute, after ten days' notice from the Police Commissioners of such use of such house, rooms or tenements, shall be deemed guilty of a misdemeanor, and upon conviction thereof shall be fined not less than $50.

> Clause 7. It shall be the duty of the Police Commissioners, whenever they become aware of the use of any house, rooms or tenement for any of the purposes mentioned in the preceding clause, to give a written notice of such fact to the owner or agent of the owner of such house, rooms or tenement.[25]

While it was the expressed intent of the *Post-Dispatch* to make public the list of the owners or owners' agents of houses of ill repute, the publication of the salient sections of Ordinance 9579 also called the attention of the public to the responsibilities of the board, which, it implied, were not being greatly exercised.

If the Morgan Boland situation and the gambling and prostitution series in the *Post-Dispatch* weren't enough, the January 1881–term grand jury presented its report to Criminal Court Judge Henry D. Laughlin on February 26. The report noted, with reference to the police department, that the previous board (Vice President David Armstrong, Basil Duke, Leslie Moffett, and John Finney) had delegated the suppression of gambling and lotteries to Vice President Armstrong. Armstrong, said the report, "failed to officially investigate charges of bribery and corruption of such serious character as to demand their immediate reference to the full Board."[26] Said the grand jury, "For failure to report charges to the full Board an indictment has been found [against Armstrong]."[27] The grand jury censured the other three board members "for neglecting to see that the instructions in respect to the suppression of gambling and lotteries were properly enforced. . . ."[28] David Armstrong was indicted for the charge of "misdemeanor in office." A trial was held in the Court of Criminal Correction on March 19. A jury acquitted him of the charge.[29]

The residency of board treasurer John Finney then became an issue. The March 1 edition of the *Post-Dispatch* included the results of an investigation to determine where Finney lived. The newspaper stated that there were those who said (and supported their statements with sworn affidavits) that Finney lived in St. Louis County. Police commissioners were, of course, required to be residents of the city of St. Louis. The affidavits were sent to Governor Crittenden for his information. A reporter checked the office of the recorder of voters and found that, in January 1881, John D. Finney had registered to vote from 2917 Laclede Avenue, the residence of well-known attorney Frank J. Bowman. Finney, stated the article, claimed that "while his family was in the country for reasons of health, he is and has been a citizen and a voter in the city."[30] The residency affidavits and the newspaper article did not bode well for Finney.

Before the March 1 meeting, there were rumors that Governor Crittenden had asked Finney and Moffett for their resignations. One "prominent city official," said the *Post-Dispatch*, claimed to have seen the letter from Governor Crittenden to Finney and Moffett. He said that the letter demanded their resignations because of "the severe censure passed upon the commissioners by the Grand Jury."[31] Both refused to resign.

On March 5, Governor Crittenden removed Finney and Moffett from the board. In a letter, John Finney appealed to his state senator, James McGrath. Senator McGrath read Finney's letter on the floor of the Senate. In his letter, Finney stated that evidence could be shown that contradicted the evidence presented to the grand jury. He asked McGrath for "a most rigid and searching investigation."[32] McGrath presented a resolution on the floor of the Senate calling for a committee of five senators to visit St. Louis "and investigate the alleged official misconduct of the late and present Board of Police Commissioners, and that this committee report the result to the Senate as early as practicable."[33] On a voice vote, the resolution was indefinitely postponed. While the investigation was not destined to happen, the entire episode gave further impetus to those in the state legislature who wanted to abolish the metropolitan police system.[34]

On March 12, the Missouri legislature passed the Police Relief Association Act. Titled "AN ACT authorizing the formation of a Police Relief Association in any City having over one hundred thousand inhabitants," it permitted the formation of the Police Relief Association under the general incorporation acts of Missouri and the creation of a fund "for the purpose of affording relief to such members of their organization as may become sick or disabled while in the discharge of their duties, or who may become incapacitated by long years of service; and for aiding the families of police officers who may die while in the service of any police department; and for such other similar purposes as may be set forth in their articles of incorporation."[35]

The second section of the act listed how the relief association would be funded. In addition to the money in the present Police Relief Fund, the act provided that money collected from the sale of unclaimed personal property, fines assessed by the board against delinquent officers, monthly and annual assessments of members, a percentage (to be determined by the board) of rewards received by officers, and the fifty cent fee then being collected by designated police officers who accepted bonds for any person charged with violating a city ordinance would be paid to the treasurer of the Police Relief Association.

The previous day, March 11, Governor Crittenden announced his new appointments to the board. He preceded the announcement by stating that he had, the previous day, also removed Morgan Boland from the board. Boland had been in office less than two months. Crittenden then announced the three nominees he wanted to join the lone surviving member, Alexander Kinkead. They were Edward C. Simmons, Samuel Cupples, and John H. Maxon.[36] They were confirmed by the Senate and received their commissions on March 14. Cupples and Simmons were appointed to complete the terms of John Finney and Leslie Moffett, which expired on January 1, 1883. Maxon would complete the term of Morgan Boland, which expired on January 1, 1885. The first board meeting was the next day.

All three were well-known merchants in St. Louis. Edward Simmons was the president of the Simmons Hardware Company. John Maxon was president of the Lindell Railway Company and a director on the boards of several corporations in St. Louis. Samuel Cupples was the senior partner in a wood and willow ware business who was known for his charitable activities.[37]

At their first meeting on March 15, Samuel Cupples was elected vice (and acting) president, and Edward Simmons bested Alexander Kinkead in the election for treasurer. Kinkead remained the purchasing member. Because the city election was to be held the next Tuesday, a day set for board meetings, the board scheduled the next regular meeting for the Saturday preceding the election.

At the Saturday meeting, the board minutes note that some citizens had intimated that "there is great danger of corrupt practices at the ballot boxes on the part of those who will have them in charge during the coming election."[38] (The incumbent mayor, Independent Henry Overstolz, was running against Republican William L. Ewing. Ewing would be the victor.) In response, the board passed a resolution instructing the captains "to designate one or more special officers of reliable character and standing" to be stationed at the ballot boxes in each precinct with instructions "to guard the same and protect the voter in the discharge of his privileges."[39]

The board called a special meeting for the Monday before the Tuesday city election. In addition to some routine business that had apparently not been addressed at the Saturday meeting, Alexander Kinkead moved that the board proceed with the appointment of a chief of detectives. The matter had obviously been discussed before the meeting; Sergeant John C. Chapman, Chief McDonough's secretary until his recent transfer to the First District, was the only nominee, and was elected to the position. His salary would be that of a captain, $150 per month. Chapman would begin his duties the next day.[40]

The board once again followed the lead of the New York City Police Department when, at the meeting of April 19, "it was ordered

Edward C. Simmons. Photograph, ca. 1900. Missouri History Museum.

Samuel C. Cupples. Photograph, ca. 1900. Missouri History Museum.

that a white helmet-shaped hat similar to the one worn by the New York police be adopted for summer wear by this department."[41]

Any complacency the board might have felt was to be short lived. On Thursday night, April 21, drivers and conductors of the various streetcar companies met at the Turners Hall on Tenth Street. They wanted to reduce the current sixteen-hour workday to twelve hours without a loss of pay.[42] The owners had refused, and the drivers and conductors, although they did not belong to a union, discussed a strike. It was decided to strike the lines on Saturday, April 23. The strikers stood solidly against the owners on the first day of the strike, although some lines ran a few cars operated by both "extras and strangers." Even the newly elected mayor, William Ewing, had to walk to city hall.[43]

Some violence occurred but was not attributed to strikers, who were at the Turners Hall meeting. A crowd estimated at five thousand gathered on Pine Street, between Fourth and Seventh streets, and pelted cars of the Mound City and Gravois lines with mud and sand. Some cars were thrown off the tracks, and some had windows broken. After the police were notified, Captain Ferd Kennett of the Central District ordered a cordon of police officers around each car as it approached. Once they reached Eighth Street, the cars were out of danger, and the officers headed back.[44] An eastbound Mound City car then came around the corner at Eighth and Pine streets. The old driver of the car was pelted with sand and cursed. Captain Kennett urged the crowd to "be quiet," but they responded by throwing dirt. Several arrests were made, and the car was reversed and sent westbound. A similar situation greeted streetcars at Ninth and Chestnut streets early in the afternoon. The police, unable to disperse the mob, were able to reverse the cars and get them out of the area.[45] Commissioner Kinkead, who was also on the scene of the disturbances, personally appealed to Vice President Cupples, who ordered a squad of mounted officers to the scene. The *Post-Dispatch* noted that the mounted officers cleared the streets within fifteen minutes of their arrival.

In spite of a greater police presence, scattered violence continued on Sunday. The board met in special session on Monday to respond to a letter signed by the presidents of six "street rail roads."[46] One signer, Police Commissioner John Maxon was the president of the Lindell Railway Company. He excused himself from the meeting. The letter informed the board that "we are prepared to operate our respective roads, as soon as the city can afford to give our employees the necessary protection."[47] After a discussion, the board instructed Chief McDonough "to employ 150 special policemen at $2 each and assign them to duty in the most available manner commencing at 6:00 AM next Thursday and to continue during the pleasure of the Board."[48] The purchasing member of the board, Alexander Kinkead, was authorized to purchase one hundred "police clubs," and Secretary Gavin was authorized to furnish each special with a police star and a commission.

The board met again the next day. Mayor Ewing attended this meeting, his first. At that meeting, the board approved and submitted for publication a special notice. It read: "Notice to the Public: All persons are hereby requested to refrain from gathering in crowds on the streets during the present excitement; as in the efforts of the police to arrest those who are violating the laws, they must necessarily use force, and in so doing may endanger the lives of innocent citizens."[49]

The board met again on Wednesday and declared that "there exists an extraordinary emergency in the peace and good order of this city, and that the exigency demands an increase in the metropolitan police of the city of St. Louis. . . ."[50] Having declared the emergency, the board then passed a resolution that called for the hiring of not more than one thousand men to "be enrolled as policemen, subject to the orders of the Board. . . ." A communication was sent to Colonel John G. Butler, commander of the First Regiment, Police Reserves, instructing him to "assemble the Police Reserves at Four Courts building to morrow — Thursday April 28/81 at 7 o'clock p.m. under arms for active service." It was signed by Samuel Cupples, vice president.[51] The board sent a telegram to Governor Crittenden requesting fifty thousand rounds of "ball cartridges (Cal 45.)" be sent by overnight train, and asked former mayor Overstolz for a list of all persons to whom he had issued a permit to carry concealed weapons.

Early on Thursday morning, police officers from the Second and Central districts and four companies of Police Reserves moved into the Four Courts building and courtyard. Vice President Cupples swore in the 150 members of the reserves as special police. The previous day, Governor Crittenden had ordered the First Regiment of the St. Louis National Guard into active service, and it formed at its armory.

Battery A of the guard had spent Wednesday night assembling and training in the handling of two caisson-mounted Gatling guns. On Thursday morning, horses were harnessed to the caissons, and the Gatling guns were moved to the courtyard at the Four Courts.[52] Each Gatling gun had ten barrels. The operator aimed the gun and turned a crank to rotate the barrels. The Gatling guns were capable of firing one thousand rounds a minute up to two thousand yards. Battery A, a light artillery unit, also moved four three-inch rifle ordinance guns, with a range of three miles, to the courtyard.[53] As it turned out, neither the Police Reserves nor the National Guard would be called from the Four Courts.

On Thursday afternoon, Governor Crittenden, who had come to St. Louis on the morning train from Jefferson City, met with the board. Also present were General Squires, National Guard; Colonel Butler, Police Reserves; Colonel Knapp, Missouri inspector general; and five of the six presidents of the street railroad lines. Commissioner Maxon was not present. Meanwhile, company presidents listed the most likely sites where assistance would be required, and Chief McDonough was instructed to provide police protection.

The first car out on Thursday morning was on the Olive Street line. The *Post-Dispatch* noted that crowds began to form on Olive Street between Fourth and Twelfth streets about 9:30 a.m., awaiting the arrival of the first car. Before it arrived, however, policemen moved into the area and soon eight officers were on every corner between Fourth and Twelfth streets, with about one hundred between Fourth and Sixth. As the first car approached, there were cheers and jeers, but no violence. A mounted police squad followed the car. Additional streetcars soon followed without incident. By agreement, no lines were allowed to operate after 7:00 p.m.[54]

The streetcars ran close to a normal schedule on Friday. Vice President Cupples announced that, pending any unusual events, the military would be withdrawn and the police would return to normal duties at 3:00 that afternoon. A mass meeting of strikers was scheduled for that evening. However, there was no meeting on Friday; the strikers' executive committee had collapsed. Another meeting was then called for Saturday morning, but it was ill attended. Most of the drivers and conductors had reached agreements with the presidents of the different lines during the previous night, and the cars were running.[55] The strike, which lasted one week, was over. Unlike the general strike four years before, the police had been prepared, with special officers, the Police Reserves, and the National Guard at the ready.

✳   ✳   ✳

Almost unnoticed during the week of the strike were some board decisions that did not concern the strike. At the meeting of April 27, several officers (on behalf of all officers) asked the board's permission to wear "citizen's dress" when off duty on Sundays. The board granted the request. This was the second erosion of the October 1867 rule that required officers to wear their uniforms at all times except when off duty at home. In July 1878, the board had ordered that officers could wear "citizen's dress" on their one day off each month.

At the meeting of May 3, the board received an application from one George Woods requesting his appointment as a detective. What made the application different from others was that Woods was black. The application was referred to Vice President Cupples, who, apparently, forwarded it to Chief McDonough for an investigation and report. The board decided at this meeting to begin meeting twice a week, the regular meeting on Tuesday and the second on Friday. No reason was given.

At the first Friday meeting, May 6, the board noted that it had received a communication from Chief McDonough recommending against the appointment of a black applicant as a regular detective on the force and stating his reasons. The files containing such communications have not been located, so these reasons are unknown. George Woods, however, did not receive the appointment.[56]

The board (by city ordinance) also had to continuously approve the use of "public stands." People wishing to be a steamboat, hotel, or railroad runner (persons who tried to get visitors to use a particular steamboat line, hotel, or railroad) had to obtain a city license and were permitted to hawk their line only in specified locations established by the board. The same held true for hacks, baggage wagons, wood and coal wagons, furniture cars, and express handcarts.[57]

The meeting of May 17 was a momentous one. Captain Warren H. Fox, commander of the Fifth (Mounted) District, recommended that the mounted force be increased by forty men and divided into three platoons serving eight hours each. This would increase the mounted police, who patrolled an area of forty-five miles, to over one hundred men and would constitute the first eight-hour shift of the police department. On motion, the recommendation was adopted and John Maxon was authorized to purchase as many more horses as would be required to carry out the recommendation. Later, Treasurer Simmons would be authorized to buy forty new sabers and belts for the mounted force, and Commissioner Maxon was authorized to transfer officers to the mounted force. The board also prepared requisitions "to be made on the Governor" for twenty additional cavalry revolvers for the mounted force.[58]

At the meeting of June 7, "a communication [from Chief McDonough] was read recommending that all the Police stations be connected by telephone. On motion referred to the Vice Pres't for enquiry and report." The first telephone had been installed at police headquarters, in the Four Courts building, in March 1878. The police telephone system would be installed in October, replacing the police telegraph system.[59]

Vice President Cupples was authorized to have a conference with all the captains to discuss the adoption of a uniform hat for officers (captains and sergeants) to distinguish them from "privates" (patrolmen). The captains were also asked to adopt a new constitution for the Police Relief Association that, by state law, had replaced the Police

Relief Fund. As a result of the meeting, an election was later held in each district to elect representatives (sergeants or patrolmen) to draft a constitution.[60]

The board then conducted some other routine business and went into executive session. The board passed two resolutions in the executive session:

> Whereas, the Board believe that it would serve the interests of the force to have a younger and more active man for Chief of Police. Therefore be it Resolved, that the Chief be respectfully requested to send in his resignation at his early convenience.

> Whereas the Board believe that it would better serve the interests of the force, that we at present dispense with a Chief of Detectives. Therefore be it Resolved That John C. Chapman be requested to send this Board his resignation.[61]

At a special meeting the next day, the board accepted the resignation of Chief James McDonough. A copy of the letter of resignation was included in the minutes of June 8. Chief McDonough's letter was very cordial, ending with an offer to assist the board "with great cheerfulness" until his successor was "appointed and installed." This was McDonough's last hurrah. He had served as the first chief of police, from April 1861 to October 1861; sixth chief, from September 1870 to March 1874; and eighth chief, from December 1875 to June 1881. James McDonough would stay in the law enforcement field. After resigning, he opened a private detective agency in downtown St. Louis. As requested, Chief of Detectives John C. Chapman also resigned from the police department.

McDonough, however, didn't have to assist the board until his successor was "appointed and installed." After the board formally accepted his resignation, the promotion of Captain Ferd Kennett to chief of police was moved, seconded, and approved, effective immediately.[62] Kennett was thirty-five years old and a relative newcomer to the police department, being appointed a special officer on October 25, 1877. He was promoted to patrolman in March 1878 and was

Ferdinand B. Kennett. Oil on canvas, ca. 1860s.
Missouri History Museum.

assigned to Chief McDonough's office. He rose rapidly through the ranks, being promoted to sergeant in November 1878 and captain in December 1879.[63]

At the meeting of July 26, Mayor Ewing moved that all meetings of the Board of Police Commissioners be open to the representatives of the city press. The mayor's motion was seconded, but lost by a three to two vote. Mayor Ewing would make the same motion two years later, under a differently organized board. On July 27, Chief Kennett departed for "an official tour to eastern cities for the purpose of forming the acquaintance of the various prominent police officials and inspecting the workings of their departments."[64]

At the meeting of October 11, the board called Chief Kennett and the captains before the board and asked if, in their opinions, the charity fund should continue to be raised by the police for distribution among the poor. The annual charity ball, sponsored by the police department each December since 1875, was the primary source of the charity fund. The minutes note that the chief and captains were opposed to the continuation of the fund. A resolution was introduced and adopted that "the custom of raising a Charity Fund by the Police Force be discontinued and the money now on hand be turned over, one half each to the Provident Association and St. Vincent DePaul Society."[65] The senior officers of the police department, according to the minutes, felt that the collection and distribution of money for the poor was "injurious to the interests of the city and the Police Dep't." The private sector assisted in filling the void. The proprietor of the Grand Opera House, for example, would present an opera in early January 1882 for the benefit of the poor.[66] Other organizations and private citizens also contributed to the relief of the poor. In reality, however, police district commanders continued to accept goods and monetary contributions at the station houses and hold them for the various charities.[67]

According to the minutes of November 1, Commissioner Kinkead was authorized to go to Cincinnati "for the purpose of enquiring into the system of police telephoning in that city, and report all the facts with the cost &c of the same to the Board as soon as possible."[68]

On Monday, November 7, the day before the next board meeting, three deputy sheriffs were marching twelve prisoners from the city jail to the Court of Criminal Correction for preliminary hearings. When the men were taken from their cells in the jail they were handcuffed in pairs. Two of the twelve, John D. Shea and Frank Fone, apparently held the backs of their hands together as if handcuffed. Someone assumed, because their hands were behind their backs, that Shea and Fone had already been handcuffed. When the procession reached the court, only ten prisoners were present. Shea and Fone were gone. Shea had been in jail for a bond default in a robbery for which he was charged. Fone had been arrested for burglary and stealing.[69]

Shortly after 9:00 that evening, several men described as a "gang of hoodlums" had gathered at Eighth and Olive streets and began to argue among themselves. A patrolman, identified only as "Officer Fine," was walking toward the group when he saw one of them move away from the others, pick up a rock, and throw it into the crowd.

The man then pulled a pistol and fired it into the air.[70] Officer Fine grabbed the man by the arm; it was John D. Shea. Shea punched Officer Fine, but "was immediately afterwards clubbed down by the officer."[71] Shea got off the ground and, accompanied by Frank Fone, who was in the group, ran east on St. Charles Street and then north on Seventh Street. Officer Fine and John Shea exchanged shots during the chase.

Patrolman Patrick Doran, who was in a business place on Seventh between St. Charles and Washington streets, heard the commotion and came out to see two men (Shea and Fone) running toward him. Before the officer could react, Shea reached Officer Doran and fired one shot into his head, killing the officer. Officer Fine again fired at Shea, but missed, and Shea turned and fired another round at Fine. A private watchman named Hill then confronted Shea. Shea pointed his revolver at Hill and twice pulled the trigger, but the revolver only clicked. Shea had fired his last round at Officer Fine. He then ran into an alley behind the Lindell Hotel; the alley ended in a closed court-yard. A patrolman identified as "Officer Walker" ran into the darkened courtyard, saw Shea's form, and fired at it. Shea immediately threw up his hands and surrendered. Officer Walker brought him out of the alley, and he was taken to the Third District station house at Seventh and Carr streets. The weapon, a .48-caliber revolver, was found in the alley. Frank Fone was arrested later that same evening.[72]

John Shea was convicted for the murder of Patrolman Doran and sentenced to death. On November 7, 1882, exactly one year to the day that Doran was murdered, Shea again escaped from jail. Two years later, it would be learned that Shea had fled to Pennsylvania and was confined in the Allegheny penitentiary after being convicted for burglary and larceny. Shea would be released from the penitentiary in 1890. St. Louis police requested that they be notified of Shea's release date so that he could be brought back to St. Louis.[73]

Doran was buried in Calvary Cemetery. Citizens made contributions to his family, and the Police Insurance Fund donated $912.[74]

✳   ✳   ✳

As with some previous boards, the Cupples board would also be accused of failing to "suppress" gambling. It began with the November 4 interview of Missouri representative (and former lieutenant governor) Charles P. Johnson by a reporter of the *Globe-Democrat*. Johnson was the author of the so-called Johnson Law that had become effective on June 26. The law elevated the establishment and operation of a gambling operation from a misdemeanor to a felony.

In the interview, Johnson attributed the extensive gambling operations to "the incapacity or wilfull [*sic*] neglect of the Police Department."[75] He pointed to a recent grand jury report that stated that police raids were ineffective at securing evidence of gambling. Johnson noted that was an accurate statement, but added that since gambling was now a felony an officer could make arrests if he had reasonable grounds to believe that a felony had been, or was being, committed.

The board asked the city counselor to define in writing the power of the board in suppressing gambling and to advise the board what, if any, special authority it possessed.[76] A week later, City Counselor Leverett Bell responded. He informed the board that an 1867 amendment to the Metropolitan Police Act of 1861 gave the board several powers with respect to the suppression of gambling, but they had been found unconstitutional in an 1879 decision of the Missouri Supreme Court. That decision was made when gambling was a misdemeanor, but still applied even though gambling was now a felony. Said Bell, "As the law now stands no action can be taken by the police authorities of St. Louis under the above provisions of the act of March 13/67. The general doctrine with reference to arrests in cases of felony is that doors may be broken open to arrest one who has committed or is in the act of committing a felony; and this may be done without a warrant."[77] In other words, the board no longer had any special powers with regard to gambling, but was to treat the violation as it would any other felony.

On December 23, the November grand jury made its report to Criminal Court Judge Henry Laughlin. Regarding the accusations made against the board, the jury reported, "We have been able to find no evidence of dereliction of duty, but, on the contrary, have found the board efficient, zealous and animated by a desire to faithfully enforce the law."[78] The grand jury reported that only five gambling houses were running in the city at the time of their report, and it had "found indictments against parties conducting the games in each of those houses."[79]

As 1881 neared an end, a new technology came to the attention of the board, one that would serve the police department for more than eighty years: police call boxes or, as they were referred to at the time, police telephone boxes. The planning, installation, and operation of the police telephone boxes (and attendant patrol wagons) would prove to be one of the most ambitious projects undertaken by any St. Louis police board in the nineteenth century.

The board, at the last meeting of 1881, approved a motion by Vice President Cupples to set aside $6,000 of the fiscal year 1881–1882 appropriations "for the purpose of instituting a system of police wagons and telephone boxes in this city, similar to that now in operation in Chicago. . . ."[80] Commissioner Kinkead and Chief Kennett were given the responsibility of obtaining "all the information possible on the subject" and submitting the information and a sketch of the proposed box locations at the next meeting, January 3, 1882.[81]

1882

Commissioner Kinkead and Chief Kennett didn't leave for Cincinnati until after the January 3, 1882, meeting. They were given a tour of the Cincinnati patrol wagon system and then traveled to Chicago to observe its system before returning to St. Louis. While both cities used the same telephone equipment, an Edison and Bell combination, Kinkead and Kennett found that the systems differed. They agreed that, while the public telephone system in Cincinnati was better managed, the Chicago Police Department had the best patrol wagon system.[82] Patrol wagons in Cincinnati were called out by public telephone, whereas Chicago wagons were called out by a private police telephone system, "with call boxes in various parts of the city."[83] The police department would use the Chicago system as a model.

Treasurer Simmons, meanwhile, submitted to the board "a communication in the name of the force" that asked that Rule 143 of the police manual be amended so that members of the force were permitted to wear "citizen's dress" when not on duty.[84] At this point, sergeants and patrolmen were permitted to wear civilian clothing only when off duty on Sundays, on their one day off each month, and in special situations after obtaining approval of their captain. The request was referred to Chief Kennett, who was instructed to consult with the captains and report at the next board meeting.

Kennett and the captains took longer than a week to reach a consensus, if, in fact, any was reached. At the board meeting of February 7, Vice President Cupples moved that the portion of Rule 143 "requiring any member of the force desiring to wear citizen's dress when off duty to make application to his Captain for permission to do so," be suspended for ninety days.[85] At the end of the suspension, the board extended the suspension another ninety days.[86] At the meeting of August 22, it was extended for a third ninety-day period. There was no mention of citizen's dress in subsequent minutes. It may be presumed that the police were no longer required to wear the police uniform when off duty. The next police manual (1890) noted that "unless otherwise ordered," officers [not assigned to the detective force or on special duty in civilian clothing] were required to wear their uniforms only when on duty or when attending court.[87]

The board moved ahead with the police telephone boxes (hereafter referred to as call boxes)[88] and regular telephone communications. At the meeting of April 4, purchasing member Kinkead sought the board's approval of a contract with the Bell Telephone Company to rent twenty-seven "hand phones and transmitters" for a one-year period ending March 1, 1883. The contract was approved. The board also approved the purchase of twenty-five "police telephone outfits" from the E. B. Chandler Company, and twenty-five "alarm boxes & lumber" from George Breckinridge.[89] The lumber would be used to build call boxes, outdoor booths in which the police telephones would be located.[90] At a special meeting three days later, the board approved the purchase of ten miles of telephone wire. John Kimpel was selected to build two new patrol wagons.[91]

In order to complete the call box circuits, the board hired "four boys" at $25 per month "to attend to the telephone boxes in connection with the patrol wagons at the Chestnut St. and 3d District stations."[92] The Central and Third districts would be the first to have call boxes, telephone operators (known for the next eighty years as "telephone boys"), and patrol wagons that could respond to a beat man's call box request. The board also began purchasing telephone poles.[93]

By the end of May, the call box–patrol wagon system was in operation in the Central and Third districts. Third District patrol wagons were also to be used to convey prisoners to the Second District police court if not otherwise engaged. In June, the board purchased three additional patrol wagons from Kimpel.[94]

As the Police Alarm and Patrol Wagon Service (its official name) expanded, the board adopted rules for the governance of the program. Those stations having a patrol wagon were assigned a signal officer, a patrolman, and a civilian driver for each of the two watches.[95] The signal officer was in charge of the patrolman and driver, the condition of the stock and apparatus,[a] and the conduct of himself and the other two men. The patrolman and the signal officer rode with the driver to each assignment:

> When the detail is directed to a box, the Signal Officer will dismount at the box and as soon as the occasion of the alarm is ascertained, and the required duty performed, he will telephone the cause of the alarm to the station.... This must be done *invariably* in order that the operator may be enabled to direct the detail to answer any other alarm which may have been received during the absence of the detail.
>
> In cases where it is necessary to leave the district, as, for instance, to go to an hospital, take an injured person home, or carry a dead body to the Morgue, the Signal Officer will stop at the first box met with in his district, on the return trip to the station, and report for orders, in order that the operator may direct him to another box

---

[a] The patrol wagon was supplied with rope (for cordoning off areas around fires), shackles, and handcuffs.

in case an alarm has come to the station during his absence from the district.[96]

The patrol wagon driver's responsibilities included one that is applicable to present patrol car drivers:

> If a driver going on duty receive from the driver being relieved from duty the custody of stock and harness without reporting any ailment or defect therein, it will be taken for granted that the ailment or defect occurred during the hours of service of the driver in whose custody the stock shall be found, when discovery is made by a superior officer.[97]

Patrol wagons had to respond to all fire alarms in the district. When necessary, superior officers could also order them into other districts.

The other half of the patrol wagon system was the telephone operator. Each district had two telephone operators, one for each watch. The operators worked the same hours as patrol wagon personnel, but they rotated once a month rather than quarterly. They were required to "keep a faithful record of all reports received by him over the telephone during his hours of duty, noting from whom received and the exact time received, upon the proper blanks furnished him for that purpose."[98]

Early in June, Chief Kennett requested, and was granted, a leave of absence "for a few weeks," for his health. The nature of his illness was not indicated.[99] Later in the month, Kennett asked for, and received, a sixty-day leave of absence with pay.[100]

The final board meeting in June lasted until after midnight and, during the meeting, Commissioners Cupples, Simmons, and Maxon decided to resign their positions as police commissioners. The *Globe-Democrat* reported that the three were upset with Governor Crittenden for pardoning several St. Louis gamblers without so much as mentioning it to the board. Governor Crittenden had been in St. Louis the previous week and had even met with Simmons and Maxon without informing them of his intentions.[101] The resignations were hand-carried by Detective William Desmond, who took the night train to Jefferson City. Desmond arrived at 2:00 a.m. and checked into a hotel. He delivered the resignations to the governor and waited for a reply, but there was none.[102]

The *Globe-Democrat* reported in the edition of July 1 that Governor Crittenden told a reporter that whomever he appointed to fill the board vacancies "would not be Sunday school men. He had tried them and had his fill. He would now appoint politicians, machine men who, while enforcing the laws and attending to the duties of these offices would look after the interests of the party."[103] That same day, Crittenden appointed three new members to the Board of Police Commissioners. They were Daniel Kerwin, who replaced Maxon; David W. Caruth, who replaced Cupples; and Frank X. McCabe, who replaced Simmons. Alexander Kinkead remained on the board.

Because the first Tuesday of July was Independence Day, there was no regular Tuesday board meeting. A special meeting was called, however, the next day. As soon as the new commissioners were seated, Kinkead nominated Daniel Kerwin for the position of vice president of the board; he was unanimously elected. Frank McCabe nominated Kinkead for the positions of treasurer *and* purchasing member. Kinkead was also unanimously elected.

The new vice president of the board, Daniel Kerwin, was an expert blacksmith and ironworker and founded the Anchor Iron Works and Bolt Factory in 1864. He had been chairman of the Democratic City Central Committee and, at the time he was appointed to the board, was chairman of the committee's subcommitee on ways and means.[104] He would later serve in the Missouri Senate.

David W. Caruth had moved to St. Louis from Louisville, Kentucky, in 1874. He had been engaged in the hardware business in Louisville and, upon moving to St. Louis, joined a local hardware business. In January 1882, that firm became the Caruth and Byrnes Hardware Company. David Caruth told a reporter, "While I am no politician, I have always taken a lively interest in the affairs of the Democratic party."[105]

Frank McCabe was a lawyer. He was born in St. Louis and graduated from St. Louis University in 1861. He soon entered the practice of law. McCabe had taken an active part in Democratic politics. At

Daniel Kerwin. Courtesy of Kevin Kerwin.

the time of his appointment to the board, McCabe was a partner in the law firm of W. C. Jones, who was the chairman of the Democratic City Central Committee.[106]

At the first meeting of the new board, Kinkead introduced a resolution that called for the reappointment of Ferd Kennett as chief of police, restored the position of chief of detectives, with current sergeant of detectives Frank Watkins in that position, and retained Secretary of the Board George Gavin. The resolution was adopted. Kinkead introduced a second resolution that the chief of detectives hold the rank of captain, a rank that paid a salary of $150 per month. This resolution was tabled for later consideration.[107]

At the next regular board meeting, July 11, the minutes of the meeting of July 5 were approved with one exception, that portion of Kinkead's resolution establishing the office of chief of detectives. Secretary Gavin was instructed to ask City Counselor Leverett Bell if the board had the power to create that office since neither the 1861 act creating the metropolitan police department nor any amendments to the act mentioned the position of chief of detectives. (Bell would later inform the board that it was his legal opinion that the only way the board could have such an office was if the board recommended it to the Municipal Assembly and the assembly passed an ordinance establishing the position.)[108] After receiving Bell's opinion, the board amended Kinkead's resolution, striking the reference to the office of chief of detectives and Sergeant Frank Watkins's appointment to that position. Watkins was then reappointed the sergeant of detectives at a salary of $125 per month.

Chief of Police Kennett appeared at that meeting and announced that he was ready to resume his duties, and the board restored him to duty. The board, meanwhile, addressed the continuing vice problems in the city. It asked each captain for a list of all gambling houses, poker houses, and houses of assignation and prostitution in their districts. The list was referred to Kennett with the instruction to proceed on the gambling and poker houses in accordance with the law.[109]

The meeting of August 1 was much anticipated by members of the police department, the press, and interested citizens. Chief Kennett had resigned, it was said, and those outside the Commissioners' Room waited to see if the board would accept his resignation and, if it did, who would be named the tenth chief of police.[110] Among the names bandied about were former chief of police Laurence Harrigan; Captain John W. Campbell, commander of the First District; and Captain Anton Huebler, commander of the Fifth (Mounted) District. Harrigan had left the police department when he resigned as chief in 1875. Captain Huebler had been an unsuccessful contender for the position upon Harrigan's resignation. Instead, James McDonough had been appointed chief for the third time. Captain Campbell was the favorite of the onlookers. Then a memorandum was handed out the door. It announced that the next chief of police would be John W. Campbell.[111] Campbell, who was thirty-five years old at the time he was promoted to chief of police, was a carpenter by trade. He was appointed to the force on May 20, 1876, and promoted to sergeant on June 1, 1879. He was promoted to captain on May 2, 1881, and assigned to the First District.[112] Like most previous chiefs, Campbell's tenure would have its share of problems.

The patrol wagon system continued to expand and, on August 22, six additional patrol wagon drivers were appointed; two of those

John W. Campbell, Chief of Police. Courtesy of SLMPD.

received appointments pending the arrival of additional patrol wagons. The board also approved payment for three hundred additional telephone poles and forty-six corrugated iron call boxes, and it ordered three more patrol wagons from John Kimpel.[113]

*   *   *

In September 1882, to honor his part in the establishment and expansion of the patrol wagon system, Alexander Kinkead's friends presented him with a gold "Commissioner's" badge with a wagon on it. Chief Campbell, meanwhile, was given a five-day leave, beginning October 19, to "visit" Chicago.[114] While the reason for the visit was not noted, it is possible that Campbell was sent to personally observe the Chicago Police Department patrol box system in action. Also in September, the proprietor of the Peoples Theatre appeared before the board and proposed to give half the theater's gross receipts for one week (ending September 16) to the Police Relief Association,

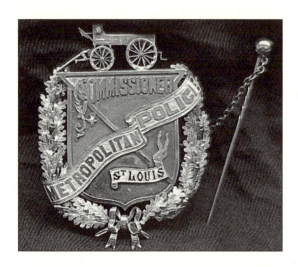

"Commissioner's" badge presented to Alexander Kinkead. Courtesy of SLMPD.

provided the police be permitted to sell tickets for the event. The board accepted the offer.[115] It would later be determined that the profit to the association was $4,893.[116] Later, the relief association would begin to produce its own annual entertainment enterprises for its benefit.

The year ended with money problems. The patrol wagon system required the purchase and installation of telephone poles, wire, call boxes, and telephone equipment for the boxes and station houses. It also necessitated the purchase of patrol wagons and the hiring of drivers, hostlers to care for the horses, and telephone boys to man the telephone equipment in the station houses. The board determined there was not enough money in the police budget to make it through the remainder of the fiscal year that ended March 31. The board asked the Municipal Assembly "to make an additional appropriation for the maintenance of the Police Force of this city, of not less than Fifteen thousand ($15,000) for the balance of the fiscal year. . . ."[117]

1883

In February 1883, the Municipal Assembly informed the board that a pending bill would provide only $10,000 of the $15,000 requested.

At its February 27 meeting, the board voted to drop a sufficient number of employees from the rolls to make up the $5,000 difference. Fourteen patrolmen and one detective were targeted to be dropped from the rolls the next day. The next day, ten patrolmen were dropped. Once into the new fiscal year, the ten (who were officially listed as dropped from the rolls "for want of means to pay them") were restored to duty.[118]

The board began its crackdown on prostitution. Chief Campbell was instructed to notify the occupants of houses of prostitution on Sixth Street, between Market and Elm, to vacate by March 1. The occupants were to be told that, if they refused to move, they would "be brought into court every day by raiding."[119] The board, however, wanted to learn just how far its powers extended. At a subsequent meeting, the board posed several questions to City Counselor Leverett Bell concerning the powers of the board and the police department under the act of March 18, 1874, or any subsequent act.[120] (In 1874, as the social evil experiment was being halted, the Missouri legislature had passed bills limiting police actions, including the prohibition of raids.)

On January 23, Leverett Bell submitted his response. He said that the offense of keeping a bawdy house or being an inmate "is a continuous one and there is no cessation in it as long as they are keepers or inmates of said houses. If arrested at any time during this period the offence for which they are arrested is [deemed to have been] committed in the presence of an officer. No warrant is necessary."[121] Bell added that arrests under these conditions were within the law.

In the meantime, the appointments of David Caruth and Frank McCabe had expired Governor Crittenden reappointed Caruth to a four-year term expiring January 1, 1887. McCabe was not reappointed. Instead, Governor Crittenden appointed Dr. Frank J. Lutz to a four-year term. The board organization, with Kerwin as vice president and Kinkead as treasurer–purchasing member, was retained.[122]

Frank Lutz was a physician and surgeon. He had a bachelor of arts degree from St. Louis University and a medical degree from St. Louis Medical College. He was affiliated with the Alexian Brothers Hospital in St. Louis and would be credited with assisting to make it the largest hospital in St. Louis by the turn of the century.[123]

Frank J. Lutz, M.D. Engraving by Mart, ca. 1921.
Missouri History Museum.

A petition from all of the turnkeys on the force was presented to the board at the meeting of February 13. The petition asked that the turnkeys be allowed one day off each month, the same as patrolmen. A motion was made, and passed, granting the request. Thus, all sergeants, patrolmen, and turnkeys were now permitted one day off each month. Two weeks later, the seven department telephone operators also asked for one day off a month. The board neither approved nor denied the request. Instead, the district captains were given the "discretionary power to act" on the request in their respective districts.[124]

The police call box system went in a different direction in March. After obviously receiving requests for the service, Commissioner Kinkead asked the board to permit the installation of police telephone boxes in banks, factories, and private residences when requested. Those making the request would pay the expenses of the equipment and connection to police telephone wires. The board approved the request.[125]

In April, after citing the benefits, the superintendent of the city fire alarm and police telegraph system recommended to the board that the telephone communication system between the various police stations be adopted in lieu of the old box telegraph system. The matter was referred to treasurer–purchasing member Kinkead for inquiry and a report concerning the expenses of a change.[126] Before April 1883 was over, the board would decide to complete the conversion from the police telegraph system to a public telephone system. While some telegraph equipment would be in use for a short time, the board approval marked the end of the police telegraph system in St. Louis.[127]

After the regular meeting of April 10, the board went into an executive session for organizational issues. Daniel Kerwin remained the vice president of the board, and Alexander Kinkead remained as treasurer and purchasing member. The board voted to retain John Campbell as chief of police, adding the supervision of the detectives to his duties. Sergeant of Detectives Frank Watkins was transferred from that position to the Chestnut Street station. Three weeks later, the supervision of the detectives would be removed from Chief Campbell and Sergeant Samuel Boyd would become sergeant of detectives.[128]

The board then considered four nominees, including incumbent George Gavin, for the position of secretary of the board. Bernard Taaffe received the most votes and was named secretary. Gavin was reassigned to clerical duties in police headquarters. At the next meeting, his salary would be generously fixed at $100 per month.[129]

Gavin's name first appeared in the minutes of the board meeting of March 25, 1865, where he was the signatory of a copy of a request for proposals for summer police uniforms. Below his name was listed "clerk of the Board of Police Commissioners."[130] On August 1, 1865, Gavin was appointed the third secretary to the Board of Police Commissioners.[131] He served as secretary for more than seventeen years.

The new secretary to the board, Bernard Taaffe, had been a colonel in the militia and, after his militia unit disbanded, held various clerical positions. At the time of his appointment, Taaffe was a justice of the peace. He had recently run a strong but unsuccessful campaign for circuit court clerk.[132]

At the last meeting in May, the board asked Secretary Taaffe to contact the city counselor to determine if it was "compulsory on the Board, under the provisions of City Ordinance No. 12,343, to regu-

Bernard P. Taaffe. Photograph, ca. 1880. Missouri History Museum.

late Private Detectives and issue licenses as such to parties apply-
ing for same or whether it is discretionary with the Board to refuse
any and all such applications?"[133] City Counselor Leverett Bell
responded that, under the ordinance, it was not compulsory for the
board to license any private watchmen, private detectives, or private
policemen. Said Bell, "No one can act in any of the capacities aforesaid without first obtaining a license from the board." On motion,
the board decided not to license any private detectives.

The meeting of July 31 was notable in two respects. First, the
board appointed former secretary to the board George Gavin a special
patrolman. Second, the board, which had replaced private watchman
stars and other private watchman badges with a standard half-moon
or crescent badge in January 1882, ordered those badges recalled.
The new private watchman badge would be oval, with the words
"Private Watchman" and a badge number on each. To demonstrate
that the board was serious, it announced that "beginning September
1, all persons using or wearing the old style badge will be arrested as

an imposter, whether or not they were performing private watchman duties, and will be prosecuted in court."[134]

The board made a second appointment at the June 26 meeting. While the Gavin appointment gained little attention, the same could not be said for the other. The board reinstated former police sergeant, and later police commissioner, Morgan Boland to the force as a patrolman. Boland's appointment was quickly followed by rumors that Governor Crittenden would ask Commissioners Kinkead and Lutz, for reasons believed connected with the Boland reinstatement, to resign.[135] The rumors offered only the barest hint of the firestorm that would consume the police commissioners and the department in the second half of 1883.

On July 9, Alexander Kinkead sent his resignation to Governor Crittenden. In his letter of resignation, Kinkead said that he wanted to devote more time to his family and "business of a more remunerative character."[136] Kinkead asked that his resignation not take effect until October 1, so that the governor would have sufficient time to choose a successor. In a letter to Kinkead dated July 10, Governor Crittenden "reluctantly" accepted the resignation effective October 1. The letter praised Kinkead's "upright conduct and faithful discharge of duty" during his time on the board.[137]

On September 11, in anticipation of the thieves that were typically drawn to the annual Agricultural and Mechanical Fair held at the fairgrounds the first week of October, Chief Campbell was authorized to invite, at the board's expense, detectives from various cities "to assist the department in the apprehension of crooks &c likely to infest this city during fair week." Two detectives would be sent from the Chicago Police Department, one from Cincinnati, one from Kansas City, and one from Louisville.[138] The assistance was helpful. By the end of the week, fifty-three arrests were made, six by the Chicago detectives. The Chicago detectives also identified two female pickpockets arrested by other officers but unknown to St. Louis police. The two, known as "Little Louise" and "Miss Jackson," were photographed by St. Louis police and placed in the rogues' gallery.[139]

On September 12, patrol wagon driver Patrick Riordan, who was seriously injured when his patrol wagon was upset in an accident at

Twelfth and Washington, died at his home later that morning. Riordan was the first fatality of a patrol wagon driver in St. Louis.[140]

On September 14, Governor Crittenden received the resignation of board vice president Daniel Kerwin. Kerwin, who had mailed his resignation the previous day, later said that he gave no reason for resigning. When asked by a reporter for the *Post-Dispatch* why he had resigned, Kerwin replied, "Because I am sick and tired of the place. I quit because there are outside influences at work all the time upon the Board, to force them to remove men that I know to be honest and capable, and to fill their places with men who would probably be dishonest. That is my reason, and my only one. I would rather be in h—l [*sic*] than in such a fix."[141]

Kerwin said that the "influences" were sometimes politicians and, at other times, gamblers. There had been an effort to remove Superintendent of Police Stables William Faulkner, said Kerwin, ever since he joined the board in July 1882. He said, however, that he found Faulkner's administration of the stables "as close and economical as could be. Why should such a man be removed to make room for some one's political pet?"[142] Kerwin added that these influences "hounded and abused [Chief of Police Campbell] as no man ever was."

Rumors began to circulate that some influential individuals held blank resignations signed by some police commissioners. If the commissioner displeased that individual, the blank resignation would be filled out and sent to Governor Crittenden. This was alleged to be the case with Alexander Kinkead, whose resignation was supposedly held by one Warren F. McChesney. It was also rumored that someone had held Kerwin's blank resignation. A source, who did not want to be identified, told a reporter from the *Globe-Democrat* that "the men who controlled Kerwin's position were making it too hot for him. He desired to do what was right, but was gradually being forced to the wall. These men have been trying to get rid of Chief Campbell for some time for the simple reason that they could not control him."[143] Kerwin supported Chief Campbell. The *Globe-Democrat* source was asked, "Who are the men who were warring on Kerwin from the outside?" He replied, "It is said that Joe McEntire and Ed Butler were two of them."[144]

The man alleged to have held Alexander Kinkead's resignation, Warren McChesney, was the co-owner of a contracting company with offices at 4 North Sixth Street. He also once had the city street cleaning contract. Edward (Ed) Butler was a blacksmith (he held the contract to shoe the horses of the police department), was a partner in the new Standard Theater, and was considered by many to be the boss of the Democratic machine in St. Louis. Joseph McEntire was the city coal oil inspector and also a partner in the Standard Theater. (The coal oil inspector was appointed by the governor.) McChesney and McEntire denied any knowledge of the blank police commissioner resignations.[145] While McChesney and McEntire would soon be forgotten, Ed Butler would be a force in the city political machinery (and the police department) for another twenty years.

Ed Butler. Steel engraving by Central Biographical Publishing Co., 1898.
Missouri History Museum.

The *Post-Dispatch* began to head columns with expressions such as "The Police Muddle" and "Police Scandals."[146] The *Globe-Democrat* simply titled the columns "The Police Board," and then listed highlights such as "Vice President Kerwin Resigns, and Charges It to Intrigue."[147] On September 20, the *Globe-Democrat* joined the afternoon paper in referring to the situation as "The Police Muddle." However one might refer to the situation, it caught the attention of the criminal court grand jury. In September, the grand jury probed "the reports of police corruption."[148] Campbell and Kinkead were the first witnesses called to testify.

The grand jury investigation was temporarily overshadowed by the appointment of a new police commissioner to take the place of former vice president Kerwin. The new commissioner, Oliver P. Gooding, was a lawyer who came to St. Louis from Indiana in 1877 and opened a law office in the Jaccard Building at 419 Olive Street. He was a graduate of West Point and had served as a brigadier general in the Union army during the Civil War. Gooding sometimes lectured on two essays he had written, and he had also composed what he called a national anthem for the United States. He attended his first board meeting on September 25, when Dr. Frank Lutz was elected interim vice president.

The grand jury completed its work and, on September 28, submitted a report of its findings to Criminal Court Judge Garrett S. Van Wagoner. The grand jury first summarized its findings:

> A well organized ring undoubtedly exists in the city in the interest of professional gamblers and lottery dealers, who are ready and willing to pay large sums of money to secure immunity from police interference, and who to this end have been aided by notorious individuals whose audacity is equaled only by their ability so far to keep themselves and their employers, with few exceptions, beyond the reach of indictment.[149]

As far as blank resignations being signed by police board aspirants, the grand jury found that "at least one if not more has been made use of...."[150] The grand jury also found that "prominent officials have been directly and indirectly approached and threatened; and the Chief of Police, Col. Campbell, has been especially marked for removal, simply because he has proved himself to be most efficient, fearless, incorruptible and determined to honestly discharge the duties of his office."[151]

The grand jury did return two indictments. Warren McChesney was indicted for "forgery in the third degree" for completing the blank resignation of Alexander Kinkead and sending it to Governor Crittenden on June 19. The indictment called the resignation a "false and forged instrument purported to be written and signed by said Alexander Kinkead."[152]

The second indictment against McChesney was for "attempted bribery." It charged that on April 16 McChesney offered Kinkead, while a member of the board, $1,000 "to vote for and to assist in the appointment of and not to oppose one Albert J. Stiles as chief of detectives of the police force of the said City of St. Louis. . . ."[153] (Stiles was the former police detective who had been dismissed from the force in 1875 for insubordination and later operated a private detective agency.) Warren McChesney was arrested that same evening.

Kinkead left the board on the effective date of his resignation, October 1. Two days later, Governor Crittenden appointed his replacement, Henry D. Cleveland. Cleveland was the superintendent of the Cass Avenue and Fair Grounds Street Railroad. He had been active in Twentieth Ward politics and was chairman of the Democratic Committee in the Third Congressional District. He took his seat as a commissioner at the next board meeting, October 9.

The meeting of October 9 was notable. After several disciplinary hearings of complaints against police officers, the board went into executive session. At the organizational session, Dr. Frank Lutz was elected vice president of the board. Henry Cleveland was elected treasurer–purchasing member. Lutz then introduced a resolution that the order of April 10, 1883, continuing John Campbell as chief of police be rescinded and that the office of chief of police be declared "vacant." The resolution was adopted by a 3–2 vote. The vote not only removed Chief Campbell, but was the first in a succession of voting issues that would see Lutz, Caruth, and Cleveland voting as a block against General Gooding and Mayor Ewing. Lutz then nominated the secretary of the board, Bernard Taaffe for chief of police. Taaffe was elected by the same 3–2 vote.

Since the board needed a new secretary, Lutz nominated C. E. Wells. With Gooding abstaining, Wells was elected by a 3–1 vote.

Mayor Ewing, who two years earlier had attempted to have the board conduct open meetings, again moved that all meetings of the board "be held with open doors."[154] The motion lost by the now familiar 3–2 vote.

Chief Campbell did not know that he had been removed until a reporter from the *Globe-Democrat* informed him. Campbell "was taken completely by surprise."[155] The chief said that he knew that former friends on the board had turned against him because of his "free utterances," but did not know that he would be so quickly deposed. When asked if he knew whether the board would assign him another position in the police department, Chief Campbell replied, "I have no knowledge of the proceedings of the board."[156]

※   ※   ※

Meanwhile, after the board had returned from the executive session, Captain Edward McDonald, Third District commander, informed the board that Sergeant Peletiah M. Jenks of the Third District, who had been shot "in the discharge of his duty" the previous evening, had died. The board passed a memorial resolution and ordered that all station houses be "draped in mourning for the space of ten days from date."[157]

Sergeant Peletiah Jenks was supervising his precinct on Monday, October 8. He was forty-two years old and had been a member of the force for sixteen years, the last fifteen years at the rank of sergeant. About 4:30 p.m., as he walked on Eighth Street near Biddle Street, a citizen approached him and told him that a black woman had been running around the vicinity for the past half hour cursing and swearing and flourishing a pistol. He asked Sergeant Jenks to arrest her as he was afraid someone would be shot. Jenks started across Eighth Street toward the woman who, when she saw the officer, raised her pistol. The reporting citizen said that "Sergeant Jenks raised his cane, a light one, as if to knock the weapon out of her hand."[158] The woman fired, striking Sergeant Jenks in the forehead. She then walked around the corner and into an alley headed in the direction of Cass Avenue. The citizen and a neighbor followed her. The woman twice turned, raised her pistol, and threatened to shoot them.

Patrolman James Condon was eating supper at Schulte's Grocery, on the northeast corner of Seventh and Biddle streets, when a little girl told him that a shot had been fired on Eighth Street. Condon quickly went up Biddle Street to Eighth Street, making inquiries as he went. He found Sergeant Jenks lying at Eighth and Biddle and asked the crowd about the perpetrator. Condon found and followed her into the basement of a house in the 1300 block of North Ninth Street, where she was sitting in a chair with her pistol pointed at him. Officer Condon pointed his revolver at the woman and told her to drop the gun, which she did. Condon placed her under arrest and took her to the Third District station at Seventh and Carr streets. The woman was identified as Sadie Hill, also known as Sadie Hayes. She was later charged with the murder of Sergeant Peletiah Jenks.

Captain McDonald, accompanied by a half dozen patrolmen, had arrived at the scene in a patrol wagon. Sergeant Jenks was taken to the city dispensary and attended by two physicians who, because of the severity of the head wound, gave him no hope of survival. A decision was made to take Sergeant Jenks to his home. Captain McDonald rode in the patrol wagon to break the news to the sergeant's family. Physicians also attended to Sergeant Jenks at his home. At approximately 10:30 p.m., he was pronounced dead. He left a wife and five children. Sergeant Jenks's funeral took place at his home, 1211 North Sixteenth Street, at two o'clock on Thursday afternoon, October 11. He was buried in Bellefontaine Cemetery.

Sadie Hill later stated that she had been having trouble with a man following her and, when Sergeant Jenks approached from behind her, she thought it was that man. She turned and fired without realizing that the man was a police officer. When asked why she was carrying a gun, Hayes replied, "'Cause I've got some enemies and I want to defend myself."[159]

* * *

On the same day that Sergeant Jenks was killed, the persons selected for the October term of the criminal court grand jury appeared before Judge Garrett Van Wagoner, who gave them instructions and charged them in their duties. Referring to the report of the previous grand jury (July), Judge Van Wagoner told the jurors: "there is a distinct allegation that a ring exists in the interest of professional gamblers and lottery dealers. . . . It is high time that the fair [name] of the citizens of St. Louis should be cleared, fully cleared, from the foul blot of this reputed pollution so graphically set forth in said report and so long whispered in muttered tones in relation to the appointment of and doings of the Police Commissioners and their reputed allies."[160] Judge Van Wagoner then cautioned the jurors "to see that no point of business transacted should be allowed to become public prematurely."[161]

Almost as if in response, the *Post-Dispatch* exploded a bombshell two days later. The newspaper had somehow obtained the testimony of then-chief John Campbell and Commissioner Alexander Kinkead presented before the July grand jury and began to print it, in question-and-answer form, on the front page of the paper. Portions of the testimony were reprinted in the *Globe-Democrat* the next morning.

Since Mayor Ewing was out of the city, deposed Chief Campbell sent a letter to Vice President Lutz informing him that the board was prohibited from removing him from office without cause. Campbell also requested that the board refrain from installing Bernard Taaffe, or anyone else, "in my office." Dr. Lutz did not reply.[162]

Sometime during the night of October 11, or very early the next morning, the office of the clerk of the criminal court was burglarized. The court stenographer conducted an inventory and found that various notes, shorthand notebooks, and certain transcripts were missing. Among the missing items were all the notes relating to the investigations of the previous grand jury. The circuit attorney, Joseph R. Harris, requested that Judge Van Wagoner order an immediate investigation.[163]

On Friday, October 12, Chief Campbell's attorneys filed a petition with the Missouri Court of Appeals in St. Louis. The petition claimed that, by removing him from office without cause, the board had violated Section 7 of the 1861 law establishing the metropolitan police and Rule 5 of the police manual. In addition, because Chief Campbell's removal was not lawful, Bernard Taaffe was now exercising the duties of chief of police without authority of law. Chief Campbell asked the court to issue a writ of certiorari, directed to the board, to certify and return to the court all proceedings concerning the removal of Chief Campbell, so that the court might declare the removal null and void.[164]

The situation worsened. The president of the Commercial Bank appeared on the floor of the Merchants' Exchange and began to circulate a petition among the members. The petition, addressed to Mayor Ewing, requested that he, as ex officio president and presiding officer of the board, exercise his authority to prevent the removal of Chief Campbell without an impartial trial. It was signed by almost one hundred businessmen and bankers.[165] The members of the Merchants' Exchange were to elect officers the next day. An estimated two thousand persons were present. The business turned to the removal of Chief Campbell. Before the meeting adjourned, the members of the exchange passed five resolutions because "the recent action of the Board of Police Commissioners, culminating in the removal of the Chief of Police because he refused to be made the tool of a corrupt combination, calls for an indignant protest on the part of the citizens against such actions."[166] The first resolution accused the board of betraying the public trust and becoming "the tools of a band of conspirators organized for plunder. . . ." The second stated that "the Police Board was not intended to be a political machine, and that any action of any members of the Board to serve the purposes of a political party is in violation of their oaths of office and in direct defiance of the law which created them."[167] The third resolution demanded that Commissioners Lutz, Caruth, and Cleveland be removed and replaced "with competent and trustworthy men." The fourth stated that recent developments "connected with the police scandal show that the individual holding the office of Coal Oil Inspector [Joseph McEntire] is intimately connected with the corrupt combination . . . is undeserving of public confidence, and ought to be removed from office." The final resolution called for the appointment of "a committee of three" to see that copies of the resolutions were printed and circulated for signatures. When a sufficient number of signatures were obtained, the petitions would be sent to Governor Crittenden.

The resolutions were amended to make the committee permanent, "a standing committee of the people of the city" to do all that was necessary to carry out the purposes stated in the resolutions, including the call for another mass meeting of citizens for consultation and advice.[168] (When the petitions were presented to Governor Crittenden on October 19, they contained an estimated one thousand signatures.)[169]

On Saturday, October 13, Judge Van Wagoner unexpectedly began a hearing in the disappearance of the July grand jury notebooks. At the hearing, Henry W. Moore, managing and city editor of the *St. Louis Post-Dispatch*, testified that he had seen nine notebooks in the office of the newspaper. A reporter for the newspaper, Florence White, then took them to another city to have them transcribed. They were then returned to the person in the criminal court clerk's office from whom they had secured the materials. Florence White did not attend the hearing and was cited for contempt of court.[170]

As the hearing was about to be adjourned for the day, an assistant to the circuit attorney, who had legitimate access to the grand jury records, admitted that he had allowed a *Post-Dispatch* reporter to have the nine notebooks. He did so because he thought it was his duty "to advise the public of a great conspiracy like the ring which now exists in this city. In no other way can it be met and fought."[171] They had been returned to him. Said the assistant, "I then secured the notes and returned them. Then comes this outrageous action of burglary."[172] The assistant submitted his resignation to the circuit attorney, who accepted it.

On Monday, October 15, Circuit Attorney Harris applied to the circuit court for an injunction against the *Post-Dispatch* to prevent the newspaper from printing any additional testimony from the July grand jury proceedings. The court ruled that (1) the circuit attorney had no standing to file for an injunction to prevent a newspaper from printing something since the publication of such information was not a crime and (2) the Missouri constitution specifically provided that "every person shall be free to say, write, or publish whatever he will on any subject, being responsible for all abuse of that liberty." The application for the temporary injunction was denied.[173]

That afternoon, the *Post-Dispatch* printed the continued testimony of Alexander Kinkead and that of former police commissioner John H. Maxon. The newspaper also reported that the president of the Cass Avenue streetcar line had notified Henry Cleveland to choose between being a police commissioner and the superintendent of the line. Cleveland's response was that he was "sick and tired of the whole business [as a police commissioner], and was anxious to get away from politics...."[174]

The next day's *Post-Dispatch* installment continued the testimony of Alexander Kinkead and included that of attorney E. J. White; Thomas E. Tutt, president of the Third National Bank; Morgan Boland; and William Ryder, former secretary with the People's Railway Company. All of the witnesses were questioned as to their knowledge of the extent that blank resignations were required for appointment to the police board. Evidence was mixed as to whether Governor Crittenden requested the resignations through third parties or whether other persons took advantage of the possibility of appointment.[175]

Governor Crittenden had requested to appear before the grand jury. On October 15, Circuit Attorney Harris granted the request and asked the governor to bring with him (1) all telegrams and other papers concerning applications for appointment, appointments to, and removals from the Board of Police Commissioners; (2) telegrams, letters, and papers surrounding the appointment of the prosecuting attorney in St. Louis; and (3) all letters, telegrams, and papers relating to the applications for pardon and the pardons in 1882 "of the following named persons convicted in the St. Louis Criminal Court of felonies under the 'gambling' and 'lottery' acts." Eleven names were listed.[176] (The *Post-Dispatch* reported that the issue surrounding the prosecuting attorney was the reported offer to a local attorney who, if he contributed $1,000, would be appointed to the position. The $1,000 would go to a local official who had great influence with Governor Crittenden. While the attorney considered the offer, someone else was appointed to the position.[177])

Former chief Campbell's fortunes took two divergent turns on Tuesday, October 16. In the morning, the Court of Appeals issued the writ of certiorari Chief Campbell had requested the previous Friday. The court made the writ returnable the following Thursday.[178] At that time, the board would be required to certify and return to the court all proceedings concerning the removal of Chief Campbell.

The Board of Police Commissioners held its weekly meeting that afternoon. Among other items of business, Mayor Ewing moved that the vote to remove Chief Campbell be reconsidered. General Gooding seconded the motion. Ewing and Gooding voted in favor of the motion, and Henry Cleveland voted against it. Lutz and Caruth abstained. Because a majority of the members present had not voted for the motion, it failed.[179]

His vote against revisiting the Campbell ouster was Cleveland's last official action. Henry Cleveland quietly and privately sent his resignation to Governor Crittenden, by emissary, the next day. The letter of resignation noted that the president of the Cass Avenue railway disapproved of Cleveland's connecting the duties of police commissioner with his duties as superintendent of the line. Cleveland added, "For this reason, and this only, I beg leave to tender you my resignation to take effect this date." Governor Crittenden accepted the resignation, "to take effect at once."[180] Cleveland had attended only two meetings of the board.

On Wednesday, the *Post-Dispatch* printed the testimony of former vice president of the Board of Police Commissioners, Daniel Kerwin; three church pastors, two of whom had assisted Alexander Kinkead obtain his appointment to the board; William Faulkner, superintendent of the mounted police stables; and James Thornton, the owner of a livery stable. Kerwin admitted that he had signed a blank resignation to show that he didn't care whether or not he would receive the appointment. Kerwin didn't know who held the blank resignation, but it was never used.

The Reverend Dr. John Vincil, who had known Alexander Kinkead for six years and who was a friend of Governor Crittenden's, stated that he had written a letter to the governor asking for Kinkead's appointment to the board. Sometime during the summer of 1883, Governor Crittenden sent the Reverend Vincil a letter requesting a meeting at the Southern Hotel. Vincil met with the governor, who "showed me a paper that had been forwarded to him by, I think, a man he called McChesney, with Alex. Kinkead's name signed to it, tendering his resignation as Police Commissioner."[181] The original date had been erased and replaced with another, said Vincil, and the body of the letter was in different handwriting than the signature—"there was no comparison."[182]

The Reverend Dr. J. W. Lewis accompanied Vincil to the meeting with Crittenden. He testified that the governor had met Kinkead after he had received the resignation in question and Kinkead said that it was a forgery. The governor then told the two pastors that he had told Kinkead to prosecute the forger or resign from the board. Lewis said, "That ended it."[183]

The *Post-Dispatch* continued printing the July grand jury testimony in the edition of October 18. Kinkead had been recalled and had testified that when Warren McChesney had asked him to sign the blank resignation, Kinkead thought that it would be forwarded to Governor Crittenden for his use. He did not know that McChesney was going to keep it. Kinkead also testified that he could recognize McChesney's handwriting, and the body of his "resignation" was in McChesney's handwriting.[184]

The same day the latest publication of grand jury testimony appeared, the return on former Chief Campbell's writ of certiorari was due in the Court of Appeals. The records requested of the board were entered, but the hearing was continued to October 23.

On Friday, October 19, Governor Crittenden appeared before the grand jury carrying a brown paper bundle, apparently the written materials requested by the circuit attorney. He testified from 10:00 a.m. until 3:15 p.m.[185] The governor's private secretary, Fine C. Farr, also had been asked to appear before the grand jury and bring with him "certain letters and telegrams which had passed between him and certain politicians and office holders of the city."[186] Farr was scheduled to appear on Wednesday, October 24.

Also testifying before the grand jury was A. A. Oldfield, a stenographer. Oldfield, after first checking with legal counsel, had transcribed the notes of the July grand jury that had been brought to him by a *Post-Dispatch* reporter. The work had been done in Godfrey, Illinois, a town about five miles south of Alton.[187]

Former Chief Campbell's writ of certiorari hearing was held on Thursday, October 25. After presentations by both sides in the case, Judge Lewis took the matter under consideration.[188]

*   *   *

Meanwhile, on Friday, October 26, 1883, a court case was heard that would further tighten the police grip on gambling in St. Louis. Judge Edward A. Noonan, presiding over the Court of Criminal Correction, had to determine whether the card game of poker was one of chance or skill. The outcome was important to gamblers in the city for, if it was demonstrated that it was a game of chance, penalties would be handed down under the so-called Johnson Law, which made gambling a felony. Judge Noonan declared, after researching case law, that poker was gambling and therefore fell within the scope of the Johnson Law.[189]

Chief of Police Taaffe issued a general order that same day. The order instructed all sergeants to "notify all proprietors, keepers and managers of poker-rooms in their respective precincts that . . . from the time of reading this notice by any Sergeant of police of this city to any proprietor, keeper or manager of aforesaid poker-rooms that the playing of such game of poker has been declared a felony . . . and [violators] will be proceeded against to the full extent of the law."[190]

*   *   *

On November 2, 1883, the October grand jury presented its report to Judge Van Wagoner. It was a scathing attack on certain members of the Board of Police Commissioners:

> A corrupt combination, composed of certain unprincipled and notorious persons, and certain persons holding offices of the State under appointment of the Governor, has for a considerable time

existed for the purpose of unlawfully controlling and using the police force of this city in the promotion and continuance of gambling and lotteries, and for other unlawful purposes. The members of this combination, outside of those belonging to the Police Board, have possessed and exercised such an influence upon its members belonging to the board that they have in many important instances dictated and controlled the policy of the board. Those Commissioners, subject to the corrupt influence and power, have latterly constituted a majority of the board, and, by either willing or forced submission to the commands and behests of the combination, have done or permitted to be done, acts which must have been contrary to their honest and upright judgment.[191]

The grand jury referred to the removal of Chief Campbell, saying that he was removed from office for no apparent cause, and that he was "solicited by members of this combination to permit the maintenance of fraudulent schemes and practices in open and direct violation of the law."[192] The grand jury reported that "members of the police force have been suspended or removed at the suggestion or request of members of the corrupt combination, irrespective of any consideration as to their efficiency, and worthless and inefficient officers have by the same powers been retained. The officers and members of the force, through like immoral and unlawful influences, have been hampered and restricted in the honest and faithful performance of their duty."[193]

Governor Crittenden received his share of criticism from the panel regarding his police board appointments and the request for blank resignations. "We have been unable to discover any lawful purpose for which these resignations have been asked and given. And in view of the uses to which they have been put, and the infamous character of those who have been permitted to hold them, the practice of requiring them must be unequivocally condemned."[194]

Because of these findings, the grand jury, as had local politicians many times in the past, recommended that the 1861 law establishing the metropolitan police be repealed. It suggested that "the office be either made elective or that the power of appointment be conferred upon the Mayor of the city, subject to the advice and consent of the Municipal Assembly, or that it be vested in the Circuit Judges of this city."[195]

The grand jury also returned indictments. Among others, politician-blacksmith Edward Butler, Coal Oil Inspector Joseph McEntire, and Police Commissioners Frank Lutz and David Caruth were indicted under the misdemeanor conspiracy law. McEntire was charged with attempting to convince then-chief Campbell to allow, without interference of the police, the setting up and keeping of gambling devices. Ed Butler was charged with threatening Chief Campbell with removal from office if he did not resign before Fair Week (the first week in October). By his own admission, the indictment against Butler was his ninth in the past seven years.[196] The indictment against Commissioners Lutz and Caruth asserted that, at the regular board meeting on October 9, 1883, "in pursuance of and in order to effect the object of said conspiracy," they voted "to arbitrarily remove, without cause and without hearing," Campbell from office "contrary to the form of the statute in such case made and provided, and against the peace and dignity of the State of Missouri."[197] The *St. Louis Globe-Democrat* noted that the indictment stated that the conspiracy was entered into on or about December 1, 1882, but Lutz was appointed to the board later.

Warren McChesney was indicted for fraud not related to the police department situation. He was alleged to have proposed to the lawyer for the beer brewers that, for $6,000, he could "fix" the decision on the test of the license fee portion of the Downing (Sunday sales) Law for them. After the brewers declined, McChesney supposedly told the lawyer that failure to pay the $6,000 would result in an adverse decision.[198]

Lutz and Caruth each filed a $50,000 damage suit in the circuit court; the defendants were members of the October grand jury. The suits stated that Lutz and Caruth "were and have been citizens of good repute in the City of St. Louis and State of Missouri." They asserted that the members of the grand jury "maliciously made, uttered and published" portions of the report they had given to Van Wagoner. Specifically cited were those portions that referred to unnamed members of the board as being part of a "corrupt combination . . . composed of certain unprincipled and notorious persons."[199] This "corrupt combination" allegedly used the police force "for the promotion and continuancy of gambling and lotteries and other unlawful purposes." Commissioners Lutz and Cauth argued that such accusations, while they might appear in the indictments, should not have been presented in open court.

On Tuesday, November 6, Judge E. A. Lewis of the Missouri Court of Appeals in St. Louis read the unanimous opinion of the court in Campbell's case against the Board of Police Commissioners. It was the holding of the court that, unless a specific term of office was set for the chief of police at the time of appointment, the term would be for four years. The board did not appoint Chief Campbell for a specified term, so it could remove Campbell from the office before the expiration of four years only for cause. The order of the board of October 9, 1883, "as declares vacant the office of Chief of Police, is reversed, quashed and annulled."[200] The regular meeting of the board began at 3:30 that same afternoon; it would not be congenial.

Since Henry Cleveland had resigned after two weeks in office and had not yet been replaced, Lutz, Caruth, Gooding, and Mayor Ewing were present when the meeting convened. They constituted two distinct voting blocks within the board: Lutz and Caruth, and Gooding and Ewing. As the meeting opened, Ewing moved that a paragraph containing a summary of Campbell's removal and the annulment of the removal order by the Court of Appeals be included in the minutes. While the motion apparently lost on the 2–2 vote, Lutz and Caruth must have acquiesced, for the summary was included in the minutes. Nonetheless, Lutz objected to Mayor Ewing voting except to break a tie vote.[201]

Chief Campbell sent a letter to Mayor Ewing stating that he was "ready now—as I have at all times on and since said 9th day of October last been ready and willing to fulfil my duties as Chief of Police of the City of St. Louis and respectfully request of you as the President of said Board that proper orders be issued enabling me without hindrance to resume the active performance of said duties."[202] Lutz moved to appeal the Campbell ruling to the Missouri Supreme Court. The motion failed on a 2–2 vote. Lutz again objected to the mayor voting except when there was a tie vote. In the meantime, Ewing instructed

Secretary Wells to notify the captains that they would be reporting to Chief of Police Campbell.

Lutz and Caruth then filed charges against Campbell for "Language & Conduct Unbecoming an Officer and a Gentleman" in violation of Rule 167 of the police manual. The charge had three specifications: (1) that Campbell stated to a newspaper reporter that James McEntire held the blank resignation of Frank Lutz and that a certain other person held the blank resignation of David Caruth; (2) that after the statements appeared in the newspapers, Campbell allowed the same to stand uncontradicted; and (3) that Campbell used threatening and insubordinate language to his superior officer, Frank Lutz, "All of which is contrary and prejudicial to the good order and discipline of the force."[203] Lutz moved that Campbell be suspended until a hearing and disposition of the charges. That motion failed by the same 2–2 vote.

In his final act as chief of police, Bernard Taaffe reported to the board that various benefits had raised $1,277 for the relief of the family of the late Sergeant Peletiah Jenks. Campbell took over the chief's office that evening.

The following Monday, November 12, Governor Crittenden appointed Tryon J. Woodward to the board. Woodward was born in Buffalo, New York. The Woodward family moved to St. Louis when Tryon was a boy. He later graduated from McKendree College in Illinois. Woodward had been a clerk in the commissioner of supplies for the city of St. Louis until Mayor Ewing's brother was appointed to his post, and he was once a member of the Democratic Central Committee. The new commissioner's first name, Tryon, was given him by his mother, a lineal descendant of Governor Tryon, the first governor of New York.[204] Woodward was the thirteenth person Governor Crittenden had appointed to the Board of Police Commissioners in the three years.

Woodward attended his first board meeting the next day. Caruth introduced a resolution to appeal the Court of Appeals's Campbell decision to the Missouri Supreme Court. This time the resolution included the wording that the expense of counsel would be paid by Lutz and Caruth and "shall in no manner be at the expense of the City of St. Louis."[205] The resolution passed by a 3–2 vote, with Woodward voting with Lutz and Caruth. Woodward later said that he voted for the appeal "because I thought it was the proper thing. The Board certainly had a right to appeal the case."[206]

Frank Lutz then introduced a resolution that the trial of Campbell be postponed until after the Supreme Court made a decision. This resolution was also adopted by a 3–2 vote, with Woodward again voting with Lutz and Caruth. Lutz then introduced a second resolution that Chief Campbell be suspended and ordered to turn over all police equipment to Taaffe, who would be chief of police. Before a vote was called for, however, Mayor Ewing, who chaired the meeting, declared that since Lutz and Caruth had preferred the charges against Chief Campbell, they were not entitled to vote. Lutz appealed the ruling, but Mayor Ewing noted that Rule 2 of the police manual stated that "the rules of parliamentary procedure as prescribed in Jefferson's Manual should, as far as practicable, guide the Board at its sessions." The mayor "happened" to have a copy of Jefferson's Manual in his pocket, and it stated that "members who are personally interested can not act as judges of their own case."[207] After further discussion, the matter was dropped. Woodward moved, and it was approved, that the board adjourn until the next day, Wednesday.[208]

At the next board meeting, November 14, Lutz moved that his appeal to the chair to allow Caruth and him to vote in the Campbell case be continued until the next meeting which, the members agreed, would be on Friday, November 16. To everyone's surprise, Woodward introduced a resolution that "all meetings of this Board be held with open doors, except for the reading of the minutes of the previous meeting and for the transaction of such business as the nature of which might endanger public interests or safety by being made public while under discussion by this Board."[209] Woodward explained that his resolution would permit reporters to be present and "thus insure accuracy in the statements of the proceedings."[210] Up to this point, the board would release a summary sheet of the meeting after each board meeting.

Caruth declared his opposition, and Lutz announced his reservations. Gooding approved of the resolution and said that he had favored it ever since he was appointed to the board. The vote was taken, and the resolution adopted with only Caruth voting against it. Only one representative from each newspaper would be permitted to attend the meeting, and a table and chairs would be provided. The board then held an election for the positions of treasurer and purchasing member of the board. Woodward was elected to serve as both.[211]

The board meeting of Friday, November 16, was the first meeting open to the press. Woodward moved that Rule 2 of the police manual (rules of parliamentary procedure should guide board meetings) be suspended. After more debate concerning the legality of temporarily suspending a rule in the police manual, Vice President Lutz produced a copy of a pocket manual for deliberative bodies written by Henry M. Roberts to rebut Jefferson's Manual. Woodward replied that Roberts was a regular army officer, a classmate of his at West Point. While Roberts was a "bright fellow," said Woodward, "he has never been out of the army and don't [sic] know anything about parliamentary law."[212] The discussion continued until the board agreed to ask City Counselor Leverett Bell for his legal opinion as to whether the board could change the rules of the police manual. Bell was also asked, "Who is the legal advisor of the Board of Police Commissioners?"[213] The city counselor later offered the legal opinion that the board was authorized, if a majority of the members were in agreement, to make such rules and regulations not inconsistent with the law, but no existing rule could be suspended without general consent.[214]

Lutz then asked permission of the board to withdraw his resolution of November 13 (that had not come to a vote) that would suspend Campbell and leave Taaffe in the chief position. There was unanimous agreement.

After the meeting concluded, Mayor Ewing was the first to leave. As he exited the boardroom he was approached by a deputy sheriff who served him with a writ of prohibition issued by the circuit court. Mayor Ewing returned to the boardroom and read the writ to the other members of the board. It was directed at all members of the board and Bernard Taaffe. The writ prohibited the board from suspending Chief Campbell and restrained Taaffe from "accepting or entering upon the duties of Chief of Police of said city until the further order of the Court in the premises."[215] The board was instructed to show cause, on or before Monday, November 19, why Chief Campbell's petition to remain as chief should not be granted. On Monday, however, an attorney representing the board asked for additional time to prepare. The case was continued until Friday, November 22.

On November 27, a jury trial began in the Court of Criminal Correction on the misdemeanor charges of conspiracy handed down by the grand jury against Commissioners Caruth and Lutz, Edward Butler, and Joseph McEntire. The trial, often before a packed courtroom, would take almost two weeks to complete. Witnesses were essentially those who had testified before the October grand jury. On December 6, after closing arguments from both sides in the case, Judge Noonan turned to the jury: "Gentlemen of the jury, the Court gives you the following instructions: Upon the evidence adduced by the State, the Court instructs the jury to acquit the defendants."[216] The jury then returned that verdict.

The board convened a special meeting shortly after three o'clock on the afternoon of December 19, with all members present. After a piece of routine business had been completed, there was a moment or two of silence. Lutz broke the silence by moving reconsideration of the vote that had delayed the trial of Chief Campbell until after the decision of the Missouri Supreme Court. After the motion was seconded, Lutz, Caruth, and Woodward voted in favor, Mayor Ewing and Gooding against. Lutz then asked permission of the board to withdraw the charges he and Caruth had filed against Chief Campbell. There was no objection, and Mayor Ewing ruled that the charges should be considered withdrawn. Chief Campbell was out of hot water for only a few moments.

As the mayor was about to adjourn the meeting, board secretary Wells announced that he had received a communication just moments before and would like to read it. The communication, from Walter F. McEntire, an attorney and the brother of the coal oil inspector, stated that "the undersigned, a citizen of the City of St. Louis, complains of John W. Campbell, Chief of Police of said city, and respectfully begs leave to present for your investigation the

charges and specifications. . . ."[217] McEntire's complaint contained
three charges: (1) conduct unbecoming an officer and a gentleman
for spreading "slanderous reports" about members of the Board of
Police Commissioners and threatening to "disembowel" one of the
commissioners for voting on a matter in opposition to Chief Campbell's request; (2) insolence, insubordination, and disrespect toward
his superior officer, for speaking contemptuously to and about the
board, and neglecting his duty by devoting time and energy to prosecuting the board while allowing "the city to be overrun with the
boldest and most dangerous of criminals"; and (3) an official indis-
cretion, by offering then-commissioner Daniel Kerwin $300 to be
returned to the rank of captain of police.[218]

The discussion after the reading of McEntire's complaint centered on precedent (since no chief of police had ever been tried by
the board, there was none) and the right to counsel. It was agreed that
Chief Campbell could be represented by counsel, as could the complainant. With the usual 3–2 vote, the trial was set for the following
Friday afternoon, December 21.[219] Because the members of the press
were now permitted to attend board meetings, all of the elements of
Chief Campbell's trial would appear in the city's newspapers. The trial
would take three days over the next week.

The board convened on Friday, December 21, but Chief Campbell was not present. Someone was sent to find him and inform him
that the board had convened. The chief and his attorneys then made
their way into the room. Procedural rules for the trial were established
by the board. The Board agreed (by a 3–2 vote) that each side could
be represented by only one attorney; all witnesses would be excluded
from the room until called to testify; each board member could ask
no more than five questions of any witness; all questions and answers
had to be germane to the subject matter; and all questions as to the
admission of testimony would be determined by a majority vote of
the board.[220]

John G. Chandler, representing Chief Campbell, then asked for
a copy of the charges. After looking at the charge sheets, Chandler
noted that, while Campbell was served with the charges, he had not

been notified in writing of the time and the place of the trial. That is why Campbell and his attorney were not present when the board convened the session. Such notice was required by the police manual.

Whether or not to postpone the trial resulted in a heated discussion among board members. Lutz moved that the objection of Chief Campbell's attorney not be sustained. Mayor Ewing, as ex officio president of the board, refused to put the objection to a vote. Lutz declared that, as vice president of the board, he would put the question. Lutz, Caruth, and Woodward voted to not sustain the objection, and Gooding voted against it. Lutz did not ask Mayor Ewing how he voted.

Woodward then offered a resolution that formally recognized what had been hinted at over the past few board meetings: "Resolved, That in the opinion of this board the President ex-officio is not entitled to vote upon any question that may come before the board except when there is a tie vote, in which case he may cast the deciding vote; therefore, the Secretary of the board is hereby instructed not to record any vote except as above provided."[221] Mayor Ewing refused to put the resolution to a vote, but Lutz called for one. Lutz, Caruth, and Woodward voted in favor, Gooding voted against. Mayor Ewing then said that he voted no. Vice President Lutz told Secretary Wells, "Don't record the Mayor's vote."[222]

Lutz then moved to adjourn until the following Thursday. Woodward objected that the matter had been "dragging on long enough," and he wanted to settle it as soon as possible. After some discussion, the trial was postponed until Thursday, December 27, at 3:00 p.m. In the meantime, Chief Campbell would be served with written notice of the time and place of the trial.[223]

Later that day, the November grand jury made its report to Criminal Court Judge Garrett Van Wagoner. Among other issues, the grand jury addressed the investigation into police matters that had been handed down to them by the previous grand jury. The members took issue with the manner in which police commissioners were appointed, noting that, in the past, some were "unfit" and their appointments (and the situations under which they resigned) "made a bad impression on the public mind."[224] While the grand jury found no collusion of Governor Crittenden with gamblers in regard to appointments, they suggested a variety of different approaches to the appointment of police commissioners, either at the state or city level.

The entire situation had demoralized the police force; asserted the grand jury, "a fine body of men, active and courageous in the performance of their duties, though discipline among them is relaxed." The grand jury found the police force too small and recommended the hiring of an additional one hundred officers. The additional money needed for the larger force could come from the increased fees paid by licensees of saloons under the recently enacted Downing Law. The grand jury added that "it is true economy to have a police [force] large enough to meet any emergency and to exercise a proper surveillance all around to the city limits. At present the outlying districts are hardly patrolable [sic] at all, and even the central districts are insufficiently patrolled. It is high time to remedy such a state of things."[225] The November grand jury report appeared to end the investigation of the police department, a situation taken up by three grand juries since July.

On Thursday afternoon, December 27, the board first met at one o'clock to conduct regular board business. In addition to routine matters, the board also agreed to change one of the rules earlier adopted for the Campbell trial: each attorney would now be granted five minutes, instead of three, for debate. Before recessing until the three o'clock trial was to begin, the board also entertained a letter from Anna C. Sneed and other members of the Woman's Christian Temperance Union (WCTU) of Kirkwood, Missouri. The signers of the letter asked the board to consider placing a matron at the Four Courts.[226] While the detailed contents of the letter are not known, the request was apparently a response to the fact that the police department had never hired a female jailer to assist in searches of, and minister to, jailed females. The letter was referred to Vice President Lutz for an investigation and report.

The board trial of Chief Campbell began at three o'clock. Campbell's attorney, John Chandler, objected to the presence of Vice

President Lutz and Commissioner Caruth. Chandler asserted that both were material witnesses in the trial and were prejudiced against Campbell. Chandler claimed that Chief Campbell could not have a fair trial with Lutz and Caruth sitting as judges. Gooding moved that the objection be sustained, but the motion was defeated by the customary 3–2 margin.

Chandler then objected to the charges and specifications preferred against Chief Campbell as they "allege no offense or misconduct on the part of the defendant either under the law or under the rules and regulations of the Board of Police Commissioners."[227] Gooding moved that the objections be sustained, but the motion lost by another 3–2 vote. Chief Campbell pleaded not guilty to all of the charges and specifications.[228] The trial began with the complainant's case. Three witnesses were called, sworn in, and testified. The trial was then recessed until that evening.

Two more witnesses were examined at the seven o'clock session. The board then adjourned until the next morning. All objections that Chief Campbell's attorney made during the two sessions were overruled by a 3–2 vote. Objections made by the complainant's attorney were sustained by the 3–2 vote.

The next morning, Friday, the board meeting was called to order at ten o'clock. The testimony of the last witness on Thursday evening was concluded and another witness recalled. The case for the defense began with the testimony of former police commissioner Samuel Cupples. Six additional witnesses testified, and the trial was continued until three o'clock. The board then approved the December payroll, excluding the salary of Chief Campbell.[229]

Three more witnesses testified for the defense at the afternoon session, all asserting that the police department was efficiently run under Chief Campbell. Lutz then moved that no more testimony concerning the efficiency of the police department be allowed. The motion was approved with the standard 3–2 vote. Campbell's attorney then offered into evidence a resolution the board adopted on December 13. In the face of Mayor Ewing's allegation that the city was "overrun with thieves," the board had passed a resolution that affirmed the efficiency of the force. In support, the board used the reports of the captains of the department that "good order and safety" prevailed in the city.[230]

Chief Campbell then took the stand. Campbell denied some of the accusations and explained others. When attorney Chandler asked the chief, "Have you so far as you know neglected your duty?" McEntire's attorney objected.[231] By another 3–2 vote, the objection was sustained and Campbell was not permitted to answer. Chandler asked, "Has the Board ever approved any pay roll for your services since the 9th of October?" Again, an objection. The objection was sustained.[232]

On cross-examination, Chief Campbell gave his version of the events of which he was accused and he denied others. The board broke for supper and then, after reconvening at eight o'clock, the cross-examination of Chief Campbell continued, most of it going over previously covered ground.[233] Two additional witnesses were called for the defense. Both sides waived closing arguments. The board then went into executive session to deliberate.

The board returned to the boardroom shortly after midnight. Mayor Ewing announced that Chief Campbell had been found guilty of all charges and specifications with two exceptions: the second specification of the first charge, that Campbell threatened to disembowel one of the commissioners, and the second specification of the second charge, neglect of duty for permitting the city to be overrun by criminals. Chief Campbell was reduced to the rank of patrolman. Captain Joseph Hercules, commander of the Second District, was named acting chief of police. The board then adjourned until Wednesday, January 2, 1884.

The next day, Captain Hercules reported for duty as acting chief of police. He did not move into the chief's office but spent his time in the Central District captain's office, the office of the chief's secretary, or in the office of the chief of detectives. Former chief Campbell was also in the Four Courts building. Campbell and Commissioner Woodward accidentally met in the office of the chief's secretary, when Woodward asked Campbell for the keys to the chief's office. Campbell refused to give them to him, and Woodward left the office.

Later in the day, Mayor Ewing received a letter from Campbell. It was addressed to the Board of Police Commissioners: "I am advised by my counsel that your proceedings of yesterday, attempting to deprive me of my office of Chief of Police, and to reduce me to the rank[s], as patrolman, are illegal and void. I therefore hold myself in readiness to discharge all the duties pertaining to the office of Chief of Police and to obey all lawful orders received from you relative to my duties as said officer."[234] A hearing was scheduled for Wednesday, January 2, 1884, in the Court of Appeals in St. Louis on a writ of certiorari filed by Campbell's attorneys.

1884

The board meeting of January 2, 1884, was significant for two reasons. First, John Campbell continued to be an issue. The board read a letter from Captain Thomas Fruchte, commander of the Central District, dated December 31, 1883. In his letter, Captain Fruchte notified the board that he had informed John Campbell that he had been assigned to duty in the Central District. Campbell "informed me that he did not intend to respect the order as he did not consider it legal."[235] The board agreed that Captain Fruchte should handle this situation according to the rules in the police manual and treat Campbell as he would any other police officer.

The second event was based upon Anna Sneed's request to the board at the meeting of December 27, 1883. At that meeting, Vice President Lutz had been given the responsibility of determining the feasibility of employing a police matron. As a result, Lutz moved that a police matron be appointed for the Four Courts for a period of three months "upon the recommendation of the ladies of the W.C.T.U."[236] The vote was unanimous. The matron would be paid a salary of $40 a month. Vice President Lutz was given the "power to act," that is, to select a woman for the position. He would also write the rules governing the new position.

After one item of business, the board went into an executive session at the meeting of January 8. With John Campbell no longer the chief of police, Woodward introduced a resolution that would rescind the order of October 9, 1883, making Bernard Taaffe the chief of police. This would clear the way for the appointment of a new chief. The resolution was adopted, with Gooding abstaining.

Woodward introduced a second resolution appointing Laurence Harrigan as chief of police "subject to removal at the pleasure of the Board of Police Commissioners. . . ."[237] The latter phrase eliminated a specific term for the chief. This resolution was adopted by a 3–1 vote. Gooding voted against it, denying that there was a vacancy in the office of chief of police and casting his vote for John Campbell. Mayor Ewing abstained. Laurence Harrigan was the chief of police for the second time.

Lutz then moved that the office of secretary of the board be declared vacant. The motion was approved by the usual 3–2 vote. Woodward moved that Bernard Taaffe be named to the post. This motion was approved by a 4–1 vote, with Gooding voting against it.

Laurence Harrigan. Photograph, ca. 1874. Missouri History Museum.

THE CRITTENDEN YEARS   239

The board returned to the open session and took up the issue of Patrolman John Campbell's failure to report for duty in the Central District. Campbell was called but did not appear. Instead, a letter addressed to the board was read. It was signed "John W. Campbell, Chief of Police." Campbell explained in his letter that he had received the charges and specifications for the hearing set this day, but they were addressed to Patrolman John W. Campbell and he was "not ready to admit that they have been served upon the proper person."[238] Campbell's letter continued that he had been advised by his counsel that the board's action of reducing him to the rank of patrolman was "illegal, null and void" and, consequently, he was still the chief of police. He had instituted a legal proceeding that would allow the courts to determine his official status. Campbell concluded that the board should defer action on the present charges and specifications until the court determined the question of the legality of his reduction in rank.[239]

Captain Fruchte was then called. Fruchte stated that, upon the orders of Acting Chief of Police Joseph Hercules, he had assigned Campbell to beat duty and had notified him of his assignment. Campbell refused the post and failed to walk the beat assigned to him.

Gooding moved that the charges and specifications against Campbell be dismissed "without prejudice." The motion lost by the usual 3–2 vote. Lutz then moved that Patrolman Campbell be found guilty of the charges and specifications and dismissed from the police force. This motion passed by a 3–2 vote.

As a result of the board's actions, both John Campbell and former board secretary C. E. Wells were without jobs. Woodward, however, introduced a resolution creating the position of assistant secretary of the board and appointing C. E. Wells to fill the position. Wells would receive $100 a month and "perform such duties as shall be assigned to him by this Board."[240] Chief of Police–elect Laurence Harrigan was then called before the board and took the oath of office.

In the meantime, a room had been prepared on the third floor of the Four Courts building for the yet-to-be named police matron. A police telephone with a direct line to the Central District captain's office was later added. On February 1, the first police matron, Louisa

Harris, was appointed.[241] Little is known about Louisa Harris. She obviously kept a journal of her daily events for, in 1893, she would write a book describing the situations of many of the women and girls she met in the course of her duties.[242] The only clue as to how she obtained the position is contained in two sentences. In 1884, "a movement was started by the W.C.T.U. for the creation of the office of Police Matron at the Four Courts in St. Louis. It was successful, and I was appointed to said office and entered upon my duties."[243]

Woodward moved that a captain be elected to replace one recently dismissed from the force. Each commissioner nominated one sergeant to fill the vacancy. On the first ballot, each sergeant received one vote. Lutz and Caruth both withdrew the names of their candidates. Lutz nominated another sergeant, Samuel J. Boyd, who was in charge of the detectives. On the next ballot, Sergeant Boyd received four votes. He was promoted to captain and assigned the First District command formerly occupied by Captain Price. The same selection process was used to select a patrolman to fill the slot left vacant by the promotion of Sergeant Boyd.[244]

The next meeting of the board began without surprise. To replace former Sergeant Boyd as "Sergeant in charge of detectives," Chief Harrigan recommended Sergeant John Burke."[b] Burke was so assigned.

Woodward then moved that Harrigan, who was selected to serve as chief of police "at the pleasure of the Board," be appointed chief for a term of four years, effective that day, March 11, 1884. With only Gooding being opposed, the appointment was approved. Woodward introduced a resolution that Vice President Lutz and Secretary Taaffe commission all officers and patrolmen for four years beginning April 1, 1884. The resolution was adopted.[245]

The minutes for the March 18 meeting refer to a petition concerning the employment of black officers: "A petition signed by a number of colored men requesting the Board to appoint Negros [sic] on the

---

[b] The titles "chief of detectives" and "sergeant in charge of detectives" were commonly used interchangeably except in the minutes of the board. There was no legal basis for a "chief of detectives," but the term was used within other areas of the police department and in the newspapers.

police force as patrolmen was read & ordered filed."[246] This was the first request that blacks be hired as patrolmen since the Republican Union of Negro Citizens of St. Louis made a similar request of the board in 1881. The board would not act on this request.

✳   ✳   ✳

On August 16, the *Post-Dispatch* reported that lottery tickets were being sold at thirty-two different locations in the city.[247] The article was referenced at the board meeting of August 19, and Chief Harrigan was directed to investigate the report and prefer charges against any member of the force found to have neglected his duty by failing the enforce the law against the sales of lottery tickets.

Chief Harrigan submitted a report to the board at the next meeting. It said, in part: "I have the honor to report for you information that upon investigation I find from the reports of Commanders of districts that no known gambling of any kind is in existence and I would state, furthermore, that efforts have been made to purchase lottery tickets from supposed lottery vendors, but without success. . . . I am unable to find any evidence against any of the officers for neglect of duty in the premises."[248]

Commissioner Gooding responded that someone must have neglected his duty. Chief Harrigan replied that he had officers "who were specially detailed to look after the lottery. They report to me that there is no lottery in the city, and that no lottery tickets have been sold. I believe the officers until I can find some evidence to the contrary."[249] When Gooding pressed the issue, Harrigan told him that if someone pays someone else a quarter and writes down three numbers, and the person receiving the quarter carries the money and the numbers to East St. Louis (Illinois), thus, "there is no violation of the law, no tickets having been sold."[250] Gooding replied that he didn't know what constituted a lottery violation; he only knew what he had seen in the newspaper.

The *Post-Dispatch*, in the edition of August 27, acknowledged that Chief Harrigan's report and the report in the August 16 edition of the newspaper were both true. The newspaper then made a distinction between a "lottery" and "policy" games. "Lottery is a scheme of chance wherein the numbers on the tickets used are printed by the managers. Policy is a lottery scheme where the player selects his own combination of numbers between one and seventy-eight, and either writes them down himself or has the vender do so for him."[251]

Gooding had called for an investigation of the "lottery" business. Chief Harrigan passed this on to a special officer who investigated such matters, and he literally interpreted it. The special officer was unable to find anyone selling "lottery" tickets.[252] The matter was allowed to drop.

St. Louis's new railroad terminal, Union Station, opened in September. Modeled after a castle in southern France, it was claimed that Union Station was the "largest railroad station in the world."[253] The terminal, and the Terminal Hotel in the west end of the building, faced Market Street and stretched from Eighteenth to Twentieth streets. A ten-acre train shed ran south along Eighteenth Street. The Romanesque style of the terminal was described as a "modern elaboration of the feudal gateway."[254] At the opening ceremony on the night of September 1, it was referred to as "the gateway to the great Southwest. . . ."[255]

The September board meetings featured a more mundane subject. Most likely for reasons of uniformity, the board ordered that no officer would be permitted to wear "any shield, star or badge of office other than that furnished by the Police Department." Captains were later excepted.[256] The order was in response to continuing requests (heretofore granted) by captains, sergeants, and patrolmen that they be permitted to wear a star or shield (usually of silver) presented to them by appreciative citizens or businessmen. The board also requested bids for, and then chose, new shields for the captains and a five-pointed star for detectives.[257] Before receiving their new detective stars, detectives probably identified themselves with a regular patrolman's star.

In response to a citizen petition that "there is more than ordinary disturbance threatened at the [general] election on Tuesday, Nov. 4," and requesting that the board employ sufficient special policemen to augment the regular officers at the polling places, the board convened a special meeting on the Saturday before the election.[258] The board voted to hire up to six hundred specials. In order to comply with the 1861 Metropolitan Police Act, the board declared that "an extraordinary emergency" existed. Vice President Lutz was then given the authority to select the men who would be employed on election day.[259] The election proceeded without any unusual incidents.

Detective star. Courtesy of SLMPD.

Governor Crittenden was not on the ballot. Opposition to his running for a second term, from a variety of sources, resulted in the Democrats nominating John S. Marmaduke. Marmaduke would win the election for governor.

At the last meeting of November, the board added another duty to the already beleaguered patrolmen. The lower house of the Municipal Assembly had passed a resolution requesting the Board of Police Commissioners to order the strict enforcement of Ordinance 12,348. The ordinance required the numbering of all houses fronting on public streets. The request was referred to Chief Harrigan "with instructions to have said ordinance enforced."[260]

The first Police Relief Association ball was held on December 11. At the board meeting of December 23, the secretary of the relief association reported a profit of $5,692.34. The Relief Association was not the only one to benefit from police selling tickets. In mid-November, the board was asked to permit First District officers to assist in the sale of tickets for the benefit of the poor in Carondelet, located at the southern tip of the city. The request was granted.[261] Later in the month, two criminal court judges asked the board to allow police officers to sell tickets for a proposed entertainment "for the benefit of the worthy poor of St. Louis." The proceeds would be divided between the Provident Association and the St. Vincent de Paul Society. The board also approved this request.[262]

The inauguration of John S. Marmaduke as governor on Monday, January 12, 1885, marked the official end of the Crittenden era. Because of the number and variety of problems with the St. Louis Board of Police Commissioners, Thomas Crittenden had found it necessary to appoint eight police commissioners to the four-man board in his first two years of office. An additional five were appointed the third year of his four-year term.

In spite of all the internal squabbles, accusations, innuendos, legal battles, and a parade of police commissioners and police chiefs, the variously occupied boards appointed by Governor Crittenden did manage to move the police department forward. A new state law permitted the old Police Relief Fund to incorporate; it became the Police Relief Association. Sergeants and turnkeys were granted one day off each month. The mounted police unit was permitted to work three eight-hour watches, rather than the usual twelve-hour shifts.

The police department abandoned the telegraph system and connected the various police station houses by telephone. Shortly after, the board began building a call box and patrol wagon system. The board tightened control of private watchmen and declined to license anyone as a private detective. It hired its first police matron in early 1884. Finally, for the first time, the board opened its meetings to the public press.

Chapter Seven

A New Board and an International Murder Case

THE YEAR 1885 WAS SPELLBINDING. Memorable events included the chief of police being put on trial before the police board, the expansion of the call box and patrol wagon systems, the enactment of a uniform requirement for private watchmen, another street-car strike, and a murder case that would see two officers go halfway around the world for an arrest.

1885

On Wednesday, January 14, 1885, the recently inaugurated governor of Missouri, John S. Marmaduke, appointed James L. Blair, Michael Callahan, and Frank Gaiennie to the St. Louis Board of Police Commissioners. He also reappointed General Oliver P. Gooding to the board.

James L. Blair, the son of General Frank P. Blair, practiced law with his brother, Frank Blair. James Blair replaced David Caruth on the board. Michael Callahan replaced Frank Lutz. At the time of his appointment, he was the superintendent of steam and gas fixtures for Cornelius Becannon and Company. For eight years before his appointment, Callahan had been the treasurer for the Democratic City Central Committee. He resigned that post a week before being nominated by Governor Marmaduke. Frank Gaiennie was a principal in the commercial merchant firm of Gaiennie and Marks. He was a longtime member of the Merchants' Exchange. Gaiennie would later become the president of the exchange as well as the vice president of the National Board of Trade. He replaced Tryon Woodward.[1]

The first meeting of the new board was Tuesday, January 20. The board immediately went into an executive session at that meeting to elect officers. Blair was elected vice president; Callahan, treasurer; and

Governor John S. Marmaduke. Photograph by Scholten, 1884–1886. Missouri History Museum.

Gaiennie, purchasing member. As was still the case, each of the four commissioners was assigned one or two districts to supervise.

At the next meeting, the board accepted the resignation of Secretary Bernard Taaffe. Two men were nominated for the open position, and Frank R. Tate was elected. The probationary term for special officers, which had been decreased from six to three months in 1883, was restored to six months.[2]

Meanwhile, the board prepared a fiscal year 1885–1886 budget that would allow completion of the expansion of the call box–patrol wagon system already under way in the Fifth Police District and begin the expansion into the Second and Fourth districts. The system would then be citywide. Chief Harrigan attested to the value of the system: "It secures the prompt arrest of crimmials [*sic*], disperses dangerous crowds, enables the officer making the arrest to remain on his beat and avoids the painful and often disgusting spectacle of drunken and violent prisoners being dragged through the streets."[3] The board also asked for an additional 101 patrolmen and 10 sergeants. Except for the addition of 39 new positions in the previous year, no additional positions had been authorized since 1875.[4]

The city election was held on April 7; the newly elected mayor was David R. Francis. The clerk of the circuit court informed the board that, on Tuesday, April 14, Mayor Francis had taken the oath given to police commissioners before their taking office.[5] On that same day, the decomposing body of a guest from England was found locked in a trunk at the elegant Southern Hotel.

The temperature was in the upper 50s on Sunday, April 12. After complaints by guests of a foul odor coming from room 144, the manager entered the room but found nothing amiss. He thought that the occupants might have left some lunch sitting out and it had decomposed. By Tuesday, the stench had worsened. Since the occupants of the room had apparently left without informing anyone, a porter was instructed to take the three large trunks in room 144 to the hotel baggage room. When it became obvious that the odor was coming from one of the trunks, it was carried outside to the sidewalk and forced open.

The decomposing body of a man clad only in white knit drawers was found inside the trunk. A piece of paper pasted on the wall of the trunk just above the victim's head contained the phrase, "So perish all traitors to the great cause." A police patrol wagon was requested, and the body, the three trunks, and all of the contents of room 144, including other smaller trunks, were put in the patrol wagon. The trunk containing the body was taken to the city morgue, the identity of the man unknown.[6] The other trunks were taken back to the office of the chief of detectives in the Four Courts.[7]

The "trunk tragedy," as it would become known, had its beginnings less than two weeks before, on Tuesday, March 31, 1885. A man who identified himself as Walter H. Lennox Maxwell, MD, from London,

England, registered at the Southern Hotel and paid for a week's stay. He was given room 144, which was located on the second floor of the hotel facing Fourth Street. Dr. Maxwell, as he was known at the hotel, was described as suave and very sociable. He visited several establishments in the city and spent much of his time at Fernow's drugstore at Broadway and Market the first three or four days.

The following Friday, April 3, the hotel received a dispatch inquiring whether Maxwell was registered at the hotel. The dispatch was signed by one C. Arthur Preller. That same evening, Preller arrived at the Southern Hotel and registered as C. Arthur Preller, London, England. He was shown to room 385, on the fourth floor.

Maxwell and Preller were seen together later that evening, and Maxwell invited Preller to stay with him in room 144. Even though he retained room 385, Preller moved in with Maxwell. The staff figured they were fellow travelers and businessmen and gave the key to room 144 to Preller whenever he came to the front desk. Maxwell later told two or three people that he and Preller were en route to Auckland, New Zealand.

As soon as the trunks and other contents from room 144 arrived at police headquarters, they were carefully examined by Sergeant of Detectives John Burke, Chief of Police Laurence Harrigan, and Captain Thomas Fruchte, commander of the Central District. Five of the trunks, all marked "C. A. Preller, London, England," were opened first. It was learned that Preller was Charles Arthur Preller of London. He was employed by J. H. Dixon, a dealer in cloths and tapestries, based in Bradford, Yorkshire, England. In late 1884 and early 1885, he had been visiting customers in Canada and the United States. Preller had planned to visit four St. Louis businesses.

A sixth trunk and two satchels belonged to Maxwell. The trunk contained a collection of medical books, various medicines, a diploma from the Royal College of Surgeons, writing ink, a prescription tablet from Fernow's drugstore, a new hat, and so forth. One of Maxwell's satchels contained a varied assortment of medicines including a half-filled vial of chloroform and a box of morphine powders.

At the morgue, the deceased was described by Morgue Superintendent John F. Ryan as being in his early twenties, having black hair, being approximately five feet, nine inches tall, and weighing about 170 pounds. A cross was carved into his chest. The time of death was estimated as ten to twelve days earlier, or between April 2 and April 4.

On Tuesday, April 14, Coroner (and former police commissioner) Dr. James C. Nidelet performed a postmortem examination. Preliminary findings indicated that death had been caused by a corrosive poison. The dead man's stomach was later sent to Dr. Charles Luedeking, at Washington University in St. Louis, for chemical analysis.

The investigation determined that, shortly after noon on Easter Sunday, Maxwell went to Fernow's drugstore and bought a four-ounce vial of chloroform. He later returned to the drugstore and obtained two additional ounces.

While not yet officially identified, it had become fairly obvious at this point that the body in the trunk was that of Charles Arthur Preller. Preller had not been seen since Easter Sunday morning, and the body fit his general description. It was equally clear that the murder suspect was Walter Maxwell. Maxwell had been seen the Monday after Easter Sunday and had told numerous persons that he was leaving on a train to San Francisco that evening. The investigation turned to westbound trains leaving St. Louis's Union Depot on Monday night, April 6, and ships leaving San Francisco for New Zealand after the train was scheduled to arrive. Maxwell arrived in San Francisco on Saturday morning, April 11.

Police in San Francisco had been alerted and had been conducting their own investigation. Captain J. W. Lees, the San Francisco chief of detectives, sent a dispatch that the suspect had bought the train ticket in St. Louis under the name "Hugh M. Brooks," but claimed to be a Frenchman and was traveling under the name of "T. C. Dauquier."[8]

On Sunday, April 12, the suspect booked passage on the steamer *City of Sydney*. It was learned that three pieces of luggage were forwarded from St. Louis under Maxwell's name on April 5. They were signed for in San Francisco by one T. C. Dauquier.

City of Sydney was bound for Auckland, New Zealand, with stops in Honolulu, Hawaii, and Tuitulla, in the Samoa Islands. It was scheduled to arrive in Honolulu on Sunday, April 19, and in Auckland on May 1. Chief Harrigan, meanwhile, sent a cablegram to Auckland, to ask the U.S. Consul there to arrest, and hold for extradition, Maxwell for the murder of Preller.

The time required for Harrigan's cablegram to be dispatched from St. Louis to Auckland is not known. The cost, however, is known. Such a cablegram cost $3.34 a word. The request for the arrest of Maxwell contained 155 words, a total of $517.70.[9] This large amount of money spent by the board attested to its determination to capture Maxwell. The *Globe-Democrat* also claimed that the message was "the most expensive police message ever sent out from a telegraph office in the United States."[10]

On the morning of April 15, a friend of Preller, James Taylor, arrived by train from Louisville, Kentucky. Taylor was shown a photograph of Preller, whom he identified as Charles Arthur Preller. He later viewed the body in the morgue and said that, to the best of his knowledge and belief, the body was that of Preller. The inquest into the death of Preller was begun on Friday, April 17, with Dr. Nidelet presiding, and continued for several days, including Sunday, before all witnesses had been questioned. The inquest was adjourned on Tuesday, April 21, pending the report of the chemical analysis of the contents of Preller's stomach.

When the inquest reconvened on Thursday afternoon, April 23, Dr. Luedeking testified that Preller's death was caused by the administration of chloroform. The six men on the coroner's jury then retired to prepare a verdict. They found that Maxwell was responsible for the death of Preller. The identification of the man in the trunk and the finding of the coroner's jury ended that aspect of the investigation.

The next problem was the disposition of Preller's body. Since there were no known relatives in St. Louis, the first consideration was to bury him in Potter's Field. A cousin of Preller in New York City, Frank Schlesinger, received a message from Preller's family in England that Schlesinger should take charge of the body. Schlesinger asked St. Louis authorities to give Preller a decent burial. He then sent a second message asking that the coroner temporarily dispose of the body pending further orders from the family. First, however, Circuit Attorney Ashley Clover asked that there be further identification of the body. Clover also wanted the teeth of the dead man in the event of the arrival of any of his relatives. The teeth were said to be peculiarly formed. Funeral services were held, and the body was placed in a vault at Bellefontaine Cemetery.

Legal measures to assure Maxwell's arrest and extradition were under way. While the case was based on circumstantial evidence, it was believed that the evidence was sufficient for Maxwell's extradition. The source of the amount of money necessary to return Maxwell to St. Louis was a potential problem. It was later determined that the governor of Missouri held a fund for "the apprehension of criminals and the suppression of outlawry." On April 21, Board Vice President Blair wrote to Governor John Marmaduke to inquire if money was available to assist in the extradition of Maxwell. Governor Marmaduke informed Blair that $10,000 had been appropriated for the fund, and $8,000 still remained. However, he said, he would not consider reimbursing any expenses until Maxwell had been returned to St. Louis.

The San Francisco police made major contributions to the investigation. Police located every place that the suspect had visited in San Francisco. They learned that the man calling himself T. C. Dauquier had exchanged a pocket watch for the one he had in his possession. The original watch was later examined by the police. Written in ink, on the inside of the brass cap that covered the face of the watch, was "H. M. Brooks," the name used by the man who had purchased the train ticket in St. Louis. Chief of Detective Lees raised the possibility that the real name of the suspect might be H. M. Brooks, not Walter H. Lennox Maxwell. It was also confirmed that he had gotten on the steamer *City of Sydney*.

On May 6, Chief Harrigan received a cablegram from the U.S. Consul in Auckland, New Zealand, that Maxwell had been arrested. The consul added that Maxwell was "disposed to give trouble." Chief Harrigan immediately replied, "Hold Maxwell by all means; evidence conclusive; State Department cables you to-day. I will send officer for him as soon as possible." Vice President Blair sent a telegram to U.S. Secretary of State Thomas F. Bayard asking that he arrange for Maxwell's detention in New Zealand until the arrival of St. Louis officers. San Francisco Chief of Police Crowley was also notified of the arrest. Circuit Attorney Clover and two assistants prepared the papers necessary for extradition. Since this was the first time that St. Louis authorities had been faced with such a case, there was some uncertainty as to all the requirements. Clover obtained a copy of the transcript of the coroner's inquest and began reducing it to affidavit form.

The time had come to indicate who would be going to New Zealand to bring Maxwell back to St. Louis. The police board was certain that the appointing power was the vice president of the board, James Blair. With that thought in mind, the board requested that Governor Marmaduke name Detective James Tracy as the state agent. Tracy, the request noted, was an experienced officer and could identify Maxwell.

Detective James Tracy. Photograph, ca. 1880s. Missouri History Museum.

Governor Marmaduke decided that only one man should go to New Zealand. The board met in special session on Monday, May 18, to discuss the issue. After the meeting, Vice President Blair sent a letter to Governor Marmaduke outlining the strain that would be felt by a lone officer in the long steamer and train journey from New Zealand to St. Louis and the possibility that, under the circumstances, the prisoner might escape. "It is also important to have someone with the officer who, as an expert witness, can prove our statute laws relating to the crime for which the prisoner is to be extradited, in order to show that the proceedings on which the acquisition are based are regular (this being essential under the treaty and laws)."[11] Vice President Blair wrote that a second state agent be named and recommended Frank R. O'Neil.

O'Neil, who had long been a newspaper man in St. Louis and was then at the *Post-Dispatch*, was described by Blair as "thoroughly competent to perform the duty, and, in every way, a reliable and trustworthy man."[12] O'Neil would be sworn in as a special officer of the police force. The board offered to pay O'Neil's expenses and suggested that Governor Marmaduke pay the expenses of Tracy and the prisoner.

A steamer bound for New Zealand, the *Zealandia*, was scheduled to leave San Francisco on June 6. The train ride from St. Louis to San Francisco would take five days. In the meantime, Frank O'Neil, who had gone to Washington, D.C., had to return from that city with the extradition papers. They would later be mailed to Governor Marmaduke. On Monday morning, May 25, President Grover Cleveland signed a warrant for the arrest of Maxwell. The warrant named Tracy and O'Neil as the persons to whom Maxwell should be delivered.

A problem quickly threatened the planned trip to New Zealand. On Wednesday, May 28, O'Neil wrote a letter to Vice President Blair stating that he had unexpectedly received a job offer from the *Missouri Republican*, a newspaper where he had previously been employed, and that he had elected to take the job. Accordingly, he resigned his commission as a special officer and would be unable to accompany Tracy to New Zealand.

Time was short. Tracy and the second unnamed officer had to be in San Francisco, with the extradition papers, in time to catch the steamer on June 6. Blair sent a telegram to Marmaduke asking for $1,500 for the expenses of the travelers and stated that he would be personally responsible for the advance. Marmaduke forwarded that amount to the board, which would pay the $1,000 round-trip expenses of the second—as yet unnamed—officer, from the regular police account.

The board then named Special Officer George W. Badger, of the Third District, to replace Frank O'Neil. On May 30, Tracy and Badger left St. Louis on the 8:25 p.m. train for San Francisco. On June 6, Badger sent a telegram to Blair informing him that he and Tracy would set sail at 2:00 p.m. on the *Zealandia*, which would reach New Zealand near the end of June.

Special Officer George W. Badger. Photograph, ca. 1880s.
Missouri History Museum.

*   *   *

With the *Zealandia* under way, the board turned its attention to a major problem that had developed the previous week. At the meeting of May 29, 1885, an affidavit was filed by previously dismissed police captain C. W. Price and read to the board by Price's attorney, John G. Chandler. It accused Chief of Police Laurence Harrigan of nine different charges, ranging from accepting bribes, gambling, inefficiency, and neglect of duty, to oppression in office and making false reports to the board. Each charge included one or more specific acts (specifications) that were meant to substantiate the charge; there were eighteen specifications.[13] Chief Harrigan was suspended from duty.

At the regular board meeting of June 2, Mayor Francis moved for the dismissal of four specifications. Callahan seconded the motion. The motion passed with Francis, Callahan, and Gaiennie voting for the motion, and Blair and Gooding voting against. Chandler then asked the board for permission to act as counsel for Price, and Harrigan asked that to be represented by attorneys Chester H. Krum and Charles P. Johnson. Both requests were approved. Chief Harrigan pleaded not guilty to all the charges, and the trial was set for Friday, June 5.[14]

Motions occupied the beginning of the trial on June 5. Fifteen witnesses were then heard for the "prosecution." At the conclusion of the testimony, two additional specifications were dropped, one by the board and the other at the request of Price's attorney, leaving twelve. The case was continued until the following Monday, June 8.[15] Eighteen additional witnesses were heard on Monday, and four more on Tuesday. The trial resumed on Friday, June 12, with the continuing testimony of the last witness on Tuesday. The complainant then rested his case. Chandler, Price's attorney, then moved that four additional charges be stricken. The board approved, leaving only the charges of inefficiency and neglect of duty, accepting a reward or remuneration, conniving at gambling, and making false reports to the board.

Six witnesses appeared for the "defense," including a former board member. Chief Harrigan also testified in his own behalf. After the defense rested its case, both sides waived closing arguments, and the board adjourned and went into executive session, which lasted five hours. Harrigan was found guilty on only one charge, violation of Rule 21, the rule that prohibited the chief of police from receiving any award or remuneration.[16] After much discussion, Chief Harrigan was fined $100 and was reprimanded. By board rules, the fine would be credited to the account of the Police Relief Association. Mayor Francis informed Chief Harrigan that he was reinstated to the force.[17]

The board, at its next regular meeting, with only General Gooding voting in the negative, allowed Chief Harrigan his pay for the time he had been under suspension.[18]

The board had also made several important policy changes during the Maxwell investigation and subsequent difficulties associated with the case. At the meeting of April 28, the board made changes regarding ranks:

1. Probationary Patrolmen. From the date of appointment to the completion of six months of service, officers would be on probation and designated by the name "probationary patrolman."

2. Emergency Specials. Men appointed for special police duty under an emergency clause would be called "emergency specials."

3. Specials. Regular patrolmen detailed for special duty would be called "specials."

4. Reappointments. Former patrolmen reappointed to the police would be reappointed at the rank of full patrolmen.

On May 5, 1885, two applicants were sworn in and appointed the first probationary patrolmen. The board next directed its attention to private watchmen. The board ordered that all private watchmen licensed by the board must wear a uniform, designated by the board, when on duty. Any failure of a private watchman to wear such a uniform would be cause for immediate revocation of the license. The selection of a uniform was left to Purchasing Member Frank Gaiennie.[19] Gaiennie had selected a uniform by the next board meeting. The uniform would consist of a blouse and cap made of gray cadet cloth trimmed with brass buttons. The board approved the selection.

The board also addressed a new law passed by the Missouri General Assembly. Effective June 23, setting up or maintaining a common house of assignation or common bawdy house within one hundred yards of any church, public school, public library, theater, city hall, or courthouse became a felony. Chief Harrigan was instructed to see that the law was strictly enforced.[20]

In the meantime, the board removed Sergeant of Detectives John Burke from that position. His replacement was Sergeant Hugh O'Neil.

*   *   *

While the *Zealandia*, with officers Tracy and Badger aboard, sailed to its first stop in Hawaii and Chief Harrigan was on trial, Acting Chief Anton Huebler received a letter from C. Arthur Preller's father. The father had received a letter from a close friend in Stockport, England, describing the evidence he had uncovered that Maxwell was really one Hugh Motham Brooks. Preller's friend stated that he would continue to gather evidence to support his statement. Chief Huebler didn't receive Preller's letter until June 10.

The *Zealandia* arrived in Auckland on June 30. Officers Tracy and Badger were met and interviewed by the Crown prosecutor. They later met with United States Consul Gamble. A hearing was scheduled for Maxwell the next day, but was continued until July 3.

At the July 3 hearing in the Auckland Police Court, Tracy testified that he had seen both Maxwell and Preller at the Southern Hotel and had been involved in parts of the murder investigation and attended part of the proceedings at the coroner's inquest. He identified the accused in the dock as Walter H. Lennox Maxwell. Tracy identified all of the legal documents and depositions in the case and produced a warrant issued by the sheriff of St. Louis, as Maxwell had fled from the jurisdiction of the criminal court.

An Auckland police detective, who had boarded the *City of Sydney* from a pilot tug outside the port of Auckland, and who had arrested Maxwell on the steamer, testified to items found on Maxwell's person as well as those found in his trunk. The testimony of the St. Louis detective and the Auckland detective constituted the case for the prosecution.

Maxwell's defense attorney attempted to show that the Police Court had no jurisdiction in the case, but his objection was over-ruled. Maxwell was then formally charged with the murder of Preller and jailed pending a warrant from the governor. The judge ruled that Maxwell was not to be handed over for fourteen days.

Tracy, Badger, and their prisoner eventually departed New Zealand, returning to San Francisco on August 10, then boarding a train to St. Louis. Maxwell, with his arms tied, sat between Tracy and Badger during the day. At night, he was chained to a lower berth. At 6:48 a.m. on Sunday morning, August 16, the train rolled into the sheds of the Union Depot in St. Louis. Approximately two thousand people awaited its arrival.

Tracy and Badger, with Maxwell between them, headed for the police department "hoodlum wagon." Crowds lined the streets along the entire route to the Four Courts. The three went directly to Sergeant of Detectives O'Neil's office where Harry Newbold, the city photographer, took four pictures of Maxwell. The following day,

Hugh M. Brooks (alias Walter H. Lennox Maxwell). Photograph, ca. 1880s.
Missouri History Museum.

Maxwell was charged with first-degree murder and then transferred from the police holdover to the city jail. In the meantime, Maxwell had retained John I. Martin as counsel. In a letter to the *Globe-Democrat* that same day, Maxwell refused to state his real name and said that he would answer to any name he was called. He also declined to state what his defense would be.

On August 19, an English citizen, Edward Morrissey, appeared at the jail and identified Maxwell as Hugh M. Brooks. He identified the prisoner's father as Samuel Brooks, who lived in Hyde. Meanwhile, Assistant Circuit Attorney Marshall McDonald became the recipient of a rather fortuitous turn of events. McDonald was in Toronto, Canada, to assist in the extradition of an embezzler. Aware that Preller had earlier been in Toronto, McDonald went to the Rossin House Hotel to make inquiries. He soon learned that Preller had stayed at the Rossin House and that a Toronto artist and photographer, John A. Frazier Jr., had been a constant companion.

McDonald went to Frazier's photography studio. He took the morgue photo of Preller from his pocket. He told Frazier that he wanted to have the picture touched up with a little color. When Frazier saw the photograph he reportedly exclaimed, "Great heavens, who are you, and where did you get this picture? Why that's Preller, who used to be here and was killed in St. Louis."[21] Frazier was called to St. Louis for Maxwell's preliminary hearing. He arrived on September 9.

The next day, McDonald, Circuit Attorney Clover, John Frazier, and an unidentified man with photographic equipment went to Bellefontaine Cemetery. En route to the cemetery, Frazier asked McDonald and Clover if anyone had noticed a scar over one of Preller's eyes, adding that he was unsure which eye. Both answered in the negative. Preller's casket was uncovered and an examination of the body revealed a perpendicular scar over the victim's left eye. Morgue photographs of the body hadn't shown the scar. The casket was stood on end against a tree, and a detailed photograph was taken. The body was then re-interred. An exhumation order from a judge was obviously not a requirement in 1885, for this was the second time that Preller's casket had been exhumed. On August 15, Clover, McDonald, and Morgue Superintendent John Ryan went to the cemetery and disinterred the body to see if it was in a condition to warrant the expense of sending for witnesses from New York and Canada.

On August 29, a *Globe-Democrat* correspondent visited Samuel Brooks in Hyde, England. Brooks was the schoolmaster at St. George's School there.[a] The correspondent had with him four photographs of Maxwell. Brooks was shown the photographs and asked if he recognized any of them as his son. Brooks looked at the photographs and then replied, "It is our Hugh."[22]

On Monday, October 12, the Maxwell case went to the October-term grand jury of the criminal court and, while witnesses were still being questioned before the grand jury, Samuel Brooks arrived from England. Maxwell was brought to the room in which Samuel Brooks was seated. After warm greetings between the two, Brooks identified the prisoner as his son. Maxwell would say nothing about his case, except that he was twenty-three years old and that his name was Hugh Mottram Brooks.

On October 30, the grand jury made its report to Judge Van Wagoner of the criminal court. The grand jury indicted Maxwell on a charge of first-degree murder. Maxwell's trial would not begin, however, for another seven months.

*　　*　　*

In the interim, two former chiefs of police were in the news. John W. Campbell, who had been demoted from chief of police to patrolman on December 29, 1883, was promoted to sergeant.[23] William Lee, former chief of police and longtime police captain, who was dropped from the rolls in 1883 because of an ongoing illness, was reported to have recovered. The board appointed him as a special officer and ordered that he report to Vice President Blair "for inspection." No documentation was found to indicate if Lee received approval from Blair to continue as a special or whether he failed Blair's "inspection."[24] Lee died of what was described as a "paralytic stroke" on November 2, 1893.[25]

---

[a] Other reports listed Samuel Brooks as the proprietor of a bank in Cheshire.

Rumor and intrigue were the order of the day as the new year approached. It was rumored that Michael Callahan, treasurer of the board, and Frank Gaiennie, purchasing member, had aroused the ire of Governor Marmaduke for voting as they had in the earlier case against Chief Harrigan. During the board's deliberation in the case, the two had voted together with Mayor Francis, and against Commissioners Blair and Gooding, on virtually every specification and charge. By the middle of December, rumor had it that Governor Marmaduke had asked Callahan and Gaiennie to resign. Both were reported to have declined.[26]

On December 17, Governor Marmaduke removed Callahan from the board and replaced him with William H. Lee (no relation to Captain William Lee). He was appointed to a term expiring January 1, 1887. Lee, about thirty-eight years of age, was the president of the

William H. Lee. Engraving, 1915. Missouri History Museum.

Midland Blast Furnace Company and was reportedly a friend of both Governor Marmaduke and board vice president Blair.[27] Lee would join the board at the next regular meeting, December 22. Gaiennie was not only retained as the purchasing member of the board, but elected treasurer. And, contrary to the rumors, Gaiennie would serve on the board for the remainder of his four-year term.

1886

The first annual physical examinations of the police force had been completed, and board vice president James L. Blair informed the board that "a large number" of patrolmen had been found incapable of performing police duties. He recommended that the board take some action in the matter, but a plan was "laid over" until the next meeting.[28] As it happened, however, the question was tabled for almost two months. At the meeting of March 2, 1886, Vice President Blair moved, and it was adopted, that he be authorized "to make provision for aged, disabled and deserving patrolmen, ascertained by the medical examination of 1885 to be physically unsound and incapable of performing police duty, by dismissing such turnkeys who have not served as patrolmen, as he may select and appointing such patrolmen to their places." Eleven turnkeys resigned, and an equal number of officers requested demotion to turnkey to fill the jobs. One patrolman was reduced to janitor.[29]

The first meeting in March dealt with gambling and offered some insight into interstate law enforcement practices in the late nineteenth century. Vice President Blair submitted a report to the board about the form of gambling called "policy." For the past two years, certain gamblers had made it a practice to have an establishment across the Mississippi River in East St. Louis, Illinois, where fictitious "drawings" occurred. Vendors in St. Louis would then sell "tickets" or "chances" that contained numbers selected by the purchaser, "who pays a certain sum of money" for the privilege of selecting the numbers. Vendors had been arrested on the Missouri side of the river, but the courts had ruled that it was necessary to establish the existence of the office in East St. Louis. Blair sent two detectives, who not only established the fact that drawings were held there but, on February 20, raided the place and succeeded in taking the gambling paraphernalia as evidence. The evidence would be presented to the St. Louis grand jury.

The board approved Blair's actions.[30] On March 10, Blair authorized the two detectives in the case to go to Belleville, Illinois, to give testimony in the raid of February 20. Indictments were later returned in both St. Louis and St. Clair County, Illinois.[31]

At the meeting of April 13, Chief Harrigan informed the board that he had been nominated by President Grover Cleveland for the position of appraiser of the port of St. Louis. Accordingly, Chief Harrigan tendered his resignation "to take effect at your pleasure." Harrigan thanked the members of the board and the officers of the department for their cooperation while he was chief of police. The board accepted Chief Harrigan's resignation, which would take effect on May 4 unless his appointment was confirmed sooner by the U.S. Senate.

There was immediate speculation as to the identity of the next chief of police. The *Globe-Democrat*, for example, maintained that it was unlikely that anyone from outside the police department would be appointed. The person appointed would be selected from among the six captains. The newspaper said that the board had earlier declared that it would make promotions based on merit. If that were the case, then Captain Anton (Tony) Huebler, commander of the Second District, was the most qualified, "though he was not of the proper political stripe."[32] (Huebler was a Republican.) Some of his close friends, however, told the *Globe-Democrat* that Huebler didn't want the job.

At the meeting of May 4, the board formally accepted the resignation of Harrigan. In executive session, two men were nominated for the position, Captain Huebler and Sergeant (and former chief of police) John Campbell. Huebler was selected and, despite the previous comments of his friends, accepted the position.[33] He had joined the police force as a patrolman on March 14, 1865, and was promoted to sergeant on July 7, 1868, and to captain on March 21, 1871. He would begin his term as chief of police on May 5.

While in executive session, and before the selection of Captain Huebler as the next chief of police, Mayor Francis and the other members of the board became involved in a dispute over some quotes in a recent newspaper article attributed to the mayor. In reply, Mayor Francis stated that he had been misquoted. Whether the newspaper quotes were a pretext for the next action of the board is not known. Over the protest of Mayor Francis, the board passed a resolution that reinterpreted a portion of Rule 12 of the police manual ("The acting President of the Board shall have a general supervision . . .") to mean that the vice president of the board was the executive officer of the board. The executive officer, stated the resolution, "shall at all times, when the Board is not in session, have the entire management and control of the Department, subject always to the approval of the Board, and further, that the Chief of Police shall between the meetings of the Board, receive and obey the orders of the Vice President only."[34] The resolution was adopted on a 4–1 vote, with only Mayor Francis voting against it.

The next day, Mayor Francis sought an injunction to restrain the board from enforcing the resolution. On May 17, Circuit Court Judge Amos Thayer rendered a decision sustaining the validity of the resolution of May 4, declaring that the same contained a lawful delegation of authority by the board.[35] Mayor Francis appealed the decision to the Missouri Supreme Court, which quickly took up the mayor's appeal and, in a unanimous decision, reversed the judgment of the circuit court. The Missouri Supreme Court found that the resolution passed by the board on May 4 was invalid because it was "in conflict with the existing state statutes and the charter of the city." The court found that "the mayor of the city of St. Louis is the chief executive officer of the city, charged to take care that the laws of the state and ordinances of the city are enforced in the city, and he cannot be deprived of his lawful control of the police force by the police board of said city."[36] This decision seemed to go to the other extreme, placing the mayor above the Board of Police Commissioners.

One reaction to the decision of the Missouri Supreme Court was the resignation of Police Commissioner William H. Lee. On June 22, Lee sent his letter of resignation to Governor Marmaduke. In the letter Lee said, in part:

> When I accepted the position I was governed by two motives— my desire to serve the State and my wish to oblige you. I accepted and am willing to hold the office only as it has been held since the

creation of the metropolitan system. The decision of the Supreme Court taking the control of the police from the Commissioners and giving it to the Mayor (for every intelligent man knows that is what the decision means and nothing else) makes it improper for me with my views to remain. The decision of the court reverses the unquestioned practices of the police department for twenty-five years and I believe is a great surprise to all of those who at any time since 1861 have been associated with the police department.[37]

The Supreme Court decision would later be appealed.

✳   ✳   ✳

On Monday, May 10, 1886, some nine months after Maxwell's return to St. Louis from New Zealand and more than a year after the murder of C. Arthur Preller at the Southern Hotel, jury selection began in his murder trial. It took more than a week to select a twelve-man jury from the three hundred men who constituted the jury pool. The jury would be sequestered on the third floor of the Four Courts building.[38]

Judge G. S. Van Wagoner's courtroom was packed on the afternoon of May 18. The state was represented by Circuit Attorney Ashley Clover and Assistant Circuit Attorneys C. Orrick Bishop and Marshall McDonald. The defendant was represented by P. W. Fauntleroy and John I. Martin. Bishop made the opening statement and read the grand jury indictment of Walter H. Lennox Maxwell (alias Brooks, alias Dauquier) for first-degree murder.[b] He then outlined the events leading to the murder, the murder itself, the details of Brooks's escape to New Zealand, and what the state expected to prove.[39]

A deputy sheriff was then asked to call the roll of the state's approximately fifty witnesses. At the conclusion of the roll call, Clover asked for the names of the witnesses for the defense; P. W. Fauntleroy replied that the defense had no witnesses.

The state's witnesses ranged from chambermaids and desk clerks at the Southern Hotel, to Detectives James Tracy and George Badger,

---

[b] From this point, Maxwell will be referred to as Brooks unless the name Maxwell is used in a direct quotation. Exceptions will be footnoted.

to Dr. Luedeking of Washington University. On the morning of the sixth day of the trial (court was in session on Saturdays), after several witnesses had testified and been cross-examined, a man in a gray suit entered the courtroom, was sworn in, and took the stand. No one besides Clover and McDonald knew the identity of the witness. As the stranger took the stand, however, it became apparent by the startled look on the defendant's face and the quick conversation with his attorneys that Brooks also knew the witness.

When asked his name by Marshall McDonald, the witness identified himself as John F. McCullough. His occupation, detective. When asked where and with whom he had been employed as a detective, McCullough replied that he had worked for three years with Pinkerton in New York, then with the United States Secret Service for the district of New York and, just before coming to St. Louis, as the chief store detective for Wannamaker and Brown. He had resigned from Wannamaker and Brown in February 1886 to accept a position with Thomas Furlong, chief of the Missouri Pacific Railroad secret service. McCullough was based in Philadelphia.[40]

In answer to questions, McCullough said that he knew Brooks, having met him "in the city jail."[41] After he arrived in St. Louis, McCullough had been introduced to Thomas Furlong, who put him on the Brooks case. He was confined to the jail for forty-seven days, posing as one Frank Dingfelder, supposedly jailed on a charge of forgery. Said the witness, "I was employed by Thomas Furlong and Mssrs. Clover and McDonald."[42] Circuit Attorney Clover was personally paying McCullough's regular salary during this time.[43]

McCullough testified that he had first met Brooks when they were routinely let out of their cells for an hour in the morning and in the afternoon. About ten days after they first met, said the witness, Brooks began to talk with him. McCullough told Brooks that he was the head of a gang of forgers and was in jail because he had been caught with a forged check in his possession. Over time, said McCullough, Brooks began to speak about his case. He gave McCullough a detailed account of how he murdered Preller, what he did in St. Louis before his trip west, and other details probably known only to Preller's killer or the police. McCullough told Brooks that he could arrange to have some members of his "gang" provide perjured alibis for him.

After forty-seven days in the city jail, Thomas Furlong arranged for McCullough to be released on bail and, later that night, to take a train to New York. McCullough did not return to St. Louis until the morning he was to testify.[44] On May 25, the seventh day of the trial, the prosecution concluded its case and court was adjourned until ten o'clock the next morning.

Attorney P. W. Fauntleroy presented the opening statement for the defense. Fauntleroy said that Preller and Brooks (using the defendant's real name) had become friends on the steamer from England to Boston. Preller had appointments in other cities, but he and Brooks had agreed to meet in St. Louis. They would then travel to Auckland together.

After they met in St. Louis, Brooks, who Fauntleroy said had considerable medical knowledge, eventually came to the conclusion that Preller was suffering from [urethral] stricture. Brooks and Preller agreed that Brooks should treat the stricture through the use of a catheter. Brooks and Preller continued their preparations for the trip to Auckland and, on Sunday afternoon, April 12, 1885, Preller went to Brooks's room to have the operation. Preller was given chloroform to render him unconscious and he died from the chloroform. Brooks tried every means to revive Preller, said Fauntleroy, but was unsuccessful. Brooks panicked. He decided to put Preller's body in one of his trunks. The defense attorney closed his statement denouncing detective John McCullough as a party to "a dastardly and damnable plot."[45]

The defendant took the stand to testify in his own behalf. He identified himself as Hugh Mottram Brooks. Under questioning by his attorney, he stated that after Preller died he began drinking and wandering the city until about nine or ten o'clock that night. He then returned to his room at the Southern Hotel. After a fitful night of sleep, Brooks decided that he had to get away. Brooks left the hotel and bought two new trunks and a ticket to San Francisco.

Brooks admitted that he had written the note attached to the inside of the trunk in which he had stuffed Preller. He said that he was under the influence of alcohol and thought that it would confuse the authorities. He had also shaved off Preller's mustache to temporarily conceal Preller's identity. Brooks also admitted that he had cut Preller's chest with a scalpel, but was unable to offer an explanation. Brooks said that he had no intention of injuring or killing Preller. The examination of Brooks by his attorney was so thorough and enlightening that the prosecution didn't raise a single objection.

Brooks testified for two additional hours the following morning before his cross-examination by Circuit Attorney Clover. During the cross-examination, Brooks admitted that he had never attended Christ Church College at Oxford University and had no degree in medicine. Brooks also had never attended the Royal College of Surgeons in London. He acknowledged that he had filled in the blank diploma from the Royal College.

In the meantime, in an effort to prove that Preller did not have a disease, his body was exhumed for the third time. Circuit Attorney Clover was accompanied by Dr. T. F. Prewitt, dean of the Missouri Medical College, Coroner Dr. James C. Nidelet, and Dr. F. V. L. Brokaw. Various organs were removed and examined by the three doctors. No stricture was found, as claimed by Brooks, nor was there any evidence that any other organs were diseased. The three doctors would later testify to these findings.

Judge Van Wagoner began the court session of June 1 by giving instructions to the jury, guiding them through all of the possible findings and verdicts from which they must decide. Both sides then made final arguments. The case then went to the jury on Friday night, June 4. Any decision would have to be unanimous. The jury returned to the courtroom at 12:15 p.m. the next day. Judge Van Wagoner asked the foreman of the jury if it had agreed on a verdict. Brooks was found "guilty of murder in the first degree."[46]

Attorney Fauntleroy stated that the case would be appealed. Brooks was later sentenced to be hanged; appeals to the Missouri Supreme Court and the United States Supreme Court would take almost two years. On June 16, the criminal case against "Frank Dingfelder" (Detective John McCullough) was nol prossed (dropped without prosecution) by Circuit Attorney Clover.

✳   ✳   ✳

The board established a regulation police revolver at the meeting of June 22. The revolver was to be a .38-caliber double-action Colt revolver with either a rubber or wooden butt and blued metalwork. The district commanders were instructed to determine and report to Chief Huebler how many of the patrolmen and sergeants did not have such revolvers. The board would determine a supplier that was inexpensive, and officers without that type of revolver would have to purchase one from that supplier. At the next meeting, Purchasing Member Gaiennie reported that he had contracted with the E. C. Meacham Arms Company of St. Louis to supply the force with the regulation revolvers. Each would cost $9.

At the meeting of July 13, Edward Wilkerson presented his commission as a police commissioner. Wilkerson was appointed by Governor John Marmaduke on July 6, to fill the unexpired term of William H. Lee, who had resigned in June. Wilkerson's term would end on January 1, 1887.

Edward Wilkerson was president of the Covenant Mutual Life Insurance Company. He was active in Democratic politics in the Eighteenth Ward of the city and was characterized by one newspaper as "one of the few strong Marmaduke men in the city during the campaign."[47]

On December 1, Chief of Police Huebler, as was the custom, was detailed by the board "to make a tour of inspection through the principal Eastern cities for the purpose of examining into the workings of various police departments. . . ."[48] This board, as had previous boards, wanted to keep the police department current on police policies, procedures, and use of constantly emerging technologies.

Chief Huebler made his report at the first board meeting of 1887. He had visited the Washington, D.C.; Baltimore; Philadelphia; New York City; Boston; Cleveland; and Chicago police departments. As a result of his trip, Chief Huebler's recommendations included an increase in the size of the police force and the number of sergeants; a reduction in duty hours; the establishment of the ranks of inspector and lieutenant; the appointment of a police surgeon; the abolition of the military drill with muskets and the substitution of exercises with the police club; the separation of the police telephone system from other city departments; and an extension of the patrol wagon system.[49]

1887

On January 14, 1887, James L. Blair and Edward Wilkerson, whose terms expired on January 1, were reappointed by Governor Marmaduke for a term of four years ending January 1, 1891. At the next board meeting, January 18, Blair was reelected vice president, Wilkerson was elected treasurer, and Frank Gaiennie was reelected purchasing member. Oliver Gooding remained a member of the board.

The board then began to implement some of Chief Huebler's recommendations. They voted for creating the position of deputy chief of police; appropriating funds for "Medical and Surgical Attendance" for members of the force, under the direction of the board; changing the police district telephone system so that all telephone communications from the various districts would go through a switchboard in the office of the chief of police; securing appropriate funds to pay for the necessary instruments and salaries of employees that would be needed to operate the new system; and erecting a new Fourth District station house.[c] The board would also ask the city's Municipal Assembly to authorize an additional one hundred patrolmen, twenty sergeants, and five detectives to the force.[50]

At the following meeting, the board removed the creation of the deputy chief of police position from the list. While neither state laws nor city ordinances provided for such a position, obtaining the appropriate legislation would not have been an insurmountable hurdle. The withdrawal more likely involved funding priorities.[51]

At the last meeting of March, the board made additional uniform changes. Upon motion of Commissioner Gaiennie, it was ordered that

---

[c] The Fourth District station, at Tenth and North Market streets, was the only station house rented by the board. Funds had already been appropriated for the purchase of land and the construction of a new station.

hereafter the sergeants be required to wear upon their coat sleeves, between the shoulder and elbow, chevrons made of blue braid and, between the wrist and elbow, service straps of blue braid, one strap for each five years served in the department.[52]

On April 12, the board amended the uniform order to include captains. Captains were also ordered to wear one service strap for each five years of service. The service straps on the captain's uniforms would, however, be gold braid. For some unknown reason the effective date of the requirement was extended. Officers didn't begin wearing the service straps until the summer of 1888, but the straps remain on dress uniforms to this day.

At that same meeting, the board received a letter from a committee of the Woman's Christian Temperance Union recommending that the police department hire two additional matrons. The police department still had only one matron, Louisa Harris. The board responded that it would recommend to the Municipal Assembly that the salary for one additional matron be appropriated.[53] At the meeting of August 16, the board announced the hiring of a second police matron, Rosetta Hainsworth, who would be assigned to the main station of the Second Police District at 714 Soulard Street.

On March 28, the Missouri General Assembly repealed the forty-year-old Sunday Closing Law and replaced it with a new closing law that would become effective in June. At its meeting of April 19, the board asked the city counselor for guidance. When would the law actually take effect? Did the law compel the board to close dram shops, beer gardens, wine shops, and other places where intoxicating liquor was publicly sold? What about theaters, baseball games, parks, and other places of amusement?

The board entered City Counselor Leverett Bell's legal response in the minutes of the meeting of June 14. The law, said Bell, would take effect on Sunday, June 19. Anyone holding a dram shop license who sold or dispensed alcohol on Sunday would be guilty of a misdemeanor and liable to a fine of not more than $50. The license would also be forfeited and the licensee would be unable to obtain a new license for two years. Cases would be heard in the Court of Criminal Correction.

As to ballparks and other places of amusement, Bell added, the new law prohibited labor on Sunday other than works of necessity or charity. Bell noted, however, that it was his opinion that several avocations could be classified as "works of necessity." Bell then listed twenty-three occupations that included livery services of every kind, omnibuses and streetcars, hotels, laundries, bakeries, meat shops, ice dealers, physicians, undertakers, and druggists. It did not include professional sporting events, theaters, or other places of amusement.

The board then ordered that, beginning June 19 and continuing every Sunday thereafter, the chief of police was to see that all persons who "shall keep open any ale or porter house, or tippling shop or shall sell or dispense of any fermented vinous or spiritous liquors" would be arrested.[54] The board also ordered that arrests be made of anyone who opened any theater, baseball park, or other place of public amusement where an admission fee was charged.

On Saturday, June 18, City Counselor Bell amended the effective date of the Sunday Closing Law to June 26. Judge Edward Noonan of the Court of Criminal Correction had informed Bell that he believed that the law took effect on Monday, June 20. He would, therefore, dismiss any cases resulting from an arrest on June 19. As with the Sunday Closing Law of 1857, the new law was not popular. The section dealing with the sale of alcoholic beverages was especially problematic and would soon cause enforcement problems. A present-day problem was also an issue: "On the motion of Mr. Vice President Blair the Chief of Police was instructed to strictly enforce the ordinances relative to the discharge of Fire Arms and Fire Works on July 4th 1887."[55]

The Sunday Closing Law had been enforced on two Sundays when Mayor Francis called a special meeting of the board for Friday, July 8. Earlier that day, a case was tried in the Court of Criminal Correction that involved the selling of beer on Sunday. The judge in the Court of Criminal Correction threw the case out, ruling that the state law did not apply to the sale of beer and wine. City Counselor Bell advised that, since subsequent Sunday law cases would go to the same court, it would be useless to enforce the law with respect to beer and wine. The board then instructed Chief Huebler to discontinue the arrest of holders of dram shop licenses who sold beer and wine.

On Saturday, July 16, Mayor Francis called another special meeting of the board to deal with enforcement of the Sunday law. The meeting resulted in a resolution that declared that, due to the actions of the prosecutor and judge in the Court of Criminal Correction, "it appears to be impossible to enforce the Sunday Law in this city."[56] The board suspended all enforcement of the Sunday law except for the selling of distilled liquor.

A group of citizens filed a writ of mandamus in the circuit court to compel the Board of Police Commissioners to enforce that portion of the new state law prohibiting the sale of wine and beer on Sunday.[57] In its response, the board replied that the statute law of the state against the sale of wine and beer on Sunday did not apply to the city of St. Louis. The board cited an act of the state legislature, "an act conferring certain powers on the citizens of St. Louis," approved March 4, 1857, and subsequent ordinances of the city, to substantiate its position.

At the writ of mandamus hearing, Circuit Court Judge Leroy B. Valliant cited various Missouri Supreme Court cases as evidence that no state law gave the city of St. Louis the power to permit the sale of wine and beer on Sunday when state law prohibited it. Judge Valliant also gave his opinion regarding several technical aspects of the case. He ruled in favor of the appellants. City Counselor Bell informed the court that the board would appeal the ruling to the Missouri Supreme Court.[58] The state supreme court would not reach a decision for six months.

On Wednesday, December 28, Governor John S. Marmaduke died of "catarrhal pneumonia." Governor Marmaduke had complained of feeling unwell for several weeks and was diagnosed with pneumonia on the Monday before his death. Lieutenant Governor Albert P. Morehouse was sworn in as governor at 11:30 a.m. the next day. Morehouse had been a schoolteacher when he began the study of law. He was admitted to the Missouri Bar in 1860 and worked as a lawyer and a real estate agent. Before being elected lieutenant governor, he served two terms as a representative in the Missouri General Assembly.[59]

Mayor Francis called a special meeting of the board on December 29 "to take suitable action in view of the death of Gov. John S. Marmaduke. . . ."[60] The board appointed a committee to draft a resolution of respect for the deceased governor and ordered that the boardroom be draped in mourning for thirty days. Mayor Francis appointed the four members of the board to be a part of the St. Louis delegation to Governor Marmaduke's funeral in Jefferson City on December 31.[61] In January 1888, "a fine portrait of the late Gov. Marmaduke was hung in the board room."[62] The portrait was the work, and a gift, of photographer Harry Newbold.

1888

In February 1888, the board asked Chief Huebler for a written report of gambling and lottery enforcement efforts. His answer summarized the problems that police faced in their gambling enforcement efforts. Said the chief, in part:

> Two officers are specially assigned to that duty and many times, other officers are called into requisition as occasion requires. Much difficulty is encountered by the officers in the prosecution of those cases, as nearly all the evidence has to be relied upon from parties other than police officers, it is invariably the custom of parties arrested to ascertain the names of witnesses and if they are not police officers it is not infrequent, that they are by either threats, or money consideration, prevented from appearing in Court.[63]

In April, the Missouri Supreme Court handed down its ruling in the Sunday Law case. It reversed the ruling of the circuit court on various points. It did, however, uphold the court's ruling that the state law regarding the prohibition of wine and beer applied to the city of St. Louis. It ordered the board to vacate its July 8, 1887, order to Chief Huebler to discontinue enforcement against the selling of beer and wine on Sunday. The circuit court was instructed to amend the alternative and peremptory writs and reissue them with only the order that the board vacate the July 8 order to discontinue enforcement of the Sunday Law against those who sold beer and wine.[64]

The circuit court issued the amended writs returnable on May 21. A special meeting of the board was called on May 18 and the order of July 8, 1887, was rescinded. Chief Huebler was instructed to enforce the law.[65] The drinking public, however, was not to be discouraged by the enforcement of the Sunday Law.

The *St. Louis Globe-Democrat* cited some examples of the measures some citizens took to get a drink on Sunday.[66] The most common, and least ingenious, method was to look for the bartender (dressed in his Sunday best) standing in front of the closed doors of the saloon. The thirsty person was required to engage the bartender in conversation and, when the bartender offered to shake that person's hand, the individual had to close his left eye and whistle the tune "I Never Drink Behind the Bar." If the bartender felt that person was "okay," he would hand him a map to the rear door of the saloon. The map likely was the admission ticket through the back door.

A more elaborate scheme was the issuance of a "latchkey." The key-holder had to first know what door to enter. After walking through the door, he had to make his way through a long, dark passage with several angles and turns. At the end of the passage was a locked door. The latchkey would unlock the door, which led to the rear of the saloon, where as many as 150 other keyholders were drinking.

Another bar had a "Young Men's Reading Room" on the second floor over a saloon. Off of the reading room was a smaller room that contained a dumbwaiter. Next to the dumbwaiter was a box filled with cards. Each card contained the name of an alcoholic drink and the price. A patron had only to take out the card listing the drink he wanted and put it on the floor of the dumbwaiter with the necessary money. A push of a button lowered the dumbwaiter. It soon returned to the second floor with the desired drink. The saloon on the first floor was closed, but the bartender was busy mixing drinks and drawing beer to place on the dumbwaiter.

Other schemes included round dinner pails with a shallow upper compartment; the area beneath it could hold a quart of beer. Some grocers would fill the bottom with beer and pour milk into the upper compartment. The *Globe-Democrat* asserted that "men who never carried a dinner bucket in their lives now find them indispensable in the household."[67] There were quart bottles labeled "Dr. Sunday's Sparkling Tonic." Some grocers maintained a thriving Sunday business refilling the bottle with more of the sparkling tonic. As Mayor Francis had earlier noted, enforcing the Sunday Law seemed impossible.

While the Sunday Closing Law took much of the board's time, the board also had to prepare for the Democratic National Convention that would be meeting in St. Louis for three days beginning June 5. During the week following the convention, St. Louis would also be the site of the twenty-fifth annual national "Saengerfest" sponsored by the North American Saengerbund. Both would be held at the Exposition Hall at Thirteen and Olive streets, now the site of the main St. Louis Public Library building.

Chief Huebler asked the board to declare an "extraordinary emergency" and appoint one hundred emergency specials for a period of twenty days commencing June 1. The board did so, setting the pay of the emergency specials at $2 per day.[68] In addition, the monthly one day off (recreation day) for those below the rank of captain was canceled for the month of June.

The need for security was greatest at the Democratic National Convention. Chief Huebler took personal charge of the security: three captains, five sergeants, and seventy-six patrolmen provided security outside the hall. A captain, three sergeants, and twenty-four patrolmen were assigned to the convention floor. At the meeting of June 19, the board declared that the emergency no longer existed and all emergency specials were asked to resign. The total cost to the board was $3,360.

✳   ✳   ✳

Meanwhile, Hugh Brooks (Walter Maxwell) had exhausted all of his appeals in the Southern Hotel murder case. In January 1888, the U.S. Supreme Court had, for lack of jurisdiction, refused to hear Brooks's appeal.[69] Brooks applied for a rehearing before the court, but that also was refused. On June 4, the Missouri Supreme Court set an execution date of July 13. Brooks's attorneys then appealed to Governor Morehouse for a thirty-day stay of execution to allow Brooks "to prepare to meet his Maker" and also give his parents time to come from England for a final visit.[70] Governor Morehouse stayed the execution for twenty-eight days, setting Friday, August 10, as the day of execution.[71]

On August 2, U.S. Secretary of State Thomas Bayard sent a note to Governor Morehouse saying that the British government had asked for a "respite" of the execution "for further inquiry."[72] Brooks's attorneys also made last-minute appeals to the governor. Governor Morehouse replied that he would announce his decision at 9:00 a.m. on August 9. A few minutes after the appointed hour, the governor stated, "I have carefully considered it, and see no reason to change my former decision. The only reason I hesitated was on account of the request of the British Government for time to investigate the case . . . I know of no new evidence, and have no cause to believe that the British Government intends to conduct an investigation of the case."[73] Governor Morehouse also informed Secretary Bayard of his decision.

The attorneys for Brooks then asked for a delay of execution so that his old father might bid his son a last farewell. Governor Morehouse replied that he had already given a four-week extension for that reason. According to the attorneys, the elder Brooks could not leave his business at that time, so the governor again considered a delay. However, Morehouse decided not to delay the execution: Brooks would be hanged at 6:30 a.m. the next day.[74]

The scaffold from which Hugh Brooks would be hung was situated in the jail yard of the Four Courts. Built in 1875, the building had an arched roof and stood on stilts. The area below the floor of the scaffold was plainly visible. The execution party would have to first walk across the jail yard and then up a planked walkway supported by sawhorses. The makeshift walkway was built to permit access to the foot of the scaffold stairs from an embankment. Seven steps led to the floor of the scaffold.[75] There would be a double hanging on August 10. Brooks would be hanged next to one Henry Landgraff, who had been convicted for the murder of his girlfriend in 1885.[76]

At 8:45 a.m., Chief Deputy Sheriff Joseph Harrington entered the jail and read the death warrants. Brooks and Landgraff were led to the gallows in a single file by Sheriff Harrington with a Catholic priest between the two and a deputy sheriff on either side. Two deputies already on the scaffold placed the nooses around each prisoner's neck. Black hoods were placed over the heads of Brooks and Landgraff. The trapdoor dropped both men at 8:56 a.m. After physicians had declared both men dead, their bodies were taken to the city morgue for a postmortem examination and then released for transfer to undertakers.[77] Brooks was later buried in Calvary Cemetery in St. Louis.

After the execution, Sheriff Harrington was besieged by relic hunters wanting a piece of the rope used in the execution of Hugh Brooks. The sheriff handed the rope to a deputy, but the deputy left without giving pieces to anyone. The noose used in the execution of Brooks would become part of the police department exhibit in the Palace of Education at the 1904 Louisiana Purchase Exposition.[78] The trunk in which C. Arthur Preller's body was found would also become a part of the police department exhibit.

✻   ✻   ✻

Mayor David Francis was elected governor of Missouri at the general election on November 6, 1888. The governor-elect attended his last meeting as a member of the Board of Police Commissioners on November 20. In the meantime, the board decided to revisit the 1886 Missouri Supreme Court ruling, from a suit Mayor Francis filed, that stated: "The mayor of the city of St. Louis is the chief executive officer of the city, charged to take care that the laws of the state and ordinances of the city are enforced in the city, and he cannot be deprived of his lawful control of the police force by the police board of said city." The board apparently filed a demurrer in the circuit court that appealed the same issues as in the 1886 decision but added the ruling of the state supreme court, which made the mayor the executive officer of the board, to the appeal. The result in the circuit court was a ruling against the board. The board appealed to the Missouri Supreme Court.

The appeal was heard in the October 1888 term of the court.[79] The ruling took a slightly different but significant view of the issues. First, it upheld the 1886 finding that the board had no authority to make the vice president of the board the executive officer of the board when it was not in session. Second, it overruled that part of the 1886 ruling that stated that the mayor of St. Louis is the executive officer of the Board of Police Commissioners when the board is not in session. The court held that Missouri laws superseded the city charter. While the city charter provided that the mayor was the executive officer of the city, state law charged the Board of Police Commissioners with establishing and operating the police force. Finally, the court added a new wrinkle to the mix. The mayor and the police commissioners were members of the board, said the court, but the board had no power to designate an individual member to perform duties ascribed by law to the entire board. In other words, the board had no executive officer. The executive officers of the police department were the chief of police and other top-ranking members of the force. This last pronouncement would cause policy changes within the department.

1889

The year 1889 started on a bizarre note. In the fall of 1888, the area of London, England, known as Whitechapel had been the scene of several murders of prostitutes by the infamous Jack the Ripper. As the new year dawned, St. Louis became the scene of a copycat malefactor. He called himself "Jack, the Kisser."[80]

This criminal, who operated in the general area of Garrison and Cass avenues (on the near north side of the city), would stop lone women on the street, ask them directions or use some other diversionary tactic, then take them into his arms and kiss them. He would then hand them a printed card titled "Compliments of JACK THE KISSER." The inscription on the card read: "Any lady who has been kissed three times by Jack and retains this card is entitled to membership in the Grand Army of the Redeemed. Jack's kiss purifies but never defiles. His mission is divine, and his kiss devoid of sensuality."[81] On the reverse side of the card were two poetic verses explaining his actions.

Newspaper reporters began to watch for him, as did several police detectives. It was even said that husbands and fathers had offered rewards for his capture, and at least one young woman was hired to decoy Jack while the husband or father of an earlier victim waited on the other side of a fence. The *Post-Dispatch* referred to Jack as the "osculatory knight."[82]

On Tuesday, January 29, the lone female reporter for the *Post-Dispatch*, Julia Hale, was given the assignment to find Jack the Kisser. She spent the next three days interviewing women who had been kissed by Jack. Descriptions of the man were virtually nonexistent, only that he was handsome and had a moustache. Hale found one woman who described Jack as tall, with gray hair and a moustache, but none of the victims had any idea whether he was "handsomely or shabbily dressed."[83]

On Friday evening, Hale, dressed in her best clothes, set out for the area of Garrison Avenue and Olive Street to find Jack. She walked down several streets in the vicinity and began walking west on Locust Street. A man rose from the stone coping around a church and stood in her path. Hale screamed, but the man said he would not harm her. He eventually kissed her several times before he was scared off by a group of young men coming up Locust Street. As he departed, Jack told her that he would meet her at the same location on Tuesday evening (February 5). Hale described Jack as about five feet, ten inches, long gray hair, with a long moustache not quite as gray as his hair, bushy white eyebrows, and "a winning smile." She was also unable to describe his clothing.[84] Julia Hale wrote her story for the following Sunday edition.

The following Tuesday, a letter signed "Jack, the Kisser" appeared in the *Post-Dispatch*. Jack said that Hale was, at first, a crude kisser, but she got better as they continued to kiss for half an hour. "Julia needed kissing," said the letter.[85]

Hale met Jack that evening. A police officer in plain clothes was stationed in a yard at Garrison Avenue and Locust Street to make the arrest, but Hale wandered away from the prescribed meeting place and out of the officer's sight. Jack refused to answer any of Hale's questions about his identity or give any straight answers as to why he went about kissing strange women. He did, however, kiss Hale until a stranger approached. He then ran from the scene.[86]

In a letter to Judge Edward Noonan of the Court of Criminal Correction, Jack the Kisser asked Noonan not to "put me down as a crank. I am only fulfilling a mission of mercy and love. I would not harm a hair of any lady's head. If fate should cast me into the dock, Judge, remember that you will have no criminal to deal with, but a gentleman who loves his fellow-beings and only desires to save them."[87]

Noonan told the press that Jack's mission would "cease for at least a year if he comes up here before me."[88] The *Globe-Democrat* noted that there were "several gentlemen along Cass avenue who are looking for Jack the Kisser and if they locate him he will hardly be able to appear outside a hospital for some weeks at least."[89]

Jack the Kisser disappeared as quickly as he had appeared. In spite of a continued vigilance by the police and the public, he was never caught. About 7:00 p.m. on Saturday, February 9, a man entered the stationery store–newsstand on the St. Louis approach to the Eads Bridge. He told the proprietor that he was leaving St. Louis but, never having crossed the bridge on foot, he decided to do so "to get a view of the river front as it appears by gas-light."[90] The man bought some stationery and began writing. He wrote for about fifteen minutes before departing the store and walking east on the bridge.

A man driving east across the bridge in his buggy reported that he met a young woman on foot hurrying toward St. Louis. The woman asked the buggy driver if there was a policeman near. He replied that there was one "a little ways back there."[91] He asked the woman what was the matter, and she said that she had met Jack the Kisser. He said he was going to East St. Louis, and then he kissed her. As he turned to continue east on the bridge Jack asked the woman if she lived in St. Louis. "If you do, you will be the last girl that Jack the Kisser will ever embrace in that city. I bid it farewell to-night. Reluctantly I do so, but duty calls me hence. Good-by, and don't forget me." As he bragged in a note found in the relay depot in East St. Louis, Jack had also kissed some young women in that city.[92]

A telegram to the *Globe-Democrat* from an unnamed Cincinnati, Ohio, source stated that a man calling himself "Jack the Kisser" had kissed several women on the streets of that city.[93] There were no further reports of Jack the Kisser in St. Louis.

*   *   *

On January 12, board vice president James Blair addressed the council committee of the Municipal Assembly in an effort to obtain an increase in the size of the police force. Said Blair, "St. Louis, with a larger area than any cities of the first class, with the exception of Philadelphia, has a force of patrolmen 135 less than Baltimore, which is one of the smallest of these cities."[94] He cited examples such as the Thirteenth Ward in the southern portion of the city: The entire Ward was patrolled by one police officer. Some of Blair's comments were particularly notable:

> The present board are unanimously in favor of shortening the hours of duty from twelve hours, the present limit, to eight hours, which is work enough for any man to do, considering the duties a patrolman has to perform. We cannot do this unless the force is increased by the addition of at least one hundred men. With this increase we can divide the force into three platoons, the first and smallest to serve from 6 a.m. to 2 p.m., the second from 2 p.m. to 10 p.m., and the third from 10 p.m. to 6 a.m. . . . At present the men have no time for recreation. It is frequently the case after being on duty all night they are obliged to be in the court rooms as witnesses or performing extra duty, such as serving notices of dog licenses, broken lamp-posts, sidewalks out of repair and reporting the sanitary conditions of alleys and backyards, and thousands of other matters with which they are charged . . . for the patrolman is the general utility man of the city.[95]

Blair made a case for additional sergeants. There was a sergeant in charge of each of the fifteen station houses and substations on both platoons. The remaining fifteen sergeants were in charge of two platoons of patrolmen. The board, said Blair, wanted to subdivide the Central District, requiring authorization for one additional captain. While only two and one-half square miles in size, the district had a population of 120,000. "This territory embraces as great a population and as large an area as are found in the limits of some large cities...."[96] Blair identified the detective force as "utterly insufficient... they have an immense amount of routine work...."[97]

Perhaps the most noteworthy of Vice President Blair's comments came in his concluding remarks:

> Policemen by the very necessities of their office have the hand of every man against them. There are times when they are obliged to be in a position of hostility to almost every man in the community. There are few of us, indeed, who do not infringe some of the laws or ordinances which it is the duty of the policeman to enforce. Unlike the Fire Department, which receives nothing but the sympathy and admiration of the community, whose duties are such as to endear them to the hearts of every citizen, the policeman has none of these consolations. From morning till night he is engaged in some disagreeable task, incurring the displeasure of somebody, and in return gets but scanty pay, double work and no sympathy.[98]

City Ordinance 14,914 would be approved on March 26.[99] The ordinance increased the authorized strength of the force by 1 captain, 15 sergeants, and 135 patrolmen. It allowed not more than 7 captains, 59 sergeants, 535 patrolmen, and 10 detectives and was only the second increase in size since the new charter took effect in 1876. Unfortunately, for Blair and the other members of the board, the passage of the ordinance was bittersweet.

A month after his inauguration, Governor Francis replaced the entire Board of Police Commissioners. On February 11, Francis appointed John H. Overall and Charles H. Turner to four-year terms to expire on January 1, 1893. On February 15, Francis removed James L. Blair, who had refused to resign,[100] and Edward Wilkerson. They were replaced by George H. Small and Julius S. Walsh, who were appointed for two-year terms. The new board would have its first meeting on Tuesday, February 19.[101]

The board went into executive session at its first meeting. John Overall was elected vice president, and George Small was elected treasurer and purchasing member. Acting Mayor George Allen nominated Henry G. Paschall as a replacement for the present secretary of the board, Frank R. Tate. Tate had been secretary since January 1885. Paschall was elected to the position effective March 1.

John Overall was a graduate of Missouri State University and Harvard. He returned to St. Louis and, after further study, began the practice of law. In 1872, he became dean of the law department of the University of Missouri–Columbia. He returned to St. Louis

John H. Overall. Steel engraving by Central Biography Publishing Company, 1898. Missouri History Museum.

two years later and joined a law firm. Overall soon formed his own law firm, Overall and Judson, where he was practicing at the time of his appointment to the Board of Police Commissioners.[102] Charles Turner was in the real estate business. He was the owner of Charles H. Turner and Company, with offices in the Turner Building at 304 North Eighth Street. George Small was described as a commission merchant who, at the time of appointment, was a principal in the firm of Small and Raisin. Small was a Democrat and had never held public office.[103] Julius Walsh held a law degree but never practiced law. Instead, he worked for his father, Edward Walsh, who was a successful merchant. In 1870, he became president of the Citizen's (Franklin Avenue) Street railway line. He later became president and principal stockholder of the Fairgrounds and also the Suburban, Union, Cass Avenue, and Northern Central lines. He sold his interest in these lines to others in December 1888.[104] On March 15, Julius Walsh

Julius S. Walsh. Engraving, 1915. Missouri History Museum.

unexpectedly resigned. He had attended only one board meeting, the organizational meeting of February 19. Walsh was reported to be in ill health, while other reports indicated that he had not really wanted the post on the board but took it at the urging of his friends and friends of Governor Francis.[105]

In Walsh's place, Governor Francis appointed Benjamin F. Hammett. In 1877, Governor Phelps appointed him to be state tobacco inspector. Hammett went into the real estate business in St. Louis two years later. He became the first person to buy and subdivide acreage in St. Louis. A year before his appointment to the board he formed the Hammett, Anderson, Wade Real Estate Company.[106]

At the meeting of March 19, Chief Huebler recommended that the board revise the police manual. While amended over the years, the police department was still using the 1874 manual. A new manual would be adopted a year after Chief Huebler's recommendation.[107]

Benjamin F. Hammett. Steel engraving by Central Biography Publishing
Company, 1898. Missouri History Museum.

The patrol wagon system continued to be expanded, but still covered only half the districts. An additional patrol wagon was purchased and considered for use in the Fifth (Mounted) District.[108] Officers from the Fifth District (some of whom were on foot) continued to patrol those areas of the city outside of the western boundaries of the other four districts. Approximately forty-five of the city's sixty-two and a half square miles (72 percent) were contained in the Fifth District. The eight sergeants and eighty-seven patrolmen were assigned to the Fifth District's main station at 2835 Market Street and to six substations ranging from the Fairgrounds and O'Fallon Park on the north side of the city, to Gravois Road and Arsenal, and Virginia and Meramec streets on the south side.[109] All of the horses were stabled at the main station on Market Street as was the Black Maria, the van that

Early patrol wagon in front of Four Courts. Baker photo, courtesy of SLMPD.

took prisoners from the various stations to the main jail at Headquarters or to the city workhouse.[110]

At the next board meeting, Sergeant (and former chief of police) John Campbell was promoted to captain.[111] Upon the recommendation of Chief Huebler, Captain Campbell was transferred to Police Headquarters for night duty. This was the first mention of a command-rank officer performing night duty at Headquarters; Campbell became the night chief of police."[112] The board also began to appoint emergency specials to fill the newly created patrolman positions. They were appointed after they had passed physical exams and had complied with Rule 96 ("Qualifications of Policemen"). Emergency specials received a monthly salary of $60 and were subject to termination at any time.

The city election was held on April 2. Former Court of Criminal Correction judge Edward Noonan was elected mayor. He would, however, not attend his first meeting as ex officio president of the board until May 7.

As had previous boards, the new board responded to calls for help. It approved a request by a delegation of citizens representing various German singing societies of St. Louis that police officers be permitted to sell tickets for "an entertainment" to be given at Exposition Hall on Monday, June 17, for the benefit of the victims of the Johnstown, Pennsylvania, flood of May 31.[113]

Also in June, apparently because of the accidental shooting of a citizen by a patrolman, the board directed the captains to check the condition of the pistols carried by their men and send a report to the board. The captains submitted their reports at the next meeting, and the board found that there were still officers possessing nonregulation revolvers in violation of the order of June 22, 1886. Permitting the Smith and Wesson .38-caliber revolver to act as a substitute if an officer already owned one, the board ordered that all officers not using a Colt or Smith and Wesson revolver must purchase a Colt .38-caliber revolver.[114]

The board appointed by Governor Francis wanted not only to have officers carrying the same make and caliber revolvers, but wanted them to present a nice appearance. At the meeting of August 6, the board read a report written by Chief Huebler reporting the findings of his recent inspection of uniforms worn by police officers. Upon Huebler's recommendation, the board established the position of inspector of uniforms. Patrolman William Parell of the Second District was appointed to fill that position.

At the final board meeting of 1889, the board passed a resolution that established a new police department policy, funeral leave. "It is ordered by the Board that in case of the death of his wife child father mother brother & sister of an officer of the force, such officer shall have leave of absence for three days without reduction of pay."[115] There would be more changes in 1890.

Chapter Eight

Entering the Gay Nineties

1890

At the end of April 1890, the board instructed Chief Huebler to notify the commanders that the rule regarding a recreation day (one paid day off each month) would be revoked effective May 1.[1] The minutes of the board meeting did not give a reason for the revocation. But it became evident when Commissioner George H. Small introduced the new police manual and a resolution "that the foregoing Rules & Regulations for the government of the Police Department of the City of St. Louis be adopted, and that all rules & parts of rules inconsistent therewith be and the same are hereby repealed." The resolution was adopted by the board and the new manual was effective that day, May 14, 1890.[2]

Among the new provisions was a rule allowing each police officer an annual vacation of eight consecutive days, the first vacation afforded members of the police force. The detective force was given a formal name, the Bureau of Criminal Investigation. The uniform for the chief of police was changed to include army-regulation colonel's shoulder straps. To this point, the chief of police had not been given a rank, only a title.

Chief Huebler would not long enjoy his new rank and shoulder straps. At the next meeting, Charles Turner noted that Huebler's four-year term had expired. He moved that a new chief of police be elected to replace him, and that two new captains be elected to replace Captains Edward McDonald and Joseph Hercules, whose four-year terms also had expired.[3] Both men were in poor health; Captain Hercules would die of cancer four months later.

George Small then moved that former Chief Laurence Harrigan be elected the new chief of police. Harrigan was unanimously elected to a four-year term. Huebler was unanimously elected to a four-year term as captain, replacing Hercules, and Sergeant Mathew Kiely was elected to a four-year term as captain. Like James McDonough before him, Laurence Harrigan was serving his third term as chief of police.

In June, the chief of police of Milwaukee, Wisconsin, requested that the board furnish him with two men from the detective force to assist him during the biennial session of the Supreme Lodge of the Knights of Pythias, convening on July 7, 1890. The request continued the unwritten mutual aid policy that saw big-city police departments sending detectives to crowded events in other cities in an attempt to identify pickpockets and other thieves who gravitated to the events from those cities. Chief Harrigan was instructed to detail two men for that purpose.[4]

The first requests for the eight-day annual vacations were granted by the board in July.[5] Officers began requesting twelve- and fifteen-day furloughs now that eight of the days would be paid. The "annual vacation furloughs" were suspended from September 1 through October 11, however, because of the annual Agricultural and Mechanical Fair and other events that required the full complement of officers.[6]

About 7:30 on the night of August 25, Patrolman Louis H. Wilmers saw a man, known to him as Louis Crabtree, in the Frisco Railroad yards near the Tower Grove station. Patrolman Wilmers approached Crabtree and was in the process of arresting and searching him when Crabtree pushed the officer away and ran down the tracks. Officer Wilmers was running past a pile of lumber when he saw "the gleam of a revolver, then a flash," and he fell to the ground, struck in the back.[7] The suspect again began running away as Patrolman Wilmers fired three shots at him. The officer's shots missed, and Crabtree made his escape.

Patrolman Wilmers was taken to his home on Old Manchester Road and medical attention summoned. The bullet had apparently struck his spine, causing paralysis in the lower half of his body. On August 29, he was moved to St. Luke's Hospital to undergo surgery. He died on September 4.[8]

Louis Crabtree, meanwhile, had hopped an outgoing Frisco freight train. It was thought that he might be going to the Missouri towns of Pacific or Union, where he had once lived, or to Dent County, in the southwestern part of Missouri. Telegrams were sent to all the small railroad stations west of St. Louis on the Frisco line alerting the stationmasters of the search for Crabtree. On August 28, Crabtree was seen in the vicinity of Salem, in Dent County. Authorities were alerted by telegram, and Crabtree was arrested. Captain Campbell left on the first train to return him to St. Louis.[9] The disposition of Crabtree's case is not known.

At the board meeting of September 16, Hugh O'Neil was relieved from duty as sergeant of detectives and assigned as a detective in the Lafayette Park substation of the Second District. It was believed that O'Neil asked to be relieved of the position because of ill health and was placed in charge of the office at the substation.[10] His replacement was Detective William Desmond, who was thirty-five years old and had been appointed to the police department in 1876, becoming a detective four years later.[11]

Another police officer was killed on October 6. Patrolman John Gaffney was attempting to move a crowd watching a fight between two men in front of Starkes's Saloon at 715 N. Eleventh Street. One of the two men fighting, Luther Duncan, shoved Gaffney. Duncan was asked to move on or face arrest. Duncan cursed the officer and refused to move. At this, the crowd moved in and, when Gaffney laid his hand on Duncan, Duncan punched the officer in the face. Luther Duncan, his brother Harrison Duncan, and others in the crowd grabbed the officer and threw him onto the streetcar tracks on Eleventh Street. They began to kick and hit Gaffney, and his baton was taken from him. There were cries from the crowd to kill the officer. Gaffney was left lying unconscious on the street.[12]

The officer recovered consciousness and, as he rose to his feet, drew his revolver. He fired twice in the air to attract the attention of other officers in the vicinity. Gaffney followed the crowd, including Luther Duncan, into the saloon and arrested him in the billiard hall portion of the saloon. Luther Duncan started to go with the officer, who still had his revolver drawn, when someone shouted, "Don't shoot." Gaffney turned his head in the direction of the shout when Harrison Duncan struck him a violent blow to the head with a billiard cue stick, causing a gash over his eye and on his head. Harrison Duncan then grabbed Gaffney's gun.[13]

Two officers, identified only as Maloney and Conners, reacted to Gaffney's shots. They entered and found Gaffney with blood streaming down his face. The officer pointed out Harrison Duncan as the man who had struck him. Patrolman Maloney, who was closest to Harrison Duncan, told Duncan to put up his hand. Duncan raised the hand in which he held Gaffney's revolver and fired two shots at Maloney and one at Conners. Both Maloney and Conners dropped to the floor and returned fire. Harrison Duncan got behind the bar for cover.[14]

Patrolman James Brady, who had also come off his beat in response to the shots fired by Gaffney outside the saloon, entered the saloon to assist. Brady approached the bar, and Duncan suddenly jumped up, fired, and again dropped behind the bar. Officer Brady yelled to Duncan to surrender. Getting no response, Brady leaned over the counter and fired one shot at Duncan. As Brady was straightening up after leaning over the bar, Duncan sprang up and fired one shot at Officer Brady, hitting him in the chest. At the same time, Officers Maloney and Conners fired at Duncan, wounding him in the side, and then rushed to assist Officer Brady. Harrison Duncan then tried to escape by slipping around one end of the bar. Officer Conners saw Duncan and, pointing his pistol at Duncan, told him to stop. Officer Conners then told Duncan, "If you raise that gun I will kill you." Duncan replied, "I've killed one; I'm satisfied," and threw Gaffney's gun behind the bar. Conners then secured him and took him to the station.[15]

William Henry Harrison Duncan was charged with first-degree murder. He was tried in Clayton, the county seat of St. Louis County, on a change of venue.[16] Duncan was defended by Walter Farmer, a black lawyer, and George Royse, a white Clayton attorney. Farmer had, the previous year, been the first black man to graduate from the law school at Washington University in St. Louis.[17] Duncan, who maintained his innocence throughout the trial, was found guilty and sentenced to death by hanging. On July 27, 1894, after exhausting all his appeals, Duncan was hanged in Clayton.[18]

The owner of the saloon where the shooting took place, Charles Starkes, died several weeks before Duncan's execution. Before he died, Starkes admitted that it was he, not Duncan, who had fired the shot that killed Officer Brady.[19] Unfortunately, this information did not become known until after Duncan's execution. The folk ballad "Brady and Duncan" grew out of the incident and "became a protest against police brutality and a song for civil rights."[20]

1891

In March, the board revisited the issue of wearing uniforms while off duty. The board had first ordered the off-duty wearing of uniforms on October 28, 1867. The board ordered a ninety-day suspension of the order on February 7, 1882, a second on May 2, 1882, and a third on August 22, 1882.

No further reference was made to the issue when the last ninety-day suspension concluded in November 1882, and the 1890 police manual did not contain any requirement that off-duty officers wear their uniforms. That changed at the meeting of March 17 when the requirement that the police uniform be worn off duty was reinstituted. The board gave no reason for its action.

The two-year terms of board members George H. Small and Benjamin F. Hammett had officially expired on January 1. It was not until March, however, that Governor David R. Francis made his decisions about replacements. Small was reappointed on March 17 for a four-year term ending January 1, 1895. On that same day, Hammett was replaced by David W. Caruth, who also received a four-year appointment. Caruth had previously been a board member, serving from January 1883 to January 1885. Hammett had asked Governor Francis not to reappoint him as his business required frequent absences from the city.[21]

On April 22, the state legislature approved an act amending a portion of the 1861 act that established the metropolitan police in St. Louis and some amendments to that act. The newly approved act was titled Support of Disabled Policemen. The first section required that the board determine the additional amount of money necessary to enable it to carry out the provisions of the act and to certify it to the Municipal Assembly. In turn, the Municipal Assembly was required to, "as soon as possible, set apart and appropriate the amount so required...."[22]

The second section was the core of the legislation: support of disabled police officers and pensions for retiring officers. The act also required that vacancies in any rank, except the chief of police, were to be filled from the next lowest rank "if competent men can be found therein."[23]

A third section concerned policemen killed in the performance of police duty or receiving injuries from which they later died. If an officer left a widow or child or children under the age of sixteen, the board was required, upon satisfactory proof of such facts, to direct that a monthly payment of one-half of the officer's salary be provided the widow until she died or remarried. Absent a widow, the child or children would receive that amount until the age of sixteen.[24]

The final section provided retirement procedures. Under the act, an officer who served for twenty years or more "may in the discretion of said board be retired from active service, and be thereafter paid during his natural life a yearly salary equal to one-half the amount of the salary attached to the rank which he may have held on such police force for one year next preceding his retirement."[25] This was not a voluntary twenty-year service retirement, but a law permitting the board to retire officers who, with twenty or more years of service, were adjudged unfit for duty because of a debilitating illness or physical disability.

The state legislature also passed an act enabling St. Louis's legislative body to pass ordinances designating some streets as "boulevards." After passage of an ordinance, a street designated as a boulevard could be developed as a major thoroughfare. Some of the first streets so designated were Delmar, Lindell, Forest Park, Page, Union, and Washington.[26]

At the last meeting of April, the board altered its vacation policy. It adopted a rule that permitted each officer one vacation day a month, except in June, September, and October, effectively increasing the paid vacation days. In addition, officers were given the option to take one day a month (except in June, September, and October), or as nine consecutive vacation days.[27]

At the last meeting of June, the board approved the addition of a sixth police district and the alteration of the boundaries of adjacent districts. The new district covered the entire northeast portion of the city north of Delmar Avenue and west of Grand Avenue, with the main station on the southeast corner of Deer Street and Easton Avenue.[28] Because the new district included the Fairgrounds and O'Fallon Park, it inherited the Fairgrounds substation and the recently constructed substation at the north end of O'Fallon Park.[29] The new district virtually cut the patrol area of the Fifth (Mounted) District in half.

1892

At the last meeting in January 1892, it was moved and adopted that the office of assistant chief of police be created, and that Sergeant Patrick Reedy, Headquarters, who had been acting "for sometime past in that capacity," be promoted to the rank of assistant chief at the salary of $2,000 a year. Reedy would retain the rank of sergeant.[30]

In November, William J. Stone, a Democrat from Vernon, was elected governor of Missouri. He was an attorney and had served three terms in the Missouri House of Representatives.

At the meeting of December 2, the Commercial Telegraph Company asked the board to issue private watchman commissions for men in their employ operating the electric burglar alarm system. While the request was refused, without comment, this was the first notation that electric burglar alarms were in existence.

1893

The terms of Commissioners John H. Overall and Charles H. Turner expired on January 1, 1893, but Governor-elect Stone had apparently asked the two to serve a while longer. Stone would not deal with appointments to the board until June.

Construction began on a combination police station, drill hall, and mounted police stables in Forest Park. In his annual report to the board, Chief Harrigan noted that "the location of the stable will also be a benefit if St. Louis County takes advantage of the provision of the [1876] Scheme and Charter under which 20 extra mounted officers can be detailed for duty in St. Louis County, at the expense of that county."[31]

Harrigan also endorsed the eight-hour watch, three platoon system, adding that additional men would be needed should that system be adopted. "Nearly every important city in the country has adopted the eight hour watch and all have found it to be a success, as the evidence has shown that a man can do better police work in eight hours than he can do in twelve."[32]

A new mayor, Cyrus Walbridge, was elected at the city election of April 4. Unlike his predecessor, Edward Noonan, Walbridge was a Republican who would serve as ex officio president of a Board of Police Commissioners of four Democrats. Mayor Walbridge would attend his first board meeting on April 25.[33]

In the early morning hours of May 13, Patrolman Lee A. Boone, assigned to the Fifth (Mounted) District, was riding his horse near the insane asylum when he came upon a man acting suspiciously. Boone called for the man to come forward, but the man began to run away. Boone started after him when the man turned and fired one shot at Boone, striking him in the hand. The officer fired four shots at the running man but did not know if any struck the man, who made his escape. Boone was treated by a physician, who believed the wound to be minor. The wound, however, became infected and, on May 16, Boone died of blood poisoning at his home. He left a wife.[34]

On June 15, the board addressed the monthly recreation day that was removed three years earlier and the recently established funeral leave. It ordered that (1) all police officers would be allowed two *consecutive* recreation days a month with pay and (2) a two-day furlough (a decrease of one day) would be allowed for attending funerals of the officers' family members, when requested. However, the furlough would be granted in lieu of recreation days. In addition, the board refined the March order concerning the off-duty wearing of uniforms: "Officers on recreation will wear their uniforms when on the street or in public places except when permission to wear citizen's clothes is given by the Chief of Police."[35]

On June 17, Governor Stone appointed Jeremiah Fruin and John A. Lee to replace John Overall and Charles Turner. Both were appointed to four-year terms that would expire on January 1, 1897. They would present their commissions and take their seats as police commissioners at the meeting of June 22.

Fruin was elected vice president of the board at the meeting of June 22. Lee would be elected purchasing member at the meeting of June 27, but the selection of a treasurer and the matter of a new secretary of the board were postponed. Fruin was vice president of the Fruin-Bambrick Construction Company. The firm operated stone quarries in St. Louis and constructed railroads and other public works throughout the country.[36] Lee had been a buyer for wholesale grocery houses in New York, Louisville, and St. Louis when he obtained a position as a buyer for a leading St. Louis grocery house. When appointed, Lee was editor of the publication *Interstate Grocer*, national president of the Travelers Protective Association of America, and a director of the Western Commercial Travelers' Association.[37]

The board read a communication from Mayor Walbridge on July 25 asking the board to consider a communication from Mrs. Louisa Harris, Central District matron. She requested that an area be prepared on the third floor of the Four Courts building as "rooms of detention for females."[38] Commissioners Lee and Small and Chief Harrigan were appointed "to act in the matter and report to the Board." Subsequent board minutes do not specifically indicate what, if any, action was taken on this request, but the board later had plans drawn by the city building commissioner to reconstruct the calaboose.[39] Female detention facilities were included in the reconstruction.

In August and September, the board received several requests from widows of policemen to be allocated pensions. The widow of Patrolman Lee A. Boone, who died from a gunshot wound received in the discharge of police duties, sent a letter to the board asking that she receive a widow's pension. Boone was the first police officer killed since the police pension bill went into effect in 1891, so the board asked City Counselor William C. Marshall for a legal opinion. Mrs. Boone had already received $1,000 from the Police Relief Association.[40] Marshall stated in his reply, "I do not think the fact that his widow has received $1,000 from the Police Relief Association deters her from the privileges as [illegible word] by this act." The board then approved the pension request. The pension entitled Mrs. Boone to a monthly payment equal to one-half the amount of the salary paid to her husband at the time of his death, to be paid for the remainder of her life provided she did not remarry.[41]

An identical request was received from the widow of Patrolman James Brady, killed at Starkes's Saloon on October 6, 1890. In this instance, City Counselor Marshall's opinion was that the 1991 law was not retroactive. No action in this case was recorded in the minutes of the board.[42] A third request, different still, was received from Caroline Crowe, the widow of Patrolman Michael Crowe. Patrolman Crowe was killed on December 12, 1892, when he was struck by a train while crossing the tracks. City Counselor Marshall, in his legal opinion to the board in this case, made a distinction between officers being killed in the discharge, or performance, of police duties and officers killed on duty from a cause "that might occasion such injury or death to any citizen." Marshall felt that the Crowe situation was the latter and recommended that the widow's application be denied.[43]

The minutes make no mention of the board's action in the Crowe request. But the three requests obviously established that, for a widow of an officer to receive a pension, the officer must have been killed or died from injuries received (1) when in the discharge of police duties and (2) after April 22, 1891, the date that the pension act was passed.

In October, Secretary of the Board Henry G. Paschall resigned. The resignation was accepted effective that day. On the motion of John Lee, Reuben H. Shotwell was appointed the new secretary and immediately began his duties.[44]

1894

In April 1894, the board received a letter from the builder of the Forest Park police station, drill hall, and stable building that an inspection of the work had been favorable. The builder reported that two flue pipes had been removed because the buildings would have steam heat.[45]

Although the minutes of the board meeting did not note what prompted it, the board asked the city counselor if it had the authority to drop police officers from the rolls, without trial, after such officers had served four or more years but had not been reappointed after the expiration of the first four years of service.[46] City Counselor William Marshall's response was lengthy. Essentially, with reference to Sections 6 and 7 of the Metropolitan Police Act of 1861, he said that officers were appointed for four years, and those who faithfully performed their duties were to be given preference in appointments to the force for the next four years. The board could drop officers after four years, subject to the preference to which they were entitled, but officers appointed for definite time periods could be dropped after such time had expired. Whether or not they were reappointed was left to the discretion of the board. The rationale apparently used by these officers (and, for that matter, by various police boards) was that the failure to formally drop them from the rolls was a de facto reappointment. The question, given these circumstances, was whether the board could drop the men from the rolls without a trial.[47]

In May, the first annual convention of the National Police Chiefs Union (United States and Canada) was held in St. Louis and hosted by Chief Harrigan. Mayor Walbridge presented the opening remarks. More than eighty persons attended.[48] The association was the forerunner to the International Association of Chiefs of Police (IACP).

Chief Harrigan's four-year term expired on May 20, 1894. At the meeting of May 22, John Lee moved that Harrigan be reappointed for another term of four years, commencing May 22, 1894. Lee's motion was unanimously adopted.

The combination police station, drill hall, and stable building in Forest Park was completed. At the last board meeting of July, Harrigan

Participants, First Annual Convention of the National Police Chiefs Union,
1894. Courtesy of SLMPD.

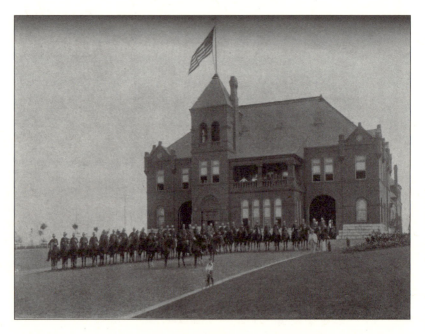

Forest Park Mounted Station. Courtesy of SLMPD.

recommended, and the board approved, redistricting of the Second,
Fifth (Mounted), and Sixth districts.[49]

The prostitution issue, a citizen complaint often raised at board
meetings, reached greater proportions in August. The Chestnut Street
Improvement Company, along with a petition signed by residents, rec-

ommended the removal of "all houses of ill-fame" in the area bounded by Market to Washington, and Jefferson to Twelfth Street.[50] Under the provisions of the prevailing city ordinance, passed in 1875, prostitutes were prohibited from walking the streets or working in various businesses. The ordinance also gave the board the power to give notice to owners or landlords who operated houses of prostitution that they had ten days to cease operation or be arrested.[51]

Accordingly, the board adopted a resolution instructing Chief Harrigan "to notify all bawds, prostitutes & Bawdy House Keepers and assignation house-keepers" residing on the listed streets to vacate on or before the stated dates.[52] The vacate order was designed to rid the entire area of "houses" by January 1, 1895. Chief Harrigan was further instructed to enforce the law and ordinances against anyone who refused to vacate and to prevent the location of bawds, bawdy houses, houses of assignation in the future in the area between Seventh Street and Jefferson Avenue (approximately twenty city blocks) and Market Street to Washington Avenue (six city blocks). This was the largest area the board had ever ordered cleared of prostitution.[53] The targeted area included that part of the city, roughly bounded by Chestnut and Market streets and Eighteenth and Twentieth streets, that was most often referred to as the "Chestnut Valley" and less often as "the sporting district."[54] Regardless of the success of this venture, a future board and chief of police would again have to deal with Chestnut Valley.

At the meeting of September 11, supported by the legal opinion of the city counselor, the board pensioned ten patrolmen at half pay. All had served twenty or more years on the police force. The board also dropped twenty-four patrolmen from the rolls without cause. Although the minutes don't offer any detail, the latter were probably dropped because of poor evaluations and the fact that they had not yet been given new four-year commissions. George Small and Mayor Walbridge voted against the action.

Small and Walbridge were also in the minority of a 3–2 vote to pension Captain (and former chief of police) Anton Huebler. Said Mayor Walbridge, "I protest against this action against a public servant of 27 years standing without a flaw in his official record or a stain upon his private life, without notice or hearing or information of any kind detrimental to him and shown by the record."[55] Captain Huebler would receive one-half the pay of a captain for the remainder of his life and would later become the city jailer.

Perhaps because of the earlier action of the board to have prostitutes and houses of prostitution moved out of such a large area (with the resulting publicity), complaints of prostitution began coming to the board from other parts of the city. There were complaints of the conduct of the inmates of houses on Sixth Street between Walnut and Poplar; of the euphemistic "disreputable citizens" living on the south side of Walnut, between Tenth and Eleventh streets; and of "bawds" on Papin Street. A petition for the removal of certain houses on South Twenty-first Street, known as "immoral resorts" (or as "Free and Easy Theaters"), was submitted. All of these were referred to Chief Harrigan with instructions to enforce the appropriate law.

At the last board meeting of 1894, Chief Harrigan reported a rather curious happening. He learned that Court of Criminal Correction Judge David Murphy had issued an order forbidding officers to appear in his court "with the arms that your rules require them to carry."[56] Harrigan was satisfied that the order was an unlawful one, and he had instructed the officers to comply with the rules of the board. Consequently, seven officers were arrested, fined, and committed to jail for contempt of court.

Writs of habeas corpus were secured from the criminal court. Chief Harrigan gave bond for the appearance of the officers, and on a hearing of the case in criminal court, the higher court decided that the order of the judge of the Court of Criminal Correction was unlawful, telling the board that "no one had the right to disarm your officers except under your rules and regulations."[57]

1895

The terms of George Small and David Caruth had officially expired on January 1, but they remained in office pending appointments that would replace them. On March 26, 1985, Small advised the board that he had resigned as a commissioner, and Governor Stone accepted his resignation. Small had served both a two-year and a four-year term on the board. His replacement was not announced. Caruth remained on the board.

> Chief Harrigan was out of the city for a time in April and Assistant Chief Reedy took some actions regarding the immoral resorts in the city. A "communication" from Reedy to Harrigan detailed exactly what illegal acts were committed in the resorts that were investigated. Reedy informed Harrigan that he had "detailed an intelligent officer to investigate and report" his findings.[58] Reedy wrote that he had proof that the business of these places depends on the sale of intoxicating liquors, and that these sales are made solely, or almost solely through the employment of Lewd Women—professional prostitutes, some of whom masquerade under the guise of actresses, their acting consisting of exposing as much of their bodies as possible, singing smutty or suggestive songs, and being the party to or making indecent remarks. These women are paid on the average of from five to eight dollars a week, and are allowed 10 to 20 per cent on all drinks they induce men to order, such drinks being charged for at from two to a dozen times the usual rates, the charges depending on the verdancy or degree of intoxication of the visitor.[59]

Reedy specifically listed seven establishments, all of which had accommodations (usually partitioned areas called "boxes") where men could have sexual relations with female employees, usually after the purchase of a $2.50 bottle of wine. Reedy described one location where the women would take their turns performing on the stage for a few minutes, "then come into the boxes clothed in short dresses, not reaching generally below the knees and not extending much above them."[60]

Reedy reported that he then "detailed some 40 officers in citizens clothes to visit these places, to become acquainted with the women, and at 9$\frac{30}{}$ PM to arrest all women who had agreed to have sexual intercourse with them."[61] A sergeant would rap his club on the street in front of each place at that time, and the arrests would be made. One officer mistook an outside noise for the sergeant's rap and began making an arrest twenty minutes or so sooner than planned. The word quickly spread among the resorts. Nonetheless, Reedy reported, thirty-five women were arrested. Reedy instigated a second attack the following Sunday. He instructed the officers "to see that all persons selling liquor in these places were arrested for violating the Sunday law."[62]

Patrick Reedy ended his report by observing that arresting the women was just "dealing with the surface of the evil. . . . To get at the root of the evil, it is necessary that the Keepers of these places be refused the privilege of selling intoxicating liquors. . . ."[63] The board then moved that a copy of Assistant Chief Reedy's communication be furnished to City Excise Commissioner Nicholas M. Bell, with a recommendation that the saloon licenses of all the places mentioned be revoked. Chief Harrigan sent such a letter to Bell asking him to revoke the licenses of the places raided the previous Saturday night.[64] The next day, Bell told a newspaper reporter that he had received the communication from the board and had notified the proprietors of all such places to appear before him and show cause why their liquor licenses should not be revoked.[65]

The following week, coincidentally, the excise commissioner sent a communication to the board concerning complaints that police officers were imposing on dram shops and obtaining free drinks and cigars. The communication was "filed."[66]

In May, the board authorized Chief Harrigan to attend the second annual National Police Chiefs Union meeting beginning on May 14 in "Washington City." As was the custom, he was given time "to make a tour of inspection through the principle [*sic*] Eastern cities for the purpose of examining the working of the various police departments."[67]

Two new commissioners came to the meeting of July 2 and presented their commissions from Governor Stone. James Bannerman and Dr. Otto E. Forster would replace George Small and David Caruth. At the next meeting, Jeremiah Fruin was reelected vice president of the board and John Lee was reelected purchasing member. The board still had not formally elected a treasurer.[68] Bannerman was a member of the wholesale saddlery and leather firm of Meyer, Bannerman and Company. In 1886, he had been elected speaker of the St. Louis House of Delegates, and in 1893, he was the Democratic opponent in the race for mayor won by Cyrus Walbridge, now the ex officio president of the board. When appointed to the board, Bannerman was the president of the ex-Confederate Association of Missouri

Dr. Otto E. Forster. Photograph by Evans, 1903. Missouri History Museum.

and was largely responsible for the home for disabled veterans at Higginsville, Missouri.[69] Dr. Forster was born in St. Louis. He attended the St. Louis Medical College for three years and then finished his medical training abroad. He returned to St. Louis and established a medical practice. About a year before his appointment to the board, Forster married the widow of former mayor Henry Overstolz.[70]

In July, the board adopted a new regulation club for use by patrolmen in the daytime. The board specified that the club be fourteen inches long and could be carried by the officer or kept in a pocket. Hereafter, said the board, a pocket would be constructed down the left seam of the uniform pants.[71]

At the last meeting of July, in order to save an estimated $25,000 in the fiscal year ending April 7, 1896, the board ordered that sergeants, patrolmen, and probationary patrolmen would each be given fifteen-day leaves of absence, without pay, during the period August 1, 1895, and March 1, 1896. Chief Harrigan was instructed to handle the details.[72]

The department armorer reported to the board on August 13 that he had tested the Columbian automatic special revolver and gave it a favorable evaluation. The board then adopted it as the regulation revolver and ordered that all officers without regulation revolvers to buy the Columbian rather than the Colt revolver.[73]

The meeting of October 15 was a busy one. First, it was moved and adopted:

> That the Board proceed to revise the entire police force, officers and patrolmen, and that all those deemed worthy whose terms have expired be reappointed and commissioned for four years as the law requires, and that all whose terms have expired and whose grading, service or records are not satisfactory and commendable be dropped from the rolls of the department and that those deemed inefficient from long service or disabled from active service be honorably retired as veterans or pensioners.[74]

Assistant Chief of Police Patrick Reedy who, on January 26, 1892, was the first to be appointed to that position, was retired because of physical infirmity. Reedy was retired effective October 17, with one-half the pay of the assistant chief of police. Captain Mathew Kiely, commander of the Fourth District, was promoted to assistant chief of police.

The year closed with an incident that is recalled to this day.[75] About 10:00 p.m. on December 25, two men, William (Billy) Lyons and Lee Sheldon were drinking in Bill Curtis's saloon on the northwest corner of Eleventh and Morgan streets (now Convention Plaza). Sheldon was also known as "Stag" and, sometimes as "Stack Lee," so called because he had been a stoker on the riverboat *Stacker Lee*. Lyons and Sheldon, who were said to be friends, had been drinking for some time. An argument ensued after their discussion had turned to politics, and Lyons snatched Sheldon's lucky hat from his head. Sheldon asked for the return of his hat, and Lyons refused. Sheldon then pulled out a .44-caliber revolver and shot Lyons once in the abdomen. After Lyons fell to the floor, Sheldon took the hat from his hand and walked out of the saloon. He was arrested that same evening. Billy Lyons died from the gunshot wound, adding another chapter to what has been referred to as the ballad of "Stagger Lee," "Stagolee," or "Stackalee." The shooting reportedly inspired a 1959 folk song "Stagger Lee" by singer Lloyd Price, which reached number one in sales that year.[76]

1896

In January 1986, the vice president of the board, Jeremiah Fruin, submitted his resignation to Governor William Stone, stating that "the demands of my business, which will require my absence from the State for the greater part of the year 1896, render this action on my part imperative."[77] The resignation was accepted on January 9. Fruin had another year left in his term.[78] It was learned that the Fruin-Bambrick Construction Company had been at work on a large street-paving contract in New York City for several months, was beginning a street-paving job in Syracuse, New York, and was building a dam across the Connecticut River near Holyoke, Massachusetts.[79]

On April 7, the size of the Fifth (Mounted) District was further reduced when, upon the recommendation of Chief Harrigan, a northern portion of the Mounted District was transferred to the Sixth District.

On April 20, Governor Stone appointed Patrick J. Kelly to complete Fruin's term. Kelly had been engaged in the livery business for the past twenty-five years, being a principal in the firm of Cullen and Kelly, liverymen and undertakers. He had been a member of the fire department in his early years and a member of the school board for ten years. He was a Democratic Party worker and was connected with a number of fraternal and benevolent organizations.[80] Kelly would be present at the board meeting scheduled for the next day.

The board meeting of April 28 would be an active meeting. After some routine business, the board went into closed session. Board Secretary Reuben Shotwell was excused from the executive session, and Chief Harrigan's secretary, James C. Espy, was brought in to record the minutes. The board first declared all elected offices of the board, including that of secretary, vacant effective May 1. The board then proceeded to elect officers. Dr. Otto Forster was elected vice president; Patrick Kelly, treasurer; and John Lee, purchasing member. James Bannerman was selected to represent the board on the city's Board of Health.

A new secretary was named to replace Rueben Shotwell. Captain John Pickel, First District, resigned his commission and was appointed secretary of the board. Former Captain William Young, who was dropped from the rolls after his commission expired on October 17, 1895, was reinstated as a captain, and assigned to the Second District. Interestingly, John Pickel had been promoted to captain when Captain Young was dropped from the rolls.

The board then adopted a resolution to request the Municipal Assembly to provide an appropriation sufficient to increase the size of the force by fifty patrolmen, five sergeants, and one captain. While the board minutes make no mention of the reason for the request, the final action in the closed session provided a clue. Each commissioner was assigned two districts at the April meeting. Dr. Forster was assigned the Fifth and Mounted districts. Since the Fifth District *was* the Mounted District, it became obvious that the board was preparing to divide the two into separate districts, thus the need for more patrolmen, supervisors, and a commander. This ultimately would prove to be the case.

The weather became an issue toward the end of May. The weather "preview" on the front page of the May 27, 1896, edition of *The St. Louis Republic* read "Partly cloudy weather continues, favorable for local thunderstorms."[81] It was sunny until about 2:00 p.m. The temperature was 86 degrees, the humidity was 95 percent, and the barometric reading was 29.92 inches. By 5:00 p.m. the barometer on the roof of the downtown post office fell to 29.65 and then to 29.35. A barometer in a house near Lafayette Park dropped to 27.30 inches, about the reading of a hurricane. It was, however, not a hurricane bearing down on St. Louis, but a tornado. At approximately 5:15 p.m., the tornado touched down in the area of Hampton Avenue and Arsenal Street in the southwest part of the city. It generally followed a southwest-to-northeast path, continuing along Arsenal Street to the hilltop known as Blue Ridge, where the city's poorhouse, insane asylum, infirmary, and the female hospital built during the social evil experiment were located. The tornado tore off the roof the female hospital and the front porch of the infirmary. Then it headed toward Henry Shaw's Garden and Tower Grove Park, snapping tree limbs. In the 4300 block of Folsom, across the tracks from the Tower Grove railroad station, a thirteen-building complex was being constructed for the Liggett and Myers Tobacco Company. Almost five hundred workers were on the site; thirteen men died when steel and wooden supports collapsed on them.

The tornado continued toward Compton Hill, where it tore roofs from approximately three hundred homes. It sped downhill toward Jefferson Avenue and, just west of Jefferson between Russell Boulevard and Chouteau Avenue, brick walls were ripped from apartment buildings and storefronts. Roofs were torn off, and many homes collapsed. Four people died in the collapse of Anchor Hall, at Jefferson and Park. At the Union Depot electric railway, at Jefferson and Geyer, three men were killed when a section of the masonry and brick structure fell on them.[82] The tornado struck Lafayette Park, the last piece of common ground left from old St. Louis. Trees were uprooted, the massive wrought iron fence flattened, and bandstands blown away. The homes facing the four sides of the park were severely damaged or destroyed. The Third District substation in Lafayette Park also suffered some damage but remained in service. Amazingly, the bronze statue of Thomas Hart Benton remained standing on its pedestal.[83]

The storm struck the City Hospital at Fourteenth Street and Lafayette Avenue. There were four hundred patients at the hospital but, in spite of the virtual destruction of the hospital, only one patient was killed. Two others died later, one of a heart attack. Two blocks east of the hospital, at Twelfth and Lafayette, St. John Nepomuk Catholic Church was virtually demolished; only a portion of the front wall of the church was left standing. The school was heavily damaged, but no students were present at that hour. (The present St. John Nepomuk Catholic Church was rebuilt on the old foundation using the original design. That portion of the front wall that had been left standing was incorporated into the rebuilt structure.)[84] The mill of the Robinson-Danforth Commission Company, at Twelfth and Gratiot streets, was destroyed. It would be rebuilt at Eighth and Gratiot streets and, six years later, would become Ralston Purina.

At Ninth Street and Park Avenue, a streetcar was blown over, crushing the motorman and the conductor. A passenger trapped beneath the car was drowned by water from a broken fire hydrant. The tornado made its way to Seventh and Rutger streets, the deadliest spot in the storm's path. Seventeen people died in the collapse of a three-story brick tenement on the southeast corner. Six more people died on the southwest corner of the intersection. The riverfront was next. Steamboats had nowhere to hide. The mooring lines of *City of Monroe*, scheduled to leave for New Orleans within the next thirty minutes, snapped. The ship was blown across the Mississippi River and beached on the East St. Louis side. A steamboat in the river collided with a towboat, and five men drowned. The storm hit the east approach to the Eads Bridge and destroyed five upper stone arches and badly damaged the sloping rail trestle, but the main span was virtually untouched. The storm then hit East St. Louis, Illinois.

In the twenty minutes it took for the tornado to sweep through St. Louis, it had flattened 311 buildings, heavily damaged 7,200 others, did significant damage to 1,300 more, and knocked out telegraph and telephone lines. The storm killed 137 people in St. Louis and another 118 in East St. Louis.

The work began for police officers, firemen, ambulance drivers, medical personnel, electrical and telegraph workers, and other personnel. Fires erupted, and live electric wires and telegraph wires were down throughout the path of the storm. The fire department was slowed by impassible streets. In addition, several fire houses sustained damage and one, Engine House 7, was demolished.

During the storm, the Four Courts building shook, and the northwest wing of the jail building caved in. The women in the female section of the jail were moved to a safer location. About seventy-five male prisoners were in the jail corridors when the storm hit. They ran in all directions, some of them into areas of falling bricks. When the jail guards were unable to contain the men, the alarm was rung and several detectives arrived and assisted in getting the men into cells. A guard of twenty-four uniformed policemen was later placed in the interior of the jail to prevent any further outbreaks.[85]

Chief Harrigan, meanwhile, had called upon the officers assigned to night duty to come in early, and day officers worked into the night. Chief of Detectives William Desmond had his detective force spread throughout the parts of the city damaged by the storm. Chicago Superintendent of Police J. J. Badenach and his inspector of detectives, John E. Fitzpatrick, were due to arrive in St. Louis on Friday morning. They would confer with Harrigan and determine how the Chicago Police Department might be of assistance.[86]

The St. Louis police department, however, was not sufficiently staffed to deal with the aftermath of such a devastating storm. The board called a special meeting the next day and declared an emergency. The declaration would permit the board to hire two hundred emergency specials for a period of thirty days, who would be subject to the rules and regulations of the department. The board further ordered that an advertisement be inserted in the daily papers for "suitable men to appear at this office Friday at 10 o'clock a.m. for examination and selection." One hundred and seventy-four emergency specials were sworn in on Friday.[87] The board continued to swear-in emergency specials and, on June 30, extended the emergency another thirty days. As some emergency specials had to return to their daily lives, others were sworn in. In July, the board declared that all emergency specials would be permitted to work for a maximum of sixty days after the date of their appointment.[88]

The police department considered the stricken area to be that between the river on the east, the Kings Highway on the west, Chouteau on the north, and Geyer on the south. Between 7:30 p.m. and 7:30 a.m., that area was patrolled by three hundred uniformed policemen, three hundred men described as "militiamen,"[a] and twenty-six detectives. Six of the latter were detectives sent to St. Louis by the Chicago Police Department. The detectives all worked in pairs, the Chicago detectives each paired with their St. Louis counterparts.[89]

In addition, Harrigan assigned 150 of the emergency specials to beats near their homes. The regular beat officers were then temporarily assigned to the stricken area.[90] The emergency specials had been selected by Commissioners Lee, Forster, and Kelly and by Chief Harrigan. After they were sworn in, each was given a badge and a copy of the police manual. They were advised to read the manual and observe the rules set forth in the manual. Harrigan advised them to be careful about the use of their revolvers and explained that their jobs were to protect people and property, not to injure anyone.[91] In addition, 1,000 citizen volunteers were patrolling the stricken area at night. They had supplied themselves with lanterns and revolvers and worked the same hours as the patrolmen and detectives.[92]

In the three days following the tornado, twenty-five persons were arrested for stealing. The targets of the thieves tended to be plumbing and copper wiring, which were easy to sell. Unofficially, it was reported that many thieves didn't come to the attention of the police. Instead, they were "dealt with roughly on the spot" by residents.[93]

The Hospital Corps of the First Regiment, Missouri National Guard, was stationed at the police station in Lafayette Park on the Thursday and Friday nights after the tornado struck. They were released after two days when it was determined that the local hospitals were able to keep up with the demand for medical services.[94]

The efforts of the police were evident throughout the stricken area. Patrolman Bart Keaney, who walked a beat in the Central District, was credited with rescuing three people who were buried under the bricks and timbers of a fallen store at 2102 Clark Avenue.[95] A detective identified only as "Detective Meany" was at Eighteenth Street and Ohio Avenue when the storm struck.[b] He noticed a building at 1806 Ohio

---

[a] The "militiamen" were probably troops of the First Regiment of the Missouri National Guard. Their armory was at Seventeenth and Pine streets.

[b] "Detective Meany" could not be located among police department listings. He might have been incorrectly identified.

Avenue swaying, with a woman and her two children on the second floor screaming for help. Running up to the second floor, he led the woman and her children to a wall that appeared to be the safest. The tornado took the roof off and spread debris around them. Detective Meany took the children in his arms, carried them downstairs, and then returned for their mother. All then went across the street and took shelter in a building that was still standing.[96]

The police were also called to the two-year-old Union Station the Sunday following the tornado when an estimated thirty thousand people filled the midway and the areas outside the train gates. Thousands who had come to the city to witness the destruction caused by the tornado were now trying to catch departing trains.[97] A large force of uniformed police and detectives were among the throngs at Union Station. On Sunday, thieves began arriving from Cincinnati, Chicago, and other areas of the country. As each element was identified, detectives quickly arrested them and placed them in the police holdover at the Four Courts.[98]

Efforts were immediately begun for the relief of the victims of the tornado. Several relief funds for the homeless and destitute were started after the tornado. Among a few of these were those of the Merchants' Exchange, the Real Estate Exchange, the Furniture Board of Trade, the *St. Louis Globe-Democrat*, and the Fairgrounds.[99] In addition to the many hours that were worked by St. Louis police officers, the officers donated $2,359.44 for the relief of victims of the tornado.[100] The Great Cyclone of 1896 would not easily be forgotten; it was the deadliest single event in St. Louis history.

*   *   *

Meanwhile, the 1896 general election was fast approaching. The board, at its meeting of October 27, declared another emergency. "Because of the smallness of the force, the large number of polling places, and the large voter registration," the board declared that an emergency existed and that five hundred emergency specials be employed to guard the polls and preserve the peace on election day, November 3rd. Advertisements to that effect would be placed in daily newspapers. Those so employed would be paid $2.50 for the day. At that election, Lawrence (Lon) V. Stephens was elected governor of Missouri.

The board apparently was not content with the work performed by the recently appointed secretary of the board, John Pickel. Pickel, the former captain of police who had served as secretary for seven months, saw the office of secretary of the board "declared vacant" effective the day of the November 17 meeting of the board. Meanwhile, the four-year term of Captain William O. Keeble, the commander of the Fifth District, had expired. The board dropped him from the rolls that same day. Former captain Keeble and former secretary of the board Pickel then switched places. Keeble was named secretary of the board, and Pickel was reinstated to the rank of captain and assigned to the Second District.

The meeting the following week concentrated on private watchmen. In 1885, the board had prescribed a uniform that had to be worn by all licensed private watchmen. At the meeting of November 17, the board changed the uniform hat from the cap made of gray cadet cloth trimmed with brass buttons to a helmet style with a gray color that had to be purchased at the company that was awarded the police hat contract. With the new helmet came new insignia. The words "Licensed Watchman" and a number corresponding with the number on the watchman's badge were to be printed in gilt letters on the front of the helmet.

Upon the recommendation of Chief Harrigan, the board adopted rules, directed at the district captains, concerning the supervision of private watchmen:

1. Captains were to prepare a list of all private watchmen in their districts, including badge number, residence, and the boundaries of their beats.

2. Captains would be required to see that each sergeant and patrol-man reported any negligence on the part of private watchmen.

3. So that private watchmen would be a strong auxiliary to the police department, they were given full police power on the territory for which they were licensed. They were expected to assist sergeants

and patrolmen in the discharge of police duty on the private watchman's beat.

The board added that the supervisory rules were to be "enforced to the letter."[101]

The board adjusted the rules for private watchmen at the next meeting. In a letter to Chief Harrigan, the board said that the previous order concerning private watchmen should have stated that it applied only to those who walked beats. Other private watchmen, those who worked inside or in a rail yard, for example, were exempt from reporting in person or by telephone or from wearing the uniform helmet. All other private watchmen were to report to the appropriate district station before going on duty and to report going off duty by telephone, provided their beats were within one mile of the station. If their beats were more than a mile from the station, they were expected to report to the beat man or the sergeant when going on duty and by telephone at the end of their duty.[102]

The board asked the city comptroller and the city counselor to attend a special meeting of the board on December 19. The board noted that it could not foresee the demands made upon the department: the tornado, the large number of conventions, and the increased protection needed at the election in November. These demands had caused the board to hire hundreds of emergency specials. The board requested that the Municipal Assembly make an additional appropriation sufficient to maintain the present force through the remainder of the fiscal year. Without an additional appropriation, it would be necessary to reduce the present force by at least sixty-four men, "which would impair its efficiency and reduce the protection of the citizens, a most unfortunate, but unavoidable, consequence."

The Municipal Assembly apparently did not pass such a bill. At a special meeting called on the last day of the year, a resolution was adopted. The resolution stated that there was the lack of sufficient appropriations to carry the present number of men employed through April 1, 1897. During January, February, and March 1897, each sergeant, patrolman, and probationary patrolman would "be laid off on furloughs for ten (10) days without pay." As it had the last time the board had a financial exigency, the details were left to Chief Harrigan to arrange so that the effectiveness of the force was minimally compromised.[103]

1897

On January 11, 1987, Lon V. Stephens was sworn in as the twenty-ninth governor of Missouri. One of the first decisions he would have to make, as far as the police department was concerned, were his appointments to the board. The terms of Commissioners Patrick J. Kelly and John A. Lee had expired on January 1.

At the meeting of January 26, Captain Michael O'Malley, who commanded the Central District, informed the board of the death of Matron Louisa Harris. Harris was appointed on January 8, 1884. In 1894, she proposed a women's detention facility, which was acted upon by the board at its meeting of August 14, 1894.

To replace the late Matron Harris, Chief Harrigan appointed Mrs. Catherine A. Gilbert. Mrs. Gilbert was the choice of the Woman's Christian Temperance Union (WCTU), at whose request Louisa Harris had been appointed. The WCTU had paid part of Louisa Harris's salary the first few years of her employment and had furnished her quarters on the third floor of the Four Courts building.[104] The board was to confirm Chief Harrigan's recommendation at the meeting of February 2. Instead, the board decided to wait. Because the terms of Commissioners Kelly and Lee had expired, it was decided that their replacements and the two remaining commissioners, Dr. Otto Forster and James Bannerman, should make the selection.[105]

Governor Stephens appointed two new commissioners, James M. Lewis and Anton C. Stuever, on January 26.[106] Stuever was confirmed by the Senate on February 10. Lewis was not so quickly confirmed. Some St. Louis Democratic Party members did not know him. Others complained about Lewis because he had never been affiliated with the local Democratic Party. There were even complaints that he might be a "sound money Democrat."[107] Lewis was, however, confirmed on February 26.

Lewis and Stuever attended their first board meeting on March 5. The first order of business at that meeting was the election of offi-

James M. Lewis. Courtesy of SLMPD.

Anton C. Stuever. Courtesy of SLMPD.

cers. James Lewis was elected vice president of the board, and Anton Stuever was elected to the dual position of treasurer and purchasing member.[108] Lewis had been a lawyer in St. Louis for several years. At the time of his appointment, he was in private practice. Stuever was a brewer and the owner of the Home Brewing Company at Salena and Miami streets in south St. Louis. Stuever had been a Democratic member of the Tenth Congressional Committee, member and treasurer of the City Central Committee, and a member of the State Committee.[109]

With a newly constituted board, the fate of Chief Harrigan became a topic of conversation. The previous board had "not been particularly favorable to him; that is, his opinions were not asked for on many occasions, and in making political appointments the wishes of Maj. Harrigan have been of very small consideration."[110] James Bannerman was apparently the only board member who favored the chief.

The newly elected mayor of St. Louis, Henry Ziegenhein, attended his first board meeting on April 20. Like his predecessor, Cyrus Walbridge, Ziegenhein was a Republican. Near the end of the meeting, the office of secretary of the board again was declared vacant. William H. Beneke was nominated and elected as secretary for a four-year term, retroactive to April 1. The ousted secretary, William Keeble, who was dropped from the rolls as a captain and appointed secretary the previous November, was assigned to duty as a sergeant and acting captain.

Meanwhile, Assistant Chief of Police Mathew Kiely had attended the meeting of the National Police Chiefs Union in Pittsburgh in early May. Kiely's report of the meeting enthusiastically endorsed a new system of criminal identification called the Bertillon system. Chief Harrigan, in turn, recommended its adoption to the board. The board agreed and, at the meeting of May 19, "it was ordered that the Bertillon System of Measurement for the identification of Criminals, be, and is hereby adopted." At the next meeting, "the Statement of Ass't Chief of Police Kiely, together with letter of Geo. M. Porteous, of Chicago, in reference to the cost of the Bertillon System, was referred to the Purchasing Member of the Board [Stuever], with full

Mayor Henry Ziegenhein. Courtesy of SLMPD.

William H. Beneke. Courtesy of SLMPD.

power to act."[111] Porteous was from the Chicago Police Department. That department had instituted the Bertillon system in 1888.

The Bertillon system had been created in 1879 by Alphonse Bertillon, who, as a French policeman, saw that criminal identification in France consisted of "bribing suspects to name each other."[112] It wasn't until 1883, however, that Bertillon's system was tested. It was successful and, in 1888, the Paris police created the Department of Judicial Identity. Bertillon was installed as the head of the new department.

Bertillon's system consisted of eleven measurements, taken with specially designed calipers and rulers, of height, head length, head breadth, arm span, sitting height, left middle finger length, left little finger length, foot length, forearm length, right ear length, and cheek width. "These body segments were selected to correspond most closely with actual bone lengths, minimizing the effects of changes in fleshiness over time. The theory behind anthropometry was that no two individuals would coincide in all eleven measurements."[113]

In St. Louis, John Haley, for a number of years a telephone operator at the Four Courts, was appointed to take charge of the system.[114] On June 30, the board appointed one Frank Anderson to the position of probationary patrolman and assigned him to Headquarters to work in the Bertillon system department.

On June 17, the police department measured its first person under the Bertillon system. He was Elmer Wainwright, alias Billy French. Wainwright had been arrested for picking pockets in the Fairgrounds on May 8. He had been given a number of hours in which to leave the city, but was again arrested on June 16. Wainwright was measured by John Haley under the supervision of George Porteous. Chief of Detectives William Desmond, Detectives Samuel Allender[c] and George Badger, and a *Post-Dispatch* reporter observed the proceedings.[115] After all the measurements had been taken and recorded on a Bertillon card, Wainwright's description (height, weight, hair color, complexion, scars, moles, or other marks) was entered on the card. Two photographs were then taken, one front

---

[c]Allender would resign his commission the next year to become the chief of detectives for the St. Louis and San Francisco Railroad.

view and one profile. After being developed, the photographs would also be placed on the card.[116]

*   *   *

The matron situation was resolved at the last meeting in June. Matron Rosetta Hainsworth, who had been hired nearly ten years earlier, was dropped from the rolls. A new matron, Mrs. Louisa Breen, was appointed and assigned to the Central District, in the Four Courts. Mrs. Catherine A. Gilbert was formally appointed and assigned to the Fourth District, replacing Rosetta Hainsworth.[117]

On August 19, the board switched the matron assignments. Breen was transferred to the Fourth, and Gilbert went to the Central District. On November 2, Louisa Breen was dropped from the rolls for neglect of duty. Rosetta Hainsworth, who was dropped from the rolls in July, was reappointed and assigned to the Fourth District, her assignment when she was dropped. After ten months, the matron issue had stabilized.

Commissioner James Bannerman, meanwhile, had not attended a board meeting since September 21. Governor Stephens received his letter of resignation on November 3 and accepted it the following day. Bannerman told a newspaper reporter that he resigned because he was "tired of the whole thing . . . to be a member of the Board of Police Commissioners requires more time and trouble and worry than I am able to give to it."[118] When asked if there had been any unpleasantness among the board members that might have precipitated his resignation, Bannerman replied in the negative. He acknowledged his friendship with Chief Harrigan and had even told the chief of his plan to resign two days before he sent his resignation to the governor.[119]

James Bannerman's unexpected resignation led to a great deal of political maneuvering. The Democratic politicians of "Kerry Patch," the north side Irish conclave, and a large number of other north St. Louis Democrats were said to favor M. J. Cullinane, of the Fourteenth Ward, for the vacant position. A strong petition urging the appointment of Cullinane had been sent to Governor Stephens just after he had taken office in January, but he appointed Lewis and Stuever.[120]

Two things immediately became clear. First, Governor Stephens had someone in mind for the appointment soon after he received James Bannerman's letter of resignation on November 4. Second, the position would not go to M. J. Cullinane. On November 5, Governor Stephens appointed Lawrence D. Kingsland to the board to complete Bannerman's term, which ended on January 1, 1899. Kingsland would attend the next board meeting, Tuesday, November 9.

Kingsland was a native St. Louisan. At the time of his appointment, he owned the Kingsland Manufacturing Company, makers

Lawrence D. Kingsland. Courtesy of SLMPD.

of engines and boilers, at 1521 South Eleventh Street. Kingsland's appointment to the board was his first public office.

At approximately 8:00 p.m. on November 15, the day before Kingsland's second meeting, three men entered Peter Heibel's grocery and saloon at 600 South Jefferson Avenue. Each had a handkerchief mask over his face, and all were armed with revolvers. Only Heibel, his wife, and two sons were in the establishment. The Heibels were told to put their hands up. While one of the men guarded the door, one of the others held Peter Heibel at gunpoint and then took the money from behind the bar. The third held Mrs. Heibel and her two sons at bay. After taking the receipts, the first robber also took Peter Heibel's watch and chain.[121]

A customer, H. W. Knost, entered the saloon-grocery unaware of the holdup. The man on guard at the door grabbed him, put a pistol to his head, and asked him for all his money. Knost gave him $5.25. The robber then made Knost stand facing a wall. Knost and the Heibels were then told to march single file into the grocery store portion of the building or they would be killed. The three robbers then ran out the side door and turned south on Jefferson Avenue. Peter Heibel quickly grabbed a revolver and gave chase. With Heibel running about a half block behind, he and the robbers continually exchanged shots.

Patrolmen Martin Delaney and Nicholas Hunt heard the shooting and took up the pursuit. At Twenty-second Street, the three robbers turned toward the railroad yards. Two of the men ran in one direction, the third in another. Delaney ran after the two who remained together, firing as he ran. Hunt followed the lone robber.

Officer Hunt fired three shots as he chased the robber through the dark railroad yards. The man suddenly stopped, turned, and fired one shot at the officer, striking him in the abdomen. Hunt fell, mortally wounded. The suspect, later identified as William C. Thornton (aliases "St. Paul Tip"; Arthur C. Webster, Connors, Knight, Frazier; and others), escaped.[122] An ambulance was called and took Hunt to St. Mary's Infirmary. At 4:30 a. m. on Tuesday, Hunt died from his wounds.

Officer Delaney, meanwhile, had captured one of the suspects. He was identified as Charles Sheldon, age nineteen. On information from Sheldon, police arrested the third robber, Frank Stetson, age eighteen, the next day.

Officer Nicholas Hunt was appointed to the force on March 15, 1895, and promoted to patrolman two weeks later. He left a wife and four children. At its meeting later on Tuesday, the board adopted a resolution commending the bravery of Officer Hunt and announcing that the entire board would attend the funeral. The resolution also directed Chief Harrigan to furnish a detail of officers, commanded by a captain, to attend the funeral.

A reward was offered for the apprehension of the slayer of Officer Hunt, and Chief Harrigan issued circulars with Thornton's picture. His picture had been in the department's rogues' gallery. It was later learned that, as he fell wounded, Officer Hunt had shot William Thornton in the back. Even though wounded, Thornton had managed to later make it to the Mississippi River where he made his escape in a flat-bottomed boat. Thornton would later be arrested in Wilmington, Delaware, for robbery. He was sentenced to five years imprisonment, but escaped. In 1899, he was arrested for a robbery in Rhode Island. He was convicted and sentenced to twenty-five years. In 1914, the governor of Rhode Island granted Thornton a pardon after serving fifteen years of his sentence. Rhode Island authorities notified St. Louis police of Thornton's impending release from Howard Prison and, on March 26, 1914, he was met at the prison gate by a St. Louis police detective. Thornton was returned to St. Louis to face charges of robbery and murder.

Meanwhile, Charles Sheldon and Frank Stetson were tried for the murder of Officer Hunt, but were acquitted. However, they both pleaded guilty to the charge of "highway robbery" and were sentenced to five years in the penitentiary.[123]

As 1897 ended, and with no additional funding anticipated, the board ordered that all sergeants, patrolmen, and probationary patrolmen be given an additional furlough of six days, without pay, commencing January 1, 1898, and ending March 31, 1898.[124]

1898

The U.S. battleship *Maine* exploded in the harbor of Havana, Cuba, on February 15, 1898. Between April 19 and 25, the U.S. Congress met and agreed to a joint resolution approving military intervention. Spain then declared war against the United States. In turn, the United States issued a formal declaration of war retroactive to April 20. The Spanish-American War had begun.

At a meeting on April 26, the Board of Police Commissioners adopted a resolution that any member of the police force who volunteered for the armed forces could be assured that, upon the expiration of his service, he could rejoin the police department "of at least equal grade and pay as that now held by him."[125]

The meeting of May 18 began with a request by Captain Reynolds of the Central District that a patrol box be erected in Forest Park, opposite the Forest Park Highlands amusement park. The board granted the request. The next item of business was the resignation of Chief of Police Laurence Harrigan. Harrigan requested that the resignation take effect on May 21. The board accepted his resignation and the effective date. The minutes of that meeting contain a glowing resolution attesting to Chief Harrigan's entire career with the police department and extended the best wishes of the Board of Police Commissioners. The resolution was unanimously adopted. Laurence Harrigan had been chief of police on three occasions since 1874. At the time of his resignation, he had been chief for eight years and had served under board members appointed by Governors Francis, Stone, and Stephens.

The board held a special meeting the following day. Captain (and former chief) John W. Campbell was elected chief of police for a four-year term to commence at noon on May 21.[126] The appointment was not without dissent. Anton Stuever wanted to delay the appointment of a new chief. It was believed that he was interested in the appointment of a former justice of the peace, Judge James McCaffery. Judge McCaffery had been endorsed for chief of police by the St. Louis delegation to the Missouri General Assembly. In spite of Mayor Ziegenhein's request to make the vote unanimous, Stuever cast the lone dissenting vote, voting for Judge McCaffery.[127]

Captain Mathew Kiely, assistant chief of police, was replaced by Captain John Pickel. Kiely was returned to a district command and commissioned for a four-year term commencing May 22. Chief of Detectives William Desmond was reappointed to his position, and Sergeant George T. McNamee was promoted to captain.

At the last meeting of June, the office of secretary of the board was again declared vacant. Stuever, seconded by Mayor Ziegenhein, nominated Judge James McCaffery. Judge McCaffery was elected the new secretary, replacing William Beneke.

On August 15, Vice President James M. Lewis sent a letter of resignation to Governor Lon Stephens. The resignation was officially accepted on August 22. That same day, Governor Stephens appointed Harry B. Hawes to replace Lewis. There was no board meeting on Tuesday, August 23, so Hawes would attend his first meeting on August 30.

Harry B. "Handsome Harry" Hawes was a young lawyer who previously had been the collector of revenue for the city of St. Louis. At the time of his appointment, he had a private practice and was vice president of the Jefferson Club. The president of the Jefferson Club

Harry B. Hawes. Photograph by Evans, 1903. Missouri History Museum.

that year was another young attorney, Joseph W. Folk. Folk, along with other Democratic businessmen and lawyers, had formed the Jefferson Club as a debating society. It soon developed into "a political organization reflecting a revolt of the younger and possibly more idealistic element among St. Louis Democrats against the notorious 'Colonel' Edward Butler, the reigning party boss."[128]

The evening of the appointment of Harry Hawes to the Board of Police Commissioners, the Democratic City Central Committee held a meeting at the Jefferson Club hall. Among the items of business was the introduction of a resolution thanking Governor Stephens for the appointment of Hawes to the Board of Police Commissioners and asserting that the selection of Hawes as vice president of the board would be to the advantage of all the people of the city. Hawes thanked the committee for the honor it had bestowed on him and then candidly indicated what the future might hold for the police department:

> As a Police Commissioner of the City of St. Louis I will never forget that I am a Democrat, and men who want appointments on the police force from me will have to come to me with the indorsements [*sic*] of their ward committeemen and their precinct committeemen. The Police Department of the City of St. Louis is attacked for its Democracy. It seems to me we might so arrange it as to not decrease its efficiency, but to make it a great aid of the Democratic party. . . .[129]

It is not known whether the statement represented a new level of politics in the police department or was simply a public affirmation of an existing situation. Because the city administration was Republican, however, Hawes's statement was an ominous one.

The board was reorganized at the meeting of August 30. Harry Hawes was elected vice president, Anton Stuever held his position as purchasing member, and Dr. Otto Forster was elected treasurer. The fourth member was Lawrence D. Kingsland.[130]

At the meeting of November 22, the board read a letter from the city auditor that it had exceeded the payrolls for commissioned officers by $16,617.66, and he would no longer audit the board if it exceeded certain stated dollar limits. Forster and Kingsland were appointed to visit the auditor and explain the position of the department. In the meantime, all detectives were given twenty days' "involuntary vacation."[131] The detectives had escaped the earlier "vacations" meted out to other members of the force.

The board began vigorously dealing with the deficit at a special meeting on November 30. Kingsland moved that, rather than lay off officers, all members of the department, except captains and chiefs, be given an extra seven days' leave of absence without pay. Said Kingsland:

> In offering this resolution I want to say I think it would be an extraordinary hardship for the men to discharge them at this season of the year. A great many have already gotten their uniforms, and are in debt for them. There is very little possible chance for them to get employment. In addition to this, when they were put on the force they understood that they were there for four years, unless discharged for cause. I think it would be an act of injustice to drop them. I think, also, it would be an illegal act on our part to drop them without trial.[132]

Vice President Hawes wanted an opinion from the city counselor whether, in view of the deficit of $16,617.66, the board could dismiss from the force a sufficient number of patrolmen and probationary patrolmen to cover this amount. If the board received a favorable reply from the city counselor, said Hawes, he would be in favor of dismissing men rather than forcing unpaid vacations on everyone. Stuever then moved that no more appointments be made on the force until there are "regular vacancies." The motion was seconded and adopted.

At the meeting of December 6, the board instructed all captains to classify their sergeants, patrolmen, and probationary patrolmen into first, second, or third classes according to their capability and to have the reports ready at the next meeting of the board. Since the board would not meet on December 13, the captains had two weeks to prepare the lists. It soon became evident that the evaluation procedure would be the way Vice President Hawes would deal with the deficit.

At the next meeting, Hawes attempted to do just that. He moved that, to cover the deficit, a sufficient number of sergeants and patrolmen on the second- and third-class lists be dismissed from the force, thus eliminating the need for involuntary furloughs. Hawes's motion died for lack of a second. The year ended on that note.

1899

The new year began with sad news. On Saturday morning, January 7, retired chief of police Laurence Harrigan died at his home, at 4412 West Belle Place, from Bright's disease and chronic heart trouble. Chief Harrigan, who had retired the previous May, had been sick for several months and had been confined to his home since the previous October.[133]

Among the telegrams of condolence received by the Harrigan family were those sent by Governor (and former mayor) David R. Francis, San Francisco Chief of Police J. H. Lees, Robert Pinkerton of the New York City Pinkerton Detective Agency office, and William Pinkerton, of the agency's Chicago office. All contained references to Chief Harrigan's high regard both nationally and internationally.[134] From early Monday morning until late that night, a constant stream of people passed by Chief Harrigan's coffin in the parlor of his home. His funeral would be the next day.

On Monday, January 9, the board called a special meeting. At the meeting, the board, with all members present, unanimously adopted a memorial to Chief Harrigan:

He was a member of the Police force of this city for over forty years, and for many years past up to his resignation was Chief of Police. In the performance of all his duties both as a private in the ranks and an officer he was always faithful to his duties, honest in the discharge of every trust, and as a Chief of Police perhaps the most distinguished and efficient in the United States.

He was the natural enemy of crime & criminals, & in the discharge of the onerous duties of his position as Chief he always exercised a wise & temperate discretion towards the unfortunate who were driven to unlawful acts by misfortune. He was fitted by nature & inclination for the duties so long exercised by him, and his mind was ever alert for the vindication of the law and the maintenance of the welfare and peace of this city.[135]

The board resolved that the members would attend as a body and further resolved that a copy of the memorial be given to the press.

On Tuesday, the funeral procession began at the Harrigan home. Mounted police headed the cortege; all wore crepe and were riding black horses. Antonio Bafunno's band followed, playing a dirge. Behind the band marched one hundred policemen from all stations in the city. The Knights of St. Patrick, of which Chief Harrigan was a member, followed the police. The empty carriages that would carry the pallbearers and friends to the cemetery were next in line, followed by the honorary pallbearers. The honorary pallbearers were, in the words of a newspaper reporter, a "body of prominent men who had been proud of the friendship of the dead chief. . . ."[136] They included at least ten former police commissioners, Sergeant of Detectives Desmond, board secretary James McCaffery, and several prominent St. Louis businessmen.

The hearse followed the honorary pallbearers. It was drawn by four black horses. Each horse was covered with a white cloth with the letter *H* embroidered on it. The pallbearers walked on each side of the hearse. They were Captains Samuel Boyd, Michael O'Malley, E. J. Phillips, and Peter Joyce and Sergeants Christ Gillaspy, James Dawson, Mathew Cummins, and Stephen Hurst. The hearse was followed by three carriages. Chief Harrigan's widow and son were in the first carriage, and other family members were in the second and third carriages. Following these three carriages were carriages "occupied by a large number of the best known people in the city."[137]

The cortege made its way to the New Cathedral "at the corner of Maryland and Newstead avenues."[138] Archbishop Kain and numerous priests were inside the chancel rail of the chapel for the solemn requiem Mass. After the last absolution, given by Archbishop Kain, the funeral cortege, estimated at 125 carriages, made its way to Calvary Cemetery. The last rites of the Catholic Church were given to Chief Harrigan, and he was laid to rest.[139]

✳   ✳   ✳

In the meantime, the front-page headline of the *St. Louis Post-Dispatch* of January 5, 1899, proclaimed that Governor Lon Stephens would, in his message to the Missouri General Assembly, request a "Lexow Probe" for St. Louis. The article explained how the city government of St. Louis would be investigated by a committee "with powers of the famous Lexow Commission[d] of New York. . . ."[140] It was said in the state capital that "the charges of corruption, bribery and boodle in St. Louis municipal affairs have become so persistent that it is time the State step in and probe the matter to the bottom."[141] The committee would investigate all municipal and state governmental units in the city of St. Louis, including the police department.

The Senate investigating committee would ultimately consist of four Democrats and two Republicans, with one of the Democrats chairing the committee. The attorney general of Missouri would act as special counsel.

The board began preparations for meeting with the Lexow committee. One of the details the board wanted to impress upon the committee was that the police department had an inadequate number of police for the geographical area of the city. To illustrate this, the board decided to conduct an experiment that demonstrated two things. First, the department had too few officers for the large area. Second, and somewhat related to the first, the board wanted to refute the charge that policemen never appear on the scene of a shooting until it is over.

About 10:30 p.m. on Saturday, January 14, Commissioners Hawes and Forster, Chief Campbell, Sergeant of Detectives Desmond, Assistant Chief Pickel, and several newspaper reporters left the Four Courts and walked south to Thirteenth and Lami streets on the near south side of the city.[142] When they reached the intersection, Commissioner Hawes and Chiefs Campbell and Pickel each fired several

---

[d]The name was derived from a similar investigation in New York City. The commission was headed by State Senator Clarence Lexow.

shots into the air, a total of twelve. Twice, a club was rapped on the pavement three times, a signal of distress that every policeman within hearing was supposed to answer. A police whistle was blown twice. The group waited for thirty minutes and then began to leave. As it left, "an octogenarian night-watchman" arrived, out of breath, and explained that he had run several miles after hearing one shot.[143] No police officers arrived even though, said Chief Pickel, there was a relief post six blocks away. Second Platoon officers were expected to relieve First Platoon officers sometime after 11:00 p.m.

At the nearby intersection of Tenth and Morrison streets, four blocks east and a dozen blocks north of the first location, four shots were fired within a span of ten minutes. A police officer arrived at the intersection within two minutes of the last shot, twelve minutes after the first. The officer stated that he was at Eleventh and Park, about four blocks away, when he heard one shot. Needless to say, the commissioners and chiefs were less than thrilled about the response. Said Desmond, "We have not seen a policeman except the one who was too late at Tenth and Morrison."[144]

At 4:00 a.m. on Tuesday, January 17, a citizen who read the newspaper account of the Saturday experiment decided to conduct his own experiment.[145] He fired five shots into the air at the intersection of Fifteenth Street and Cass Avenue, just north of downtown, and then stepped into a hallway. He reported that he heard the approaching steps of policemen "in less time than it takes to tell it."[146] They made such a racket, said the citizen, that he first thought that it was a company of soldiers. None of the officers discovered the shooter in the hallway. But citizen heard the officers' conversation. The responding officers thought that it might have been the commissioners and chiefs "putting up a job" on them. After looking about for a while, the officers separated and returned to their beats.

On January 19, the Jefferson Club held its annual election. Since president Joseph W. Folk was not running for reelection, the field was open. The vice president of the Jefferson Club, Harry B. Hawes, was elected president. Joseph Folk was elected one of the seven directors. Harry Hawes was now president of the Democratic Jefferson Club and vice (and acting) president of the Board of Police Commissioners. Hawes apparently aspired to be president of the police board, however, not vice president. Since, by state law, the mayor was ex officio president of the board, it would be necessary to change the law.

Chapter Nine

Preparing for the New Century: The Police Act of 1899

IN A LETTER TO THE PUBLIC printed by the various city newspapers in December 1898, board Vice President Harry B. Hawes announced his proposal to go to the state legislature for a revision of the Metropolitan Police Act of 1861 and the subsequent amendments to that act. The department policing the fourth-largest city in the country needed more men, said Hawes. Providing data from other large cities, he asserted that St. Louis had about half the number of men needed to serve the city. "According to its size and population, St. Louis should not have less than 1200 patrolmen. With such a force the eight-hour system could be placed into operation and a reserve force maintained at all the stations to deal with riots and other emergencies."[1]

City ordinances authorized 685 patrolmen, and Hawes was recommending that the state legislature, rather than the city assembly, fix the number. There would be more in the proposed legislation than Hawes had provided in his public letter.

On the morning of January 4, 1899, the *Globe-Democrat* published an article indicating that the police were raising a "slush fund" to "assist in securing the passage of a bill at Jefferson City providing for an increase of salary for patrolmen and Sergeants."[2] The newspaper claimed that the fund was supposedly being raised without the knowledge of the heads of the department. A patrolman from each police district was elected by his peers to represent them on the committee. Patrolman Jacob Horine, Central District, was believed to be the head of the committee. Everyone interviewed by the *Globe-Democrat* reporter told him they knew nothing about such a committee. Assistant (and Acting) Chief of Police John Pickel also "professed ignorance of all that was going on."[3]

That afternoon, a reporter for the *Globe-Democrat* went to the Mounted Police station in Forest Park in the hope of interviewing Patrolman Horine. The reporter had learned that Horine was in a meeting in the second-floor assembly room.[4] The reporter went to the room and asked one of the clerks in the rear of the hall if he might speak to Patrolman Horine.

While he waited, the reporter saw Assistant Chief Pickel sitting next to Patrolman Horine. They were facing thirty or so police officers who were sitting in a semicircle in the front of the assembly hall. Chief Pickel had earlier, of course, told a *Globe-Democrat* reporter that he was unaware of any fund-raising efforts among the police.[5]

Instead of Horine, Captain George McNamee, commander of the Mounted District, came to the back of the hall. The reporter told him that he wanted to talk to Patrolman Horine. At that point, the reporter heard the secretary of the committee and Chief Campbell's secretary, Charles H. Jones, begin reading the minutes of the last meeting, December 22, 1898. Jones read the names of those present at the previous meeting; among them were Assistant Chief Pickel and Chief of Detectives William Desmond. The secretary then read the minutes of the first order of business at the previous meeting. "It was moved and carried to assess patrolmen $5 each," read the committee secretary, before he was stopped by Captain McNamee. The reporter was asked to leave, and Captain McNamee escorted him to the door. The *Globe-Democrat* published an account of the meeting in an article headlined "POLICE SLUSH FUND."[6]

When later interviewed, Jones denied any knowledge of any organization formed to assess police officers for lobbying efforts. When asked about the organizing efforts and the meeting at which he was reading the minutes, Jones replied, "What organization?"[7]

Needless to say, the newspaper pursued the story. In a subsequent edition under the same headline, the *Globe-Democrat* reported that the evidence indicated that the fund was wider in scope than simply a means for patrolmen to amass a fund to lobby for a bill that would benefit them. The newspaper asserted that the evidence suggested that commissioned members of the force were being assessed for a different reason. Said the newspaper, "The circumstances surrounding the whole business indicate that it has been resorted to as an additional means of drawing from the police an additional assessment for the [Democratic party] campaign fund."[8] The *Globe-Democrat* calculated that the assessment of turnkeys, probationary patrolmen, patrolmen, sergeants, detectives, and all officers above those ranks could yield a monthly "slush fund" of $5,010.[9]

The new police bill, Senate Bill 118, was authored by Senator John W. Drabelle, a Democrat from St. Louis. It repealed (and rewrote) the 1861 police act and all amendatory acts, and it was quite lengthy. It had thirty-six sections covering approximately ten printed pages. The act provided for some sweeping changes and appeared to favorably address a list of concerns of police boards that had accumulated over the previous thirty-eight years. Many of the listed features continue in the police department to this day, while others laid the groundwork for the present organization of the metropolitan police department:

1. The mayor of St. Louis, while still an ex officio member of the board, would no longer be the president; the president would be elected by the members of the board.

2. The president of the board, or vice president during the absence of the president, would be the executive officer of the board and act for it when the board was not in session.

3. The governor would appoint four board members for terms of four years each; there was no provision for staggered terms. Present commissioners would serve until the expiration of their terms.

4. Beginning with the effective date of the new law, the board was "required to appoint, enroll and employ a permanent police force."

5. The number of policemen to be appointed to the permanent police force was required to "be not less than" 850 patrolmen and 250 probationary patrolmen. The number of detectives to be appointed could be no fewer than 25.

6. The number of turnkeys appointed could not be less than thirty-five, and retired and disabled policemen were to be given preference.

7. Patrolmen, detectives, and turnkeys were to be appointed for four years, subject to removal only for cause after a hearing by the board.[a]

8. The bill gave military-style ranks to all "officers of police" and restored the rank of lieutenant of police. The chief of police would hold the rank of colonel, the assistant chief would be a lieutenant colonel. The chief of detectives would be a major, and the assistant chief of detectives, a lieutenant. The office of inspector of police was created, the inspector holding the rank of major.

9. The position of secretary to the chief of police was created, as was the position of superintendent of the Bertillon system.

10. The bill provided for an assistant chief of police and a chief of detectives, positions that did not exist under the old law. (While not in the old law, the board had created the position of assistant chief of police in 1892.)

11. The bill called for twelve captains, twelve lieutenants, and one hundred sergeants, each to receive commissions for four years unless removed by the board for cause.

12. Any vacancy in a rank had to be filled from the next lowest grade.

13. Probationary patrolmen had to serve at least one year before being eligible for promotion to patrolman. Patrolmen had to serve at least three years before being eligible for promotion to sergeant. Sergeants and lieutenants had to serve one year in their ranks before being eligible for promotion to the next rank. To be eligible for promotion to detective, patrolmen were required to first serve three years in that rank.

---

[a] In a speech before the Jefferson Club the following year, Harry Hawes referred to this section as "the civil service amendment" (Hon. Harry B. Hawes, *A Noonday Discussion of the St. Louis Metropolitan Police Law,* St. Louis: E. J. Schuster Printing Co., 1900, 23).

14. The appointment of a chief of police could no longer be made from outside the police department. The chief and the assistant chief of police had to be selected from members of the force, and they could only be chosen from those holding a rank not lower than captain. The inspector could only be chosen from those holding the rank of lieutenant or higher.

15. The act provided that the city should be divided into twelve districts with, if necessary, a station house or houses in each.

16. The board was required, on March 31 of each year, to prepare an estimate of the sum of money deemed necessary to discharge the duties imposed upon it for the next year. The Municipal Assembly was required to set that amount aside after first deducting from the city revenue the amount necessary to pay interest on indebtedness, the expenses of the city hospital and health department, the amount necessary for lighting the city, and any sum required by law to be placed to the credit of the sinking fund of the city.

17. Any officer or servant of the mayor or Municipal Assembly, or any other person, who violated any provision of the act was liable to a penalty of $1,000 for each and every offense. In addition, such person "shall forever thereafter be disqualified from holding or exercising any office or employment whatsoever under the mayor or municipal assembly of the city."

18. The board was authorized to appoint, mount, and equip as many policemen as deemed necessary for duty in the parks, outskirts, and such other portions of the city.

19. The president or acting president of the board was given the authority, upon knowledge "or satisfactory information," to issue search warrants to seize any gaming table or device or apparatus used in gambling, or any books, instruments, boards, or devices used to record bets. The act authorized the police to arrest any persons owning or operating such gambling devices.

20. The officer charged with execution of such warrant was given "the power to break open doors for the purpose of executing the same

and for that purpose may have the assistance of the whole police force."

21. The president or acting president of the board was constituted a magistrate and, upon complaint being made on oath that any personal property had been stolen or embezzled, and "the complainant suspects that such property is concealed in any particular house or place" in such city and, satisfied that there was "reasonable ground for suspicion," could issue a warrant in the same manner as a justice of the peace.

22. The act declared that members of the police force were officers of the city and officers of the state of Missouri and were to be recognized as such by all courts having jurisdiction of offenses against the laws of the state or ordinances of the city.

23. The act reiterated the power of the board to regulate and license all private watchmen, private detectives, and private policemen serving in the city. Failure to obtain the written license of the board was deemed a misdemeanor.[10]

Problems connected with the passage of the police act were mostly partisan. They centered on (1) how the bill was favorable to Democrats; (2) the loss of any input into police operations by the (currently Republican) Municipal Assembly of St. Louis; (3) the desire (mostly by Republicans) to create a bipartisan board; (4) the requirement that the city appropriate the amount submitted by the board; and (5) the levying of a $1,000 fine and the disqualification of the offending party from forever holding any office under the mayor or Municipal Assembly.

Senator Drabelle "expended six weeks in amending the bill, drawing up substitutes and making any and all changes he saw fit in the bill."[11] Republican Senator James M. Rollins offered an amendment providing for a bipartisan board. It would have two members of the board, one Democrat and one Republican, appointed by the governor. Two additional members would be selected by the mayor, one from each party, with the advice of the Municipal Assembly. It was voted down by the predominantly Democratic Senate. Later, Republican

Charles Busche would offer the same bill in the House of Representatives. Busche's amendment also failed.[12]

The Senate passed the police bill on February 21. The vote, along party lines, was nineteen to six, the former number cast by Democrats.[13] While the Democrats held a 61 percent majority in the House of Representatives, House passage of the bill would be more difficult.

The fight for passage of the new police act was unseemly. Some of the actions involving members of the police department were difficult to accept even in the political times. The intense scrutiny of the St. Louis newspapers, some of which were against the bill, also disclosed some indelicate features of the police department.

The police department heavily lobbied for the bill. In addition to the assessments, patrolmen presented petitions to businessmen on their beats. The petitions, allegedly endorsing the bill, were given to the Missouri House after the bill had passed the Senate. It was asserted later that the signatures, many of them of the most prominent businessmen in the city, were obtained under the impression that a signature endorsed only an increase in the number of patrolmen. All the signers contacted by reporters from the *Globe-Democrat* disavowed being in favor of the bill.[14]

It was reported that police commissioners, the chief, captains, sergeants, detectives, patrolmen, and even special officers personally appeared at the Capitol in Jefferson City, pushing for the passage of the bill.[15] At a meeting of the St. Louis Bar Association on March 6, former police commissioner James L. Blair referred to the lobbying efforts. Blair said that the force was working under many disadvantages. He cited

the existing system of appointment and promotion on purely political grounds, irrespective of merit; the practice of assessment for political purposes, which is, of course, a most iniquitous abuse of power. It goes without saying that the demand made by the constituted authorities that captains should contribute $25 each, sergeants $10 and patrolmen $5, as has recently been done in order to raise a fund for promoting the passage of the pending bill; that the chief, captains and sergeants should be taken from their duties to Jefferson City for the purpose of influencing the passage of the bill, and that the entire force of patrolmen should be employed in obtaining the signatures of citizens to petitions urging its enactment into law, must produce great demoralization.[16]

The new police bill was given final approval on March 15. Under Missouri law, it would take effect ninety days after the adjournment of the General Assembly, or August 20. The act applied to all cities having 300,000 or more inhabitants.[17] Incidentally, St. Louis was the only city in Missouri having 300,000 or more inhabitants.

The provision of the act authorizing the strength of the department to be not fewer than 850 patrolmen and 250 probationary patrolmen caused a high demand for police appointments. It was reported that, even before the bill passed the Missouri House, board vice president Hawes was so besieged by people wanting a job on the police force that he had to leave his office (in the Lincoln Trust Building, at Seventh and Olive streets) and go to the sixth-floor office of a friend.[18]

Rumors of appointments to the board abounded. Thomas J. Ward, who had lobbied for the bill in Jefferson City, was deemed a replacement for Dr. Otto Forster when his term expired. Ward, however, had earlier sided with Ed Butler's organization against the election of John Drabelle (the author of the new police bill) to the Missouri Senate. Hawes worked for the election of Drabelle, beating the Butler machine.[19]

At the meeting of April 19, the board deemed it "desirable & necessary" that the police department be reorganized. Since the board had been informed that "the department in Cincinnati is conducted upon modern lines and is noted for its efficiency & effectiveness" and, since Cincinnati chief of police Deitsch had extended an invitation, it was resolved that the four board members, Secretary of the Board McCaffery, Chief Campbell, Chief of Detectives Desmond, Superintendent of Police Stables Faulkner, and board stenographer Roscoe T. Shaw go to Cincinnati for two days, beginning April 26. At the same meeting, the board established the first awards system since the Honor Roll that was instituted in May 1873. The board passed a resolution that, at the end of each year, the Board of Police Commissioners would award two gold medals. A gold medal would be presented to the police officer displaying the greatest amount of courage during the year, and another to the officer making the most important arrests. On a lesser note, the board ordered that all captains, sergeants, patrolmen, and probationary patrolmen wear black shoes while in uniform.

At the meeting of April 25 the board, in executive session, wrestled with a notification from the city auditor that the salaries of patrolmen and probationary patrolmen was far in excess of the regular appropriations and that, in the future, he would refuse to allow the monthly payrolls if the amount requested exceeded the monthly share of the annual appropriation. Payday for the police was less than a week away. In response, the board adopted a resolution addressed to both the city council and the House of Delegates of the Municipal Assembly. The resolution stated that, unless additional money was appropriated, the board would, on May 1, "dispense with the services of all probationary patrolmen, 131 in number...."[20] The board added that the present force "is insufficient and the taking of any of the force would be unwise & a calamity to the community...."[21]

The resolution to both houses of the Municipal Assembly had an impact. As the *Globe-Democrat* pointed out the following day, "In almost every appointment made during the past few months, the probationary has been a man possessing political pull. These men are not expected to submit cheerfully to the wholesale suspension, and a powerful influence will be brought to bear upon the powers that control the Police Board."[22] Despite this, all probationary patrolmen were suspended from duty effective May 1. Vice President Hawes noted that when the new police act became effective, all of the suspended probationary patrolmen "who are worthy" would be promoted to patrolmen.[23]

On May 31, the board established a uniform fund. All members of the force would be assessed twenty-five cents a month for a fund that would keep "the clothing of the members of the force in first class condition *viz* cleaning, pressing & mended whenever necessary." At later meetings the board placed a patrolman (who likely had been a tailor before joining the department) in charge of the police tailor shop[24] and announced that the secretary of the board, the recipient of the uniform fund assessments, would pay all bills for the tailors' material and salaries out of the fund collected from members of the department.[25]

The board also accepted the resignation of Secretary McCaffery, effective May 31. The appointment of McCaffery as president of the Board of Election Commissioners would be announced by Governor Lawrence Stephens on July 17. The Board of Election Commissioners, three men appointed by the governor, had been established by the passage of the so-called Nesbit Election Law, and it replaced the election commissioner appointed by the mayor.

Thomas Ward was elected to succeed McCaffery, his appointment to take effect on June 1. As noted earlier, Ward had been an active lobbyist for passage of the new police act, and he was even mentioned as a possible police commissioner. One newspaper wryly noted

Thomas J. Ward. Courtesy of SLMPD.

that "from a financial standpoint the position is much more 'desirable' than membership in the board, as the secretary receives $2500 a year, while the Commissioners receive $1000 each."[26]

At the meeting of July 11, the board announced that clerks would receive two recreation days a month. This was the first time that civilian employees of the department had been given days off.

On July 17, Governor Stephens announced his appointments to the Board of Police Commissioners, effective August 20. They were Harry B. Hawes, Anton C. Stuever, Dr. Otto E. Forster, and William E. Atmore. All but Atmore, of course, were on the present board. Atmore replaced Lawrence Kingsland. Governor Stephens had appointed Kingsland, like McCaffery, to the Board of Election Commissioners.[27] Kingsland would attend his last board meeting on August 16 and would then resign to accept his new duties, which began on August 20. At the time of his appointment, Atmore had been a resident of St. Louis for fifteen years. In 1884, he had come to St. Louis from Louisville, Kentucky, as the city passenger agent for the Louisville and Nashville Railroad. He held that position when appointed to the board.[28]

On August 1, the board prepared for the implementation of the new police act by establishing an "examining committee" to screen new applicants for the department. The committee would be expected to prepare an examination that would demonstrate the applicant's proficiency in reading, writing, spelling, and elementary arithmetic. Members of the committee would include Chief Campbell, a captain, two sergeants, and one patrolman. Three physicians would also be appointed to pass upon the physical condition of all applicants. Five hundred and seventy applicants ultimately passed through the "Mental Examining Board." Of those, 466 passed and progressed to the physical examinations. A total of 346 applicants passed the physical.[29]

Among those passing both the mental and physical examinations were two black men, Hugh V. Allen and James A. Gordon. Five black men had applied, but only Allen and Gordon were successful.[30] The police department had no black officers, but Chief Campbell spoke highly of both of the successful applicants, especially Allen. Campbell called Allen one of the most intelligent men he had ever met, that he had a "remarkable aptitude."[31] Despite Chief Campbell's confidence that both men would be assigned to police duty, Allen and Gordon would not be among the one thousand patrolmen and probationary patrolmen sworn in later in the month.

On August 16, four days before the act of March 15, 1899, was to become effective, the city's Republican administration moved to stop it. A temporary injunction was applied for, and issued, by a St. Louis circuit court judge. The injunction restrained the members of the police board from reorganizing the police force or taking any action under the act of March 15.[32] Two days later, attorneys for the board appeared before a member of the Missouri Supreme Court and sued for a writ to prohibit the judge from enforcing his injunction. The state supreme court judge issued the writ prohibiting the lower court judge from enforcing his injunction and directing that it be dissolved.[33] The circuit court judge had failed to ask the board to respond to the issues before he had handed it down.[b]

Atmore attended his first board meeting on August 21. The first order of business was the reorganization of the board under the new police act. The board went into executive session to elect officers. The mayor would no longer be the ex officio *president* of the board, but an ex officio *member*, so the first office for which a member would be elected was that of president of the board. Hawes was elected president of the board; Atmore, vice president and treasurer; Stuever, purchasing member; Forster, member; and Ward, secretary. In conformance with the police act of 1899, the board declared the following officers "elected." Commissions were issued and the oath of office administered to

Colonel John W. Campbell, Chief of Police,

Lt. Colonel John N. Pickel, Assistant Chief of Police,

Major Edward L. Lally, Inspector of Police,

Major William Desmond, Chief of Detectives,

Lieutenant James H. Smith, Assistant Chief of Detectives,

Dr. Fred D. Johns, Superintendent, Bertillon system.[34]

---

[b] The city administration used the same approach (and the same judge) in an attempt to stop the Board of Election Commissioners from taking their seats on August 20. The election commissioners were also successful in having the injunction dismissed.

Major Edward L. Lally. Courtesy of SLMPD.

Dr. Fred D. Johns. Courtesy of SLMPD.

In addition, the board elected twelve captains, twelve lieutenants, and one hundred sergeants. Commissions were issued to those officers and the oaths of office were administered. The board then "enrolled and employed as a police force for the City of St. Louis and the oath of office . . . administered to" 850 patrolmen, 250 probationary patrolmen, 25 detectives, and 35 turnkeys. The total number of commissioned officers now stood at 1,289.[35]

The board met on August 18 to redistrict the city and assign six captains and ten of the twelve lieutenants. As the new law dictated, twelve districts were formed: the First through the Tenth districts, a Central District, and a Mounted District. Each district would be commanded by a captain in the daytime and a lieutenant at night.

The city, however, was not yet ready to give up its efforts to stop the police act from being implemented. On September 1, the board certified the payrolls, the amount due each member from August 1 through August 19, at the salary fixed by law up to that time, and the amount established under the act of March 15 for the period August 20 through August 31. The city auditor, Isaac Mason, refused to audit the payrolls on the grounds that the police act of March 15 was unconstitutional, that no appropriation had been made, and that the board had not certified the estimated amount of funds required by the act.[36]

On September 12, the board prepared a new estimate, in writing, of the amount necessary for the current fiscal year ending March 31, 1900. It certified the payrolls to the Municipal Assembly and delivered them to the city auditor. The auditor still refused to audit the new payrolls. The board then filed an alternative writ of mandamus setting out the above facts.[37] In his return, Mason substantially admitted the facts as stated, but claimed for a variety of reasons that the act of March 15 was unconstitutional. The case went to the October term of the Missouri Supreme Court.

Later in September, the board made some minor firearms and uniform changes. On September 19, the minutes of the board contain one sentence about the police sidearm: "The Smith and Wesson 38 cal. revolver was adopted for use in the Department."[38] There was no indication that the Smith and Wesson revolver replaced the others previously announced as the regulation revolver. All the newly hired patrolmen and probationary patrolmen would, however, have to outfit themselves with the Smith and Wesson revolver. At the meeting of October 31, the board also adopted the "Dwyer Strap and pistol holder," a belt and holster manufactured in St. Louis.[39] This was the first time that the department had gone to a holster on the outside of the uniform.

A special meeting was called for October 6 after the board learned that city comptroller wouldn't allow "secret service" money to be used in procuring the necessary evidence to close the poolrooms and to secure such legal assistance as deemed necessary. The poolroom, a place where offtrack betting operations took place, was a form of gambling new to St. Louis. The usual response of the board had been to retain persons unknown to the gambling operators to act as undercover (secret service) officers. They would enter the establishment and get enough evidence to provide "reasonable grounds" for the issuance of a warrant or for forced entry by police. The board paid them through a secret service account.

The members of the board were so adamant about closing the poolrooms that they decided to hire former Missouri lieutenant governor Charles P. Johnson, a lawyer, to represent them in matters related to the closings.[40] The police then began to raid the poolrooms, followed by saloons a week later. Eleven slot machines were confiscated. Under the provisions of the new police act, if the person permitting a gambling device on his or her premises was convicted in court, the president of the board could cause a notice to be posted on the place where the device was found. The notice gave the owner five days to appear before the president and show cause why the device should not be burned. Failure of the owner to appear or to show cause before five days resulted in the slot machine being burned.[41]

Because of the pending Missouri Supreme Court decision, meanwhile, the police had been working without pay since August 21. In the minutes of the meeting of November 7, the board noted two actions by merchants in the community to assist the unpaid police force. One local merchant offered underwear and other goods on account for any officer recommended by any member of the board "until such time as these men have been reimbursed for their service by the City. . . ." P. J. Dwyer offered "to furnish each policeman in the City of St. Louis, with the Dwyer Holster and Belt." Dwyer said that he would not require payment for the belt and holster until "the Supreme Court of Missouri passes upon the constitutionality of the Police Bill now before them. . . ." He added that if the bill was further contested, no money would be necessary until the final settlement.

At the meeting of November 21, Paul Arendes, who had a uniform contract with the department, offered credit to all officers (with no deposit required), so that they could call for their uniforms. On December 5, the board accepted an offer from the M. Goettler Hat Company to allow all captains, lieutenants, and sergeants to pick up the hats they had previously ordered without paying for them. The officers only needed to sign an agreement to pay for them when they were paid.

The Police Veterans' Association was organized at a meeting in Wenzel's Hall, Eighth Street and Franklin Avenue, with thirty-nine charter members. The purpose of the organization was "to promote fraternal relations among members and to provide relief in case of sickness."[42]

On December 19, the Missouri Supreme Court ruled in the case of *The State ex rel. Hawes et al. v. Mason*. The court, in a unanimous decision, ruled, "In our opinion it [the act of March 15] is a valid and constitutional law of this State, and as such is entitled to cheerful obedience by all persons and especially all officers, state and municipal."[43] The court directed the city auditor to audit the police department payrolls and draw a warrant on that amount. Said the court, "The fact that the whole police force has for three months guarded the city and protected its peace without one dollar of remuneration speaks volumes for their patriotism and fidelity to duty. Had they for one night refused to perform their duty, on account of the default in paying their salaries, one is appalled at the carnival of crime which would have resulted in our great metropolis."[44] It was a positive note for the dawning of the year 1900.

Chapter Ten

Policing "The Future Great City of the World"[a]

THE FIRST YEAR OF THE NEW millennium would be a violent one in St. Louis. The month of May saw yet another streetcar strike. What began as rock throwing and the cutting of trolley wires after striking workers were replaced, escalated to the dynamiting of rails and the shooting of pistols at the so-called scab motormen and conductors. The police board began hiring emergency special officers to augment the regular force and, ultimately, summoned a posse comitatus of one thousand men. The strike resulted in the deaths of a police officer and an emergency special officer and the wounding of three other officers. A patrolman would be shot to death in August, and another in October. It was a shocking year that began quietly enough, with the police board addressing two perennial problems.

1900

The board met on the second day of 1900, conducting a dozen trials of officers charged with a variety of complaints. Half of the twelve involved complaints of intoxicated officers, including one sergeant, four patrolmen, and a probationary patrolman. All six were found guilty; the sergeant, who was also charged with conduct unbecoming an officer, was dismissed from the force.

---

[a] L. U. Reavis coined the phrase when he wrote the 1870 book *Saint Louis: The Future Great City of the World*.

The board then addressed the continuing gambling problem in the city and the issue of intoxicated officers. Both had been addressed by virtually all boards since 1861. As earlier noted, gambling in

> St. Louis had even seen some Board members and at least one Chief of Police accused of being soft on the offense. The present Board addressed both problems with resolutions.

> Be it Hereby Resolved, that the Chief of Police is instructed to prefer charges against all sergeants and officers on whose precincts and beats gambling is discovered, for neglect of duty in reporting same.[1]

In the past, officers had been held accountable for omissions such as failing to find burglaries during their beats. The board now added gambling to that list. In addition, precinct sergeants were now to be held accountable for the failure of their beat men to report gambling on their beats or failing to report gambling that had been reported to them by their beat officers.

Said the resolution regarding intoxicated officers: "Be it Hereby Resolved, that all officers brought before the Board on a charge of intoxication, and the charge is proven, shall be dismissed from the force: and that such officers shall not be eligible for reinstatement."[2] While the latter resolution sounded ominous, all previous police manuals had prohibited drinking on duty and listed the maximum penalty as dismissal from the force. In addition, board resolutions on March 7, 1871, and August 1, 1893, prohibited the reinstatement of officers dismissed from the force.

The February term of the grand jury made its report to Criminal Court Judge David D. Fisher on March 26. One of Judge Fisher's charges to the grand jury in February had been to direct its attention to the alleged inefficiency of the police department and the prevalence of crime in the community. The grand jury reported, "We regret exceedingly to be obliged to state that no one has appeared before this Grandjury [sic] to substantiate such charges. . . . On the other hand, the police officials appear to be anxious for a thorough investigation of the department."[3]

The grand jury report stated that the police claimed to be aware of one of the causes of crime. The cause was "what is known as criminal suggestion and that the detailed description of crime is almost certain to be followed by similar crimes. The force of suggestion has been known to result in epidemics of crime."[4] Thus, the police suggested that the public might direct its attention to the newspapers and their detailed accounts of criminal activity as a cause for increased crime rates.

The February grand jury also pointed at another possible source: the police courts:[b]

> When offenders are subject to frequent arrests and when a system prevails under which they are either set free, fined simply the costs of the case, or when fined have their fines stayed; when grafters and professional bondsmen have it in their power to fix matters without the defendant being obliged to go to court; when wholesale arrests result in absolutely nothing, the administration of the law becomes a farce and the law itself is brought into ridicule and contempt.
>
> We approve of the system now introduced, to take the personal bonds of these unfortunates and release them on their own recognizance.[5]

✳　　✳　　✳

In the meantime, the transit workers in St. Louis were increasing their organizing efforts. On May 8, after their bosses allegedly had reneged on an agreement, over three thousand St. Louis Transit Company workers went on strike.[6] The president of St. Louis Transit, Edwards Whitaker, brought in strikebreakers from Cleveland to operate the streetcars. "Strikers, their wives, children, and sympathizers threw dead frogs and water-soaked bread at the scab motormen and rocks at the cars at first, then they graduated to cutting trolley lines, block-

---

[b] Police courts are today known as city courts. They handle traffic cases and city ordinance violations.

ing the tracks with rubbish and stones, and building bonfires on and dynamiting the rails."[7]

At 9:00 a.m. on May 9, the board met in a special meeting. Mayor Henry Ziegenhein was absent. Commissioner Atmore, who was ill, was excused. President Harry Hawes summoned Chief Campbell, Assistant Chief Pickel, Chief of Detectives Desmond, and all twelve captains before the board. Hawes, speaking for the board, set out three rules in dealing with the situation:

1. Use utmost care and diligence in dispersing riotous assemblages and to preserve peace and order at any cost.

2. Furnish extra ammunition to the men and instruct them to "use their revolvers and clubs freely on all occasions when it was deemed necessary."

3. Suspend any officers derelict in their duties or who show any signs of leniency toward the rioters and charge them with cowardice. Tell the men that anyone charged with cowardice would be summarily dismissed from the force at the first meeting of the board.[8]

The board would hold another special meeting that afternoon. At 2:00 p.m., the board met (with Mayor Ziegenhein again absent and Atmore excused because of illness) to discuss letters received from Edwards Whitaker and former police board member Charles H. Turner, president of the St. Louis and Suburban Railway Company.

Whitaker felt that the police force was inadequate to preserve the peace unless its numbers were increased or augmented by some other force. Whitaker added, "We have the men to operate our cars and will resume operation as soon as proper protection to employees and passengers is afforded."[9]

Turner's letter was short, but most descriptive of the dangers. He wrote that mobs hurled missiles of every description and often fired pistols at the motormen and conductors. Turner requested that the board declare an emergency and increase the size of the force.

In a communication to the board dated May 9, Chief Campbell replied that he had 1,078 men working two twelve-hour shifts. On May 8, the first platoon (day watch) worked twenty-four hours. Chief Campbell issued clubs to the men on the day watch to retain until the end of the strike, asserting that the strike area was so large that it was "absolutely impossible for me to prevent violence on all the roads with the men at my command."[10]

Another special board meeting was called on May 14. The minutes of that meeting contained a copy of a letter to Mayor Ziegenhein complaining of the condition of the streets where streetcars were operated. There were rocks and other refuse on the tracks and the street causing danger to citizens and police. Many police officers had already been badly injured, said the board, "and our mounted horses could not be used today."[11]

The board instructed Chief Campbell to advertise for, and employ, 2,500 men to serve as emergency special officers. The chief was also instructed to purchase five hundred revolvers and one thousand clubs for use by the specials.[12]

On May 21 a fifty-three-year-old widower, Duncan K. MacRae, was sworn in as an emergency special. Two days later, he was assigned as a guard on the Cass Avenue line. As the eastbound car approached the intersection of Cass Avenue and Cleary Street, a man stepped out of the crowd at the intersection and fired three shots at the Cass Avenue car.[13] On the third shot, MacRae, who had been riding on the rear platform, fell to the floor and shouted that he had been shot. The bullet had entered his right arm and passed through his body. The car was stopped and an ambulance summoned, but MacRae died before it arrived. Three officers in the crowd pursued the assailant south on Cleary Street and into an alley, but the suspect made good his escape.

The violence continued. At a special meeting called on May 30, John H. Pohlman, sheriff of the city of St. Louis, was called upon to summon a posse comitatus of one thousand able-bodied men "to act under the direction of the Board as conservators of the public peace in the city of St. Louis and during the continuance of the existing emergency . . . and that [Pohlman] shall, with his posse comitatus [*sic*] report forthwith." While the board acted under the provisions of Section 6219 of the 1899 Missouri Revised Statutes, there were those who thought that the formation of the posse took the heat off Harry Hawes and put it on the Republican sheriff just before the primary elections.[14]

The board held another special meeting the next day, May 31, and ordered Sheriff Pohlman to summon 1,500 additional men for the posse, bringing the number to 2,500.[15]

About 11:30 p.m. that night, Sergeant H. E. Lucy, who was supervising a squad of twenty officers guarding the streetcar powerhouse near Broadway and Osage Street, had his attention drawn to shots being fired nearby.[16] Sergeant Lucy, accompanied by three patrolmen, headed in the direction of the shooting. At Broadway and Osage they saw a man, later identified as Arthur Koenig, pointing a double-barreled shotgun at Patrolman Dennis Crane, who was standing near a wall of the Alexian Brothers Hospital. Koenig was said to have spent much of the evening drinking at the saloon at that intersection. The *Post-Dispatch* reported that Koenig had earlier been armed with the shotgun, which he had fired off at intervals. It was also reported that he had a revolver in his possession.

Crane ordered Koenig to "put up that gun," but Koenig replied with a "defiant exclamation" and began to advance on Crane. When he got within about ten feet of the officer, Koenig fired both barrels of the shotgun at him. Patrolman Crane fell to the ground, and Koenig ran back to the saloon with the officers in pursuit. Gunfire was exchanged in the saloon, and Koenig was shot to death by Officer Patrick Maher.

Crane died at the nearby Alexian Brothers Hospital at approximately 3:00 a.m. on June 1. He left a wife and two children. One of his two brothers, Jerry Crane, was a patrolman assigned to the Central District. Dennis Crane was buried in Calvary Cemetery on June 2.

At the board meeting that afternoon, on motion of Dr. Otto E. Forster, Chief Campbell was instructed to purchase 2,500 police riot guns and deliver them to Sheriff Pohlman for the use of the posse. The shotguns would remain the property of the police.[17]

On that same day, attorney Joseph Folk and the Reverend Willard Boyd, representing the workers, made a tentative settlement with the St. Louis Transit Company that affirmed the original agreement. While Folk was garnering praise from both labor and the newspapers, Edwards Whitaker kept hiring nonunion workers and, after a week, the strike resumed.[18]

The strike was taking a terrible toll. At the board meeting of June 8, the captains reported, in addition to the deaths of Patrolman Crane and Emergency Special Officer McRae, a total of nineteen officers were injured, three officers shot, and two officers assaulted.

Yet another probe of the police department was undertaken by the June term of the grand jury. One instruction given the June term was to investigate the police's handling of the transit strike. The grand jury presented its final report on July 6. The jury attacked the 1899 police law, the inefficiency of the police force, and the "refusal" of the police to protect the citizens of the city: "We lay the blame for much of the utter lawlessness that has occurred to the iniquitous police law which was passed by the last legislature, which takes the control of the police department entirely out of the hands of the citizens."[19]

The "hands of the citizens" was probably a reference to the removal of the mayor as ex officio president of the board, although the mayor remained on the board. The grand jury either ignored or didn't know that Mayor Ziegenhein seldom attended a board meeting. The grand jury report also ignored the fact that the four appointed members of the board were also citizens of the city.

The law was criticized for placing control of the police department in the hands of the president of the board rather than the chief of police:

It gives the president of the board authority to assume charge of the police force, although his previous education may not have specially fitted him for these duties. It allows him to supercede in authority the chief of police, who by virtue of his appointment under the law, must be experienced in the duties of the office; this same officer ... is deprived of using his judgment in the placing of proper men on the force, and is denied the power of removing others useless as police officers.[20]

The grand jury reproved the patrolmen and their superiors on the street: "We wish to condemn the patrolmen and officers who have so openly violated their oath of office in refusing to protect the citizens of this city from mob violence, which began on the 8th of May, and continued for so many days thereafter. We regret that we are compelled to publicly acknowledge the inefficiency of our police department...."[21]

Finally, the grand jury suggested that a committee be formed, consisting of two representatives each from the bar association, the Merchants' Exchange, the Commercial Club, the Business Men's League, and the St. Louis Manufacturers' Association, "to frame a new law to be presented to the next general assembly eliminating all [political] parties and political features."[22]

The next day, Harry Hawes publicly defended the police department. He also attacked the grand jury system: "A body of 12 men sit behind closed doors and hear one side of the case. The man who is accused is never allowed an opportunity to be heard...."[23] Hawes said that some of the statements were "absurdly ridiculous" and showed "an absolute lack of knowledge of the facts...."[24] He pointed out that the only real changes between the police laws of 1861 and 1899 were to increase the authorized number of police and to place "a civil service classification in the department which prevented politicians from interfering to a large extent with its operation."[25]

Hawes denied that the board interfered with the chief of police at any time during the transit strike. "He [Chief Campbell] had his own way from the start."[26] Hawes found the suggestion that the chief of police should appoint men to the force "amusing to anybody acquainted with the police systems of the United States. I challenge any member of the grandjury [*sic*] to name a single police department in the United States, no matter how small or how great it may be, where the chief of police has the power to appoint or the power to remove a police officer."[27]

Said Hawes in conclusion, "Hasty denunciation and unjust criticism does not elevate or improve the public service, but, on the contrary, it discourages proper effort, and our men who are now in the hospital and the friends of those who were killed will not sympathize with a report based on the information which brought about this one."[28] The emergency specials were dismissed that same day. Any additional problems concerning the transit system would be handled by the regular police force.

*　　*　　*

At the meeting of July 10, upon the recommendation of Chief Campbell, membership in the Police Relief Association became mandatory. Those not enrolled were given sixty days to do so, and all new appointees to the force would be given an application for the association at the time of appointment. Campbell estimated there were about 1,050 members, leaving about 200 not enrolled. He made the recommendation because "it affords every officer an opportunity, at the very lowest rate, to protect himself and his family."

Chief Campbell's words were prophetic. Seventy men were on duty in the Fourth District on the night of September 3. The standard operating procedure required that each officer call the station once each hour. Beat officers used call boxes to contact the telephone boys who manned the switchboards at the district stations. The officer first unlocked the box, then picked up the telephone, and then turned a crank to notify the district switchboard that there was an incoming call from a call box.

The beat officers in the Fourth District had no way of knowing that an electric wire at Eighth and Carr streets had dropped onto one of the police call box lines. It was later learned that the insulation had worn off the electric line and was sending approximately 3,300 volts through one of the Fourth District call box circuits.[29] When the news was first received at the Fourth District station that officers were receiving shocks from the call boxes, three men were sent out to tell the beat men not to use the call boxes.

About 7:15 p.m., Patrolman Nicolas F. Beckman went to the call box on Eighteenth Street between Wash (now Cole) and Carr streets to make his hourly call. A man who lived across the street, Daniel

Brothers, later described how he saw the officer unlock the box and immediately fall backward, screaming with pain. Brothers ran to the fallen officer and dragged him from the call box. Beckman was then carried across the street to Protestant Hospital. He died about fifteen minutes later without regaining consciousness.

Officers all along that particular call box line, which took a circuitous route over more than forty city blocks, were calling into the district station and receiving various degrees of electric shock. All who were shocked had their hands burned. Many were also knocked unconscious.

At 8:00 p.m., Patrolman John P. Looney used the call box at Twelfth (now Tucker) and Morgan (now Delmar). He was knocked to the ground and did not regain consciousness. Efforts were made to resuscitate him at the city dispensary, but Looney died a few minutes later.

After news of the fatal shocks to Officers Beckman and Looney reached the station house, a patrol wagon was sent out to spread the warning. In all, two officers had been killed and thirteen others injured (eleven patrolmen, the Fourth District telephone boy, and the city inspector of wires). An inquest held later found that the wires carrying the electricity had not been hung according to specifications, which called for a clearance of fourteen to eighteen inches between lines. Witnesses testified that the electric wire was hung approximately one inch to one and one-half inches above the police call box line.

Patrolman Beckman was twenty-six years old and was described as "a hero of San Juan Hill" in the Spanish-American War.[30] He was single and lived with his widowed mother and had been on the police force for just over a year. Patrolman Looney was forty-one years old and had been a member of the force for seven years. He was married and had two children. Both men were buried on the following Wednesday, September 5. Beckman was buried in Bethany Cemetery, Looney in Calvary Cemetery.

A day after the funerals, police officers began to publicly complain about a 20 percent pay "assessment" taken from their August salaries, levied by the State Democratic Committee. The *Globe-Democrat* was quick to point out that the secretary of the Board of Police Commissioners, Thomas Ward, was a member of the state committee.[31] Officers were also apparently not thrilled with the July 10 order that all officers were required to join the Police Relief Association.

A sergeant and a probationary patrolman, whom the newspaper did not identify, told a *Globe-Democrat* reporter why the policeman's lot was not always a happy one. Said the sergeant, in part:

> I am earning $115 per month as a Sergeant. On the first of the month I contributed $23 to the Democratic State Committee for the expenses of the campaign, that being 20 per cent of my pay for August. I was told this was expected of me, and I know too much to refuse. Of course, it is a voluntary contribution to the cause of Democracy. If I should fail to contribute I might not be dismissed from the department for it, but—well, I don't care to take any chances. . . . The first of next month it is a "cinch" that we will be assessed again for at least 20 per cent of our wages by the state committee, and by that time the city committee will be after us for nobody knows how much, and the same dose will probably again be given us November 1.[32]

The probationary patrolman said:

> I am only making $60 per month as a probationary policeman, and four months ago I was forced to join the Police Relief Association. Since then it has cost me $32, including my membership fee, a pretty steep figure for a third of a year's life insurance on a $2000 policy when I am less than 25 years old. Out of my $60 for August $12 went to the Democratic State Committee. If the city committee and the state committee both get in the first of next month, and I have to pay $9 to $12 for $2000 life insurance, I will be lucky if I can keep my wife and baby from going hungry until another pay day rolls around.[33]

The officer stated that probationary officers were young and ambitious and would "pay up our assessments and say nothing. But we do kick on the insurance feature which makes us pay just as much as the man 60 years old, and when it is by no means certain that we will remain a lifetime on the force."[34]

At the meeting of September 15, the board demonstrated that the requirement that officers wear uniforms off duty away from their homes, or without permission, was still in force. A patrolman was fined $20 for "donning citizens clothes without permission."

In late August, Chief Campbell learned that some slot machines came up with more than cherries and oranges. The police began investigating the so-called picture slot machines that were being "displayed in summer gardens, saloons and mutoscope parlors."[35] After depositing a coin, one could watch what were described as "risqué" pictures. Chief Campbell stated that the board would not appoint a censor from the ranks. Instead, each patrolman would judge for himself if the picture slot machines on his beat were "fit to be offered to the public gaze. The courts will have to decide later how nearly his judgment is correct."[36] Beat men would be required to inspect all the machines on their beats and prepare a written report concerning what was exhibited. If the views were represented as indecent, Chief Campbell stated, he would apply for warrants against the exhibitors.

Mutoscopes aside, gambling and prostitution continued to be issues. In October, the *Post-Dispatch* reported that policy games, which first appeared in St. Louis in March 1886, were operating daily in the city.[37] The newspaper reported the names of six "companies" that were operating games. Persons at the various policy shops told the reporter (who was not likely to have identified himself as a reporter) that there were at least two hundred places in St. Louis where policy tickets could be purchased. The *Post-Dispatch* printed the addresses of several of them.

The next day, the newspaper was pleased to report, police raided "all the policy shops that could be quickly located."[38] The order from Acting Chief Pickel was to close all the shops and arrest the dealers.

＊　　＊　　＊

Alexander M. Dockery was elected governor of Missouri at the November general election. Since the terms of Commissioners Anton Stuever and Dr. Otto Forster expired January 1, 1901, Governor Dockery would be, at the very least, replacing half of the board.

Just as important was the election of Joseph Folk to the office of circuit attorney. The circuit attorney was the Missouri counterpart of a district attorney. Folk, the former president of the Jefferson Club, had been elected when two major Democratic figures, Harry Hawes and Ed Butler, agreed to support Folk's nomination. Folk's election to the office of circuit attorney was his first step toward reform and the governor's mansion. For Hawes and Butler, Folk's reform efforts would later illustrate the adage, "Be careful what you wish for."

Another grand jury investigation closed out the year 1900. It began on Saturday night, December 15, when two prostitutes were being released on bond from the police holdover in the Four Courts.[39] One mentioned to the other that she would not have been arrested if she had given a certain officer a Christmas present. The desk sergeant heard the remark and immediately took the women to the lieutenant on duty, James Johnson. The women told their stories to the lieutenant. Because they were black prostitutes, they did not expect the police to believe them, so they said that they could prove that bribes were being taken if officers would accompany them to their house and lay in wait.

Assistant Chief Pickel and Lieutenant Johnson went to the house with the women and were secreted in a kitchen closet, which had an opening from which they could watch. An officer did come to the house and spoke with the women but, it was obvious from the women's questions and his responses, that he suspected some type of trap. He left the house after denying everything to the women.

Chief Campbell was informed the next morning and approved another watch at the women's house. About 11:30 p.m., this time in civilian clothes, Pickel and Johnson again hid in the closet. They had given the women two $5 bills from which they had recorded the serial numbers. About 11:45 p.m., a different officer came to the house and asked for $20. They replied that they only had $10. The officer took the two $5 bills and put them into his vest pocket after they told him they would give him the other $10 the next morning. Pickel and Johnson emerged from their hiding place when the officer turned to leave the house. The officer was placed under arrest and transported to the Four Courts building, where he was taken before Chief Campbell.

When Campbell asked the officer for his money, he handed over his pocketbook. Campbell asked the officer if he had any more money; the officer didn't answer. Pickel then told the officer to empty his vest pockets. The officer produced two $5 bills and gave them to Campbell. Before Campbell looked at the bills, Pickel gave him a memorial upon which the serial numbers of the bills were recorded; the numbers on the bills matched those in the memorial. The officer was ordered to take off his star and was taken into custody.

The two women were shown into Chief Campbell's office and identified the officer as the one to whom they had given the two $5 bills. In their statements, the women named other prostitutes who were paying police officers. A roundup of the others began immediately. Other officers were named, and all of the evidence was turned over to the December-term grand jury on Monday morning. The officer arrested by Pickel and Johnson and three other Central District patrolmen were indicted that afternoon, charged with accepting bribes and conduct unbecoming officers. Bench warrants for the arrest of the officers were given to the sheriff's department for service. Charges and specifications were also prepared for presentation to the board. Neither legal nor administrative dispositions of the cases have been located.

1901

The new year opened with a death. The vice president and treasurer of the board, William E. Atmore, died at his home on Saturday afternoon, January 5, 1901. Atmore had been ill since March 1900 with what was described as "an aneurism of the aorta."[40] He missed few meetings during that time even after his vocal cords became partially paralyzed and he had to communicate in writing. All flags on police department buildings were lowered to half-staff, and Atmore's chair was draped in black.[41] He was the first police commissioner to die while in office.

On January 7, Atmore's remains were removed from his residence on Cleveland Avenue and taken to the Masonic Temple at 1042 North Grand Avenue, accompanied by Chief Campbell, four captains, four lieutenants, sixteen sergeants, thirty-six mounted officers, and two hundred patrolmen. The commissioner's funeral was held on the third floor of the Masonic Temple that afternoon. The pallbearers were all members of Missouri Lodge No. 1, AF and AM. Antonio Bafunno's band led the funeral cortege to Bellefontaine Cemetery. The body was temporarily interred in a vault at the cemetery until Atmore's family from Louisville made a final determination of a resting place.

In February, the *Globe-Democrat* began publishing articles about the running of poolrooms in the city. Acting Chief of Detectives James Smith told the *Globe-Democrat* reporter that "raiding the pool rooms as it is now done is all a farce. We get into a place, make arrests, and then before the patrol wagon has left the rooms are running in full blast again with new men taking bets."[42] Smith explained that officers in plain clothes had to be brought from other districts so that the operators did not recognize them as police. Now, said Smith, "anyone who wants to enter has to be vouched for by one of the managers of the room or by some well-known player before he can get into the room."[43]

Chief Campbell said, "It is almost impossible for us to get a man into the pool rooms. When he does get in he makes his bet, puts up his money, but receives no written ticket to certify to his wager. . . . Then, when one of our men figures in a prosecution, his future usefulness in that line is ended."[44] Campbell added that there were over fifty cases pending in the Court of Criminal Correction against poolroom men. Nonetheless, raids of poolrooms began within days of the *Globe-Democrat* articles.

Governor Dockery made his appointments to the Board of Police Commissioners on February 19.[45] All were appointed to terms ending January 1, 1905. Harry B. Hawes was reappointed to the board. Hawes would be joined by Theodore R. Ballard, Andrew F. Blong, and William F. Woerner. All were confirmed by the Senate on February 21.[46] Ballard was a member of the grain commission firm of Messmore and Ballard. He was second vice president of the Jefferson Club and first vice president of the Merchants' Exchange. Blong was a member of the firm of James S. Dowling and Company, painting contractors, and an active Democratic politician. He was identified

Theodore R. Ballard. Courtesy of SLMPD.

Andrew F. Blong. Courtesy of SLMPD.

with the Barrett-Lemp faction of the Democratic Party, described as opponents of the Jefferson Club. The *Globe-Democrat* described Woerner as "a prominent attorney and a wealthy man."[47] His late

William F. Woerner. Photograph by Gerhard Sisters, early 20th century. Missouri History Museum.

father had been a judge of the probate court and a prominent representative of the southside Democrats. This new member of the board was a Democrat, but he had never held public office or participated in party politics.

The board held its first meeting on February 26. Mayor Ziegenhein, who seldom attended a board meeting, was present.[c] Ziegenhein, who was nearing the end of his term, had decided to attend future

[c] While the general public was probably unaware of Mayor Ziegenhein's absenteeism, he would be remembered for his comment concerning the fact that two-thirds of the city were still not lighted in 1900. Said the mayor, "We got a moon yet, ain't it?" (*St. Louis Post-Dispatch,* September 8, 1900, p. 1).

meetings of the board.[48] The meeting started on a routine note: the organization of the board. Hawes was elected president, Woerner was elected vice president and treasurer, and Blong was elected purchasing member of the board. Thomas Ward continued as secretary.

The board then went into an executive session. It quickly became apparent that the business conducted in the closed session had been orchestrated.[49] The first item on the agenda was the consideration of a request from Chief Campbell. In a letter to the board, Campbell asked for a reduction from his present rank of chief of police to captain of police. Ziegenhein moved that Campbell be permitted to come before the board and make any statements he cared to about the request. Chief Campbell said that he had nothing to say beyond what was contained in his letter. It was moved and seconded that Campbell be reduced to the rank of captain. The motion passed on a 4–1 vote, with Ziegenhein voting against it.[50]

Next, the former superintendent of stables, William Faulkner, now the general manager of police proprieties, appeared before the board on behalf of the Assistant Chief Pickel, stating that Pickel also wished to be reduced to the rank of captain. "His Honor Mayor Ziegenhein made the same objection as he did to the reduction of Chief Campbell."[51] It was moved and seconded that Pickel be reduced to captain. The motion was approved on the same 4–1 vote.

Hawes moved that the board proceed to the election of a new chief and assistant chief. Woerner objected to the motion because he had not had time to look into the merits of the various captains. Ziegenhein also objected. Nonetheless, Hawes declared that nominations for chief of police and assistant chief were open. Ballard nominated Captain Mathew Kiely. Ziegenhein nominated Captain William Young. Kiely was elected the new chief of police on a 3–1 vote, Ziegenhein voting for Young, and Woerner abstaining. Woerner then placed Young's name in nomination for assistant chief. Hawes nominated Captain Christ G. Gillaspy. Gillaspy was elected assistant chief of police on a 3–2 vote, with Woerner and the mayor voting for Young. The changes would take effect on March 1. The board then adjourned until the next afternoon.[52]

Chief Mathew Kiely. Courtesy of SLMPD.

Assistant Chief Christ G. Gillaspy. Courtesy of SLMPD.

His unexpected appearance at the board meeting suggested that Mayor Ziegenhein had been alerted that Campbell and Pickel were going to ask for reductions in rank. The mayor likely wanted to get Captain Young an appointment to one of the positions. As earlier noted, Vice President Woerner had never participated in party politics and had never held public office. He was probably surprised by the politics of the whole situation. The actions of the board at the first meeting he attended were likely the catalyst for Woerner's imminent departure.

The next day, February 27, the board found the intoxication issue literally in front of them. Of the twelve disciplinary cases heard by the board, seven were for being intoxicated on duty. Ignoring the resolution adopted by the board a year earlier that any officer found guilty of intoxication would be dismissed from the force, the board applied that action to just one of the seven cases. One probationary patrolman was dismissed, one was fined $65, and five patrolmen were fined $90 each and reprimanded. On the heels of these actions, the board ordered "that the punishment for Intoxication in the future be <u>absolute</u> <u>dismissal</u> from the force and that the order to this effect be read at all roll calls for the next 30 days."[53]

In March, the Jefferson Club organized a "colored auxiliary."[54] Police officers, who had been complaining to the newspapers about the assessments that they had to pay to the Jefferson Club, were upset because they thought the auxiliary would increase their assessments. One officer who had recently resigned from the police department wrote to the *Globe-Democrat*. In part, he said, "I felt that I had been bled until I couldn't stand it any longer. I was born in Missouri, of Democratic parents, and have been a Democrat all my life, but I don't believe in machine politics or in the methods employed by the police department in taking money from its men . . . I felt I owed it to my wife and babies to get off the force."[55] The officer claimed that many other officers were also "disgusted" with the situation. Later in the year, another police officer would complain: "We have always considered it wrong to assess us to keep up the Jefferson Club, a purely political organization, maintained for the benefit of a few well-known politicians. But we have been compelled to meet these assessments promptly or else lose our jobs. . . ."[56]

On March 28, the police department followed the lead of the Jefferson Club. Two black men, Andrew J. Gordon, a shoemaker, and Allen W. Wilkinson, a barber, were appointed probationary patrolmen. They were assigned as special officers under Chief of Detectives

Andrew J. Gordon. Courtesy of SLMPD.

William Desmond. Chief Kiely told the *Post-Dispatch* that the two officers "were appointed to work on cases among negroes" and "may never appear in uniform."[57] No board meeting was held the day they were appointed, and the minutes of the board meetings made no mention of the appointments of Gordon and Wilkinson.

In an editorial, the *Globe-Democrat* pointed out, "The appointment of deserving negroes to responsible positions under proper conditions must have everyone's unqualified approval. It is much-needed opportunity tardily given."[58] However, the editorial continued, "the

Allen W. Wilkinson. Courtesy of SLMPD.

appointment at this particular time by such a power bears only one interpretation."[59] The inclusion of the phrase "at this particular time" referred to the fact that the city's general election was less than a week away and, among other offices, the Democrats wanted to wrest the mayor's office from the Republicans. Most black St. Louisans were Republicans.[60] There was even some speculation that, after the city election, Gordon and Wilkinson would be let go.[61] Not only did that not happen but, two years later, Gordon would receive an award from the police department.[62]

On March 9, Governor Dockery received the resignation of board vice president and treasurer Woerner. Woerner, who had been a member of the board a little more than a month, told the *Post-Dispatch* "that he never intended to remain permanently on the board. . . ."[63] He wanted to quit before the city primary election was held so that Republicans wouldn't have the opportunity to cry that he quit the board because of election frauds. His resignation was officially accepted by Governor Dockery on April 14. Woerner had attended three board meetings.

The city election, to elect a mayor, the members of the city council, and the members of the Board of Education, was April 2. It was a city election different from any others. Hawes continued his alliance with Butler. For mayor, the Democrats chose Rolla F. Wells, the president of the American Steel Foundry Company. Wells was the son of the highly respected Erastus Wells, the city alderman and member of

Rolla F. Wells. Steel engraving by Central Biographical Publishing Co., ca. 1890. Missouri History Museum.

the U.S. House of Representatives who had written the 1861 Metropolitan Police Act. Rolla Wells would win the election.

The next day, Governor Dockery appointed William G. Frye to the Board of Police Commissioners to fill the vacancy left by Woerner. Frye, forty years old, was president and treasurer of the Philibert and Johanning Manufacturing Company, where he had been employed for twenty years.[d] He was also president of the Millman's Association, an organization that included all the window and door

---

[d] In January 1902, the firm became the Frye Manufacturing Company.

manufacturers in the city, and he president of the Western Sash and Door Association.[64]

The meeting of April 19 marked the first appearance of Frye and Mayor Wells. Mayor Wells would remember his first board meeting; he was refused admission to the boardroom. The mayor had arrived

William G. Frye. Courtesy of SLMPD.

several minutes after the other members, and the janitor guarding the door didn't recognize him. Mayor Wells wasn't admitted until a passing police officer, who knew the mayor, vouched for him.[65]

President Hawes requested that he be allowed to resign as president of the board so that the two new members would have a voice in the selection of the president. His request was granted. Andrew Blong also resigned his position as purchasing member. Frye then nominated Hawes for the presidency, Mayor Wells seconded the nomination, and Hawes was unanimously reelected. Frye was unanimously elected vice president, and Blong, purchasing member. The position of treasurer was temporarily left open. Theodore Ballard would be elected to that position a month later.

On May 3, the board appointed Chief Kiely, Inspector of Police Edward Lally, and Captains Peter Reynolds, Peter Joyce, and Edmond Creecy to a committee to draft a new police manual and present it to the board as soon as possible. The board, which had been meeting on Fridays since April 19, also officially moved the weekly meetings from Tuesdays to Fridays. With slight variations, the Board of Police Commissioners had been meeting on Tuesdays since 1869.

At the next meeting, the board instructed Chief Kiely and Chief of Detectives Desmond to go to Cincinnati and Boston to "investigate the departments" and then attend the National Association of Chiefs of Police convention at New York City, which began on May 28. In addition, the board ordered that, "if there is nothing against an officer," all those appointed probationary patrolmen on August 21, 1899, would be given preference in promotion to the rank of patrolman until all had been promoted.[66]

On June 15, LuLu Brooks entered the Fourth District station at Seventh and Carr streets and informed Captain Samuel Boyd that a man she identified as William Turner had beaten her and threatened to stab her with a knife. Patrolmen Richard Delaney and Nicholas Roach were instructed to escort Brooks to Turner's home and arrest Turner.[67]

The officers arrived at the Turner home, at 1315 North Sixth Street, about 6:30 p.m. Officer Delaney prepared to enter the front door, telling Officer Roach to go to the back door. LuLu Brooks started into the house behind Delaney. She later said that she saw Turner with a revolver and that the officer had also drawn his revolver. Brooks said she didn't know who fired the first shot, but she ran from the house as soon as a shot was fired. A detective later searching for Turner found her several blocks from the scene.

Roach later said he had barely reached the backyard when he heard several shots. Unable to get into the house through the back door, Roach ran to the front. When he reached the sidewalk, he saw Delaney backing down the front steps. As Delaney fell to the ground, he told Roach that he was shot and to get Turner. Roach ran into the house, but Turner was gone. Captain Boyd and several officers ran from the station to the scene. An ambulance was called, but Delaney was dead.

Turner was arrested in East St. Louis, Illinois, about two hours later. After the shooting, he had taken the North Market Street ferry across the river. He had been shot in the leg, and he claimed that he had returned fire after the officer had shot him. An ambulance picked him up and returned him to the city. After his leg wound was treated at the city dispensary, he was jailed. Turner was later convicted and sentenced to ten years in prison.

Patrolman Delaney was twenty-nine years old and had been one of the many probationary patrolmen appointed to the force on August 21, 1899. He was first assigned to the Sixth District and, in March 1900, had been transferred to the Fourth District. He was survived by a wife and two children and was buried in Calvary Cemetery on June 18.

Sometime during the year, the board authorized the formation of a gambling squad. While the board minutes make no mention of its formation, the minutes of the board meeting of December 4 indicate that Lieutenant James Johnson was in charge of the squad.

In anticipation of the Louisiana Purchase Exposition scheduled for Forest Park in 1903, the board met on December 6 to clean up a part of the city to which visitors would immediately be exposed. The board adopted the following preamble and resolution:

> Whereas, Chestnut Street and part of Pine Street, extending from the vicinity of Union Station to Jefferson Ave. is and has been for some time ocupied [sic] almost exclusively by prostitutes and lewd women so that it has become known as the Scarlet or "Tenderloin District" of the City; many complaints having been filed with the department because of the nearness of this district to the Union Station; because Pine and Chestnut streets will be, during the World's Fair period, the two principal highways to that exhibition, and because the locality, by changed conditions, has become more conspicuous than desirable; be it hereby, Resolved, ... [68]

What the board then resolved to do was sure to create controversy. First, the board wanted to determine if "citizens and representatives of different organizations social, business and religious" wanted to move the prostitutes and lewd women from that area. Second, if removal was desired, it would be necessary to select a district "where the unfortunate women may reside, as experience has shown both the futility and harm which follows an attempt of an order of general removal without indicating in some manner the locality to which it seems desirable they should go as being the least objection-able to the general public and best removed from thoroughfares largely used by the public."[69]

The area in question, Chestnut Valley, was the city's "sporting district." To obtain feedback from the public, the board scheduled a meeting for December 18. Secretary Ward was directed to notify the presidents and secretaries of the various social, business, and religious organizations and societies in the city of the purpose of the meeting and request that said representatives participate in the inquiry by written statement or by attending the meeting. Approximately 228 invitations would be mailed.[70]

The December 18 meeting was attended by about thirty persons, "for the most part ministers and representatives of district improvement societies."[71] President Harry Hawes explained to the attendees that if it was determined at the meeting that the designated area should be cleared of prostitutes, the next step would be to determine a district where the prostitutes could be relocated. The latter issue would be discussed at a second meeting.

Several of the clerics spoke to the issue, all in favor of cleaning Chestnut Valley of prostitutes. At the conclusion of the meeting, the board noted, "Upon hearing from all attending said meeting it was the unanimous opinion that all lewd women and prostitutes should be placed in a district and moved from pine [*sic*] and chestnut [*sic*] streets."[72]

1902

On January 15, 1902, the board held the second Chestnut Valley meeting to suggest various locations where the prostitutes might be relocated. This was also an open meeting, and a crowd filled the Four Courts an hour before the scheduled starting time.

Ultimately, fourteen locations were suggested at the meeting. Several different persons suggested areas in the oldest part of the city from Sixth, Fourth, Third, or Second streets to the Mississippi River, and from Market, Walnut, Lombard, or Clark streets to Chouteau. Others proposed areas several blocks farther west.

A third meeting concerning Chestnut Valley was held at the boardroom on January 22 to allow persons who lived or owned property in each proposed location to speak. As before, the boardroom was filled and overflowed into the adjacent hallways. After each district was announced and objections heard, Secretary Ward listed the number of objections for each.[73] After all the objections were heard, the board adjourned the session. The board stated that it would later announce the selected location. For reasons to be later noted, however, the date of the Louisiana Purchase Exposition would be postponed until 1904. The area into which the women of Chestnut Valley would be moved was never revealed.

The new police manual, which had been in the works for two years, was the subject of a special session of the board on Monday, May 5. The board reviewed, and then adopted, the 1902 manual. The major change was organizational: the formation of two "bureaus." Uniformed officers were placed in the Patrol Bureau, and detectives in the Secret Service Bureau.[74] The new manual noted that meetings of the board would be held on Fridays.

On June 27, Captain John W. Campbell, commander of the Tenth District, resigned "to accept a responsible position with the Etna Life Insurance [Company]."[75] His resignation was accepted at the board meeting that afternoon. Campbell was appointed to the police force in 1876. He had been chief of police on two different occasions. Said Campbell, "While the offer made me [by Etna] was quite flattering, I did not take this step hastily, but after careful consideration. I leave the department with the kindliest feelings for everyone connected therewith."[76]

In September, a committee composed of Commissioners Frye, Ballard, and Blong was appointed to considering the feasibility of forming a bicycle corps in the police department.[77] The minutes of the meeting of October 10 note that "the committee appointed in reference to forming a bicycle core [sic] in the department, recommended having two stationed at head quarters."[78]

At that same meeting, a committee was established for awarding gold medals to officers in various categories. The five-member committee would consist of the president of the Merchants' Exchange, the president of the Business Men's League, the president and vice president of the Board of Police Commissioners, and the chief of police. Gold medals were awarded in a ceremony at the second annual review and parade held on October 21.

Less than a week after the annual review and parade, pomp and circumstance gave way to sorrow. Early on Sunday morning, October 26, Robert C. Walsh, a clerk in the drugstore on the southwest corner of Tenth Street and Cass Avenue, was awakened by the sound of breaking glass. Walsh, who lived across the street from the drugstore, looked out the front window and saw three men in front of it. One was breaking the glass while the others acted as lookouts. Walsh waited until the first man had crawled into the store and then opened the door for the other two. Walsh then leaned out his window and began shooting at the burglars.

Fifth District patrolman Michael Reedy, who walked a beat on Cass Avenue, heard the shots being fired and ran toward Tenth Street. As Reedy turned the corner onto Tenth Street, one of the shots fired by Walsh struck Reedy in the chest. Reedy was taken to City Hospital in a carriage, where he was admitted in critical condition.[79] He died in the hospital at approximately 8:00 p.m. on Monday, October 28. According to the *Post-Dispatch*, "In an ante-mortem statement Reedy exonerated Walsh."[80] Patrolman Reedy was thirty-five years old and unmarried, and he resided with his sister. He was buried in Calvary Cemetery on October 31. Three men suspected of the drugstore burglary were later arrested.

In the days following his nomination for the post, Circuit Attorney Joseph Folk had repeatedly promised to do his duty if elected, a promise made by virtually everyone running for office. But Folk meant it. "Years later it was common to attach much significance to Folk's routine assertion, the implication being that it was a sort of warning all along that he intended to reform the St. Louis government."[81] Harry Hawes's police department would not be immune to Folk's reform efforts.

1903

On February 26, 1903, the February grand jury indicted a syndicate, consisting of four men, who were charged with renting houses and filling them with young female prostitutes. The charges were misdemeanors punishable only by fines or sentences of less than one year in the city workhouse. The houses were located on Linden (now Gamble) near Twelfth Street, and on High Street (now Twenty-third Street) between Morgan (Delmar) and Lucas. All were in the Fourth District commanded by Captain Samuel Boyd. On March 2, Captain Boyd was indicted on two counts of neglect of duty in connection with the houses of prostitution operated by the syndicate. Like those handed down against the four members of the syndicate, the indictments were for misdemeanor violations.

The following day, after conferring with President Hawes, Chief Kiely suspended Captain Boyd from duty pending the outcome of the trial. Hawes then released a statement to the press. In it, Hawes said that a jury would determine Boyd's guilt or innocence. He praised Boyd for his thirty-three years of service during which "not one dishonorable act [has] been charged against him."[82]

Captain Boyd's trial was set for March 7 in the Court of Criminal Correction but, at the request of the defense, the case was continued to March 30. At the second setting, the prosecuting attorney "asked that a nolle prosequi be entered in the two cases charging Samuel Boyd, captain of police, with neglect of duty."[83] The reason, said the prosecuting attorney, is "that it is the desire of the State to substitute one broader in scope and of a different nature."[84] The substance of any new charge was not learned. Nonetheless, Boyd was "exonerated by the court of criminal correction."[85] Chief Kiely reinstated Boyd.

In the meantime, the Jefferson Club sent a letter to the members of the police department soliciting contributions to aid the Democrats in winning the city election on April 7. Approximately eight hundred members of the department were members of the Jefferson Club. The letter stated that, while a contribution was sought, there would be no lists passed around on which to pledge a donation.[86]

In the early morning hours of Sunday, May 16, Probationary Patrolman Hugh McCartney, for reasons that were not determined, was involved in a violent struggle with a group of men near the cracker factory on Clark Street, near Fourteenth Street. McCartney was shot in the abdomen by one of the men, supposedly one William Washington. McCartney returned fire and killed Washington. The officer was taken to City Hospital where, on May 31, he died. McCartney, who had just been appointed to the force in January, was married and had three children. He was buried in Calvary Cemetery on June 2.[87]

In June, the U.S. Congress approved a one-year delay of the Louisiana Purchase Exposition. Some state and federal exhibit structures were not likely to be ready by the original opening date of April 30, 1903, and several nations were not certain that they would be able to meet the deadline and were sending regrets. However, the ceremonial dedication of the World's Fair, from April 30 through May 2, 1903, would proceed as scheduled.[88]

At the meeting of June 26, the board ordered that all members of the police force be subject to a physical examination. Commissioners Frye and Blong and Mayor Wells were appointed to provide for the exams, which would report the age, height, weight, and physical condition of each officer. As a result of the physical examinations, the board took action against one hundred members of the department. Two sergeants, thirty-six patrolmen and probationary patrolmen, and seventeen turnkeys were dropped from the rolls of the department. Twenty-three sergeants and three detectives were reduced to the rank of patrolman. Seventeen patrolmen were reduced to the rank of turnkey, and two patrolmen were retired on physical disabilities.[89]

Virtually all of the remaining members of the police force were commissioned for four years effective September 1.

At the meeting of October 2, the board declared vacant the office of superintendent of the Bertillon system. Dr. Fred D. Johns, the superintendent, was dropped from the rolls. He was replaced by John M. Shea, who was promoted to detective just three days earlier. Johns had been appointed the first superintendent of the Bertillon system in

John M. Shea. Photograph, ca. 1900. Missouri History Museum.

1899. The new superintendent was generally referred to as "Camera Eye" Shea. It was said that he had the photographs of forty thousand criminals in his head and could "recall a face or feature he has seen on a photograph with remarkable agility."[90]

At the board meeting of October 16, the number of black policemen on the force was reduced by 50 percent. After a hearing, Special Officer Allen Wilkinson was dismissed from the force for "conduct unbecoming an officer." A saloon keeper filed a complaint against Wilkinson for interfering with his business, after he had ordered a crowd from a saloon for disturbing the peace and had arrested one of the patrons. Residents in the area of the saloon had complained of the noise to Wilkinson, who also lived in the area.[91] Wilkinson and the other black officer on the force, Andrew Gordon, had been appointed in March 1901. Wilkinson would be replaced by the appointment of another black officer in November.

The annual inspection and parade was held on October 20. Gold medals for the "best arrests" were presented to Detective Michael Cremin and Special Officer Andrew Gordon, who was the first black officer to receive the award.[92] The gold medal for "greatest act of bravery" was presented to Patrolman James F. Dockery of the Fourth District, who had rescued two small boys from drowning in the Mississippi River at the foot of Carr Street.[93] On November 25, the board

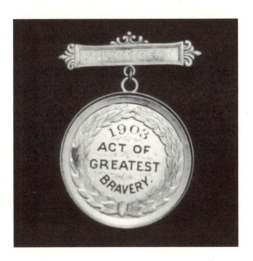

Patrolman James F. Dockery's medal. Courtesy of SLMPD.

appointed another black applicant, Hugh V. Allen. In December, the president of the Louisiana Purchase Exposition Company, David R. Francis, met with the board to discuss how many "custodians of the peace" would be required at the fair and who would pay them.[94] The Louisiana Purchase Exposition Company wanted the city to pay. However, at other expositions in the country, the exposition management had paid the bill. The exposition company had created a unit called the Jefferson Guard to police the grounds but, at this point, the members of the Jefferson Guard had yet to be given any powers, and they considered themselves watchmen.[95]

It was estimated that the number of extra police officers that would be needed to provide coverage of the forty-seven acres of fairgrounds would "be in the neighborhood of 500."[96] The estimated cost was not less than $300,000. No decision had been made at the conclusion of the meeting, but a careful study would be made of the plan executed at the 1893 World's Columbian Exposition in Chicago.

In the meantime, the enmity between Harry Hawes and Joseph Folk was coming to a head. Folk had investigated and successfully prosecuted election fraud in St. Louis and had sent "boodlers" (bribers and those bribed) to prison, regardless of political party affiliation or social status in the community.[97] Folk had been urged to run for governor and, at the Democratic Convention in Jefferson City in July, overwhelmingly beat Harry Hawes, whose name had also been placed in nomination.[98]

On December 16, Hawes resigned from the board. In a telegram to Governor Dockery, Hawes asked that his resignation be immediately accepted. Governor Dockery obliged, and then appointed Richard Hanlon to complete Hawes's term, which would end on January 1, 1905. There was speculation that Hawes wanted to run for governor of Missouri in 1904.[99] While he did not make an official announcement, Hawes released a statement to the press that many people had asked him to seek the nomination for governor and he had always replied, "I would resign [from the board] if I entered the field and would make a canvass of the state."[100] Hawes added that he would make an official announcement at a later date.

Richard Hanlon was forty-nine years old. For many years, he was employed by the Levis-Zukoski Mercantile Company of St. Louis. In 1902, he organized his own company, the Richard Hanlon Millinery Company, at Twelfth and Washington. While Hanlon had not been active in Democratic Party politics, he was a member of the board of directors of the Jefferson Club, having been a member since the club was organized. Governor Dockery stated that Hanlon had been "suggested and indorsed [sic] as Mr. Hawes' successor by Mayor Wells and Commissioners Frye, Ballard, and Blong, and that he is a representa-

Richard Hanlon. Courtesy of SLMPD.

tive business man and loyal Democrat."[101] Hanlon would attend his first board meeting on December 18.

In the meantime, the *Sunday Magazine* supplement of the *St. Louis Post-Dispatch* outlined how Chief of Detectives Desmond was preparing to deal with the criminals from all over the world who would descend upon the World's Fair. Chief among the tools was a combination of the rogues' gallery and photographs of known criminals. The photograph would be pasted to the blank side of the Bertillon card so that one card would contain all of the identifying physical information and the latest photograph.[102]

The various metropolitan police departments in the United States were asked to put together exhibits for the World's Fair that told the stories of the most infamous crimes and criminals with whom each police department had dealt. Chief of Detectives Desmond prepared the St. Louis exhibit. Among the items in the exhibit was the rope used to hang Hugh M. Brooks, convicted of murdering C. Arthur Preller

Chief William Desmond's collection of burglars' tools and criminal curios displayed at the Louisiana Purchase Exposition. Photograph by Byrne's Photographic Company, 1904. Missouri History Museum.

William Desmond, Chief of Detectives. Photograph by Byrne's Photographic Company, 1904. Missouri History Museum.

in the Southern Hotel in 1885, and the trunk that Brooks used to conceal Preller's body. Desmond also had prepared a cabinet containing a collection of burglar tools and revolvers that figured in a number of murders.[103] A rogues' gallery would be on display, as would an exhibit of the Bertillon system of measuring and photographing criminals and a demonstration of the police telephone system.[104]

Police departments from the major police systems of the world were sending detectives to assist in dealing with the international pickpockets, con men, and thieves. Among these were detectives from the gendarmerie of Paris; Scotland Yard in London; Berlin; Vienna; and St. Petersburg, Russia. All would serve under Chief Desmond. The Louisiana Purchase Exposition, the 1904 World's Fair, was about to get under way.

Chapter Eleven

1904: The Year the World Came to St. Louis

IT WOULD BE A MOMENTOUS year for St. Louis. The eyes of the world would be turned toward the 1904 Louisiana Purchase Exposition (the World's Fair), if not also toward the Democratic National Convention that would be held in July. For the police department, it would be a year to remember.

The preparations continued for the opening of the Louisiana Purchase Exposition on April 30, 1904. The principal "boulevard" to the World's Fair would be Chestnut Street, which would be paved with asphalt from Broadway to Grand Avenue. Two streets, Lindell and West Pine, continued west from Grand Avenue directly to Forest Park. At Eighteenth and Market streets, Union Station faced Chestnut Street, just one short block north: All visitors who came by rail would travel west on Chestnut to the fair. Before they got to the fair, however, the first impression made on the visitors would be the saloons and houses of prostitution in the Tenderloin section of Chestnut Valley. The Board of Police Commissioners would again have to broach this situation. The board would also have to come to grips with the need to add a sufficient number of officers so that both the city's beats and the grounds of the World's Fair were adequately staffed. The addition of five hundred officers had been previously suggested.

The Jefferson Guard, who would number six hundred on opening day, would handle many of the duties on the World's Fair grounds. The exposition company had advertised nationwide for young men to join the guard. They would receive $50 a month and free lodging at a barracks on the grounds. The cost of uniforms would be deducted

Union Station. Photograph by A. W. Sanders, 1904.
Missouri History Museum.

from wages each month, but the costs would be refunded at the expiration of their service.[1] Exposition president David R. Francis would later describe the members as ex-soldiers who had been in the Spanish-American War six years earlier and students who wanted to take part in the exposition and see it on a daily basis. Said Francis, "The Jefferson guard was composed of young men much above the average in intelligence, address and deportment."[2] Two hundred members of the guard were sworn in as special private watchmen and had the power of arrest.

Unlike regular private watchmen, however, they had many other duties. They were available to answer visitors' questions, they acted as honorary escorts on special days and for special functions, they were instructed in the use of fire apparatus, and they protected the property against theft and burglary.[3] The Jefferson Guard was commanded by regular U.S. Army officers who were transferred from army bases

Jefferson Guard and officers. Photograph by Byrnes Photographic Company, 1903. Missouri History Museum.

for the duty. The guard would augment the regular police officers who would be assigned to World's Fair duty for the duration. It became apparent, soon after the exposition opened, that there was an insufficient number of Jefferson Guards. Their number would be increased from six hundred to eight hundred and their salary from $50 to $55 per month.[4]

At the first meeting in March, the board adopted a resolution specifying the manpower needs of the police department for the exposition. Following a preamble citing the need for additional forces, the board resolved that "an extraordinary emergency exists, and it is hereby determined that the said extraordinary emergency does and will require additional Patrolmen during the said period of the said exposition, and the police force of the City of St. Louis, is hereby increased by the addition of the following members to the said force, to wit: 500 Special Emergency Probationary Patrolmen."[5]

The board began advertising in the local newspapers and, at the meeting of April 1, listed the names of 397 men who were appointed as emergency special policemen at a salary of $65 per month.[6] Before the fair began on April 30, the board would list 59 more emergency specials.

Each applicant first had his weight and height checked, and was then examined for reading and writing proficiency. Those who passed reported to Dr. A. C. Robinson, the department surgeon, for a physical examination. Passing the exam led to an order for a police uniform, paid for by the applicant, and a six-month commission.

The new emergency specials were provided with police manuals, enrolled in the School of Instruction, and attended a two-week session

Dr. A. C. Robinson. Courtesy of SLMPD.

of military drills at the Chestnut Street station. Successful completion led to a one-week assignment to a beat with an experienced officer and then to an individual assignment. The specials would take the place of the regular officers who would be assigned to the exposition.[7] Four black applicants, Addison (or Adderson) Logan, Noah Warrington, Ollie Washington, and Joseph Wilson were appointed emergency special officers. Logan, Warrington, and Wilson would later be appointed to the force as probationary patrolmen.[8]

The mounted police headquarters and stables, near the southeast entrance to the grounds, were to serve as World's Fair police headquarters. Chief of Detectives William Desmond would be in charge of the fairgrounds. Anyone arrested on the grounds would be confined in the cells in the mounted police facility.[9]

Before the World's Fair began on April 30, however, there was the Democratic city primary. The race between former police board president Harry B. Hawes and his onetime friend Circuit Attorney Joseph W. Folk would decide who would go to the Democratic state convention in Jefferson City with the support of his home city. The primary would cause more problems for the police department than the hundreds of people attending the Democratic National Convention and the nearly 20 million people who would pass through the gates of the Louisiana Purchase Exposition.

The primary election was held on Saturday, March 12, from 1:00 to 8:00 p.m. Hawes resoundingly defeated Folk by a vote of 13,205 to 2,801. Folk won only 10 of the 121 St. Louis delegates. He won by only one vote in his home precinct and ward. Democratic "boss" Edward Butler's "Indians"[10] were expected to operate as usual in the downtown wards but, unexpectedly at this election, Indians invaded the tony west end.[11] The newspapers reported numerous irregularities. In addition to the fraudulent voting, men were constantly being put at the head of the line. At one voting place, the polls closed while legitimate voters, who had waited in line for an hour or more, never had a chance to vote. Said one column headline, "Police Do Nothing."[12]

The following Monday, Governor Dockery ordered the president of the board, William G. Frye, to "convene your board forthwith, investigate fully and impartially each of these charges, and if any police officer is found guilty of intimidating voters or willful neglect of duty, or violation of duty, dismiss him from the force at once. Kindly report to me the result of your investigations at the earliest practicable moment."[13]

Dockery had sent a letter to President Frye before the election to impress upon him that the duty of the police at the polls was to maintain law and order. The letter was read aloud to the board by President Frye, in the presence of all the police captains, at the regular board meeting on March 11. In addition, Dockery had personally contacted Assistant Chief of Police Christ Gillaspy on election morning to impress upon him the necessity of seeing that voters were not intimidated and that repeat voters were arrested.[14]

The February term of the grand jury had reconvened on Monday, March 14, by calling three members of the board, William Frye, Richard Hanlon, and Mayor Rolla F. Wells. The board members met with the grand jury for about ten minutes.[15] Other witnesses also appeared before the grand jury that day testifying about police officers who had physically assaulted them at a polling place or who had seen officers stand by while others were assaulted. One of the witnesses gave the grand jury the numbers on the stars worn by the officers.[16]

On Wednesday morning, March 16, forty police officers who were on duty at polling places in the Twenty-fifth and Twenty-eighth wards were called before a first-time joint session of the board and the grand jury. Citizens who claimed they had been assaulted by the police at the polls or claimed that officers neglected their duty, and the citizens who had obtained star numbers, were also called before the joint session to identify the officers. The forty police officers were lined up for identification.[17] Scores of police officers and witnesses would be called before the grand jury before it ended its session.

On Thursday, March 17, the board convened a special meeting. Based upon a complaint, the board adopted a resolution that charges be preferred against all of the officers stationed at the Twenty-eighth Ward polling place at Taylor and Delmar avenues, in the Eighth Police District, during the hours the polls were open. The board met sporadically, on an informal basis, over the next week.

The grand jury presented its final report to circuit court judge Daniel G. Taylor on March 31. It investigated only three precincts, but it found that "the police in some precincts were in connivance with the ruffians."[18] The report praised the individual members of the police department and said that the police department would be considered an excellent one if the officers were to attend only to police duties. The grand jurors added that the "police force is used now more as a political machine than a means to enforce the law.[19] The grand jury stated that it favored state control of the police under a nonpartisan Board of Police Commissioners: "We lean to the theory that policing is a function of the State and that power to control should be lodged with the Governor, but we do strongly believe, for the best interest of the city, in the exercise of that power through the Police Board, partisan political influence should be entirely eliminated, and this can only be done through a nonpartisan Board of Police Commissioners."[20] To show that the request for removal of the police from political influences did not have any partisan motives, the report called to Democratic governor Dockery's attention that only one of the twelve grand jurors was a Republican.

The grand jury also investigated gambling in the city. It found that "policy playing" was extensively operated "without any apparent effort toward suppression."[21] It didn't find this to be true with other forms of gambling. The grand jury said that, as a result, it lacked confidence in the "efficiency and honesty of purpose" of the police gambling squad.[22]

The grand jury returned indictments against the central committeeman of the Twenty-eighth Ward and seventeen police officers, including three sergeants. Additional complaints from other precincts would be heard by the next grand jury.

The 111 delegates that Harry Hawes won in the March 12 primary would be the only delegates he would garner. On April 27, he dropped out of the race for governor. Hawes said that "the people of Missouri were running an 'ideal and imaginary' Folk and that they would soon tire of the real man. . . ."[23] Nonetheless, Hawes said he would support Folk if he were nominated.[24] Later, the progressive, anti-corruption Joseph Folk handily won his party's nomination for governor.

The Board of Police Commissioners, meanwhile, continued preparations for the World's Fair. At the board meeting of April 29, a day before the exposition would open, the board transferred officers to a new police district. The commander of the World's Fair Police District was Third District Captain William Young. He would be assisted by Lieutenant Patrick McKenna, of the Central District, and Lieutenant Joseph N. Schoppe, of the Tenth District. Eighteen sergeants and 275 patrolmen, chosen by Chief Mathew Kiely and Captain Young, completed the initial transfers.[25] Officers would be transferred in, and out, of the World's Fair Police District for the duration of the fair. The men would be divided into three platoons.[26]

As the opening of the exposition approached, the police department had to deal with another potential problem, speeding automobiles. Park Commissioner Robert Aull said that he had witnessed many narrow escapes in Forest Park. Some autos were being driven "at the speed of a passenger locomotive."[27] Chief Kiely issued an order, with a copy of the appropriate city ordinance attached, instructing all captains to see that their officers arrested "all parties found to be running their machines at a higher rate of speed than that prescribed by law."[28] The city speed limit was eight miles per hour, six miles per hour in city parks.

It was up to the mounted police to deal with speeding autos in Forest Park. Chasing the speeding autos on horseback was the usual, but not always successful, means of apprehension. Patrolman John Brandt of the World's Fair Police District, however, had a different idea, a method of timing speeders that is still in use today, although now more sophisticated. Brandt noted that "chauffeurs" tended to speed on a certain part of a street within his beat. He measured and clandestinely marked a 220-yard (one-eighth of a mile) section of the street. Brandt would look at the second hand on his pocket watch as an auto hit the first marker and again when it crossed the second. He noted the difference and calculated the speed. Brandt would then stop the auto and arrest the chauffeur. The first person brought into court under Brandt's system was charged with driving fifteen miles per hour in the park.[29]

The *St. Louis Post-Dispatch* opined that "it would not be an unwise policy for the [police] department to have officers of the law operate horseless carriages so that they might lessen the chance of escape of those who exceed the speed limit."[30] This was also reported to be the position of the general manager of police property, Dr. William Faulkner.[31] The board authorized Faulkner to purchase two high-speed automobiles, which were delivered on Saturday, July 9. The next day, the members of the board and Chief Kiely witnessed a demonstration of the two-passenger autos in Forest Park.[32]

The two automobiles were apparently not purchased by the board as the press reported. Subsequent newspaper articles refer to "the automobile" purchased by the police department to catch "scorchers."[33] A photograph of the "skidoodle wagon" in the *Post-Dispatch* the following Thursday showed an automobile driven by a civilian chauffeur, William Sleuter, with two uniformed officers, James Cooney and William Stinger, of the Mounted District, in the backseat.[34] A flag on a pole, rising slightly above the two officers, stood at the right rear of the auto. The accompanying article described the flag as a red warning flag. The skidoodle wagon had a speedometer and a bell, which was rung to get the attention of the driver of the auto being pursued. After getting his attention, the officers used hand signals to have the scorcher pull over to the side of the road.[35]

The auto, a 1904 St. Louis, was manufactured by the St. Louis Motor Carriage Company at 1211–19 North Vandeventer Avenue.[36] It had a seven-horsepower engine capable of speeds up to fifteen miles per hour[37] and ran on "stove gas," also referred to as "white gas," a common fuel that was readily available.[38] It would be another year before gasoline made any inroads as a motor fuel.

Dr. Faulkner claimed that the police department "was the first on record to use automobiles as a means of catching speed ordinance violators. . . ."[39] Faulkner noted that "he had already received communications from several cities requesting him to notify them if the venture in St. Louis proved successful.[40]

The 1904 "skidoodle wagon," the first car used by the St. Louis Police
Department. The two officers in the rear seat are Patrolmen
Cooney and Stinger; the officer in the front seat, Captain John Pickel,
commander of the Mounted Police; and chauffeur William Sleuter.
Photograph, ca. 1904. Missouri History Museum.

One week before the opening of the World's Fair, Chief Kiely
issued orders to the police patrolling Pine and Chestnut streets to close
all houses of ill repute in the Tenderloin District. The order specified
the closing of houses between Twentieth Street on the east and Jefferson Avenue on the west, a distance of six blocks. It was estimated that
this area contained approximately 250 houses and 2,000 women.[41]
The 1902 question was revisited: Where would these women go? In
the end, they were absorbed into the community; they were not sent
to any specific part of the city.

The board suddenly found that it had to deal with opening-day
security. Six months earlier, the board had informed exposition company president David Francis that the city of St. Louis was financially
unable to properly police the World's Fair grounds. The board was now
informed that the exposition company had not provided for opening-

day security, in the belief that the police department was going to handle it. The board resolved to provide opening-day security "consistent with our resources and our duty to other interests of the City."[42] In the end, a police force of 150 men, assisted by the Jefferson Guard, would be present for opening ceremonies on April 30.[43]

On May 6, one of the two black officers on the force, Hugh Allen, resigned. Allen, who had been on the force less than six months, later stated that he resigned "because he found the political influences in the department too strong for him."[44] In December, the board appointed a black porter, Reece Evans, to replace Allen.[45]

Two weeks after the opening of the fair, Chief of Detectives Desmond asked for "100 additional men in Citizens clothes."[46] Desmond already had one hundred patrolmen in civilian dress: Half were assigned to the World's Fair grounds, and half, under Assistant Chief of Detectives John Keely, operated throughout the remainder of the city. Desmond also had thirty to fifty experienced detectives from other large cities in the United States and others from London, Paris, and Berlin. Chief Desmond needed the additional men to police the exposition and the city streets.[47] The board allowed him an additional fifty men.

The police department set up an exhibit in the Palace of Education at the World's Fair. It was not installed, said Chief Kiely, "with a view of appealing to the morbidly curious, but rather to educate the public in the tricks and wiles of the under world."[48]

Chief of Detectives William Desmond, meanwhile, had adopted a vigorous crime prevention stance. He had several resources: plainclothes St. Louis officers and detectives, and detectives from other cities. Local detectives were stationed on the exposition grounds, along with police officers from foreign cities, but detectives were also watching arrivals at Union Station; were present in hotel lobbies; and kept an eye on the main "highways" into the city, the locations criminals were known to frequent, and even streetcar terminals. A duplicate of the Headquarters's rogues' gallery was kept at the World's Fair Police District station.[49]

Crime on the grounds of the World's Fair was kept in check. It was reported that the losses to thieves and pickpockets on the grounds were estimated at less than $1,500 for the duration. Most of that loss was attributed to a series of petty thefts by employees on the grounds.[50] Meanwhile, there were 1,400 arrests. While there likely had been other thefts not reported to the police, the small number of losses, coupled with a relatively small number of arrests, was laudatory. During the seven months of the World's Fair, almost 20 million visitors had passed through the turnstiles.[51]

Throughout the city, thieves, pickpockets, and other criminals from other cities were identified and arrested "on general principles." They were taken to the Four Courts, where they were booked as "Hold for the Chief." It is unknown whether "the Chief" was Chief of Police Kiely or Chief of Detectives Desmond. If such a suspect forthrightly answered questions, he would then be returned to his cell. The words "1st clause" would be added to the booking sheet, which meant that the suspect was to be sent to police court (on a charge of "idling") with a recommendation that the judge give the suspect a certain number of hours to leave the city. The police court judge invariably followed the recommendation, and a detective was assigned to make certain that the person left St. Louis.[52] Those who refused to answer questions, were evasive, or were otherwise uncooperative were held at the Four Courts while the Bertillon system records were checked. It was claimed that, in 90 percent of those cases, those so held were wanted on fugitive warrants from other locations.[53]

In addition to the thefts, however, some violent crimes were committed on the exposition grounds. For example, a guide in the Jerusalem concession shot and killed the proprietor of the grocery booth in the same concession. The killing apparently occurred after an argument between the two as to which one was "king of the gamblers."[54] Also, two armed, masked men held up a train on the miniature railroad at the fair. The robbers got a small amount of money and a gold watch from the three passengers. The manager of the miniature railroad bought a new watch for the one passenger and reimbursed the monetary losses of all.[55] A watchman for "Mysterious Asia on the Pike" shot the manager of the Temple of Mirth, a part of Mysterious Asia. The manager had demanded an apology from the watchman for allegedly insulting the manager's mother. The watchman attempted to escape the grounds, but was stopped and disarmed by Sergeant Fred Armstrong of the World's Fair Police District.[56] These crimes, and others, stood in contradiction to Chief Kiely's statement in the 1905 annual report that "the Fair can be said to have been absolutely free from crime."[57]

Crimes were not, of course, limited to the grounds. Chief of Detectives William Desmond authored an article in the *Post-Dispatch* warning visitors of an area he called the "bad lands":

> The new criminal region created on the outskirts of St. Louis, extending westward from within a few rods of the World's Fair gates, is full of peril. The fact should be impressed upon the minds of World's Fair visitors. They are safe in St. Louis. They are unsafe when they venture among the criminals who have congregated just beyond the city limits. Beware of the "bad lands." Crime lurks there, waiting for World's Fair victims to be enticed within its reach.[58]

The bad lands, according to Chief Desmond, extended as far as Creve Coeur Lake, several miles northwest of the grounds. Gambling was the principal venture and, according to Desmond, "The victim has no chance against them, for the game is crooked from start to finish and they're as sure of his money as if he turned it over to them without going through the form of a gamble."[59] Desmond explained what his office was doing to lessen the dangers of the bad lands. Said Chief Desmond, "Delmar Garden, only a few hundred yards distant from the Fair, is in the county, but I have assigned a number of my men to duty there, and whenever they spot a suspicious character they await a chance when, crossing the line that brings him within the St. Louis jurisdiction, they can arrest such a character and bring him to me."[60]

One such incident involved St. Louis police detective Frank McKenna, who was assigned to the area to get evidence that might help break up the gambling and the shows.[61] McKenna decided that he would trail two female dancers who, in deference to the costumes they wore in a show, were referred to as "the girl in red" and "the girl in green." He would follow them out of the county to see if some evidence could be collected for which they could be charged in St. Louis.

For several nights, he watched the exits of the place for signs of the two women. He never saw them leave. After several nights with the same results, Detective McKenna checked to see if the women stayed at the place; he had no other explanation for their ability to get past him every night. He even considered the possibility that there might be an underground tunnel.

Finally, on July 19, McKenna was watching the men file out after the show and noticed one who bore a resemblance to the girl in green. Thinking it might be her brother, he followed the man into the city to a saloon on Market Street. That man was soon joined by another. Detective McKenna struck up a conversation with the two men and mentioned his admiration for the girl in green. The man McKenna had followed to the saloon then told him, "Why, I'm the girl in green." The other man added, "And I'm the girl in red."[62] They were, in the words of the *Post-Dispatch*, "feminine impersonators." Both were taken to the Four Courts and placed in the holdover, marked "Hold for the Chief."

Both men appeared in police court the next day to answer to the charge of "idling." The man referred to as the "girl in red" stated that he only donned a Turkish costume and danced in the free show outside the establishment and never took part in the performances inside. He was fined $100 and costs. The judge offered to suspend the fine if the defendant left the city by noon the next day. It is likely that, as was typically the case, he was escorted to the train station or city limits by a detective. The case of the girl in green was continued until the next day so that he could bring some character witnesses to court. At the trial, the girl in green was also fined $100 and costs. The judge issued a stern lecture and then stayed the fine so long as the defendant refrained from further dancing. No more was heard from either of the dancers.

A highlight of the World's Fair was the display of the English crown jewels. Among the Scotland Yard detectives sent to St. Louis to guard the crown jewels was John Kenneth Ferrier. In 1902, Scotland Yard had discarded the Bertillon system of identification in favor of the new Henry fingerprint system.[63] In addition to guarding the jewels, Ferrier promoted the fingerprint method of identification by giving demonstrations. He "took a number of inked prints, left the room, had one person leave another print, and then matched the unknown print to its correct owner. . . ."[64] The New York State Bureau of Prisons, which, the previous year, had instituted the first fingerprint system for criminal purposes in the United States, also had a display at the World's Fair.[65] Personnel from Scotland Yard also gave a fingerprint system demonstration to the members of the International Association of Chiefs of Police (IACP), who were holding their annual meeting in St. Louis.[66] The National Association of Chiefs of Police had become the IACP in 1902. The IACP had been asked to coordinate the crime and law enforcement exhibits for the World's Fair.[67]

A fingerprint demonstration at the World's Fair. Scotland Yard Detective John Ferrier is on the left. Photograph, 1904. Missouri History Museum.

Although the fingerprint system would not be formally approved by the board until October, the first prints were taken by St. Louis police on Saturday, August 6, 1904. The superintendent of the Bertillon system, John M. Shea, had studied the system with Scotland Yard detective Ferrier that week. The first set of fingerprints were those of May Hollis. Memphis, Tennessee, police had notified the St. Louis department that Hollis was wanted in that city. An officer identified only as "Sergeant Hoffman of the central district" was at Sixth and Pine streets when he recognized Hollis from a photograph and placed her under arrest.[68] "She had had her photograph and measurements taken for several rogues' galleries, but the finger-print system was new to her, and for several minutes she stoutly refused to go through the ordeal. She spoiled several 'blanks' by her manner before Supt. Shea finally secured a good impression with a duplicate copy."[69]

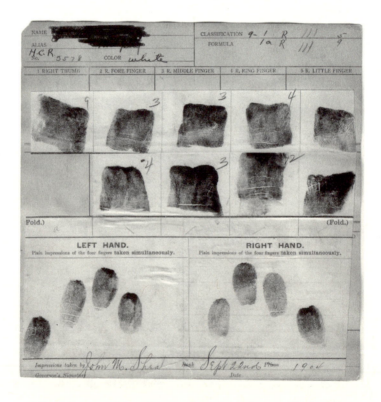

A fingerprint card, dated September 22, 1904, signed by Bertillon Superintendent John Shea. Courtesy of SLMPD.

The second person to be fingerprinted was Richard Walsh, alias Edward Cotton, who was in the city jail awaiting trial on a charge of attempted burglary. Walsh, it was reported, also had his picture in many rogues' galleries and had served time in the prison at Joliet, Illinois. Walsh asked many questions as his impression was being taken, and when told of the new method, replied that "he guessed he would have to cut his fingers off if he wanted to avoid detection."[70]

Bertillon Superintendent John Shea established a routine for those arrested by the police. The fingerprints of the prisoner were first taken, followed by the front and profile photographs, and then the Bertillon measurements and descriptions. All were incorporated on one card. Superintendent Shea later installed the fingerprint system at the state penitentiary in Jefferson City.[71]

The St. Louis Metropolitan Police Department became the first police department in the United States to adopt fingerprinting as a means of criminal identification. The police department would be first in another fingerprint category the following year.

✳   ✳   ✳

Events were unfolding, meanwhile, that would lead to the worst disaster in the history of the police department. On August 1, 1904, an Illinois Central passenger train left Chicago and headed south. Three men got on the train just as it was pulling out of the station at Harvey, Illinois, about twenty miles southwest of Chicago. Passengers were riding in a day coach and three Pullman coaches. Since it was about 10:45 p.m., many of the passengers in the Pullman coaches had retired for the night. One of the three men held the brakeman at gunpoint until the train cleared the Harvey depot. All three, who were armed with pistols, then began to walk through the cars forcing the passengers to surrender any money and valuables. It is unknown whether the train had been forced to stop after the robbery, but the three men got off the train and began walking in an easterly direction.[72]

Based on bits of information they had gathered and pieced together, St. Louis police detectives Joseph H. James and John J. "Crab" Shea, Special Officer Thomas Dwyer, and Kansas City, Missouri, detective

Edward Boyle[a] deduced that the three train robbers were heading for St. Louis. Sometime in early October, Detective James got a tip as to the whereabouts of the men. On October 18, he located them, sharing a room on the first floor of a three-story brownstone rooming house at 1324 Pine Street.[b] Detectives James and Shea, Special Officer Dwyer, and Detective Boyle were joined by Special Officer James McCluskey in a surveillance of the house. On Thursday afternoon, October 20, one man left the house and the police followed, but the man escaped. He later returned to the house.

About 4:00 the next afternoon, October 21, the five officers prepared to enter the house. When a man identified as Harry Vaughn came out the front door, he was arrested after a brief struggle. Detectives James and Boyle walked Vaughn west on Pine to the intersection with Fourteenth Street and held him there until the other two men could be arrested.[73] Special Officer Dwyer, followed by McCluskey and Shea, entered the unlocked front door of the building and went to the door of the room where the other two suspects were believed to be located. Dwyer entered the room and, before his eyes adjusted to the dark, he was shot in the abdomen. McCluskey, immediately behind Dwyer, was also shot. Both wounded officers continued to advance into the room, firing at two dim figures highlighted by the flashes from their pistols. Detective Shea was wounded before he could step across the threshold into the room. He also returned fire and was struck a second time.[74]

Upon hearing the shots, Boyle ran to the house and entered the hallway just as a second bullet struck Shea, who was in the doorway. Boyle assisted Shea into the hallway and then returned to the room, where he emptied his revolver at the two suspects. The shooting stopped. Detective Shea was dead, as was one of the two suspects, Albert Rose, alias Albert Rosenaur. Officers Dwyer and McCluskey were rushed to City Hospital, as was the other suspect, William Brice

---

[a] Detective Edward Boyle was detailed to St. Louis for World's Fair duty. He was working with Detective James.

[b] The building was located on the south side of Pine Street. That is now the north entrance to the Soldiers' Memorial.

The house at 1324 Pine Street, where a shoot-out resulted in the deaths of three police officers and two train robbers. Courtesy of SLMPD.

Morris, alias C. C. Blair. Dwyer died at the hospital an hour after his arrival. At 9:00 p.m. the next day, October 22, McCluskey died of his wounds. In the meantime, Morris had a four-officer detail guarding him around the clock.[75]

While still in the hospital, William Morris admitted to committing several train robberies. Questioned by Chief of Detectives William Desmond, Morris said that the latest robbery, that of the Illinois Central train outside Harvey, Illinois, was committed by him, Albert Rosenaur, Harry Vaughn, and a man named Rogers, alias Collins, who was currently under arrest in Chicago. Morris, Vaughn, and Rosenaur had been identified by the members of the train crew. On October 24, Morris died of his wounds.[76] Vaughn, whose arrest had preceded the shoot-out at 1324 Pine Street, was ultimately tried, convicted, and sentenced to twenty-seven years in prison.[77] In November 1905, he would lead a revolt at the Missouri State Penitentiary that resulted in the deaths of several guards. He was hanged.

Shea was thirty-two years old and unmarried and supported his mother and sister. Dwyer was thirty-five years old and married. McCluskey, who was about forty years old and lived with his aunt,

Detective John J. Shea. Courtesy of SLMPD.

Special Officer Thomas Dwyer. Courtesy of SLMPD.

Special Officer James McCluskey. Courtesy of SLMPD.

was an Eighth District patrolman who had been assigned to Headquarters at the beginning of the World's Fair.[78] The funerals of Shea and Dwyer were held at the St. Alphonsus "Rock" Church on Monday, October 24. An estimated ten thousand persons paid their respects to the two slain officers. The double funeral was called one of the largest in the history of St. Louis. After a solemn High Mass, the funeral cortege made its way to Calvary Cemetery. Seymour's military band led the march, followed by thirty-six mounted officers, two platoons of police officers, a company of soldiers, and hundreds of carriages. All city offices were closed until noon, and flags were hung at half-staff.[79]

McCluskey's funeral was held the following day at a packed St. Kevin Church at Cardinal and Park avenues. The cortege from St. Kevin to Calvary Cemetery was much like that from the funeral of Shea and Dwyer. In addition, however, there were seventy-six members of Marquette Council 606, Knights of Columbus, of which McCluskey had been a member. McCluskey was laid to rest in a plot near those of Shea and Dwyer.[80]

The board adopted a resolution of respect for the three officers, taking notice of the strain imposed upon the police by the surge in population brought about by the World's Fair:

> Resolved, that the Board of Police Commissioners of the city of St. Louis deeply deplore the killing of Detective John J. Shea and Special Officers Thomas Dwyer and James A. McCluskey by desperate criminals. . . . The unflinching fidelity of these three officers to the service of the public prompted them to willingly risk their own lives, and to sacrifice themselves in order that the lives and property of others might be more secure. The act of these men was the act of brave men. While this Department and the public have sustained an irreparable loss in the death of these three officers, yet in their sacrifice the public have gained in greater security, and the Department has been raised to a higher standard of action.[81]

The board further resolved that copies of the resolution be sent to the press and to the families of the three officers, "to whom we extend our heartfelt sympathy in their deep sorrow."[82] Individuals and businesses began making cash contributions to aid the families of the slain officers, and the board received numerous offers to perform benefits.[83]

*　　*　　*

Meanwhile, the police department had to prepare for the general election on November 8, 1904. The fraud in the Democratic primary election, including the indictment of police officers, required extraordinary steps to prevent a recurrence. On November 4, Chief Kiely called all of the captains together and, in the presence of the board, gave them their orders for election day. The orders included the scheduling of officers on both watches so that, the night before the election, only a minimum number of officers, "enough men to keep a lookout for fires, etc . . . ," would be working.[84] The entire command, less the "fire watch," would report to the station houses for election day duty at 5:30 a.m.

A minimum of two officers were to be detailed at each polling place in the city, and they were to remain on duty until the polls closed. Enough officers were to be kept in reserve to relieve polling place officers for meals and give them time to vote. While they were at the polls, officers were to arrest all law violators, be on the lookout for concealed weapons, and see that the one-hundred-foot rule (no electioneering within one hundred feet of the polling place) was obeyed.[85]

Said Chief Kiely to the captains, "Instruct your men as to their duties on election laws, so there will be no doubt in their minds as to what will be expected of them."[86] To make the order more compelling, Chief Kiely told the captains that they would be held responsible for the discipline maintained in their districts on election day, adding that "it is in your best interest to see that the men under you know just what their duty is and just what will be expected of them."[87] Chief Kiely assigned over fifty detectives and special officers to be on hand in certain wards and polling places. In addition, Kiely applied to the Democratic clerks and judges for permits to station the detectives and special officers inside the polling places, a course "never before heard of in the history of the city."[88] Chief Kiely said that he did not want "one single dishonest vote cast."[89]

At 7:00 p.m. on election day, Chief Kiely detailed all detectives and special officers to the various polling places. Each had permits to enter the polling places. They were to observe the counting of ballots and, if irregularities were observed, to gather evidence of the incidents to present before a grand jury.[90]

With the exception of one ward, the election was held with few of the problems that arose in the Democratic primary election. In addition, Democratic boss Ed Butler refused to allow his Indians and the election officials in the wards controlled by him to "go down the line," that is, pad the registration or falsify the returns.[91] Republican Joseph Folk actually ran ahead of his ticket in each of the so-called Butler wards. Said the *Globe-Democrat*, "That the election was quiet and uneventful is proven by the police records, for, in spite of the army of policemen thrown into each of the wards, scarcely an arrest was made during the day."[92] The newspaper asserted that, if Democrat Butler's Indians had been working for the Republicans (as Harry Hawes had earlier claimed), the police holdover would have been overcrowded with Indians.[93]

The result was a resounding victory for Democrat Folk. Republicans were elected to all other major offices. "Despite the fact that Folk had campaigned for governor almost solely on the anti-corruption issue and had qualified as a progressive more by association than by any clear exposition of his views, there was never any doubt that his victory was interpreted as a general mandate for reform."[94] The police department would not be overlooked in Folk's reform movement.

The ranks of the Jefferson Guard began thinning during the last month of the Louisiana Purchase Exposition. Men resigning from the guard were not replaced. The army's Sixth Infantry would remain on the grounds, as would approximately four hundred police officers assigned to the World's Fair Police District. To augment this force, two regular army infantry battalions from Fort McPherson, Georgia, were brought in to assist in guarding the exhibits until all had been removed.[95]

The term of the emergency special officers was due to expire after the closing of the Louisiana Purchase Exposition on December 1. At its regular meeting a week before the World's Fair closed, the board declared "that an [extraordinary] emergency still exists" and resolved that one hundred of the emergency special officers "be retained until such time as the Board may determine they are no longer needed."[96] The board held a regularly scheduled meeting the day after the World's Fair closed. The board ordered all emergency specials appointed after April 1 dropped from the rolls the next day, "there being no further use for their services."[97] The last of the emergency special officers (seventy-four) would not be dropped from the rolls until May 31, 1905.[98]

The World's Fair Police District was abolished on December 9. Captain William Young, 6 sergeants, and 146 patrolmen were returned to their regular districts. One lieutenant, 2 sergeants, and a handful of officers remained on the grounds while the exhibits were dismantled.[99] On January 6, 1905, the remaining officers were returned to their districts. The policing of the World's Fair had been successfully completed.

*   *   *

The gambling specter, however, again raised its head. Along with the visitors to the World's Fair, a new form of gambling had made its appearance in St. Louis. Previously, anyone wishing to bet on horse races being run outside of the city had to use the services of a "poolroom," which was especially created for betting on horse races around the country. The new form of betting on horse races was called a "handbook." The *Post-Dispatch*, which published several articles in December chronicling how reporters had made bets on horse races through the new medium, explained to the readers that the handbook was virtually the opposite of a poolroom. "It usually is conducted as an adjunct to a barroom, a cigar store, a laundry or barber shop, or in a so-called club, where gambling is conducted. On the bookmaker's desk or counter lies a copy of a published racing 'form sheet' with the names of the horses, the odds and other information."[100]

The bettor would pick the horse he or she wished to bet on and give the "handbook maker" his money. The handbook maker would write down the track, the race, the horse, the amount bet, and a name or mark that would identify the bettor to the bookmaker. This could be done in person or by telephone. If by telephone, the amount to be wagered had to be sent to the bookmaker before the bet was phoned in. The next day, the bookmaker would consult the *Chicago Racing Form*, which published the official winners of the races the previous day and the odds. Using the *Racing Form*, the bookmaker would determine the winners in his book, and then calculate the amount each successful bettor had won. The newspaper reported that in most cases the bookmaker was not ready to pay winners until after 11:00 a.m.[101]

Post-Dispatch reporters spoke with Chief Kiely. He replied that he was unaware of the new scheme until he had read about it in the newspaper. He referred the reporters to the detective heading the eight-man gambling squad, Thomas McGrath. Detective McGrath explained that his squad could not make an arrest without observing the bets being placed. The newspaper articles put the handbook operators on notice, said McGrath, and they were taking bets only from people known to them. No bets were made when detectives were in the business place.[102]

Earlier in the year, said McGrath, members of the gambling squad had placed bets themselves and made about thirty arrests. "But the cases were thrown out of court, the judge holding that it was no violation of law for a man engaged in a legitimate business—such as selling cigars or running a saloon, for instance, to accept a bet. It was held that the 'business' had to be primarily a poolroom or gambling place."[103] An assistant prosecuting attorney contacted by a reporter merely confirmed that securing a conviction in a handbook case was very difficult.[104]

Kiely then personally investigated the alleged bookmaking operations and, on December 13, called Detective McGrath into his office. After the conference, McGrath got his squad together, "secured a patrol wagon and made the rounds of the various suspected places. The patrons in the places were not molested, but told to hurry home."[105] Five men, however, were arrested and taken to the Four Courts.

＊　　＊　　＊

The year ended with an old problem and a new problem. The old problem, one that persists to this day, was that of New Years revelers celebrating by discharging firearms. A number of men, women, and children were in a west-end street blowing horns, ringing cowbells, and shooting revolvers. One woman was killed by a stray bullet as she and a friend crossed the street shortly after midnight. Police were unable to locate the shooter. Another woman, several blocks west of the first, was watching the crowds from her second-floor window. She was struck on the knee by a bullet that went through the wall of her house. She was only slightly injured. Again, no one was able to tell the police who fired the shot.[106]

The new problem was unique. On the evening of December 20, 1904, one H. M. Noel reported to Chief of Detectives William Desmond that his automobile had been stolen. Noel told Desmond that he had ridden in his auto "to 3635 Washington boulevard, and, knowing that he was coming out within a few minutes, left the controller on the auto, making it easy for any person to operate it and run it away."[107] The auto was described as a 1904 Oldsmobile bearing license number 49. Police were not immediately able to locate the auto, but detectives didn't believe that it would be hard to find. "It is too big for sale in a pawnshop and is not so easy to dispose of as a horse."[108]

Chapter Twelve

After the Fair Was Over: Reformation

1905

ON JANUARY 9, 1905, Joseph Wingate Folk was inaugurated as the thirty-first governor of Missouri.[1] In his inaugural speech, he continued the anti-corruption theme of his campaign: "Those who believe in the righteousness of the people are looking to see their theory vindicated; those who hold that corruption is a necessary incident of government, and that the 'Missouri idea' is only a passing virtuous spasm are awaiting the result to sustain their position. Missouri is now on trial."[2]

Governor Folk promised to enforce every law: "Every rumor or official venality would be promptly investigated, and the neglected laws prohibiting state officials from accepting railroad passes would be made effective. . . . "[3] He advocated home rule for large cities, the improvement of election laws so that there would be honest elections, especially in the cities, and repeal of the law legalizing gambling on horse races. Folk's message was one of reform and progress. By the end of the year, reform would lead to unintended or, at least unexpected, consequences.

The St. Louis Board of Police Commissioners was one of the first places Governor Folk would apply his reform message. The terms of all four members of the board, William G. Frye, Theodore R. Ballard, Andrew F. Blong, and Richard Hanlon, had expired on January 1, 1905. Before he left office, however, and while the General Assembly was in recess, Governor Dockery reappointed Hanlon to the board. The Senate confirmed Hanlon on January 20, 1905.[4]

Governor Joseph W. Folk. Photograph by J. C. Strauss, 1903.
Missouri History Museum.

Technically, Governor Folk could withdraw any so-called recess appointment, including Hanlon's. He would not, he said, asserting, "Withdrawals amount to a removal from office, and such action, dictated purely by a desire for spoils, would be manifestly improper."[5] Folk, however, attached a condition to Hanlon remaining on the police board. He announced that an appointee to the board could not be a police commissioner and an officer of the Jefferson Club or any other political organization. Folk said that Hanlon would have to resign from one office or the other.[6] He did not resign; less than a week later, he was elected the first vice president of the Jefferson Club.[7]

That same day, January 20, Governor Folk announced the appointments of two new board members: Alphonso C. Stewart, for president of the board, and John W. Fristoe. Each was appointed for a four-year term ending January 1, 1909. This was the first time that a governor made an appointment to the board and designated the position the appointee should hold. The same day, Richard Hanlon was confirmed to the board by the Senate. The length of Hanlon's term was not noted.[8]

Stewart was a lawyer with firm of Stewart, Cunningham and Eliot, located in the Security Building at Fourth and Locust streets, and he also served as counsel for the Union Trust Company. Fristoe was the president of the Moss Tie Company located on the southwest corner of Twelfth Street and Washington Boulevard. Their first board meeting would be February 3.

Alphonso C. Stewart. Courtesy of SLMPD.

John W. Fristoe. Courtesy of SLMPD.

In the meantime, Governor Folk had instructed Chief Mathew Kiely to close all "wine rooms," places where women served drinks and engaged in acts of "immorality." Beginning Saturday, January 21, 1905, the police began raiding wine rooms and arresting the women working in them. Seventy-two women were arrested that night, and forty-eight were arrested on Sunday.[9] Most of the women failed to appear in court and defaulted on their bonds. The police viewed the defaults as evidence that the women had either left the city or did not intend to again work in wine rooms.[10]

Chief Kiely told a newspaper reporter that the order he had prepared for the raids on the wine rooms was a copy of the order he had drawn up when he was acting chief of police in March 1897. Kiely explained that, in spite of the raids conducted then, the wine rooms continued. "At that time political influences were too strong for me to combat and the places sprang up again. Now it is different. With

Joseph W. Folk Governor, I know that I will be supported in any movement for the betterment of the city and I shall allow no political influence to move me from my purpose to rid the city of these places."[11] At the same time, Chief Kiely also put gamblers on notice. Kiely promised to fight the gamblers "every minute in the day until they are driven from the city."[12]

Governor Folk called his new board appointees, Stewart and Fristoe, to Jefferson City on January 26. The governor and his appointees discussed the police situation in St. Louis and Governor Folk outlined the measures he wanted to see enforced in the city. It was the first time that Governor Folk and the two police commissioners-elect had an opportunity to speak with one another.[13]

Three days later, Chief Kiely was called to Jefferson City by Governor Folk and asked for a report on the closings of wine rooms, dance halls, and gambling dens. Kiely reported that Governor Folk had congratulated him on the work done thus far, but told him to continue to raid the places until they were wiped out: "As to the future policy of the police department, the governor instructed me to see that all forms of gambling are suppressed; to see that the law prohibiting the carrying of concealed weapons is rigidly enforced, and, above all, to keep the police department out of politics. The governor told me that it was one of the aims of his administration to keep the police department free from any political influences whatever."[14] Governor Folk, it appeared, was intent on immediately putting his reform measures into operation.

Neither Andrew F. Blong, who had yet to be replaced, nor Mayor Rolla F. Wells were present at the first meeting of the board attended by Stewart and Fristoe. But Acting Mayor Joseph L. Hornsby was substituting for Mayor Wells, and the board had a quorum. Alphonso Stewart was elected president of the board. At Stewart's suggestion, the election of the remaining officers was postponed until a board meeting at which all were present.[15] After that first meeting, President Stewart told the press, "It will be one of the first duties of the new police board to see that the police are taken out of politics, and any officer found guilty of indulging in party affairs beyond casting his vote will be dismissed."[16]

All board members were present at the meeting of February 17. Hanlon was elected vice president, and Fristoe was elected purchasing member. The board minutes made no mention of a treasurer. Hanlon, who had been treasurer under the previous board, might have retained that position as well as taking on the vice presidency.

The last meeting of February was momentous in several respects. First, the board passed two resolutions that were steps toward removing politics from appointments and promotions; the board would make appointments and promotions based solely on the merit of the individual. When appointing probationary patrolmen, said the first resolution, "this Board will consider all applications and any other known available material, and select for appointment only such as shall appear to a majority of the Board to be the best qualified for the position. Before any such selection shall be commissioned, he shall appear before the Mental Examining Board . . . and if, on such examination shall make an average percentage less that 65, shall not be commissioned."[17]

The board adopted a resolution that before any promotion was made, the chief of police had to first obtain from the captain of each district a report of one man from each district, who, in the opinion of the captain, was best qualified to fill the vacancy. The reports of the captains and the recommendation of the chief of police "shall be placed before the Board, and from the whole number of names thus reported and recommended, a majority of the Board shall determine who is the best man to fill the vacancy, and such only shall be promoted."[18]

Next, the board opened nominations for the positions of chief of police and assistant chief of police. Mayor Wells nominated Mathew Kiely for chief of police. He was unanimously elected for a new four-year term effective February 27, 1905. Richard Hanlon nominated Christ G. Gillaspy for assistant chief of police. Gillaspy was also unanimously elected for four more years.[19]

For their part, the officers on the beat were taking a "wait and see" attitude regarding the removal of politics from appointments and promotions. Said one, "We've heard those tales before, that is, those of us who have been in the business long have, and the change was never noticeable. Now most of us come from Missouri and we've got to be shown. That's a good system, but—well, we are waiting."[20]

The newly organized board, like previous boards, needed to address the problem of intoxicated police officers. The previous board had passed a resolution that all officers found guilty of intoxication would be dismissed. Like several boards in the past, however, the announced punishment was not applied to all officers. Ironically, it was a member of the previous board, Andrew Blong, who presented an identical resolution that "any member of the Police force who is charged before the Board with being intoxicated and is found guilty, shall be dismissed from the force and the Chief Of Police is hereby directed to have the order read at each roll call for three consecutive days."[21] This board, however, began enforcing the rule. By the end of April, five officers had been found guilty of intoxication. All were dismissed from the force.

In March, the board appointed a black applicant, Noah Warrington, a probationary patrolman.[22] Warrington had served as an emergency special officer during the 1904 Louisiana Purchase Exposition. Like all the black officers appointed to the force, he was to work as a plainclothes special officer.[a]

In April, the board put its merit promotion announcement into effect. Chief Kiely was instructed to have each of the captains of the First, Sixth, and Ninth districts submit the name of one probationary patrolman who warranted promotion to patrolman. The three named officers were then to be examined by the board. After the examination, each of the recommended officers was promoted. The process was later repeated for the captains of the Second, Fourth, Seventh, Eighth, and Mounted districts. The commander of the Central District was asked to recommend two. After examination by the board, all were promoted to patrolmen.[23]

On May 12, the board ordered that the last of the emergency special officers hired for the Louisiana Purchase Exposition be dropped from the rolls of the department effective May 31."[24]

---

[a] Black officers would not be put into uniform until 1921.

Chief Kiely and Chief of Detectives Desmond were granted a thirty-day leave of absence, beginning May 20, to attend the annual convention of the International Association of Chiefs of Police. It was ordered that, at the close of the convention, the two proceed to the cities of Baltimore, Philadelphia, New York, and Boston "to examine Police and Police department matters in said cities for the purpose (of) ascertaining what improvements can be introduced in this Department."[25] Upon their return, the board expected a full report, including recommendations as to what the board might consider for the St. Louis department.

On June 2, the board authorized the general manager of police properties, Dr. William Faulkner, to purchase an additional automobile for the sum of $1,800. From the specifications described in the newspapers, the second skidoodle wagon, like the first, was built by the St. Louis Motor Carriage Company.[26] It was accepted on a ten-day trial basis on August 9, 1905. It was larger than the first auto, capable of seating a chauffeur and four passengers, and was more powerful then its predecessor. It had a thirty-five-horsepower engine capable of reaching speeds of fifty miles per hour, and it was equipped with a speedometer and a powerful searchlight. Mounted officers William Stinger and James Cooney, who had ridden in the first skidoodle wagon, were assigned to the new vehicle, along with civilian chauffeur John W. Gardner.[27]

On June 16, the board appointed another black applicant, Joseph Wilson, to the position of probationary patrolman.[28] The addition of Wilson brought the number of black officers on the force to four. He would also be assigned as a special officer. Wilson had also served as an emergency special officer during the Louisiana Purchase Exposition.

In July, the board made preparations for the completion of a new police station on the east side of Newstead Avenue, just north of Forest Park Avenue, the home of the new Eleventh District. The boundaries of the new district were established, and the boundaries of adjacent districts were redrawn to conform to the new addition.

In a letter to the board read at the meeting of September 1, Dr. Faulkner reported that he had inspected the new station. He called it "a strictly first class model Police station" and said that "I do not hesitate to say that the Eleventh District Station House surpasses anything of its kind in the Country." On motion, the station house was accepted.

New Eleventh District station. Courtesy of SLMPD.

In October, the judges of the circuit courts requested that the portion of the Four Courts building occupied by the police department be vacated so that the area could be used by the courts. At the board meeting of October 9, Mayor Wells moved that since it was "absolutely necessary for the Police department to be in close proximity to said Courts, for the purpose of properly transacting their business," the Board of Police Commissioners proceed to make arrangements as soon as possible to procure a suitable location for the police department "for the purpose of erecting a building for headquarters on same."[29] The motion was carried. The board would later select a site on the east side of Twelfth Street, in the block north of the Four Courts.[30]

On November 17, the police department became the target of yet another grand jury investigation. Amid rumors of graft and misconduct up and down the ranks of the police department, Circuit Attorney Arthur Sager had, for several weeks, been personally conducting an investigation into the conditions within the police department. The information he secured was turned over to the October-term grand jury. Assistant Chief of Detectives Keely, two former sergeants, and a patrolman who quit after charging political oppression by their superiors, as well as special officer Andrew Gordon, were among witnesses who testified on the first day of the grand jury investigation. Gordon was under suspension at the time, accused by the police department of "grafting."[31] More officers, including six captains, were subpoenaed to appear before the grand jury over the next two days.[32]

Governor Folk made his next move in November. On November 20, police commissioner Blong received a telephone call from board president Stewart asking Blong to come to his office. When he arrived, Stewart asked him if he would resign. There was no particular reason, said Stewart, but if Blong didn't resign, the governor would remove him. Stewart told Blong that he had nothing to do with the request but was merely carrying out the instructions of Governor Folk. Blong refused.[33]

Governor Folk had asked the opinions of the Missouri attorney general and a Boonville, Missouri, judge regarding the power of the governor to remove a board member. Both advised him that the law that provided for the appointment of police commissioners by the governor "contemplates also their removal by the Governor."[34] On November 22, Governor Folk removed Blong from the board and appointed George P. Jones as his replacement.[35]

Speculation and rumors began shortly after the announcement that Blong had been removed from the board. It was reported that a close friend of Governor Folk's said that the governor's next move in reorganizing the board would be to ask Vice President Richard Hanlon for his resignation.[36] When Hanlon was later asked if he would resign if asked by the governor, he replied that it "might depend on the humor I was in at the time . . . I will not lose much sleep over any threatened dismissal from the Board, and it wouldn't take much for me to resign anyway."[37]

George P. Jones was quickly confirmed by the Senate and attended his first board meeting of November 24. Jones was forty-nine years old and the owner of the George P. Jones Oil Company at 704 North Main Street. He had started the company at the age of twenty-four.

Among other organizations, Jones was a member of the Mercantile Club, where he played billiards or pool every day with board member John Fristoe. Jones was a Democrat, but his only involvement with

George P. Jones. Courtesy of SLMPD.

politics was to cast his vote on election days. The appointment to the Board of Police Commissioners was his first public office.[38] Jones's term would expire on January 1, 1907.

Special Officer Andrew Gordon, who was under suspension for suspected grafting, and his partner, Special Officer Noah Warrington, had both earlier been charged with conduct unbecoming an officer. The charges arose from a complaint that Gordon had assaulted a man in July. Warrington's charge was based on his supposed complicity in the incident. The board tried the pair at the meeting of November 17. Gordon was found guilty and fined $25. Warrington was found not guilty.[39]

At the first board meeting attended by George Jones, on November 24, a resolution was presented and adopted that *all* proceedings of the board, with the exception of executive sessions, be open to the general public. The meetings had been opened to the press in 1883. The board closed disciplinary hearings portions of the meetings to everyone, including representatives of the press, in 1897.[40] The resolution opened even these hearings to the public. Excluded from the order were witnesses in cases on trial who, unless otherwise ordered by the board, had to remain outside the room until called to testify.[41] The doors of the meeting room were immediately opened after adoption of the resolution.

Two disciplinary hearings were held at that meeting. In the first, an officer was charged with "failing to pay a just debt." The other involved the trial of Andrew Gordon for "grafting from negro clubs."[42] At least four proprietors of such clubs had filed affidavits with Assistant Chief of Detectives John Keely, accusing Special Officer Gordon of collecting sums varying from $1 to $3 for protecting gambling games.[43]

At Gordon's trial before the board, his former partner, Hugh Allen, testified for the defense. Allen said, "We [Allen and Gordon] could never make a case, because after we would make an arrest, some clubman or politician would go to the front for the prisoner and secure his release. I got sick and disgusted with this kind of work and quit."[44] Noah Warrington also testified in Gordon's defense.

After the completion of Gordon's trial, the board found him guilty, and he was dismissed from the force.[45] Exactly two weeks later officer, Noah Warrington would be tried for withholding important information from the board at Gordon's trial. He was found guilty by the board and dismissed from the force, reducing the number of black police officers to two.[46]

The grand jury made its report to Judge Matthew G. Reynolds on December 2. Simultaneously, Governor Folk arrived in St. Louis to discuss with the board the accusations that had prompted the grand jury investigation.[47] The grand jury report noted that it had found it difficult to obtain evidence from witnesses because the witnesses were afraid of retaliation by the police. Said the report: "The fact that the police commit perjury and suborn witnesses in cases in which they are interested—offering protection to, or menacing those whom they seek to use, was well established before this jury. . . . There exists, too, a feeling on the part of the police, which seems general, that anything is excusable in the defense of a brother officer."[48] The grand jury indicted two former police officers for perjury, stating that the police department was "in a state of disorganization and demoralization, quite unparalleled in its history, and that this condition is due largely to the fact that the police have been used in politics."[49] The grand jury determined that, at one time, every member of the department was a member of a political club [the Jefferson Club], even those who were not Democrats, to avoid problems within the department. The grand jury bluntly stated that

 The evidence is convincing that the department has been made a political machine, and the police have either actively assisted in the perpetration of election frauds or have connived at them. Many of these outrages are fresh on the public mind and that the police are responsible is fully established by the fact that under the administration of the present Police Board the last election was void of the scenes that marked former contests at the polls.

A feeling pervades the department that security of office and preferment are not guaranteed by merits and service, but are matters affected by pull and influence.[50]

The attention of the grand jury had been directed to many cases of inebriated officers. In the past, they said, high officials in the police department tended to lightly treat the situation if the drunken officer was considered an otherwise good officer. The grand jury stated: "We condemn this stand and protest against it. We are pleased that the members of the present police board have made drunkenness a ground of dismissal from the force."[51]

Many members of the detective force were described by the grand jury as "unfit for police duty."[52] The grand jury characterized the standards of the detective department as "low." The final responsibility, they said, rested with the police board: "They cannot be expected to reform in a day conditions that have existed for years, or correct all these evils by a single proclamation. But in that body lies the absolute power, and the credit or discredit of successful administration must there fall."[53] The grand jury expressed confidence in the present board, "and in that confidence have made suggestions and furnished them information in the privacy of the jury room, which it would not be proper to embody in this report."[54]

Governor Folk, who was staying at the Planters Hotel when the grand jury report was released, told a newspaper reporter, "I want the Police Department renovated from top to bottom."[55] Graft and mismanagement were to be eliminated, said Folk, and the police department "cannot and will not be run in [the] future as an adjunct of any political machine."[56] Folk stated that announcements of changes within the department would come from the board. In response to further questioning, it became apparent that the last holdover commissioner, Richard Hanlon, would soon be leaving the board. It was rumored that the removal of some top-ranking officials was also in order. Folk returned to Jefferson City the next morning.

Unknown to Governor Folk and questioning newspaper reporters, Hanlon had already resigned in a letter Folk dated December 1.[57] In his letter, Hanlon took Folk to task on several issues. Among other things, he accused the governor of managing the police department from Jefferson City and attempting to make the police department "a Folk political organization."[58] Hanlon also reminded Governor Folk that Folk was president of the Jefferson Club when "all the police officers were taken into the club at that time, with your consent and approval. . . . "[59]

Hanlon expressed concern that the governor's public expressions about politics were different from those he discussed with some of his political leaders. Governor Folk denied the accusations. He added, "Changes in the board are made not to build any machine, but because it is manifestly impossible to get the best results from a board composed of those hostile to the governor or controlled by his enemies."[60] Folk then requested that his recently appointed president of the St. Louis Board of Election Commissioners, Andrew C. Maroney, meet with him that evening in Jefferson City. Governor Folk was unsure whether Maroney would accept, but he offered to appoint him to take Hanlon's place on the police board.[61] Maroney did accept the appointment, and he was confirmed by the Senate in time for the next board meeting on December 8. Maroney was a lawyer who had served as an assistant circuit attorney under then-circuit attorney Joseph Folk. Maroney was described as "a devoted enough reformer to accept a job paying $1000 a year [the annual salary of a police commissioner] when he had no private funds. . . . "[62]

The first order of business at Maroney's first board meeting was to fill the vacancies of vice president and treasurer. Maroney was elected vice president; Jones was elected treasurer. Meanwhile, the December-term grand jury was organized and received instructions from circuit court judge James E. Withrow. The newly impaneled grand jury was to continue the police inquiry begun by the October-term grand jury.

A few days after the December grand jury began its work, the board and Chief of Police Kiely were visited by the ghost of elections past. The last witness before the October-term grand jury had been Sergeant Harry Dorsey of the Mounted District. He had testified that in the September 1902 primary elections, he had observed a man being assaulted by another at the polling place on the 5800 block of Delmar, and he arrested the man, described as a Democratic leader. Dorsey said he was then approached by Chief Kiely and ordered, "Release that man. He is not the right party."[63] The October grand jury relayed this information, and additional details, to the December grand jury, and Sergeant Dorsey was called before the new body. He basically repeated the same story before the grand jury and Circuit Attorney Arthur Sager.[64]

Circuit Attorney Sager gave the information to the president of the board, Alphonso Stewart. Sergeant Dorsey was then charged with filing a false report. Ironically, the man assaulted at the polls in September 1902 had since become President Stewart's son-in-law. Stewart recused himself from the case. The new vice president of the board, Andrew Maroney, would preside over the board trial of Sergeant Dorsey.[65]

Sergeant Dorsey's trial was held at the board meeting of December 22. Dorsey testified at the hearing that in February 1905 (more than two years after the incident occurred) Chief Kiely asked him to prepare a report of the assault. Dorsey said that Kiely helped refresh his memory of the incident to the effect that Kiely had ordered the arrest of the assaulter but the assaulter was released because the victim could not identify him. Dorsey told Chief Kiely that the chief's version was inaccurate. Nonetheless, Sergeant Dorsey prepared the report the way Chief Kiely had described the incident. In November, after Dorsey had been subpoenaed to appear before the October grand jury, Chief Kiely asked that Dorsey meet him at the Newstead Avenue station. There, testified Dorsey, Kiely gave him a copy of the February report and told him, "Read this report over carefully and stick to it."[66] After Dorsey's testimony had been completed and the hearing had concluded, the board met and unanimously voted that Dorsey be dismissed from the force. There was speculation that Chief Kiely would soon face a similar fate.[67]

Meanwhile, the grafting investigations continued. On December 29, Captain Patrick J. Gaffney, commander of the Ninth District, personally completed an investigation within his district and suspended four patrolmen for suspicion of grafting.[68] Chief Kiely immediately issued a written order to all district commanders to send him "without delay" a list of all sergeants, patrolmen, and probationary patrolmen in their districts and to designate the precincts the sergeants supervised and the beats walked by the patrolmen and probationary patrolmen. Chief Kiely said that with that list, to which was added the number of each officer's star, he would be able to quickly identify who patrolled the areas where "dives and immoral houses are located" and quickly put "his finger on an accused officer in a few minutes."[69]

It was evident that, with Joseph Folk as governor, the board appointed by him was essentially beginning a crusade. The next day, the *Globe-Democrat* even printed a box score of the "shake-up and reorganization" of the police force.[70] The list included the dismissals of one sergeant, two patrolmen, and six detectives, and the suspensions of six patrolmen.[71] The "shake-up and reorganization" would next embrace the Chief of Police.

1906

The new year would be just over a month old before the board resolved to remove Chief Kiely. Kiely was called to meet with the board at the executive session held immediately after the open board meeting of February 2, 1906. Chief Kiely was asked to resign as chief of police and, reportedly, Kiely asked the board that he be given a captaincy. Without that stipulation, said Kiely, he was not inclined to resign. President Stewart asked Kiely to call on him at his business office the following morning (Saturday) to further discuss the situation. Kiely met with Stewart and again was asked to resign. Kiely repeated his offer to resign if he were given the rank of captain. Stewart replied that Kiely would not be permitted to remain on the force.[72]

That evening, Chief Kiely sent a letter to President Stewart's home. Kiely stated in the letter that he had continuously been a member of the police department since 1875, and he outlined the dates of his promotions. The letter noted that, at the meeting that morning, Kiely asked Stewart if there were any charges of graft or dishonesty against him and Stewart had replied that there were none:

> Should I now retire upon the request of the board, the general public would be justified in thinking that I was ashamed of my record and afraid to stand trial. My record has been an open book. I have grown old in the service and have nothing but my reputation. This, to my family and myself, is sacred. I also owe something to the citizens of St. Louis, who have honored me for so many years.
>
> Whatever may be the result, I feel it my duty to my family, my friends and myself to have all the facts made public, and to that end I demand a specification of charges and a speedy public trial, where I shall be confronted with the witnesses. I respectfully request that at such trial I be accorded the privilege of counsel.[73]

Chief Kiely would receive a response the following Monday.

The December-term grand jury made its final report to Judge James Withrow the same morning that Chief Kiely called at President Stewart's office. The grand jury reported that, while there was evidence of wrongdoing, it was "not indictable by a grand jury."[74] That evidence was furnished to the board, in which the grand jury expressed confidence. Nonetheless, said the report, the grand jury believed that one way to prevent a recurrence of the past problems was "the enactment of a law placing the board of police commissioners on a strictly non-partisan basis."[75]

At a special meeting the following Monday, February 5, the board suspended Chief Kiely pending the formal filing of charges. Kiely repeated his request that he be allowed counsel at the trial. President Stewart would later tell a newspaper reporter that Chief Kiely would not be permitted counsel. "He is to be tried under the rules in the police manual, just the same as any other officer. He has no more right to counsel, under the rules, than those ranking below him."[76] No date was set for the trial. Assistant Chief Christ Gillaspy was called to the Four Courts and installed as acting chief of police.[77]

On February 16, Chief Kiely was served with a copy of the formal charges and specifications. There were two charges: "neglect of duty" and "conduct unbecoming an officer." The neglect of duty charge contained eight specifications that included Chief Kiely's knowledge that some officers were taking money and other valuable things from prostitutes and other criminals and wouldn't aid the board in determining whether such allegations were true; assigning a sergeant with a reputation of being a "masher" to the Union Station where women and girls who were strangers to the city, and women visitors, were common; permitting houses of ill repute that recruited girls under the age of eighteen to operate in the Fourth District; and permitting Captain Samuel Boyd to remain in charge of the Fourth District after Kiely well knew the notorious condition of the district.[78]

The conduct unbecoming an officer charge had five specifications. Four of those involved Chief Kiely's conduct in the assault case at a polling place in September 1902. Chief Kiely was accused of inducing Sergeant Harry Dorsey to make a false police report of the incident; failing to suspend Sergeant Dorsey for making a false report; ordering Dorsey to release the man he had arrested for the assault; and trying to induce Dorsey to testify falsely before a grand jury. The fifth specification was that, anticipating violence at the primary election of

March 12, 1904, Chief Kiely requested permission (which the board granted) to leave the city.[79]

After Chief Kiely again requested that he be permitted counsel and was refused, he filed for and received a preliminary writ of prohibition that compelled the board to show cause why he should not be so represented. The case went to the Missouri Supreme Court where, after a hearing, Chief Kiely was granted the right to counsel.[80] The board called a special meeting for the next day, February 27, to begin the board's trial of Chief Kiely.[b]

The trial began at 1:30 p.m. Chief Kiely was represented by attorneys Walter H. Saunders and John S. Leahy. Second Associate City Counselor Charles P. Williams represented the board. Kiely's attorneys first moved for a continuance so that they could adequately familiarize themselves with the case and prepare a defense. The request was denied. On motion, the board permitted Kiely's counsel to read all objections to the charges and specifications. Counsel was also permitted to read an affidavit, signed by Kiely, that Vice President Maroney was prejudiced against him and should be disqualified from participating in the trial. President Stewart ruled that the board had no authority to disqualify Maroney, as he held his commission from an act of the legislature. However, Stewart left open the possibility that the objection might later be considered.[81]

President Stewart proceeded to read the charges and specifications, and Kiely entered a plea of "not guilty" to each. After the first witness for the board had been called and testified, one of Kiely's attorneys, John Leahy, entered the room and informed the board that a writ of prohibition had been issued "temporarily restraining the Board from further proceeding with the case."[82] The board suspended the trial until further notice.

On March 12, circuit court Judge Walter B. Douglas overruled a motion by the board to vacate Kiely's writ of prohibition. Judge Douglas also invalidated six of the eight specifications listed under the first

---

[b] The order of the Missouri Supreme Court had a secondary effect, the assistance of counsel at board trials. At subsequent board trials the minutes of the board noted the names of counsel retained by accused officers.

charge, neglect of duty, and four of the five specifications under the second, conduct unbecoming an officer, ruling that the board couldn't try Kiely for offenses he was alleged to have committed before he was reappointed chief of police on February 27, 1905.[83]

Three charges remained:

Charge 1, Specification 5. That, knowing of the existence of notorious saloons, gardens and dance halls, he failed to do his duty in suppressing them between February 27, 1905, and the date of his suspension

Charge 1, Specification 6. That, knowing or having the means of knowing of where men were robbed almost daily, he failed, between February 27, 1905 and June 1, 1905, to do his duty in suppressing these places.

Charge 2, Specification 4. That, knowing that Sergeant Harry B. Dorsey had been summoned to testify before the grand jury, he met Sergt. Dorsey by secret appointment at the Newstead Avenue Station and instructed him to make his testimony before the grand jury agree with the false report made in reference to the assault on George B. Williams at a primary election Sept. 16, 1902.[84]

Two days later, Judge Douglas dissolved the temporary writ of prohibition granted to Chief Kiely and replaced it with a permanent writ that prohibited the board from trying Kiely on any but the three remaining charges.[85] While not directly stated in either of Judge Douglas's actions, a precedent may have been established: the right of police officers to have charges against them reviewed by the courts.[86]

✳   ✳   ✳

At the next board meeting, the resignation of one of the two remaining black officers on the force, Reece Evans, was accepted while he was under charges. At the same meeting, Allen Wilkinson, who had been dismissed in 1903, was reinstated as a probationary patrolman.[87]

The board also began moving police officers out of nonpolice roles within the department, ruling that no officers at the rank of probationary patrolman or higher could be assigned to clerical or mechanical duties "unless effective police service requires such assignment."[88] Instead, the board established three grades of civilian clerks. The highest level, first-class clerks, would receive a salary of $90 a month. Second-class clerks would receive $75 a month, and third-class clerks would receive $60. Newly hired clerks would enter at the third-class level. Vacancies in the first- or second-class levels would be filled from the level below. All civilian clerks would serve at the pleasure of the board.[89]

Twelve patrolmen performing clerical duties were returned to beat duty. Nine additional patrolmen serving as clerks resigned and were appointed first-class clerks. Five patrolmen, two serving as painters, two as carpenters, and one as an armorer, were permitted to resign. They were then rehired as civilians, at the same salary, to continue the work they were doing. All of the changes were effective April 1.[90]

The board also created a new professional position in April. Dr. A. C. Robinson, who had served as the department physician and held the rank of patrolman, was slated for the position of surgeon of the police department if he resigned his patrolman rank. Dr. Robinson resigned his commission and was appointed to the office.[91]

Vice President Maroney, who had been on the board only six months, resigned on June 2. Governor Folk immediately reappointed him to the presidency of the Board of Election Commissioners. Maroney told the press that it had been his understanding that he would be on the Board of Police Commissioners only for a few months to conduct the inquiry into police graft and other abuses.[92] Maroney said he had wanted to resign from the board in March, but was "prevailed upon," apparently by Governor Folk, to remain until June 1.[93] There had been many dismissals from the force during his tenure.

Meanwhile, patrolmen in the Central District formed an organization, the "Three-Platoon System club" that was formed "for the purpose of preparing a communication to be presented to the board of police commissioners, petitioning them to establish the three-platoon system."[94] Men from the other eleven districts would later join their colleagues in the effort. The officers of the organization claimed that the eight-hour system could be installed with the addition of few, if any, officers and would greatly increase the efficiency of the force.[95] The club began securing reports from the other districts to determine how officers would be scheduled and how many additional officers might be required. These were to be forwarded to the chief of police for his approval before being presented to the board.[96]

Former Missouri senator John W. Drabelle, who was an attorney, was asked to write a bill for introduction into the next legislative session. Drabelle had written, and fought for, the 1899 police act under which the department was then operating. The new bill would (1) divide the officers of the department into three platoons that worked eight hours each; (2) add 250 patrolmen and 50 probationary patrolmen to the strength of the department; and (3) add 2 captains, 2 lieutenants, and 30 sergeants.[97] Also in the bill was a paragraph that would prevent the dropping of officers from the rolls by simply failing to renew their four-year commissions. The bill stated that officers could only be removed for "cause" and after a hearing by the board: "They [all officers in the department] shall have commissions issued to them by the board of police commissioners, and those hereafter commissioned shall serve while they shall faithfully perform their duties, and possess mental and physical ability, and be subject to removal only for cause after a hearing by the board, who are hereby invested with the exclusive jurisdiction in the premises."[98]

The bill would pass, with these sections included, on March 15, 1907.[99] The three-platoon system would not be put into effect by the board until November 1, 1907.[100]

On June 16, two more black applicants, Ira Cooper and W. W. Crockett, were appointed probationary patrolmen. Cooper was believed to be the first college graduate appointed to the force, having a degree in ophthalmology from Northern Illinois College in Chicago. He came to St. Louis to practice his profession, but decided to join the police department "after starving for a year."[101] Cooper would become the first black sergeant (in 1923) and first black lieutenant (in 1930) in the police department.[102]

Governor Folk appointed Maroney's replacement, Theodoric R. Bland, on June 28. Bland, at twenty-eight years of age, was likely the youngest man appointed to the board. He was a former college foot-

Ira Cooper. Courtesy of SLMPD.

Theodoric R. Bland. Courtesy of SLMPD.

ball player and college football coach who held a law degree from Saint Louis University and practiced in the St. Louis law firm of Rhodes E. Cave. When Governor Folk announced Bland's appointment, Folk instructed him to "at once begin energetic and aggressive prosecution of the bucket shops and the clubs illegally selling liquor, and not to let up in his efforts until both are suppressed and driven out of business."[103]

Ironically, Bland had been among the victims of assaults at the Democratic primary of March 1904. He was pushed to the ground and later knocked into the gutter at Taylor and Delmar avenues. He told a reporter for the *Globe-Democrat* that the incident would have no effect on his duties on the board: "My efforts will be directed toward keeping the department in line with the statutes and keeping good men on, as well as bad men off the force."[104] Bland attended his first board meeting the next day and, since the position of vice president of the board was left vacant by Maroney's resignation, Bland was elected to that office.

In August, the board granted permission for the second annual "base ball contest" between the police department and letter carriers of the U.S. Post Office.[105] The first game, held in August, was for the benefit of the Police Relief Association; the second game would be played for the benefit of the *Post-Dispatch* Free Ice and Pure Milk Fund.

At the meeting of July 27, the board, at the suggestion of the St. Louis Board of Health, voted to appoint a department chemist. While the minutes of the meeting gave no indication of the work the chemist would perform, a *Globe-Democrat* article the next day said that the board was reacting to Acting Chief Christ Gillaspy's "crusade . . . against opium sellers and smokers."[106] The duties of the chemist, said the newspaper, would "consist in part in discovering the difference between 'hasheesh' and opium."[107]

The case of Chief Kiely was then called, but Acting President Bland continued the case to September 11. The counsel for Chief Kiely filed a motion for an immediate trial, but Bland replied that the board was not ready for trial because of the absence of two of its members, Alphonso Stewart and George Jones. Mayor Wells was also absent, but was represented by Acting Mayor Hamilton A. Forman.

Mathew Kiely's attorneys filed a formal written protest, stating that their client was ready for trial. Acting President Bland replied that the protest would be made part of the record, but he preferred that the full board be present for the trial. Amended charges, conforming to the orders of the circuit court, were filed against suspended Kiely on July 31 and served on him that same day.

In the meantime, Acting Chief Christ Gillaspy quite possibly added a new word to the English language. Two mounted patrolmen were brought before the board on a charge of "conduct unbecoming an officer." When the board asked Gillaspy the nature of the misconduct, he replied that the officers were "lollygagging" with two young women. Asked to explain what he meant by lollygagging, Chief Gillaspy defined lollygagging as "standing about idly, chatting and laughing and talking about nothing in particular, but anything but business."[108] After hearing the explanations of the officers, the board found both guilty. The board reprimanded them for their conduct and "dismounted" the two officers. Captain McNamee of the Mounted District was ordered to assign the men to foot duty "for a while."[109]

The trial of suspended Chief Mathew Kiely began on September 12. After a reading of the three charges, Kiely pleaded "not guilty" to all. The trial would end on September 19, after having met for six seven-hour days. Thirty-six witnesses testified against Kiely, sixty-eight for him, and forty-two businessmen were called as character witnesses. Kiely was in the witness chair for ten hours.[110]

Both sides were asked if they wished to make closing statements. The board's attorney, Charles Williams, declined. After closing arguments by Kiely's attorneys, the members of the board went to lunch at about 1:00 p.m. They returned at 2:00 p.m. and began their deliberations behind locked doors.[111] Kiely was found guilty on all charges and was dismissed from the force.

The board then proceeded to fill the office of chief of police. Captain Edmond P. Creecy, commander of the Seventh District, was promoted to the position effective that day, September 19.[112] Creecy was fifty-three years old, married, and had seven living children. Born in North Carolina, Creecy enlisted in one of the home regiments of the Confederate forces at the age of fifteen. He fought in the Civil

War and was captured and imprisoned for one year at Point Lookout, Maryland. He was released in a prisoner exchange and, after the war, was trained and worked as a civil engineer. He made a trip to St. Louis in 1870, then moved there in 1876 and was appointed a special officer

Chief of Police Edmond P. Creecy. Courtesy of SLMPD.

on the police force the following year. He resigned in 1881, accepting an offer to do some civil engineering in Colorado. He was reappointed to the force the following year. In 1883, he again resigned, returning in 1885. He was reappointed to the force that year and had continuously served since.[113]

The policemen on the beats, meanwhile, continued to perform their daily duties. While walking his beat on Hunt Avenue on September 29, Patrolman Humphrey O'Leary, assigned to the Seventh District, saw a live electric wire dangling across the sidewalk. Borrowing a pair of rubber gloves from a resident of the neighborhood, O'Leary began to coil the wire around a telegraph pole until the electric company could be notified. There was a "sudden blinding flash," and O'Leary fell to the sidewalk.[114] He was quickly taken to a physician's office, but was pronounced dead. O'Leary, whose brother was a sergeant in the same district, was twenty-seven years old, married, and the father of a six-month old baby.[115] He was buried in Calvary Cemetery.[116]

The annual police review and parade were altered for 1906. Instead of marching downtown, the review and parade were held in conjunction with the unveiling of the bronze statue of St. Louis at the top of Art Hill in Forest Park. Six companies of patrolmen and four platoons of mounted police, about 450 policemen in all, passed before the board's reviewing stand.[117]

Chief Creecy's first challenge lay ahead: the general election on November 6. Creecy had a meeting with all of the captains on November 1. He said that he didn't anticipate any trouble at the polls but, if there was trouble, "it will be suppressed immediately, or there will be an investigation as to why it was not. I mean to have a clean election if the police can make one."[118]

After meeting with the board the next day, Creecy announced that saloons would be closed on election day. The closing of saloons on election days had been sporadically enforced over the past several years but, said Creecy, "A great deal of the rowdyism and trouble which occur at the polls is, I believe, the result of too much liquor drank by the offenders. If they get it this year they will have to buy it Monday and carry it around in bottles."[119] In addition, every police officer was to work on November 6, with two officers being assigned to each polling place at all times. Extra men would be assigned to those polling places where trouble might be suspected.[120] To emphasize his point, Creecy ordered the transfer of the Fourth District commander to the Tenth District and the Tenth District commander to the Fourth District. The Fourth Ward, which was in the Fourth Police District, had been the scene of election irregularities in St. Louis for years. The newly transferred Fourth District commander had orders to see that there were no problems in the polling places in his district.[121]

The excise commissioner began sending notices to saloon keepers that their businesses must be closed during the hours that the polls were open. At the same time, election board president and former police commissioner Andrew C. Maroney spoke to several hundred election officials in the rotunda of city hall. Maroney told them that no liquor was to be allowed in any polling place. He also forbade the use of so-called poor boxes. It had been the practice of election judges and clerks in some parts of the city to put boxes in the polling places where donations could be deposited for the lunches of the officials and to permit the officials to buy drinks.[122]

Chief Creecy, who had ordered the saloons closed from midnight on Monday until midnight on Tuesday, modified his order to close them only during the hours that the polls were open: 6:00 a.m. to 7:00 p.m.[123] The day before the election, Circuit Attorney Arthur Sager sent a communication to Chief Creecy that Section 3011 of the Missouri Revised Statutes required that dramshops be closed "upon the day of any general election in this state. . . . "[124] Sager interpreted "day" to mean twenty-four hours, from midnight to midnight. Chief Creecy stood pat, however, and Circuit Attorney Sager sent him a second communication that he would "vigorously prosecute" any dramshop keeper who remained open after midnight on Monday or opened his doors before midnight on election day. Sager quoted Governor Folk: "The law does not consider fractions of time."[125] In the end, both viewpoints were enforced. Saloons were closed only during the hours that the polls were open. Circuit Attorney Sager, with the current grand jury in his office, gave the sheriff's department the order to visit any saloon that had opened after the polls closed. Deputies were to inform the proprietor that he had to remain closed until midnight. Deputies were to "gather evidence" of the selling of alcoholic beverages of those who refused to close and present it to the grand jury.[126]

Sager personally took the initiative. He and grand jury foreman Horace Rumsey went to Fourth and Morgan and began walking west on Morgan. Sager walked on one side of the street and Rumsey the other. Each saloon that was open was requested to close until midnight. They visited from twenty to thirty saloons before they stopped at Seventeenth Street. All of them closed after the request. The saloon keepers in the downtown area of the city remained open. It was not known whether sheriff's deputies had paid any of these a visit. Ironically, and despite telephone messages from the circuit attorney's office, one saloon that did not close was at Twelfth and Clark streets, directly across from the Four Courts building that housed the circuit attorney's office.[127]

At the last board meeting of November, President Stewart announced that gambling in all forms was going to be suppressed even if the police had to conduct raids and destroy the gambling paraphernalia. He concluded, "And we mean to carry out our plans."[128] The board also discussed the suggestion of Chief Creecy that the gambling squad be abolished. President Stewart was in favor of transferring all current members out of the squad and appointing a new squad.[129]

Two weeks later, the gambling squad was abolished. In an order to all captains, Chief Edmond Creecy stated: "Henceforth the abatement of gambling in your district will be under your direction. You will hold the sergeants and patrolmen responsible for failure to discover gambling. Failure to detect crime on a patrolman's beat is made the basis of charges, as provided in the manual."[130]

The board also promulgated a new rule concerning private watchmen. The rule was instigated by the application for a private watchman's license by a former police detective who had been dismissed from the force. The board refused to approve a license for the former detective and then announced that no officer who had been dismissed from the force would be eligible for a private watchman's license.[131]

Before the year was out, former chief of police Mathew Kiely joined a private detective agency operated by former police detective Lee Killian. Through an agreement, Kiely became the senior partner in the Kiely and Killian detective agency in the Nulsen Building at Sixth and Olive streets. Kiely had also made a claim against the board for $3,200 in pay he believed was due him for the time he was under suspension.[132]

That the police department was in the process of reformation became clear when the treasurer of the Jefferson Club, the Democratic club that almost all police officers had joined during the board presidency of Harry Hawes, complained that the police members weren't paying their dues. Said Chief Creecy, "The police are out of politics.

If they want to pay, they can. I will not stop them, but there will be no orders from this office directing them to settle club dues. Those days are past and gone."[133]

The Jefferson Club also complained to the Board of Police Commissioners, but the board did not consider the complaint.[134] As the editors of the *Globe-Democrat* had commented two months earlier, "The new police era now begun is most welcome, for it is hopeful.[135]

Epilogue

IT IS DIFFICULT, FROM AN EARLY twenty-first century perspective, to imagine how a police department could become so deeply enmeshed in party politics. In his work concerning the history and future of policing, Victor G. Strecher posed salient questions: Was policing in the United States during this time "deviantly political or simply part of an era which was inherently political"?[1] What was the political norm from which the police department would have to deviate in order to be considered "deviantly political?" Was this an era in history that was "inherently political?" To determine if the police department was "deviantly political," one must first determine if it was "inherently political."

This account of the St. Louis Metropolitan Police Department has described a time in Missouri when there weren't open primary elections. Democrats and Republicans held separate primaries. A person who registered and voted in the Democratic primary was considered a Democrat. The same was true for the Republican Party. It was not difficult to determine, when party affiliation was a requisite for a job or in the awarding of a contract with the city or the state, who was a Republican and who was a Democrat. This was a time of party bosses, machine politics, the bribery of state and local officials for the passage of laws favorable to certain interests (boodling) and the stuffing of ballot boxes by men (known in St. Louis as "Indians") who were paid to falsely represent themselves, in as many voting places as dictated, as different registered voters. This aspect of the political system was not unique to St. Louis; similar incidents took place all across Missouri and the rest of the country.[a]

---

[a] See, for example, the reprint of Lincoln Steffens's *The Shame of the Cities*, New York: Hill and Wang, 1957.

Politics ruled in the everyday operations of city government and in elections. And, while not technically an arm of city government, the police department operated within the same environment. The police department wasn't created in a social vacuum; politics was a reality with which the department had to deal. This was an era, to answer Strecher's question, that was inherently political; the police were simply a part of that era.

St. Louis grand juries, especially in the latter part of the nineteenth century, constantly investigated the actions of individual police officers and members of the Board of Police Commissioners. However, this was equally true of other city (and state) departments. That the times were inherently political, and that the way the system operated was well understood by politicians, can be illustrated by two examples. "Colonel" Ed Butler was the Democratic Party boss in St. Louis during much of the era described in this book. After the Republicans won the state general election in 1904, Butler candidly admitted to a *St. Louis Post-Dispatch* reporter that he had been "stealing elections from the Republicans of this city for 30 years, and I have decided to quit."[2] Butler said that "St. Louis [like Missouri] is Republican, too, and if things were on the level here the Democrats could never have elected any mayor save Joe Brown [in 1871]. Joe was elected twice honestly—and he is the only Democrat who did carry St. Louis on the square since the civil war."[3] When the reporter asked Butler if he could quote him publicly, Butler replied "It's all right. Go ahead, I know what I am talking about, and every man in politics knows the same thing, too."[4]

Some twenty-four years later, former police board president Harry B. Hawes allegedly made a similar admission. In 1928, Hawes was a U.S. senator from Missouri. He and friends of fellow senator James A. Reed had persuaded Reed to run for president. Hawes called Lee Meriwether, an unsuccessful candidate for mayor in St. Louis in 1901, and asked him to come to Washington, D.C., and manage Reed's campaign.[5] Meriwether consented. Later, at a meeting attended by Meriwether, Hawes, Reed, and others in Washington, the men began reminiscing about past political campaigns. Hawes, said Meriwether, "referred to the time [1901] Rolla Wells was given the office to which the people elected me . . . Hawes then told us how the 'trick was done'—how the police gave protection to election crooks while they stuffed the ballot boxes and counted my votes for Mr. Wells."[6] Meriwether said that Reed later told him "he was surprised to hear so frank an admission of so outrageous a wrong."[7] Meriwether later wrote that "the judicious were severe in condemning Hawes, but that he was in accord with the political morals of that day seems shown by the fact that, well known as his record was, a majority of the people of Missouri chose him as their representative in the United States Senate."[8] Nineteenth- and early-twentieth-century politics embraced a set of standards that are no longer the norm.

And, while the metropolitan police system was generally viewed with favor, the Board of Police Commissioners was constantly under attack. The way in which board members were selected, by appointment of the governor with the consent of the Missouri Senate, was criticized by various St. Louis mayors, members of the city legislative body, and grand juries. Those who found disfavor with the board selection process recommended such disparate repairs as election of board members by the people of the city; gubernatorial appointment of some members, mayoral appointment of the remainder; and various other combinations of popular election and appointment. Sometimes mentioned was the abolition of the metropolitan police system, with the control of the police department returning to the mayor.

That the Board of Police Commissioners *was* the police department could easily be observed. The board established policy and made the rules that were duly printed in the rule manuals supplied to each member of the department. The board appointed every member to the police department, from the chief of police to janitors. It decided who would be promoted, and it had the final word on transfers. It conducted disciplinary hearings of all accused police officers, determined guilt or innocence, and, if guilt was established, set the punishment.

In addition, it had no small amount of power in the city. A member of each board was selected to sit on the city's Board of Health. The police board alone licensed private watchmen and private detectives and could revoke the licenses. It approved or disapproved applications for liquor licenses, theater licenses, the licenses of hotel and steamboat runners,[1] pawnshop licenses, and even licenses required of ragpickers.

Unfortunately, the last board of the nineteenth century and the first of the twentieth century took politics to the extreme. These were the boards that apparently appointed only applicants who were Democrats. It was under these boards that police officers felt compelled to join the Democratic Jefferson Club. It was while these boards were in charge that police officers were assessed a fee each month to be contributed to the state and city Democratic committees. These kinds of circumstances contributed to the election of Joseph Folk, a former circuit attorney in St. Louis and a reform gubernatorial candidate, and his subsequent appointment of reform-minded men to the board.

The last board in this account, that headed by Alphonso C. Stewart, led the police into the reform era. Did this reform mark the end of politics in the police department? If that was the case, says Strecher, "the influence of politics [would be] eliminated, reduced or displaced by some other social mechanism. [The George Kelling/Mark Moore three eras of American policing model] failed to distinguish between the primitive sorts of corrupt and machine politics prevalent during the formative years of American local governments and the [only slightly] more subtle but no less prevalent political incursions into policing known throughout the subsequent periods termed 'reform' and 'community.'"[9] Politics remained in the police department, but would not be nearly as pervasive or as debilitating as in the political era.

What was in the immediate future for the St. Louis Metropolitan Police Department? In 1907, the department would move from the Four Courts building to its new headquarters at 208 South Twelfth Street. Since 1872, the police had shared the Four Courts building with the city jail and three courts; the police department would be the only occupant of the new headquarters building. In 1927, the police department would begin construction of the current headquarters at Tucker Boulevard and Clark Street. In its continuing effort to control auto speed, the police department bought its first motorcycle in 1907.

New police headquarters at 208 South Twelfth Street. Courtesy of SLMPD.

By far, however, the most momentous event occurred on March 15, 1907. On that date, the state legislature approved Senate Bill 13, the bill that would change the workday of the force from a two-platoon, twelve-hour day to a three-platoon, eight-hour day. Additional men would be needed, so the bill increased the number of

Patrolman Willard Pritchard, the first motorcycle officer in the St. Louis Metropolitan Police Department. Courtesy of SLMPD.

patrolmen from 1,000 to 1,250 and the number of probationary patrolmen from 100 to 150. The bill also provided for 2 additional captains and lieutenants (from 12 to 14) and an increase in the number of sergeants from 100 to 130. To further gladden the hearts of the members of the force, the bill also did away with the a time limit on their commissions.[10] While the authorized number of officers has changed over the years, the foundation of Senate Bill 13 remains in force to this day.[11]

St. Louis Boards of Police Commissioners, 1861–1906

Name	Appointing Governor	Date Appointed or Confirmed	Term of Appointment	Date Left Office	Reason
McLaran, Charles	Claiborne Jackson	Apr. 4, 1861[1]	2 years	Aug. 30, 1861[1]	Removed by Prov. Gov. Gamble
Brownlee, John A.	Claiborne Jackson	Apr. 4, 1861[1]	2 years	Aug. 21, 1861[1]	Resigned
Carlisle, James H.	Claiborne Jackson	Apr. 4, 1861[1]	4 years	Aug. 30, 1861[1]	Removed by Prov. Gov. Gamble
Duke, Basil Wilson	Claiborne Jackson	Apr. 4, 1861[1]	4 years	Aug. 30, 1861[1]	Removed by Prov. Gov. Gamble[a]
Duke, Basil	Claiborne Jackson	May 23, 1861[1]	To Apr. 4, 1865	Sep. 9, 1861	Removed by Governor Gamble
How, John	Hamilton R. Gamble	Aug. 24, 1861	To Apr. 4, 1865	Jan. 25, 1865	Removed; state law vacated board[b]
Patrick, William	Hamilton R. Gamble	Sep. 2, 1861	Unknown[c]	Jan. 25, 1865	Removed; state law vacated board[b]
Riggin, John	Hamilton R. Gamble	Oct. 18, 1861	To Apr. 4, 1865	Jan. 25, 1865	Removed; state law vacated board[b]

Meyer, Ferdinand	Thomas C. Fletcher	Jan. 31, 1865[1]	4 years	Feb. 2, 1869	Term expired; reappointed for 4-year term
Jameson, E. H. E.	Thomas C. Fletcher	Jan. 31, 1865[1]	4 years	May 7, 1866	Resigned
Clark, N. H.	Thomas C. Fletcher	Feb. 2, 1865[1]	2 years	Feb. 2, 1867	Term expired
Laibold, Bernard	Thomas C. Fletcher	Feb. 2, 1865[1]	2 years	Mar. 23, 1865[1]	Resigned to become chief of police
Corbett, James M.	Thomas C. Fletcher	Mar. 24, 1865[1]	To Feb. 2, 1867	Apr. 3, 1866	Resigned
Conrad, Joseph	Thomas C. Fletcher	Mar. 5, 1865[1]	To Jan. 31, 1869	Nov. 1, 1866	Resigned
Eaton, Lucien	Thomas C. Fletcher	Apr. 6, 1866[1]	To Feb. 2, 1867	Feb. 2, 1867	Term expired; reappointed for 4-year term
Irwin, Charles W.	Thomas C. Fletcher	Jan. 22, 1867[1]	To Jan. 31, 1869	Jan. 29, 1867[1]	Resigned
Codding, John O.	Thomas C. Fletcher	Jan. 30, 1867[1]	To Jan. 31, 1869	Jan. 31, 1869	Term expired

Name	Appointing Governor	Date Appointed or Confirmed	Term of Appointment	Date Left Office	Reason
Eaton, Lucien	Thomas C. Fletcher	Jan. 31, 1867[1]	4 years	May 29, 1867[1]	Resigned
Hequembourg, William	Thomas C. Fletcher	Jan. 31, 1867[1]	4 years	Sep. 24, 1870[1]	Removed by Gov. McClurg
Lademann, Otto C.	Thomas C. Fletcher	May 30, 1867[1]	To Jan. 31, 1871	Feb. 8, 1870[1]	Resigned
Meyer, Ferdinand	Joseph C. McClurg	Feb. 2, 1869[1]	4 years	Sep. 24, 1870	Removed by Gov. McClurg
Bonner, Samuel	Joseph C. McClurg	Feb. 2, 1869[1]	4 years	Oct. 31, 1870[1]	Resigned
Hunicke, Julius	Joseph C. McClurg	Feb. 16, 1870	To Jan. 31, 1871	Sep. 24, 1870[1]	Removed by Gov. McClurg
Baker, William B.	Joseph C. McClurg	Sep. 24, 1870[1]	To Jan. 31, 1871	Jan. 31, 1871	Term expired
Randolph, S. Martin	Joseph C. McClurg	Sep. 24, 1870[1]	To Feb. 2, 1873	Feb. 13, 1871	Removed by Gov. B. Gratz Brown

Moran, William	Joseph C. McClurg	Sep. 24, 1870[1]	To Jan. 31, 1871	Jan. 31, 1871	Term expired
Rosenblatt, William A.	Joseph C. McClurg	Oct. 31, 1870[1]	To Feb. 2, 1873	Feb. 17, 1871	Resigned
Patrick, William	B. Gratz Brown	Feb. 2, 1871	4 years	Feb. 2, 1873	Reappointed by Silas Woodson to complete term
Ferguson, William F.	B. Gratz Brown	Feb. 13, 1871	To Feb. 2, 1873	Feb. 7, 1873	Term expired
Hunicke, Julius	B. Gratz Brown	Feb. 17, 1871	4 years	Jan. 27, 1873[1]	Resigned
Filley, Oliver B.	B. Gratz Brown	Feb. 17, 1871	To Feb. 2, 1873	Jan. 17, 1872[1]	Resigned
Pulitzer, Joseph	B. Gratz Brown	Jan. 19, 1872	To Feb. 2, 1873	Feb. 2, 1873	Term expired
Rainwater, Charles C.	Silas Woodson	Feb. 2, 1873[1]	4 years	Mar. 27, 1877	Term expired
Patrick, William	Silas Woodson	Feb. 2, 1873[1]	2 years	Feb. 2, 1875	Term expired

Name	Appointing Governor	Date Appointed or Confirmed	Term of Appointment	Date Left Office	Reason
Armstrong, David H.	Silas Woodson	Feb. 17, 1873[1]	2 years	Feb. 17, 1875	Term expired
Dorsheimer, Lewis	Silas Woodson	Feb. 2, 1873[1]	4 years	Feb. 27, 1877	Term expired
Nidelet, James C.	Charles Hardin	Feb. 2, 1875	4 years	Apr. 15, 1879	Term expired
Priest, John G.	Charles Hardin	Feb. 16, 1875	4 years	Apr. 22, 1879	Term expired
Duke, Basil	John Phelps	Jan. 1, 1877	4 years	Jan. 25, 1881	Term expired
Armstrong, David H.	John Phelps	Jan. 1, 1877	4 years	Oct. 14, 1877[1]	Resigned; appointed to U.S. Senate[d]
Bent, Silas	John Phelps	Oct. 15, 1877[1]	To Jan. 1, 1881	Apr. 15, 1879	Unknown[c]
Armstrong, David H.	John Phelps	Apr. 16, 1879	To Jan. 1, 1881	Jan. 25, 1881	Term expired

Name	Appointed by	Date appointed	Term	Date left	Reason
Finney, John D.	John Phelps	Apr. 16, 1879	To Jan. 1, 1883	Mar. 5, 1881[1]	Removed by Gov. Thomas Crittenden
Moffett, Leslie A.	John Phelps	Apr. 16, 1879	To Jan. 1, 1883	Mar. 5, 1881[1]	Removed by Gov. Thomas Crittenden
Boland, Morgan	Thomas F. Crittenden	Jan. 25, 1881	To Jan. 1, 1885	Mar. 11, 1881[1]	Removed by Gov. Thomas Crittenden
Kinkead, Alexander	Thomas F. Crittenden	Jan. 25, 1881	To Jan. 1, 1885	Oct. 1, 1883	Resigned
Cupples, Samuel	Thomas F. Crittenden	Mar. 14, 1881[2]	To Jan. 1, 1883	Jul. 1, 1882[1]	Resigned
Simmons, E. C.	Thomas F. Crittenden	Mar. 14, 1881[2]	To Jan. 1, 1883	Jul. 1, 1882[1]	Resigned
Maxon, John W.	Thomas F. Crittenden	Mar. 14, 1881[2]	To Jan. 1, 1885	Jul. 1, 1882[1]	Resigned
Caruth, David W.	Thomas F. Crittenden	Jul. 1, 1882[1]	To Jan. 1, 1883	Jan. 1, 1883	Term expired; reappointed for 4-year term
Kerwin, Daniel	Thomas F. Crittenden	Jul. 1, 1882[1]	To Jan. 1, 1885	Sep. 14, 1883[2]	Resigned

Name	Appointing Governor	Date Appointed or Confirmed	Term of Appointment	Date Left Office	Reason
McCabe, Frank X.	Thomas F. Crittenden	Jul. 1, 1882[1]	To Jan. 1, 1883	Jan. 23, 1883	Term expired
Caruth, David W.	Thomas F. Crittenden	Jan. 1, 1883[1]	4 years	Jan. 10, 1885[1]	Resigned
Lutz, Frank	Thomas F. Crittenden	Jan. 1, 1883[1]	4 years	Jan. 14, 1885	Resigned
Gooding, Oliver P.	Thomas F. Crittenden	Sep. 24, 1883[1]	To Jan. 1, 1885	Jan. 14, 1885	Term expired; reappointed for 4-year term
Cleveland, Henry D.	Thomas F. Crittenden	Oct. 3, 1883[1]	To Jan. 1, 1885	Oct. 17, 1883[2]	Resigned
Woodward, Tryon J.	Thomas F. Crittenden	Nov. 12, 1883[1]	To Jan. 1, 1885	Jan. 14, 1885	Term expired
Blair, James L.	John S. Marmaduke	Jan. 14, 1885	2 years	Jan. 14, 1887	Term expired; reappointed for 4-year term
Callahan, Michael	John S. Marmaduke	Jan. 14, 1885	2 years	Dec. 17, 1885[1]	Removed by Gov. John S. Marmaduke

Name	Governor	Date appointed	Term	Date ended	Disposition
Gaiennie, Frank	John S. Marmaduke	Jan. 14, 1885	4 years	Feb. 5, 1889	Term expired
Gooding, Oliver P.	John S. Marmaduke	Jan. 14, 1885	4 years	Feb. 5, 1889	Term expired
Lee, William H.	John S. Marmaduke	Dec. 17, 1885[1]	To Jan. 1, 1887	Jun. 26, 1886[1]	Resigned
Wilkerson, Edward	John S. Marmaduke	Jul. 6, 1886[1]	To Jan. 1, 1887	Jan. 14, 1887	Term expired; reappointed for 4-year term
Blair, James L.	John S. Marmaduke	Jan. 14, 1887	4 years	Feb. 15, 1889[1]	Removed by Gov. David R. Francis
Wilkerson, Edward	John S. Marmaduke	Jan. 14, 1887	4 years	Feb. 15, 1889[1]	Removed by Gov. David R. Francis
Overall, John H.	David R. Francis	Feb. 11, 1889	4 years	Jun. 15, 1893	Term expired
Turner, Charles H.	David R. Francis	Feb. 11, 1889	4 years	Jun. 15, 1893	Term expired
Small, George H.	David R. Francis	Feb. 15, 1889[2]	2 years	Mar. 24, 1891	Term expired; reappointed for 4-year term

Name	Appointing Governor	Date Appointed or Confirmed	Term of Appointment	Date Left Office	Reason
Walsh, Julius S.	David R. Francis	Feb. 15, 1889[2]	2 years	Mar. 15, 1889[1]	Resigned
Hammett, Benjamin F.	David R. Francis	Apr. 2, 1889	To Jan. 1, 1891	Mar. 17, 1891[2]	Term expired
Caruth, David W.	David R. Francis	Mar. 17, 1891[2]	4 years	Jun. 25, 1895	Term expired
Small, George H.	David R. Francis	Mar. 17, 1891[2]	4 years	Mar. 18, 1895[1]	Resigned
Fruin, Jeremiah	William J. Stone	Jun. 17, 1893[3]	To Jan. 1, 1897	Jan. 9, 1896[3]	Resigned
Lee, John A.	William J. Stone	Jun. 17, 1893[3]	To Jan. 1, 1897	Feb. 11, 1897	Term expired
Bannerman, James	William J. Stone	June 24, 1895[1]	To Jan. 1, 1899	Nov. 4, 1897[1]	Resigned
Forster, Otto E.	William J. Stone	June 24, 1895[1]	To Jan. 1, 1899	Feb. 19, 1901[f]	Term expired

Name	Governor	Date appointed	Term	Date	Disposition
Kelly, Patrick J.	William J. Stone	Apr. 20, 1896[1]	To Jan. 1, 1897	Feb. 11, 1897	Term expired
Lewis, James M.	Lon V. Stephens	Jan. 26, 1897[2]	To Jan. 1, 1901	Aug. 22, 1898[1]	Resigned
Stuever, Anton	Lon V. Stephens	Jan. 26, 1897[2]	To Jan. 1, 1901	Feb. 19, 1901	Term expired
Kingland, Lawrence D.	Lon V. Stephens	Nov. 5, 1897[1]	To Jan. 1, 1899	Aug. 16, 1899	Resigned
Hawes, Harry B.	Lon V. Stephens	Aug. 22, 1898[1]	To Jan. 1, 1901	Feb. 19, 1901	Reappointed by Gov. Dockery to 4-year term
Atmore, William E.	Lon V. Stephens	Aug. 20, 1899[2]	To Aug. 21, 1903	Jan. 5, 1901	Died in office
Hawes, Harry B.	Alexander Dockery	Feb. 19, 1901[2]	To Jan. 1, 1905	Dec. 16, 1903[1]	Resigned
Blong, Andrew F.	Alexander Dockery	Feb. 19, 1901[2]	To Jan. 1, 1905	Nov. 22, 1905[1]	Removed by Gov. Joseph W. Folk[g]
Woerner, William F.	Alexander Dockery	Feb. 19, 1901[2]	To Jan. 1, 1905	Apr. 14, 1901[1]	Resigned

Name	Appointing Governor	Date Appointed or Confirmed	Term of Appointment	Date Left Office	Reason			
Ballard, Theodore R.	Alexander Dockery	Feb. 19, 1901[2]	To Jan. 1, 1905	Feb. 3, 1905	Term expired			
Frye, William G.	Alexander Dockery	Apr. 15, 1901[1]	To Jan. 1, 1905	Feb. 3, 1905	Term expired			
Hanlon, Richard	Alexander Dockery	Dec. 16, 1903[1]	To Jan. 1, 1905	Dec. 7, 1905[1]	Resigned[h]			
Stewart, Alphonso C.	Joseph W. Folk	Jan. 20, 1905[2]	To Jan. 1, 1909					
Fristoe, John W.	Joseph W. Folk	Jan. 20, 1905[2]	To Jan. 1, 1909					
Jones, George P.	Joseph W. Folk	Nov. 22, 1905[1]	To Jan. 1, 1907					
Maroney, Andrew C.	Joseph W. Folk	Dec. 7, 1905[1]	To Jan. 1, 1907	Jun. 2, 1906[1]	Resigned			
Bland, Theodoric R.	Joseph W. Folk	Jun. 28, 1906[1]	To Jan. 1, 1907					

Sources:

[1] Date validated by documents in the Missouri State Archives as date of confirmation by Senate.

[2] Date validated through newspaper reports as either the date of appointment or of confirmation.

[3] Appointment or resignation date listed in the minutes of the Board of Police Commissioners. (All other dates are based on attendance records in the minutes and usually indicate the date of the first or last meeting attended.)

Notes:

[a] Basil Wilson Duke purportedly resigned on May 25, 1861, but was officially removed on August 30.

[b] The Act of January 25, 1865, amended the original police bill regarding police board appointments, and the sitting board was declared vacant.

[c] No documentation was found indicating the length of William Patrick's appointment. It was probably until January 1, 1865.

[d] David Armstrong was appointed by Governor John Phelps to complete the unexpired term of Senator L. V. Bogy, who died in office.

[e] After David Armstrong completed his term as U.S. senator, Silas Bent either resigned or was removed for Armstrong's reappointment to the board.

[f] There was no documentation to indicate that Dr. Otto Forster was reappointed. He did, however, remain two years past his initial term.

[g] Andrew Blong had apparently been appointed to an additional two-year term beginning in January 1905.

[h] "Lame duck" governor Alexander Dockery reappointed Richard Hanlon to a term of unknown length during a December 1904 legislative recess.

Chiefs of Police, 1861–1906

Name	Date Appointed	Resigned or Removed
McDonough, James	April 10, 1861	October 18, 1861
Couzins, John E. D.	October 18, 1861	March 20, 1865
Laibold, Bernard	March 20, 1865	October 22, 1866
Fenn, William P.	October 22, 1866	June 30, 1868
Lee, William	July 1, 1868	September 26, 1870
McDonough, James	September 30, 1870	March 10, 1874
Harrigan, Laurence	June 1, 1874	November 18, 1875
McDonough, James	December 1, 1875	June 8, 1881
Kennett, Ferdinand B.	June 8, 1881	August 1, 1882
Campbell, John W.	August 1, 1882	October 9, 1883
Taaffe, Bernard P.	October 9, 1883	November 6, 1883
Campbell, John W.	November 6, 1883	December 29, 1883
Harrigan, Laurence	January 8, 1884	May 4, 1886
Huebler, Anton	May 4, 1886	May 20, 1890
Harrigan, Laurence	May 20, 1890	May 21, 1898
Campbell, John W.	May 21, 1898	February 28, 1901
Kiely, Mathew	March 1, 1901	September 19, 1906
Creecy, Edmond P.	September 19, 1906	April 9, 1910

Source: Annual Reports of the Board of Police Commissioners, Minutes of the Board, and St. Louis newspapers.

Notes

Notes from Introduction

1. Samuel Walker, *The Police in America: An Introduction*, 2nd ed. (New York: McGraw-Hill, 1992).

2. Ibid., 5.

3. Roger Lane, "Urban Police and Crime in Nineteenth-Century America," in *Modern Policing*, eds. Michael Tonry and Norval Morris (Chicago: The University of Chicago Press, 1992), 5.

4. James F. Richardson, *Urban Police in the United States* (Port Washington, NY: Kennikat Press, 1974), 21–22.

5. Eric H. Monkkonen, "History of Urban Police," in *Modern Policing*, eds. Tonry and Morris, 553.

6. David R. Johnson, *American Law Enforcement: A History* (St. Louis: Forum Press, 1981), 25.

7. Ibid., 28.

8. Eric H. Monkkonen, *Police in Urban America, 1860–1920* (Cambridge, Eng.: Cambridge University Press, 1981), 30.

9. Ibid., 53.

10. Ibid.

11. Ibid., 55.

12. Ibid., 57.

13. George L. Kelling and Mark H. Moore, "The Evolving Strategy of Policing," in *Perspectives on Policing*, no. 4 (Washington, DC: National Institute of Justice, 1988).

14. Raymond B. Fosdick, *American Police Systems* (New York: The Century Company, 1920).

15. Ibid.

16. Ibid., 2–4.

Notes from Chapter 1

1. James Neal Primm, *Lion of the Valley: St. Louis, Missouri*, 2nd ed. (Boulder, CO: Pruett, 1990), 88. Bates was probably referring to a "dirk," which *Webster's New Collegiate Dictionary* (8th ed.) defines as "a long straight-bladed dagger."

2. Board of Police Commissioners, *History of the Metropolitan Police Department of St. Louis* (St. Louis: Author, 1910), 107–108.

3. Primm, *Lion of the Valley*, 123.

4. Board of Police Commissioners, *History*, 109–110.

5. Maximilian Ivan Reichard, *The Origins of Urban Police: Freedom and Order in Antebellum St. Louis* (Ann Arbor, MI: Xerox University Microfilms, 1975), 178–179.

6. Ibid., 208.

7. The bicameral form lasted until 1859, when the city reverted to a board of aldermen. The bicameral form reappeared in 1876 and lasted until 1914, when it again returned to a board of aldermen. The singular house remains to this day.

8. Ordinances of the City of St. Louis, 1839–1840 (St. Louis: publisher unknown), 78–80f.

9. Ibid., Sec. 1.

10. Reichard, *Origins of Urban Police*, 230.

11. Ordinances of the City of St. Louis, 1839–1840, Sec. 7.

12. Charles van Ravenswaay, "The Pioneer Photographers of St. Louis," *Bulletin of the Missouri Historical Society* 10, no. 1 (October 1953): 48–49.

13. *St. Louis Globe-Democrat*, August 30, 1891, 8.

14. The St. Louis rogues' gallery began with daguerreotypes, and then moved to tintypes (ferrotypes), ambrotypes, and photographs.

15. This was one year after the formation of the New York City Police Department. Whether the part of the St. Louis reorganization concerning the police department was a natural progression or was generally modeled after the New York City department, or both, is unknown.

16. Revised Ordinances of St. Louis, 1843, Sec. 15.

17. *Missouri Republican*, March 25, 1849, 2.

18. Ibid.

19. This account of the fire is from Charles van Ravenswaay, *Saint Louis: An Informal History of the City and its People, 1764–1865* (St. Louis: Missouri Historical Society Press, 1991), 383–390.

20. According to Primm, *Lion of the Valley*, 171, in 1840 "the 'Native American' party was formed in St. Louis as in other cities. Locally it was first just a pressure group within the Whig Party, anti-Irish, anti-German, anti-Catholic—appalled by the prospect of being dominated by the 'dirty' Irish and 'Dutch.'"

21. Van Ravenswaay, *Saint Louis*, 391.

22. William B. and Marcella C. Magnan, *The Streets of St. Louis: A History of St. Louis Street Names* (St. Louis: Virginia Publishing, 1996), 46. Primm, *Lion of the Valley*, 180, further describes the block as a line of two-story rooming

houses. Battle Row is now some lofts and a parking lot on the south side, and the Union Market, on the north side of Lucas Street between Broadway and Sixth streets.

23. Van Ravenswaay, *Saint Louis*, 391.

24. Primm, *Lion of the Valley*, 174.

25. Ibid.

26. The Revised Ordinances of the City of St. Louis, Ord. 2410, "An Ordinance Establishing and Regulating the Police Department," approved April 1, 1850 (St. Louis: Chambers & Knapp, City Printers), 326–335.

27. Ibid., Sec. 25.

28. Board of Police Commissioners, *History*, 112.

29. City of St. Louis, Mayor's Message, with Accompanying Documents, Submitted to the City Council of the City of St. Louis, at the Opening of the First Stated Session (St. Louis: *Missouri Democrat* office, May 8, 1854), 4–5.

30. *The Republic*, January 31, 1897, 35.

31. Except where otherwise noted, this account of the nativist riot is from van Ravenswaay, *Saint Louis*, 433.

32. Primm, *Lion of the Valley*, 179.

33. Ibid.

34. Ibid., 197.

35. Ordinance Regulating the Police Department of the City of St. Louis and Rules and Regulations for its General Government (St. Louis: The *Republican* office, 1856), 1–32. The original ordinance (#3599) had the police department divided into three "divisions" of eight hours each, beginning with the first division from 8:00 p.m. until 4:00 a.m. Because of the cost the ordinance was revised to reflect two shifts. It also cut the authorized number of police by thirty.

36. Ibid., Sec. 2.

37. Walter B. Stevens (*St. Louis, The Fourth City, Volume 1* [St. Louis: The S. J. Clarke Publishing Co., 1911], 97) says that Mayor George Maguire (1842–1843) "appointed a young college graduate, John F. Long, Chief of Police," and that Mayor John M. Wimer (1843–1844) "chose a young carpenter, James McDonough [as chief]." Since the term "chief of police" did not appear in city ordinances until 1856, it is more likely that Long and McDonough were Captains of the Guard.

38. A news item in the *Missouri Republican* of May 18, 1861, refers to a writ of replevin from the United States District Court being served by "Marshal Rawlings."

39. Ibid., Sec. 21.

40. Ibid., Sec. 38.

41. Ibid., December 15, 1859, 2.

42. Late in the previous session (1858–1859), the Missouri General Assembly had approved a two-year term for the mayor of St. Louis. This also benefited police officers who, all else being equal, could hold their jobs longer than one year.

43. *Daily Missouri Democrat*, December 12, 1859, 2.

44. State of Missouri, Journal of the House of Representatives of the State of Missouri at the Adjourned Session of the Twentieth General Assembly (Jefferson City, MO: W. G. Cheeney Public Printer, 1860).

45. Rolla Wells, *Episodes of My Life* (St. Louis: W. J. McCarthy, 1933).

Notes from Chapter 2

1. Primm, *Lion of the Valley*, 1990, 246.

2. Claiborne F. Jackson, "Inaugural Address, January 2, 1861," in Charles D. Drake, *Autobiography: 1811–1867* (Columbia, MO: Western Historical Manuscript Collection), 663b.

3. Robert J. Rombauer, *The Union Cause in St. Louis in 1861* (St. Louis: St. Louis Municipal Centennial Year, 1909), 135.

4. Drake, *Autobiography*, 667.

5. Galusha Anderson, *The Story of a Border City During the Civil War* (Boston: Little, Brown, 1908), 58.

6. Rombauer, *The Union Cause*.

7. Journal of the Senate of Missouri at the First Session of the Twenty-First General Assembly (Jefferson City, MO: W. G. Cheeney, Public Printer, 1861).

8. Journal of the House of Representatives of the State of Missouri at the First Session of the Twenty-First General Assembly (Jefferson City, MO: W. G. Cheeney, Public Printer, 1861).

9. State of Missouri, Laws of the State of Missouri passed at the Regular Session of the Twenty-First General Assembly (Jefferson City, MO: W. G. Cheeney Public Printer, 1861).

10. Ibid., Sec. 16.

11. *Missouri Republican*, March 10, 1861, 3.

12. Ibid., February 22 and February 27, 1861.

13. *Missouri Democrat*, March 26, 1861.

14. State of Missouri, Journal of the Senate of Missouri at the Called Session of the Twenty-First General Assembly (Jefferson City, MO: J. Ament, Public Printer, 1861).

15. Primm, *Lion of the Valley*, 247. Also, Basil Duke listed (in *Reminiscences of General Basil W. Duke, C.S.A.* [Garden City, NY: Doubleday, Page, 1911], 43–44) the names of the police commissioners appointed by Governor Jackson in 1861 and said, "All were Southern in sentiment."

16. Duke, *Reminiscences*, 38.

17. See Duke, *Reminiscences*; Primm, *Lion of the Valley*; and Anderson, *Border City*.

18. *Missouri Democrat*, April 6, 1861, 2.

19. Primm, *Lion of the Valley*, 247.

20. According to the April 15 minutes of the Board of Police Commissioners, (St. Louis: Missouri History Museum), "B. Wilson Duke appeared and took his seat as a member of the Board. Commissioned by the Governor and duly qualified according to law." The *Missouri Democrat* (April 11, 1861) reported that Duke was one month short of the three-year city residency requirement and the appointment would have to "stand for a month or so. . . ." Duke later noted that, in early April, he was on the trip to meet with Jefferson Davis and secure the artillery needed for the assault of the arsenal.

21. Ibid., April 10, 1861.

22. Reichard, *The Origins of Urban Police*, 258–260.

23. Minutes of the Board, April 15, 1861.

24. *Missouri Republican*, May 7, 1861, 2.

25. Ibid.

26. Henry Boernstein, *Memoirs of a Nobody,* trans. and ed. Steven Rowan (St. Louis: Missouri Historical Society Press, 1997), 267.

27. Ibid., 268.

28. Ibid.

29. Ibid., 269.

30. Ibid., 269–270.

31. Minutes of the Board, April 19, 1861.

32. Letter to General Harney, reproduced in Minutes of the Board, April 21, 1861.

33. Reply of General Harney, reproduced in Minutes of the Board, April 22, 1861.

34. Board "Order" and Chief's "Notice" reproduced in Minutes of the Board, April 24, 1861.

35. Ibid.

36. Minutes of the Board, April 27, 1861.

37. *Missouri Republican*, May 4, 1861.

38. Ibid.

39. Ibid., May 1, 1861.

40. Lindell Grove was a wooded area between Grand Avenue, Garrison Street, Olive Street, and Laclede Avenue.

41. Duke, *Reminiscences*, 43–51. The boat was the *J. C. Swon.*

42. General John C. Frémont, who would become the commander of the Department of the West in July, later wrote that the police board paid the freight charges to have the artillery shipped from New Orleans and detailed policemen to guard the movement of the artillery from the levee to Camp Jackson. Other sources claim it was the Brownlee Guard. (See Christopher Phillips,

Damned Yankee: The Life of General Nathaniel Lyon, Columbia: University of Missouri Press, 1990, 181).

43. Ibid., 50–51.

44. In the early morning hours of April 26, the arsenal had been emptied of all guns except those that were immediately needed to arm the volunteers that Captain Lyon was gathering. Ironically, the German American volunteers who guarded the shipment to Alton, Illinois, were commanded by Henry Boernstein, the theater owner and newspaper publisher.

45. If informants hadn't told Lyon, he could have read about the shipment in the *Missouri Democrat* on Friday morning, May 10. A notation on page 3 of that edition states, "It is said the J. C. Swon brought in yesterday morning a large quantity of arms in boxes and barrels, which were marked 'marble,' 'sugar,' &c."

46. J. Thomas Scharf, *History of St. Louis City and County* (Philadelphia: Louis H. Everts & Co., 1883), 500.

47. Ibid., 501.

48. Anderson, *Border City*, 102.

49. Marshall D. Hier, "Basil Wilson Duke, Legend Made Vivid," *The St. Louis Bar Journal* (Fall 1996): 45–46.

50. *Minutes of the Board,* May 21, 1861.

51. Ibid. Also, *Missouri Republican*, June 16, 1885.

52. *Missouri Democrat*, June 20, 1861, 3.

53. Ibid., June 18, 1861, 2.

54. Ibid., June 20, 1861, 3.

55. Ibid., June 29, 1861, 3.

56. *Missouri Republican*, June 18–July 7, 1861.

57. Ibid., July 7, 1879.

58. *Missouri Republican*, July 7, 1861, 3.

59. Over time, the *Missouri Republican* spelled the last name of the defendant several different ways: Zuckwag, Suchwartz, Zuckschwerdt, Tuckschwerdt, Zuchswart, and Zuckswart. The last spelling, Zuckswart, was chosen for this account because it was the spelling most often used by the *Republican* and the only one used by the *Missouri Democrat*.

60. *Missouri Democrat*, July 30, 1861.

61. *Missouri Republican* and *Missouri Democrat*, July 6–July 31, 1861.

62. Primm, *Lion of the Valley*, 252.

63. Van Ravenswaay, *Saint Louis*, 501.

64. *Missouri Republican*, August 15, 1861, 2.

65. Ibid.

66. Primm, *Lion of the Valley*, 256. .

67. Letter from Maj. General J. C. Frémont to Gov. Hamilton Gamble, dated August 18, 1861 (St. Louis, Missouri History Museum).

68. *Missouri Democrat*, August 31, 1861, 4.

69. *Minutes of the Board*, September 24, 1861.

70. *Minutes of the Board*, October 18, 1861.

71. Reichard, *Origins of Urban Police*, 257–258.

72. Couzins was also the captain of the night guard during John How's first term as mayor.

73. Letter from James O. Broadhead to Hon. Thomas W. Palmer, U.S. Senate, dated St. Louis, February 13, 1888, reproduced in Memorial, J. E. D. Couzins Papers (St. Louis, Missouri History Museum), 3.

74. This information was found in the city residential and business directories from 1860.

75. Ibid.

76. Police Commissioners' Report dated April 29, 1862, in City of St. Louis, Mayor's Message with Accompanying Documents, First Stated Session, May 12, 1862 (St. Louis: George Knapp & Co., Printers and Binders, 1862), 20.

77. *Webster's New Collegiate Dictionary* (8th ed.) defines a "slungshot" as "a striking weapon consisting of a small mass of metal or stone fixed on a flexible handle or strap."

78. *Missouri Republican* of December 11, 13, 28, 1861, and *The Republican*, July 7, 1879.

79. No copies of the 1861 manual were found by the author.

80. Minutes of the Board, November 28, 1862.

81. Gerald L. Phelan, "St. Louis' Rogue Gallery—1850s thru 1860s" (unpublished manuscript, Phelan Collection, Missouri History Museum, 1997).

82. *St. Louis Globe-Democrat*, August 30, 1891, 8.

83. Van Ravenswaay, *Saint Louis*, 49.

84. *Laws of the State of Missouri Passed at the Twenty-Second General Assembly*, Jefferson City, MO: W. A. Curry, Public Printer, 1864.

85. Ibid.

86. *State, ex rel. the Police Commissioners of the City of St. Louis, Relators, v. the County Court of St. Louis County, Respondent*, 546 Mo.S.C. Reports XXXIV (1864).

Notes from Chapter 3

1. Primm, *Lion of the Valley*, 275–280.

2. Van Ravenswaay (*Saint Louis*, 528) says that the two factions of the Republican party were divided over the manner in which emancipation of the slaves was executed. Conservatives favored an orderly program with slaveholders receiving compensation; radicals wanted immediate emancipation.

3. Couzins would later become the U.S. Marshal for the Eastern District of Missouri.

4. Minutes of the Board, March 16, 1865.

5. Ibid., March 16 and 25, 1865.

6. Ibid., March 20, 1865.

7. Van Ravenswaay, *Saint Louis*, 536.

8. *Missouri Democrat*, April 22, 1865, 4.

9. "Report of the Police Commissioners," Mayor's Message with Accompanying Documents, May 1865, 70.

10. According to Primm, *Lion of the Valley*, Lafayette Park is the only remaining portion of the original common fields of the village of St. Louis, 18.

11. *Missouri Democrat*, May 16, 1865, 3.

12. Ibid.

13. Minutes of the Board, June 5, 1865.

14. Ibid., April 20, 1865.

15. Ibid., June 15, 1865, and Report of Police Commissioners and Chief (annual report), May 6, 1867.

16. Minutes of the Board, August 9, 1865.

17. "Hydrophobia" was the term used for what is now known as rabies.

18. *Missouri Democrat*, July 10, 1865, 4.

19. City Ordinance No. 5,604, reprinted in the *Missouri Democrat*, July 20, 1865. (The newspaper erroneously identified the ordinance as 6,604.)

20. Mayor's Proclamation, July 20, 1865, reprinted in the *Missouri Democrat* on that date.

21. *Missouri Democrat*, July 24, 1865, 4.

22. Ibid.

23. *Missouri Democrat*, July 27, 1865, 4.

24. Letter from Mayor Thomas to Common Council dated July 28, 1865, reprinted in *Missouri Democrat*, July 29.

25. Minutes of the Board, July 24, 1865.

26. The board regularly met on Monday and Thursday. Prior to this, mail addressed to the board was opened at the next meeting. After this incident the board gave the secretary of the board the authority to open mail addressed to the board upon its arrival at the police office.

27. *Missouri Democrat*, September 7, 1865, 4.

28. Ibid.

29. Ibid.

30. Ibid.

31. *Missouri Republican*, September 12, 1865, 3.

32. Minutes of the Board, November 1, 1865.

33. Ibid.

34. Minutes of the Board, November 16, 1865.

35. *Missouri Republican*, February 14, 1868, 1.

36. Ibid.

37. Minutes of the Board, December 11, 1865.

38. Report of the Joint Committee of the General Assembly Appointed to Investigate the Police Department of the City of St. Louis (St. Louis: Missouri Democrat Book and Job Printing House, 1868), xiii.

39. Minutes of the Board, November 13, 1865.

40. *Missouri Democrat*, July 16, 1868, 4.

41. Ibid., November 23, 1865.

42. Minutes of the Board, February 23, 1866.

43. Ibid.

44. Minutes of the Board, March 13, 1866.

45. No one, inside or outside of the police department, questioned this arrangement. It is likely that several express company agents, who came to St. Louis to assist in the investigation, stayed at the Lindell Hotel. It is not known whether they occupied that room or whether it was used exclusively for interrogation.

46. Minutes of the Board, March 19, 1866.

47. Ibid., March 26, 1866.

48. The board sometimes went into "executive session" after the regular board meeting. There is no evidence of any minutes of executive sessions. While unusual, the board may have resolved the matter in executive session.

49. *Missouri Democrat*, March 9, 1866, 4.

50. Minutes of the Board, March 28, 1866.

51. Ibid., April 2, 1866.

52. Ibid., June 4, 1866.

53. Two derivations of the expression "Black Maria" have been discovered. According to Carl Sifakis (*The Encyclopedia of American Crime* [New York: Facts on File, 1982], 80) the term was coined in Boston in the 1840s. The name referred to a black woman, Maria Lee, who ran a lodging house for sailors. She was called Black Maria, and her establishment was among the most unruly in the city. Says Sifakis, "It was assumed that a police van loaded with boisterous offenders was coming from Black Maria's." The cable television History Channel reported on July 9, 1999 (*Modern Marvels*; "The Police Car"), that the Black Maria name originated in Detroit in 1871. The police wagon was named after a woman of ill fame who was a frequent rider in the wagon and always wore black. (The latter is obviously incorrect, as the St. Louis Board of Police Commissioners used that expression in the minutes of the board meeting of April 9, 1866.)

54. Minutes of the Board, April 12, 1866.

55. W. A. Swanberg, *Pulitzer* (New York: Charles Scribner's Sons, 1967), 7–8.

56. Laibold was elected marshal at the November 6, 1866, election, winning by a wide margin.

57. John Kenneth Maniha, *The Mobility of Elites in a Bureaucratizing Organization: The St. Louis Police Department, 1861–1961* (Ann Arbor, MI: Xerox University Microfilms, 1984), 91.

58. Minutes of the Board, October 22, 1866.

59. According to the minutes of the board of January 17, 1867, N. H. Clark stated that, because of his business interests, he would decline reappointment to the board. Clark and Laibold had been appointed for two years in accordance with the stagger system of appointments.

60. Minutes of the Board, February 18, 1867.

61. *An Act Amendatory of and Supplementary to an Act Entitled 'An Act Creating a Board of Police Commissioners, and Authorizing the Appointment of a Police Force for the City of St. Louis,' Approved March 27, 1861*, Section 3, Approved March 13, 1867, 178.

62. Ibid.

63. Report of Board of Police Commissioners, *Mayor's Message with Accompanying Documents* (St. Louis: Missouri Democrat Book and Job Printing House, May, 1868, 39.

64. *An Act Amendatory*, 179.

65. Ibid.

66. Minutes of the Board, April 8, 1867.

67. The western city limits were actually 660 feet west of Grand Avenue. By extending the city limits slightly west of Grand, those living on the western side of the street were also included in the city.

68. Minutes of the Board, October 21, 1867.

69. Ibid.

70. Report of Board of Police Commissioners, 39.

71. Minutes of the Board, November 11, 1867.

72. Ibid., November 4, 1867.

73. As reported in the *Missouri Republican*, February 14, 1868, 1.

74. Ibid.

75. Minutes of the Board, January 22, 1868.

76. City Ordinance 5421, Section 1, Article 9, approved September 3, 1864.

77. *Missouri Democrat*, February 13, 1868, 4.

78. Report of the Joint Committee of the General Assembly, iii.

79. Senator Evans was from Phelps County, in the south-central part of the state, and represented Missouri's twenty-second senatorial district. Representative

Stafford was from Pettis County, in the west-central part of the state about fifty miles southwest of Jefferson City. Representative Hickman was from Worth County, in the northwest part of the state adjacent to the border with Iowa.

80. The Joint Committee's report precedes the "Proceedings of the Investigating Committee" and is found on pages iii–xiii.

81. Report of the Joint Committee of the General Assembly, vi.

82. Ibid., vii.

83. Ibid., viii.

84. Ibid.

85. Ibid.

86. Ibid., xii.

87. Ibid., xiii. Actually, the minutes of the board for 1865 list Mayor Thomas as present at thirty-two meetings. He attended eleven meetings in 1866, counting one special meeting in his office and three occasions on which he appeared late.

88. Ibid.

89. *Missouri Republican*, September 3, 1868, 2.

90. Ibid.

91. Report of the Chief of Police, in *Report of Board of Police Commissioners, Mayor's Message with Accompanying Documents*, 46.

92. Ibid.

93. While no accounts of the incident indicate that Officers Skinner and Miller were in uniform, the circumstances, waiting for a train to arrive, would suggest that the officers were performing a crime prevention/peace-keeping role, one that they would likely perform in uniform. In addition, there were no accounts of the incident stating that the officers were conducting an undercover operation or were detectives.

94. *Missouri Democrat*, June 17, 1868, 4.

95. Board of Police Commissioners, *Reasons for the Dismissal of William Fenn, Late Chief of Police of the City of St. Louis* (St. Louis: Missouri Democrat Print, 1869).

96. Minutes of the Board, June 30, 1868.

97. William P. Fenn, *Reply of Colonel William Fenn Ex-Chief of Police in Answer to a Pamphlet Entitled "Reasons for the Dismissal of William Fenn, Late Chief of Police of the City of St. Louis" As Published by the Board of Police Commissioners* (St. Louis: R. P. Studley & Co., Printers, 1869).

98. Ibid., 4.

99. Ibid., 20.

100. Ibid., 22.

101. Ibid., 23.

102. *Missouri Democrat*, February 19, 1869, 1.

103. *Missouri Democrat*, July 12, 1868, 4.

104. *Missouri Republican*, November 2, 1868, 4.

105. Ibid.

106. Ibid.

107. *Missouri Democrat*, November 5, 1868, 4.

108. *Missouri Democrat*, January 20, 1869, 4.

109. Ibid.

110. In the minutes of this meeting the board passed a resolution testifying to Codding's "efficiency as a member of the Board; and in view of the esteem that the Board have for him. . . " requested Codding "to retain and wear his badge of office, and to have free access to and through the Police Department." This is the first time that it is noted that a former board member would retain his commissioner's badge (and wear it).

111. *Missouri Democrat*, January 24, 1869, 4.

112. Ibid., April 13, 1869, 4.

113. Mayor Thomas's successor would also not be in office when the building was completed. Construction on the new building began in February 1869 and was completed in the autumn of 1871. Nathan Cole was elected mayor in April 1869, serving one two-year term.

114. *Missouri Democrat*, February 3, 1869, 1.

115. Scharf, *History of St. Louis*, 734.

116. No copy of the 1861 rules and regulations has been located. The board minutes of January 3, 1862, note the approval of payment to the "Republic Office" for printing five hundred copies.

117. Board of Police Commissioners, *Manual of the Board of Police Commissioners of the City of St. Louis, State of Missouri* (St. Louis: Missouri Democrat Print, 1869), 71–72.

118. Ibid.

119. Minutes of the Board, August 31, 1869.

120. Ninth Annual Report of the Board of Police Commissioners, in *Mayor's Message, with Accompanying Documents, May, 1870* (St. Louis: George Knapp & Co., Printers and Binders, 1870), 233.

121. Minutes of the Board, September 29, 1869.

122. Ibid., October 19, 1869.

Notes from Chapter 4

1. Primm, *Lion of the Valley*, 298.

2. An act approved by the state legislature on March 15, 1866, empowered the St. Louis City Council to increase the size of the police force at any time to any number recommended by the Board of Police Commissioners. The same

act gave the City Council the power to increase or diminish the pay of officers upon the recommendation of the board, and provided that the city could raise taxes to pay for increases in manpower or salaries.

3. Tenth Annual Report of the Board of Police Commissioners, in *The Mayor's Inaugural Address & Message to the City Council of the City of St. Louis* (St. Louis: St. Louis Times Company, City Printers, May, 1871), 328fn.

4. The Wedge House was located on the appropriately shaped property where Laclede Avenue split from what was then Manchester Road. In 1870, Market Street terminated at Jefferson Boulevard and continued west as Manchester Road. The wedge location no longer exists; Laclede Avenue now begins at Ewing.

5. Ferdinand Meyer ran for county sheriff in the November election as a Liberal Republican, the same party as gubernatorial candidate B. Gratz Brown. Meyer lost by 1,395 votes out of just more than 22,000 votes cast.

6. *Missouri Republican*, September 26, 1870, 2. The legislature had, during Governor McClurg's term, changed gubernatorial elections from quadrennial to biennial. Thus, McClurg had to run for reelection in November 1870.

7. St. Louis City Plan Commission, *History: Physical Growth of the City of St. Louis* (St. Louis: Author, 1969), 18.

8. Minutes of the Board of Police Commissioners (September 26, 1870, 9:00 a.m. meeting).

9. *Missouri Democrat*, September 27, 1870, 4.

10. Ibid.

11. In an editorial, the *Missouri Democrat* stated that McDonough was not the board's first choice for chief of police. The three newly appointed members, whom the *Democrat* referred to as "McClurgites," first wanted a man named McMurtry, a salesman in a clothing store, to be the new chief. Mayor Cole, the editorial said, "entered so strong a protest that the faction did not dare to go before the public in the face of it, and reconsidered the appointment." October 2, 1870, 2.

12. *Missouri Republican*, September 25, 1870, 2.

13. Primm, *Lion of the Valley*, 202.

14. *Missouri Democrat*, November 1, 1870, 4.

15. Ibid., October 26, 1870, 4.

16. Ibid.

17. Ibid.

18. In the second edition of their book *Streets of St. Louis* (St. Louis: Virginia Publishing, 1996, 35), William B. and Marcella C. Magnan note that Green Street was originally named after a tree, as were all east-west downtown streets; it was called Prune Street. Prune was later changed to Christy, and then to Green. Today, it is named Lucas.

19. Tenth Annual Report of the Board, 317.

20. Ibid.

21. Ibid., 318–319.

22. Duane R. Sneddeker, "Regulating Vice: Prostitution and the St. Louis Social Evil Ordinance, 1870–1874," *Gateway Heritage* 2, no. 2 (1990), 22.

23. Ibid.

24. *Report of the Joint Committee of the General Assembly Appointed to Investigate the Police Department of the City of St. Louis* (St. Louis: Missouri Democrat and Job Printing House, 1868), 29.

25. Ibid., 315.

26. *Missouri Democrat,* July 21, 1870, 4.

27. Sneddeker, "Regulating Vice," 23.

28. Ibid.

29. *Missouri Democrat,* July 21, 1870, 4.

30. Ibid., July 22, 1870, 4.

31. Ibid., July 23, 1870, 4. The first district extended from the southern city limits to Park Avenue; the second from Park Avenue to Clark; the third from Clark to Olive Street; the fourth from Olive Street to Morgan Street (now Delmar); the fifth from Morgan to Cass Avenue; and the sixth from Cass to the northern city limits.

32. Ibid., July 21, 1870, 4.

33. Sneddeker, "Regulating Vice," 24.

34. *The Revised Ordinances of the City of St. Louis* (St. Louis: George Knapp & Co., 1871), 439.

35. Annual Report of the Board of Police Commissioners of the City of St. Louis, in *The Mayor's Inaugural Address & Message with Accompanying Documents* (St. Louis: St. Louis Times Company, 1871), 311–328.

36. Hunicke was referred to in the board minutes of April 6, 1871, as "the purchasing committee."

37. Harrigan had resigned from the force the previous September in protest of the removal of three of the board members by then-governor McClurg. He had also resigned in the spring of 1867, under then-chief Fenn, but was reinstated, as a sergeant, in November of that same year.

38. The 1861 act establishing the metropolitan police department specifically permitted the board to drop officers from the rolls for inefficiency.

39. Minutes of the Board, June 27, 1871.

40. Ibid., June 30, 1871.

41. Ibid.

42. Elm Street no longer exists. It ran from the riverfront to Seventh Street, between Clark and Walnut Streets. In *Streets of St. Louis*, the Magnans note (34–35) that, between 1764 and 1826, French street names had been used. In the latter year an ordinance was passed adopting the Philadelphia system of naming

streets. At that time, the western city limit was Seventh Street. The northern boundary was where Biddle Street is today, and the southern boundary was approximately where the Poplar Street Bridge now stands. North-south streets were, beginning at the river and going west, given numbers. Twelve streets north of Market Street and twelve streets south of Market were given the names of trees. Fewer than a dozen of these "tree streets" still exist.

43. *Official Proceedings of the National Police Convention Held at the City of St. Louis, Missouri on the 20th, 21st and 23d of October, 1871* (St. Louis: R & T. A. Ennis, Stationers and Printers, 1871).

44. Ibid., 19.

45. Minutes of the Board, October 10, 1871.

46. Swanberg, *Pulitzer*, 3–12.

47. Minutes of the Board, February 6, 1872.

48. *Eleventh Annual Report of the Board of Police Commissioners of the City of St. Louis* (St. Louis: St. Louis Times Co., 1872), 93–99.

49. Ibid., 75–84.

50. *St. Louis Democrat*, March 15, 1873, 2.

51. Ibid., January 29, February 27, and March 5, 7, 8, 10, 13, 14, and 24, 1873.

52. These accounts of the railroad strike were excerpted from the March 18–21, 1873, issues of the *St. Louis Democrat*.

53. *Twelfth Annual Report of the Board of Police Commissioners of the City of St. Louis* (St. Louis: St. Louis Times Co., 1873), 41–43.

54. Minutes of the Board, April 22, 1873.

55. Ibid., May 7, 9, 27, 1873.

56. Ibid., July 15, 18, 1873.

57. Ibid., August 29, 1873.

58. Ibid.

59. Ibid., August 29 and 30, and September 1, 1873.

60. Ibid., notation on bottom of page after regular meeting of March 3 and before regular meeting of March 10, 1874. There was no fourth captain; he had previously been dismissed from the force and had not yet been replaced.

61. *St. Louis Democrat*, March 7, 1874, 4.

62. Sneddeker, "Regulating Vice," 40.

63. *Thirteenth Annual Report of the Board of Police Commissioners of the City of St. Louis* (St. Louis: St. Louis Times Printing House, 1874), 45.

64. Sneddeker, "Regulating Vice," 30–41.

65. Ibid., 38–41.

66. John C. Burnham, "The Social Evil Ordinance—A Social Experiment in Nineteenth Century St. Louis," *Bulletin of the Missouri Historical Society* (April 1971): 213–217.

67. Minutes of the Board, September 16, 1874.

68. Turnkeys were normally assigned to guard prisoners in the police department "jail" or "holdover."

69. Minutes of the Board, November 24 and December 22, 1874. The board ordered the closing of the Third District soup house the next month. Turnkey Little was transferred to the Second District, where he probably returned to regular turnkey duties until the opening of a soup house in the Second District.

70. Ibid.

71. Ibid., March 18, 1875.

72. Ibid., April 20, 1875.

73. Ibid., April 3, 1875.

74. Ibid.

75. Primm, *Lion of the Valley*, 315–316.

76. Ibid., 317.

77. *St. Louis Democrat*, April 21, 1875, 4.

78. Ibid.

79. Ibid.

80. Revised Ordinances of the City of St. Louis—1875, Ord. #9579, Section 7, Approved July 1, 1875.

81. Minutes of the Board, July 27, 1875.

82. Ibid.

83. Ibid., August 3, 1875.

84. Ibid., August 10, 1875. The names listed: A. G. Edwards, William E. Burr, Enos Clark, Rodley & Essen, Edw. Whitaker, Leonard Matthews, George W. Gill, John W. Andrews, J. Alkire, W. A. Kingdon, A. G. Mermod, J. S. Warren, Henry J. Mudd, Henry W. Wough, and J. L. Mills.

85. Ibid.

86. *St. Louis Globe-Democrat*, January 5, 1877, 3.

87. *A Brief History of the Kirkwood Police Department*, typescript, n.a., n.d. Obtained from Kirkwood Police Department.

88. June Wilkinson Dahl, *A History of Kirkwood Missouri, 1851–1965* (Kirkwood, MO: The Kirkwood Historical Society, 1965), 60–61.

89. *St. Louis Dispatch*, September 10, 1875, 1.

90. *St. Louis Republican*, September 11–13, 1875.

91. Minutes of the Board, September 14, 1875.

92. Ibid.

93. *St. Louis Globe-Democrat*, November 12, 1875, 4.

94. Ibid., October 31, 1875, 6.

95. Ibid., November 1, 1875, 8.

96. *St. Louis Globe-Democrat*, November 7, 1875, 4.

97. Minutes of the Board, November 6, 1875.

98. Ibid.

99. *St. Louis Globe-Democrat*, November 11, 1875, 3.

100. Ibid., November 12, 1875, 4.

101. Minutes of the Board, November 11, 1875.

102. Ibid., November 18, 1875.

103. Ibid.

104. Ibid., September 28, 1875.

105. Ibid., November 9, 1875.

106. Ibid., October 19, 1875.

107. Ibid., January 4, 1876.

108. Ibid.

109. Ibid.

110. Ibid., March 7, 1876.

111. The minutes of the board for April 4, 1876, list the total number of officers as 417. This number included 1 chief, 6 captains, 43 sergeants, 348 patrolmen, 5 detectives, 11 turnkeys, 2 officers serving as clerks, and 1 officer serving as the department carpenter.

112. *St. Louis Globe-Democrat*, June 28, 1876, 5.

113. Minutes of the Board, September 5, 1876.

114. Ibid., October 10, 1876.

Notes from Chapter 5

1. Primm, *Lion of the Valley*, 315.

2. Ibid., 321.

3. Ibid., 323.

4. Ibid.

5. *Scheme for the Separation and Reorganization of the Governments of the City and County of St. Louis and the Adjustment of Their Relations* (St. Louis Public Library, www.slpl.lib.mo.us/cco/charter/data/scheme.htm, November 4, 1999), 9–10.

6. St. Louis City Plan Commission, *History*, 42–43.

7. *St. Louis Globe-Democrat* (date unknown), in Primm, *Lion of the Valley*, 325.

8. Secretary George Gavin's nineteenth-century handwritten minutes were not always readable. While the applicant's name appears several times in the minutes of the next few weeks, it always appears to be William "Berzery." No such name appears in city directories of the time. A political science graduate student (and former newspaperman), Benjamin Israel, who was researching the hiring of blacks in the early years of the St. Louis Metropolitan Police Depart-

ment, suggested to me that the applicant might have been William H. Berzey. A William H. Berzey appears over the years in the city directories as a clerk, a laborer, a waiter, and, in the late 1880s, a deputy sheriff in St. Louis.

9. The minutes do not indicate who made the motion to hire Berzey but, in a December 24, 1880, interview in the *Globe-Democrat* (p. 7), Mayor Henry Overstolz is quoting as saying that "at one time he had a colored detective appointed."

10. Minutes of the Board, December 26, 1876.

11. *Republican*, December 23, 1876, 4.

12. Minutes of the Board, December 19, 1876. Subsequent board minutes do not mention the removal of the officer from Bridgeton, so it is unknown how long he served there. He was likely removed at the same time that the separation of the city and county forced removal of the officers from Kirkwood, if not sooner.

13. According to the Smithsonian Institution (http://americanhistory.si.edu/csr/harris.pdf, December 4, 2001), "The papyrograph was a stencil duplicating system devised and patented by Eugenio de Zuccato in Britain and the United States beginning in 1874. Writing was done in caustic ink on a lacquered sheet of thin paper. The ink attacked the lacquer, creating a porous stencil. The stencil sheet was then used with a pad saturated with writing ink to produce multiple copies of 'hand written' letters."

14. Minutes of the Board, March 27, 1877.

15. *St. Louis Globe-Democrat*, April 11, 1877, 4.

16. Ibid., July 7, 1880, 5.

17. Michael G. Tsichlis, "Calamity and Glory: Phelim O'Toole, Mike Hester, and the Legacy of Heroism at the Southern Hotel Fire," *Missouri Historical Review* XCVIII, no. 3 (April 2004): 229.

18. Ibid.

19. Ibid., 241–244.

20. *St. Louis Globe-Democrat*, April 11, 1877, 4.

21. Minutes of the Board, April 24, 1877.

22. Ibid., May 15, 1877.

23. Primm, *Lion of the Valley*, 327.

24. Ibid.

25. David T. Burbank, *Reign of the Rabble: The St. Louis General Strike of 1877* (New York: August M. Kelley, 1966), 27.

26. Primm, *Lion of the Valley*, 328.

27. Ibid.

28. Ibid., 329.

29. Ibid., 330.

30. Ibid.

31. Ibid., 130.

32. Ibid., 140.

33. Ibid., 141.

34. Ibid.

35. Primm, *Lion of the Valley*, 330.

36. Burbank, *Reign of the Rabble*, 143.

37. Ibid.

38. Ibid.

39. Board of Police Commissioners, *Manual Containing the Rules for Governance of the Police Department of the City of St. Louis* (St. Louis: Times Book and Job Printing House, 1874), 36. Disciplinary problems within the police department during the years encompassed by this book appear in a later chapter.

40. Minutes of the Board, August 10, 1877.

41. Ibid.

42. Ibid., August 31, 1877.

43. Ibid., September 11, 1877.

44. *Seventeenth Annual Report of Board of Police Commissioners of the City of St. Louis* (St. Louis: John McKittrick & Co., 1878), 40.

45. Minutes of the Board, September 3, 1877.

46. William Hyde and Howard L. Conard, *Encyclopedia of the History of St. Louis*, Vol. 1 (New York: The Southern History Company, 1899), 133.

47. The entire account of this incident is from the *Globe-Democrat* editions of November 17–23, 1877; November 25, 27, and 28, 1877; and December 4, 1877.

48. Ironically, Sergeant Jenks would be killed in the line of duty six years later.

49. *St. Louis Post-Dispatch*, March 7, 1884, 1.

50. Minutes of the Board, December 11, 1877.

51. Ibid.

52. *Seventeenth Annual Report of Board*, 42.

53. *St. Louis Globe-Democrat*, January 4, 1878, 8.

54. Ibid., January 5, 1878, 8.

55. Ibid., January 7, 1878, 8.

56. Minutes of the Board, May 14, 1878.

57. Ibid., March 19 and 26, 1878.

58. Ibid., July 16, 1878.

59. Ibid., June 25, July 16, July 30, and August 27, 1878.

60. Ibid., July 30, 1878.

61. Ibid.

62. Ibid., August 27, 1878.

63. *St. Louis Globe-Democrat*, October 9, 1878, 7, 9.

64. Minutes of the Board, September 10, 1878.

65. Ibid., October 1, 1878.

66. Ibid., February 12, 1878.

67. Thomas M. Spencer, *The St. Louis Veiled Prophet Celebration: Power on Parade, 1877–1995* (Columbia: University of Missouri Press, 2000), 8.

68. Ibid.

69. *St. Louis Globe-Democrat*, October 9, 1878, 2.

70. Ibid.

71. Ibid.

72. *St. Louis Post and Dispatch*, December 28, 1878, 5.

73. Ibid.

74. *St. Louis Globe-Democrat*, January 5, 1879, 1.

75. Ibid., February 12, 1879, 4.

76. Ibid., February 18, 1879, 1.

77. *St. Louis Post and Dispatch*, February 18, 1879, 1.

78. Ibid., February 19, 1879, 5.

79. Ibid., February 17, 1879, 1.

80. *St. Louis Globe-Democrat*, February 25, 1879, 3.

81. Minutes of the Board, February 27, 1879.

82. *St. Louis Post and Dispatch*, February 17, 1879, 1.

83. Ibid.

84. Ibid.

85. Ibid.

86. Ibid., March 4, 1879.

87. Ibid.

88. *St. Louis Globe-Democrat*, April 20, 1879, 9.

89. Minutes of the Board, April 22 and 29, 1879.

90. Ibid., May 1, 1879.

91. Ibid., January 27, 1880.

92. *St. Louis Post and Dispatch*, May 1, 1879, 1.

93. Ibid.

94. Ibid.

95. Ibid.

96. Ibid.

97. Ibid.

98. Ibid.

99. Ibid.

100. Ibid.

101. *St. Louis Globe-Democrat*, June 3, 1879, 2.

102. Ibid., June 2, 1879, 4.

103. Ibid.

104. Ibid., June 3, 1879, 2.

105. Ibid.

106. Ibid.

107. Ibid.

108. Ibid., June 2, 1879, 4.

109. Ibid., June 5, 1879, 5.

110. Ibid., June 2, 1879, 4.

111. Minutes of the Board, July 15, 1879; January 25, 1881; October 25, 1881.

112. Ibid., May 15, 1883.

113. *St. Louis Globe-Democrat*, June 5, 1879, 5.

114. Minutes of the Board, October 25 and 28, 1879.

115. Ibid., January 13, 1880.

116. Ibid., June 25, 1879.

117. Ibid., August 25, 1879.

118. Ibid., September 2 and 16, 1879.

119. Ibid., October 28, 1879.

120. Annual Report of the Board of Police Commissioners, in *The Mayor's Message with Accompanying Documents to the Municipal Assembly of the City of St. Louis* (St. Louis: Woodward, Tiernan & Hale, 1880), 481.

121. Minutes of the Board, April 29, 1879.

122. Minutes of the Board, June 30, 1879.

123. Ibid., June 7, 1879.

124. Ibid., July 1, 1879.

125. Ibid., July 29, 1879.

126. Annual Report of the Board (1880), 469.

127. Ibid., 468.

128. Ibid., 470.

129. Ibid., 468.

130. The rank of sergeant of detectives had been abolished on January 4, 1876. It apparently was resurrected between that date and the meeting of November 25, 1879, but board minutes do not indicate when that happened.

131. Minutes of the Board, November 25, 1879.

132. Annual Report of the Board (1880), 467–483.

133. Ibid., 478. It should also be noted that, contrary to the annual report that this was the sixth annual Charity Ball, it was the fifth ball, having begun in 1875.

134. Minutes of the Board, January 13, 1880.

135. Ibid., December 7, 1881.

136. Ibid., November 18, 1879; April 13, 1880.

137. Ibid., March 30, 1880.

138. Ibid., April 6, 1880.

139. Ibid., May 18, 1880.

140. Ibid., unknown date in September 1880. The meeting in question was a special board meeting that occurred between the regular meetings of September 14 and September 21. The secretary of the board had entered the time of the special meeting, 11:00 a.m., but not the date. Because the meeting was held in the morning and, because of the history of past special meetings, this meeting was likely held on Saturday, September 18.

141. Ibid., March 1, 1881.

142. Ibid., March 14, 1882.

143. Ibid., February 13, 1883.

144. *The State ex rel. the Attorney General v. France*, 72 Mo. 41; 1880 Mo. LEXIS 153 (April 1880).

145. Minutes of the Board, June 17, 1880.

146. Ibid., July 15, 1880.

147. *Murray and another v. Overstolz and others*, 8 F. 110; 1880 U.S. App. LEXIS 2746, 1 McCrary's Cir. Ct. Repts. 606 (September 1880).

148. *France v. Missouri*, 154 U.S. 667; 1880 U.S. LEXIS 1561 (October 1880).

149. Minutes of the Board, June 15, 1880.

150. Ibid., July 30, 1880.

151. St. Louis City Plan Commission, *History*, 23.

152. Minutes of the Board, November 16, 1880.

153. *St. Louis Globe-Democrat*, January 6, 1881, 3.

154. Barbara Miksicek, David McElreath, and Stephen Pollihan, *In the Line of Duty: St. Louis Police Officers Who Made the Ultimate Sacrifice* (St. Louis: St. Louis Metropolitan Police Department, 1991), 13.

155. The police department lists only six officers killed during this time (see Miksicek, McElreath, and Pollihan, *In the Line of Duty.*). Patrolman Nehemiah Pratt, killed on the balcony of the Recorder's Court on June 17, 1861, and Patrolman Thomas Kirk, killed during an arrest attempt on July 5, 1861, were uncovered by this author while researching other aspects of the early history of the police department.

156. The remainder of the account of Patrolman Walsh's death was taken from the *St. Louis Post-Dispatch* editions of December 6, p. 7; December 8, p. 4; and December 9, p. 8.

157. *St. Louis Post-Dispatch*, December 8, 1880, 4.

158. Ibid., December 9, 1880, 8.

159. Minutes of the Board, June 15, 1880.

160. Gary R. Kremer, *James Milton Turner and the Promise of America: The Public Life of a Post-Civil War Black Leader* (Columbia: University of Missouri Press, 1991), dustcover.

161. Ibid., 98.

162. *St. Louis Globe-Democrat*, January 4, 1881, 8.

163. Ibid., December 24, 1880, 7.

164. Ibid.

165. Ibid. If the detective was William Berzey, the time of appointment would have been in the first year of Mayor Overstolz's term. The board minutes of that period, as noted earlier, indicate that Berzey served as a special officer on temporary duty and was employed for almost three weeks.

166. *St. Louis Post-Dispatch*, January 3, 1881, 1.

167. Ibid.

168. Minutes of the Board, January 3, 1881.

Notes from Chapter 6

1. *St. Louis Post-Dispatch*, January 12, 1881, 1.

2. *St. Louis Globe-Democrat*, January 13, 1881, 2.

3. Ibid.

4. Ibid., January 21, 1881, 2.

5. Minutes of the Board, February 1, 1881.

6. Ibid.

7. Ibid.

8. *St. Louis Globe-Democrat*, February 4, 1881, 7.

9. Minutes of the Board, February 8, 1881.

10. Ibid., February 15, 1881.

11. Ibid.

12. *St. Louis Globe-Democrat*, February 4, 1881, 7.

13. Ibid., February 5, 1881, 6.

14. Ibid., February 20, 1881, 11.

15. Ibid., February 26, 1881, 9.

16. Ibid., February 10, 1881, 8.

17. Ibid.

18. Ibid.

19. Ibid., March 29, 1881.

20. Minutes of the Board, April 2, 1881.

21. Ibid., May 2, 1882.

22. Ibid., February 6, 1883.

23. *St. Louis Post-Dispatch*, February 22, 1881, 5.

24. Ibid., March 1, 1881, 5.

25. Ibid.

26. Ibid., February 26, 1881, 8.

27. Ibid.

28. Ibid.

29. Ibid., March 19, 1881, 4.

30. Ibid., March 1, 1881, 10.

31. Ibid., March 3, 1881, 5.

32. *St. Louis Globe-Democrat*, March 6, 1881, 7.

33. Ibid.

34. Ibid.

35. *Laws of Missouri Passed at the Session of the Thirty-First General Assembly* (Jefferson City, MO: Tribune Printing Company, 1881).

36. *St. Louis Post-Dispatch*, March 11, 1881, 8.

37. Ibid.

38. Minutes of the Board, April 2, 1881.

39. Ibid.

40. Ibid., April 4, 1881.

41. Ibid., April 19, 1881.

42. *St. Louis Post-Dispatch*, April 22, 1881, 1.

43. Ibid., April 23, 1881, 4.

44. Ibid.

45. Ibid.

46. Minutes of the Board, April 25, 1881.

47. Ibid.

48. Ibid.

49. Ibid., April 27, 1881. The "Notice to the Public" was prepared on April 26 but was not noted in the minutes until the following day.

50. Ibid.

51. Ibid.

52. *St. Louis Post-Dispatch*, April 28, 1881, 1.

53. Ibid., April 29, 1881, 4

54. Ibid.

55. Ibid., April 30, 1881, 8.

56. Minutes of the Board, May 6, 1881.

57. The Twenty-first Annual Report of the Board of Police Commissioners of the City of St. Louis, in *The Mayor's Message with Accompanying Documents* (St. Louis: A. Ungar & Co., 1882), 466. "Hacks," or hackney carriages, were two-horse vehicles for carrying passengers. "Furniture cars" were heavy-duty rigs for moving any type of heavy load. Wood and coal wagons were used to hawk those products for heating. The definition of the term "baggage wagons" could not be found.

58. Minutes of the Board, May 17 and June 7, 1881.

59. St. Louis Board of Police Commissioners, *History of the St. Louis Metropolitan Police Department: 1810–1910* (St. Louis: Skinner and Kennedy, 1910), 123.

60. Minutes of the Board, June 7, 1881.

61. Ibid.

62. Ibid., June 8, 1881.

63. *The Republican*, August 2, 1882, 5.

64. Minutes of the Board, July 19, 1881.

65. According to the board minutes of November 1, 1881, the amount held by the police department was $1,027.61.

66. Minutes of the Board, November 8, 1881.

67. *St. Louis Globe-Democrat*, January 9, 1885, 10.

68. Minutes of the Board, November 1, 1881.

69. *St. Louis Post-Dispatch*, November 7, 1881, 8.

70. Ibid., November 8, 1881, 8.

71. Ibid.

72. Ibid.

73. *St. Louis Globe-Democrat*, April 17, 1885, 8.

74. Minutes of the Board, December 13, 1881.

75. *St. Louis Globe-Democrat*, November 5, 1881, 9.

76. Minutes of the Board, November 29, 1881.

77. Ibid., December 7, 1881.

78. *St. Louis Globe-Democrat*, December 24, 1881, 9.

79. Ibid.

80. According to John J. Flinn and John E. Wilkie, *History of the Chicago Police* (New York: Arno Press, 1971, 212), the "signal patrol service" was introduced in Chicago in 1880. The authors termed the introduction of the signal service "the most important event of the year."

81. Minutes of the Board, December 27, 1881.

82. *St. Louis Globe-Democrat*, January 9, 1882, 2.

83. Ibid.

84. Minutes of the Board, January 10, 1882.

85. Ibid., February 7, 1882.

86. Ibid., May 2, 1882.

87. Board of Police Commissioners, *Manual Containing the Rules for the Government of the Police Department of the City of St. Louis*, Rule 22, Sec. 10, "Wearing Uniforms, etc.," 29.

88. The Twenty-second Annual Report of the Board of Police Commissioners of the City of St. Louis lists the location of the "patrol wagon alarm boxes" in the Central and Third districts and "the respective 'call' number of each box." It might be presumed that the later use of the expression "call box" emanated from this terminology.

89. Minutes of the Board, April 4, 1882.

90. *St. Louis Globe-Democrat*, September 18, 1883, 8. In an interview by a reporter, Chief of Police John W. Campbell described how he and another person were on Market, between Sixth and Seventh streets, and he needed to contact headquarters. Campbell noted that he "was detained in the box for about three minutes . . . but when I came out of the box. . . ."

91. Ibid., April 7, 1882.

92. Ibid., May 23, 1882.

93. Ibid.

94. Ibid., June 20, 1882.

95. Twenty-second Annual Report of the Board, 435–436.

96. Ibid.

97. Ibid.

98. Ibid.

99. Ibid., June 6, 1882.

100. Ibid., June 27, 1882.

101. *St. Louis Globe-Democrat*, June 28, 1882, 8.

102. Ibid., June 29, 1882, 5.

103. Ibid., July 1, 1882., 4.

104. Ibid., July 2, 1882, 3.

105. Ibid.

106. Ibid.

107. Ibid., July 5, 1882.

108. Ibid., July 24, 1882.

109. Ibid., July 18, 1882.

110. While the next chief of police would be the tenth appointed, it should be remembered that James McDonough was appointed chief on three occasions.

111. *The Republican*, August 2, 1882, 5.

112. Ibid.

113. Minutes of the Board, August 22 and 29, September 8, 1882.

114. Ibid., October 17, 1882.

115. Ibid., September 8, 1882.

116. Ibid., September 19, 1882.

117. Ibid., December 19, 1882.

118. Ibid., April 2, 1883.

119. Ibid., January 2, 1883.

120. Ibid., January 16, 1883.

121. Ibid., January 23, 1883.

122. Ibid., January 30, 1883.

123. Hyde and Conard, *Encyclopedia of the History of St. Louis*, vol. 3, 1,330.

124. Minutes of the Board, February 27, 1883.

125. Ibid., March 20, 1883. It should be noted that there were few regular telephones in service in 1883.

126. Ibid., April 10, 1883.

127. Ibid., April 17, 1883.

128. Ibid., April 10, 1883.

129. Ibid., April 17, 1883.

130. Ibid., March 25, 1865.

131. The first secretary to the board was James Loughborough. He was appointed at the first board meeting, April 10, 1861. The minutes of May 21, 1861, simply noted that Loughborough had resigned but gave no date of resignation. Henry F. Watson was, that same date, appointed the second secretary of the board. Watson apparently remained in that position until a new board took office on February 3, 1865. At that time, one of the police commissioners, E. H. B. Jameson, was elected treasurer and secretary of the board. On August 1, 1865, board clerk George Gavin was promoted to secretary.

132. *St. Louis Post-Dispatch,* October 12, 1883, 5.

133. Minutes of the Board, May 8, 1883.

134. Ibid., July 31, 1883.

135. *St. Louis Globe-Democrat,* July 3, 1883, 4.

136. Ibid., July 13, 1883, 8.

137. Ibid.

138. Minutes of the Board, September 11, 1883.

139. *St. Louis Post-Dispatch,* October 5, 1883, 8.

140. Minutes of the Board, September 18, 1883.

141. *St. Louis Post-Dispatch,* September 14, 1883, 2.

142. Ibid.

143. Ibid.

144. Ibid.

145. Warren McChesney's denial of any knowledge of blank resignations first appeared on page 2 of the *Post-Dispatch* of September 14, 1883. Joseph McEntire's denial appeared on page 2 of that newspaper on September 18.

146. *St. Louis Post-Dispatch*, September 17, September 18, 1883, 2.

147. *St. Louis Globe-Democrat,* September 15, 1883, 6.

148. *St. Louis Post-Dispatch*, September 21, 1883, 7.

149. *St. Louis Globe-Democrat*, September 29, 1883, 7.

150. Ibid.

151. Ibid.

152. Ibid.

153. Ibid.

154. Minutes of the Board, October 9, 1883.

155. *St. Louis Globe-Democrat*, October 10, 1883, 3.

156. Ibid.

157. Minutes of the Board, October 9, 1883.

158. *St. Louis Globe-Democrat*, October 10, 1883, 12. This account of the incident is taken from the October 9 and 10 editions of the *Globe-Democrat* (pp. 4 and 12, respectively) and the October 9 edition of the *Post-Dispatch*, p. 2.

159. *St. Louis Globe-Democrat*, October 9, 1883, 4.

160. Ibid., 12.

161. Ibid.

162. Ibid., October 13, 1883, 4.

163. *St. Louis Post-Dispatch*, October 12, 1883, 2.

164. Ibid.

165. Ibid.

166. Ibid., October 13, 1883, 2.

167. Ibid.

168. Ibid.

169. Ibid., October 18, 1883, 2.

170. Ibid., October 13, 1883, 2.

171. Ibid.

172. *St. Louis Globe-Democrat*, October 14, 1883, 7.

173. *St. Louis Post-Dispatch*, October 15, 1883, 2.

174. Ibid.

175. Ibid., October 16, 1883, 1.

176. *St. Louis Globe-Democrat*, October 16, 1883, 12.

177. *St. Louis Post-Dispatch*, October 16, 1883, 8.

178. Ibid.

179. Ibid., October 17, 1883, 2.

180. *St. Louis Globe-Democrat*, October 26, 1883, 12.

181. Ibid., October 17, 1883, 1.

182. Ibid.

183. Ibid.

184. *St. Louis Post-Dispatch,* October 18, 1883, 1.

185. Ibid., October 19, 1883, 2.

186. *St. Louis Post-Dispatch,* October 23, 1883, 3.

187. Ibid., October 20, 1883, 8.

188. Ibid., October 26, 1883, 9.

189. Ibid., October 27, 1883, 12.

190. Ibid.

191. Ibid., November 3, 1883, 4.

192. Ibid.

193. Ibid.

194. Ibid.

195. Ibid.

196. Ibid., December 22, 1883, 10.

197. Ibid.

198. Ibid.

199. Ibid., November 4, 1883, 7.

200. Ibid., November 7, 1883, 8.

201. To this day, the Board of Police Commissioners consists of five members, the mayor, and four residents of the city appointed by the governor. Interestingly, the mayor today typically votes only when there is a 2–2 tie vote.

202. Minutes of the Board, November 6, 1883.

203. Ibid.

204. *St. Louis Globe-Democrat*, November 13, 1883, 8.

205. Minutes of the Board, November 13, 1883.

206. *St. Louis Globe-Democrat*, November 15, 1883, 7.

207. Ibid., November 14, 1883, 8.

208. Minutes of the Board, November 13, 1883.

209. Ibid., November 14, 1883.

210. *St. Louis Globe-Democrat*, November 15, 1883, 7.

211. Minutes of the Board, November 14, 1883.

212. *St. Louis Globe-Democrat*, November 17, 1883, 8.

213. Minutes of the Board, November 16, 1883.

214. Ibid., December 13, 1883, 12.

215. *St. Louis Globe-Democrat*, November 17, 1883, 8.

216. *St. Louis Globe-Democrat*, December 7, 1883, 8.

217. Ibid., December 20, 1883, 8.

218. Minutes of the Board, December 19, 1883.

219. *St. Louis Globe-Democrat*, December 20, 1983, 8.

220. Minutes of the Board, December 21, 1883.

221. *St. Louis Globe-Democrat*, December 22, 1883, 10.

222. Ibid.

223. Ibid.

224. Ibid., 2.

225. Ibid.

226. Minutes of the Board, December 27, 1883.

227. Ibid.

228. Ibid.

229. Ibid., December 28, 1883.

230. *St. Louis Globe-Democrat*, December 29, 1883, 8.

231. Minutes of the Board, December 28, 1883.

232. Ibid.

233. *St. Louis Globe-Democrat*, December 29, 1883, 8.

234. Ibid., December 30, 1883, 6.

235. Minutes of the Board, January 2, 1884.

236. Ibid.

237. Ibid., January 8, 1884.

238. Ibid.

239. Ibid.

240. Ibid.

241. The Twenty-third Annual Report of the Board of Police Commissioners of the City of St. Louis, in *The Mayor's Message with Accompanying Documents to the Municipal Assembly of the City of Saint Louis at its Session May, 1884* (St. Louis: Woodward & Tiernan, 1884), 480.

242. Louisa Harris, *Behind the Scenes or Nine Years at the Four Courts of St. Louis* (St. Louis: A. R. Fleming & Co., 1893).

243. Ibid., 13.

244. Minutes of the Board, March 4, 1884.

245. Ibid., March 11, 1884.

246. Ibid., March 18, 1884.

247. *St. Louis Post-Dispatch*, August 16, 1884, 2.

248. Minutes of the Board, August 26, 1884.

249. *St. Louis Post-Dispatch*, August 27, 1884, 8.

250. Ibid.

251. Ibid.

252. Ibid.

253. William Barnaby Faherty, S.J., and Eileen Nini Harris, *The St. Louis Portrait* (Tulsa, OK: Continental Heritage, 1978), 105.

254. Primm, *Lion of the Valley*, 311.

255. Ibid., 312.

256. Minutes of the Board, September 15, 1884. The order excepting captains was announced at the meeting of December 9, 1884.

257. Ibid., September 30, 1884.

258. Ibid., November 1, 1884.

259. Ibid.

260. Ibid., November 25, 1884.

261. Ibid., November 11, 1884.

262. Ibid., December 30, 1884.

Notes from Chapter 7

1. Biographical information obtained from the January 14, 1885, issues of the *St. Louis Post-Dispatch* (p. 1) and the *St. Louis Globe-Democrat* (p. 10), and vol. 2 of Hyde and Conard, *Encyclopedia of the History of St. Louis*, 858–859.

2. Minutes of the Board, January 27, 1885.

3. *The Mayor's Message with Accompanying Documents to the Municipal Assembly of the City of St. Louis at Its Session May, 1885* (St. Louis: Wm. Biebinger & Co., 1885), 506.

4. Ibid., 496.

5. Minutes of the Board, April 21, 1885.

6. *St. Louis Globe-Democrat*, April 15, 1885, 4. The entire account of this crime is taken from the pages of the *Globe-Democrat* and the *St. Louis Post-Dispatch* between April 15, 1885, and August 15, 1888, unless otherwise noted.

7. The police department was authorized not to have a chief of detectives, but a sergeant in charge of detectives. Nonetheless, the press commonly referred to the position as "chief of detectives," a position created in the 1870s but then removed when a legal opinion of the city counselor stated that such a position was not authorized by the Police Act of 1861 or any subsequent amendments.

8. The name assumed by the man believed to be Walter H. Lennox Maxwell is spelled several different ways in the newspapers. The spelling that appears in each report is reproduced here.

9. Minutes of the Board, April 21, 1885.

10. *St. Louis Globe-Democrat*, April 17, 1885, 8. While the *Globe-Democrat* agreed

with the board that the cost was $3.34 a word, it reported a different word count than that reported in the board minutes. This edition of the newspaper reported the message contained 133 words, for a total of $444.22.

11. Minutes of the Board, May 18, 1885.

12. *St. Louis Post-Dispatch*, May 18, 1885, 2

13. Minutes of the Board, May 29, 1885.

14. Ibid., June 2, 1885.

15. Ibid., June 5, 1885.

16. *St. Louis Globe-Democrat*, June 13, 1885, 9.

17. Ibid., June 14, 1885, 22.

18. Minutes of the Board, June 16, 1885.

19. Ibid., May 23, 1885.

20. Ibid., May 12, 1885.

21. *St. Louis Globe-Democrat*, September 12, 1885, 2.

22. Ibid. September 14, 1885. 10.

23. Ibid., September 9, 1885, 12.

24. Minutes of the Board, October 20, 1885.

25. *St. Louis Post-Dispatch*, November 2, 1893, 2 and 5.

26. *St. Louis Globe-Democrat*, December 14, 1885, 10.

27. Ibid., December 18, 1885, 12.

28. Minutes of the Board, January 26, 1886.

29. Ibid., March 30, 1886.

30. Ibid., March 2, 1886.

31. Ibid., March 30, 1886.

32. *St. Louis Globe-Democrat*, April 12, 1886, 7.

33. Minutes of the Board, May 4, 1886.

34. Ibid.

35. Ibid., May 18, 1886.

36. *Francis, Mayor, Appellant, v. Blair, et al (1886) 89 MO 291* (April term, 1886).

37. *St. Louis Globe-Democrat*, June 29, 1886, 7.

38. The *Globe-Democrat*, in the issues of May 10–18, 1886, listed the names of each prospective juror questioned and excused and the reason why each was excused.

39. The accounts of the Maxwell/Brooks trial are taken from the pages of the *St. Louis Globe-Democrat* unless otherwise noted. Quotations are cited regardless of the source.

40. Thomas Furlong, *Fifty Years a Detective* (St. Louis: C. E. Barnett, 1912), 17.

41. *St. Louis Globe-Democrat*, May 25, 1886, 4.

42. Ibid.

43. Furlong, *Fifty Years a Detective*, 17.

44. Ibid., 29.

45. *St. Louis Globe-Democrat*, May 27, 1886, 4.

46. Ibid., June 6, 1886, 4.

47. Ibid., July 7, 1886, 8.

48. Minutes of the Board, November 9, 1886.

49. The Twenty-sixth Annual Report of the Board of Police Commissioners of the City of St. Louis, in *The Mayor's Message with Accompanying Documents, to the Municipal Assembly of the City of Saint Louis at Its Session, May, 1887* (St. Louis: Nixon-Jones, 1887), 442.

50. Ibid., 443.

51. Minutes of the Board, January 25, 1887.

52. Ibid., March 29, 1887.

53. Ibid., April 12, 1887.

54. Ibid., June 14, 1887.

55. Ibid., June 28, 1887.

56. Ibid., July 16, 1887.

57. *The State ex rel Wear et al. v. Francis et al., Police Commissioners of St. Louis, Appellants* (1888) 95 Mo. 44; 8 S.W. 1; 1888 Mo. LEXIS 219, decided April 1888.

58. *St. Louis Globe-Democrat*, September 6, 1887, 12.

59. Ibid., December 29, 1887, 1.

60. Minutes of the Board, December 29, 1887.

61. *St. Louis Globe-Democrat*, December 30, 1887, 1.

62. Ibid., January 25, 1888, 12.

63. Minutes of the Board, February 28, 1888.

64. *The State ex rel Wear et al.*, 1888.

65. Minutes of the Board, May 18, 1888.

66. *St. Louis Globe-Democrat*, June 17, 1888, 30.

67. Ibid.

68. Minutes of the Board, May 22, 1888.

69. *Brooks v. Missouri* (1888), 124 U.S. 394; 8 S. Ct. 443; 1888 U.S. LEXIS 1874; 31 L. Ed. 454, decided January 23, 1888.

70. *St. Louis Globe-Democrat*, July 13, 1888, 1.

71. Ibid.

72. Ibid., August 10, 1888, 1.

73. Ibid.

74. Ibid.

75. Ibid., 2.

76. Ibid.

77. Ibid., August 11, 1888, 8.

78. Furlong, *Fifty Years a Detective*, 38.

79. *Mayor Francis, v. Blair et al., Police Commissioners, Appellants* (1888), 96 Mo. 515; 9 S.W. 894; 1888 Mo. LEXIS 76, decided October 1888.

80. *St. Louis Globe-Democrat*, January 30, 1889, 12.

81. Ibid.

82. *St. Louis Post-Dispatch*, February 3, 1889, 3.

83. Ibid.

84. Ibid.

85. Ibid., February 5, 1889, 5.

86. Ibid., February 6, 1889, 4.

87. Ibid.

88. Ibid., January 30, 1889, 12.

89. Ibid.

90. *St. Louis Globe-Democrat*, February 10, 1889, 20.

91. Ibid.

92. Ibid.

93. Ibid.

94. *St. Louis Post-Dispatch*, January 12, 1889, 5.

95. Ibid.

96. Ibid.

97. Ibid.

98. Ibid.

99. Minutes of the Board, April 2, 1889.

100. *St. Louis Globe-Democrat*, February 16, 1889, 8.

101. Minutes of the Board, February 19 and 26, 1889.

102. Obituary in *St. Louis Post-Dispatch*, December 23, 1903, 1.

103. *St. Louis Globe-Democrat*, February 16, 1889, 8.

104. Ibid.

105. *St. Louis Republic*, March 8, 1889, 2.

106. James Cox, ed., *Old and New St. Louis: A Concise History of the Metropolis of the West and Southwest, with a Review of Its Present Greatness and Immediate Prospects* (St. Louis: Central Biographical Publishing Co., 1894), 318.

107. Minutes of the Board, May 14, 1890.

108. Ibid., March 7, 1889.

109. The Twenty-eighth Annual Report of the Board of Police Commissioners of the City of St. Louis, in *The Mayor's Message with Accompanying Documents, to the Municipal Assembly of the City of Saint Louis at Its Session, May, 1889* (St. Louis: Nixon-Jones, 1889), 435.

110. *St. Louis Post-Dispatch*, February 19, 1889, 3.

111. Minutes of the Board, April 5, 1889.

112. *St. Louis Globe-Democrat*, September 17, 1890, 4.

113. Minutes of the Board, June 11, 1889.

114. Ibid., July 16, 1889.

115. Minutes of the Board, December 24, 1889. Board secretary Tate failed to place any commas in the new order.

Notes from Chapter 8

1. Minutes of the Board, April 29, 1890.

2. Ibid., May 14, 1890.

3. Ibid., May 20, 1890.

4. Ibid., June 24, 1890.

5. Ibid., July 15, 1890.

6. Ibid., August 19, 1890.

7. *St. Louis Post-Dispatch*, September 4, 1890, 5.

8. Ibid.

9. Ibid., August 29, 1890, 2.

10. *St. Louis Globe-Democrat*, September 17, 1890, 4.

11. Ibid.

12. *The State v. Duncan, Appellant* (No Number in Original), 116 Mo. 288, 22 S.W. 699, 1893 Mo. LEXIS 288, decided May 30, 1893.

13. Ibid.

14. Ibid.

15. Ibid.

16. Ibid.

17. John A. Wright, *Discovering African American St. Louis: A Guide to Historic Sites*, 2nd ed. (St. Louis: Missouri Historical Society Press, 2002), 18.

18. Miksicek, McElreath, and Pollihan, *In the Line of Duty*, 21.

19. Wright, *Discovering African American St. Louis*, 18.

20. Ibid.

21. *St. Louis Globe-Democrat*, March 18, 1891, 9.

22. *Laws of Missouri Passed at the Session of the Thirty-Sixth General Assembly* (Jefferson City, MO: Tribune Printing Company, 1891).

23. Ibid., 185.

24. Ibid.

25. Ibid.

26. St. Louis City Plan Commission, *History*, 24.

27. Minutes of the Board, April 28, 1891.

28. Ibid., June 30, 1891.

29. The Thirty-first Annual Report of the Board of Police Commissioners of the City of St. Louis, in *The Mayor's Message with Accompanying Documents, to the Municipal Assembly of the City of Saint Louis at Its Session, May, 1892* (St. Louis: Nixon-Jones, 1892), 497–498.

30. Minutes of the Board, January 26, 1892.

31. The Thirty-second Annual Report of the Board of Police Commissioners of the City of St. Louis, in *The Mayor's Message with Accompanying Documents, to the Municipal Assembly of the City of Saint Louis at Its Session, May, 1892* (St. Louis: Nixon-Jones, 1893), 532.

32. Ibid., 533.

33. Minutes of the Board, April 25, 1893.

34. Taken from accounts in the *St. Louis Post-Dispatch*, May 13, 1893, p. 5, and Miksicek, McElreath, and Pollihan, *In the Line of Duty*, 23.

35. Minutes of the Board, June 15, 1893.

36. Hyde and Conard, *Encyclopedia of the History of St. Louis*, vol. 1, 842–843.

37. *St. Louis Post-Dispatch*, June 18, 1893, 3.

38. Minutes of the Board, July 25, 1893.

39. Ibid., August 14, 1894.

40. Ibid., August 1, 1893.

41. Ibid.

42. Ibid., August 7, 1893.

43. Ibid., September 19, 1893.

44. Ibid., October 10, 1893.

45. Ibid., April 3, 1894.

46. Ibid., May 1, 1894.

47. Ibid., May 22, 1894.

48. *St. Louis Post-Dispatch*, May 8, 1894, 2.

49. Minutes of the Board, July 31, 1894.

50. Ibid., August 14, 1894.

51. Revised Ordinances of the City of St. Louis—1875, Ord. #9579, Section 7, Approved July 1, 1875.

52. Minutes of the Board, August 14, 1894.

53. Ibid.

54. Michael Lerner, "Hoping for a Splendid Summer: African American St. Louis,

Ragtime, and the Louisiana Purchase Exposition," *Gateway Heritage* 19, no. 3 (Winter 1988–1999): 34.

55. Minutes of the Board, September 11, 1894.

56. Ibid., December 26, 1894.

57. Ibid.

58. Ibid., April 23, 1895.

59. Ibid.

60. Ibid.

61. Ibid.

62. Ibid.

63. Ibid.

64. *The St. Louis Republic*, April 25, 1895, 4.

65. Ibid.

66. Minutes of the Board, April 30, 1895.

67. Ibid., May 21, 1895.

68. Ibid., July 9, 1895.

69. *The St. Louis Republic*, June 25, 1895, 3.

70. Ibid.

71. Minutes of the Board, July 17, 1895.

72. Ibid., July 23, 1895.

73. One source—Julian S. Hatcher, Frank J. Judy, Joe Weller, *Firearms Investigation Identification and Evidence*, ed. Thomas G. Samworth (Harrisburg, PA: The Stackpole Company, 1957), 43—states that the Iver Johnson Company and others advertised "automatic" revolvers. "However, these were simply double action topbreak revolvers; the 'automatic' referred to the ejection of the shells, which were automatically ejected when the revolver was opened." The English firearms manufacturer Webley also produced a revolver, the authors said, where the recoil pushed the entire barrel back over the butt, cocking the hammer and, at the same time, revolving the cylinder for the next shot.

74. Minutes of the Board, October 15, 1895.

75. This account is taken from the December 26, 1895, edition of the *St. Louis Globe-Democrat*, p. 7, and from Wright, *Discovering African American St. Louis*, 18. For a historic study of the "Stagger Lee" folklore ballad see Cecil Brown, *Stagolee Shot Billy* (Cambridge, MA: Harvard University Press, 2003).

76. Joe Sonderman, *St. Louis 365: Intriguing Events from Each Day of the Year* (St. Louis: Stellar Press, 2002), 256.

77. *St. Louis Globe-Democrat*, January 10, 1896, 9.

78. Minutes of the Board, January 21, 1896.

79. Ibid.

80. *St. Louis Globe-Democrat*, April 21, 1896, 12.

81. Tim O'Neil, "The Great Cyclone of 1896," *St. Louis Post-Dispatch Magazine*, May 26, 1996, 8. Unless otherwise noted, the account of the tornado is excerpted from pp. 5 to 15.

82. Julian Curzon, ed., *The Great Cyclone at St. Louis and East St. Louis, May 27, 1896* (Carbondale: Southern Illinois University Press, 1997), 111.

83. Ibid., 85–91.

84. *St. Louis Review*, June 11, 2004, 5.

85. *St. Louis Globe-Democrat*, May 28, 1896, 4.

86. Ibid., May 29, 1896, 5.

87. Minutes of the Board, May 28, 1896.

88. Ibid., July 21, 1896.

89. *St. Louis Globe-Democrat*, May 31, 1896, 2.

90. Ibid.

91. Ibid., May 30, 1896, 6.

92. Ibid., May 31, 1896, 2.

93. Ibid.

94. Ibid.

95. Curzon, *The Great Cyclone*, 152–153.

96. Ibid., 332–333.

97. Ibid., 262–265.

98. Ibid., 286–289.

99. *St. Louis Globe-Democrat*, June 1, 1896, 2.

100. Minutes of the Board, November 9, 1897.

101. Ibid., November 17, 1896.

102. Ibid., November 24, 1896.

103. Ibid., December 31, 1896.

104. *St. Louis Globe-Democrat*, January 21, 1897, 12.

105. Minutes of the Board, February 2, 1897.

106. *St. Louis Globe-Democrat*, January 27, 1897, 7.

107. Ibid. Those who favored a gold standard were sometimes referred to as "sound money" men.

108. Minutes of the Board, March 5, 1897.

109. *St. Louis Post-Dispatch*, August 14, 1898, 18.

110. *St. Louis Globe-Democrat*, January 27, 1897, 7.

111. Minutes of the Board, May 25, 1897.

112. Simon Ablon Cole, "Manufacturing Identity: A History of Criminal Identification Techniques from Photography Through Fingerprinting" (Ph.D. diss., Cornell University, 1998), 77.

113. Ibid.

114. *St. Louis Post-Dispatch*, June 17, 1897, 12.

115. Ibid.

116. Ibid.

117. Minutes of the Board, June 30, 1897.

118. *St. Louis Globe-Democrat*, November 4, 1897, 12.

119. Ibid.

120. Ibid.

121. Taken from accounts in *The St. Louis Republic*, November 16, 1897, pp. 1–2, and Miksicek, McElreath, and Pollihan, *In the Line of Duty*, 27.

122. *The St. Louis Republic*, August 13, 1899, 4.

123. Ibid.

124. Minutes of the Board, December 28, 1897.

125. Ibid., April 26, 1898.

126. Ibid., May 19, 1898.

127. *The St. Louis Republic*, May 20, 1898, 3.

128. Louis G. Geiger, *Joseph W. Folk of Missouri* (Columbia: The Curators of the University of Missouri, 1953), 14.

129. *St. Louis Globe-Democrat*, August 23, 1898, 9.

130. Minutes of the Board, August 30, 1898.

131. Ibid., November 22, 1898.

132. Ibid., November 30, 1898.

133. *St. Louis Post-Dispatch*, January 7, 1899, 1.

134. *St. Louis Globe-Democrat*, January 8, 1899, 12.

135. Minutes of the Board, January 9, 1899.

136. *St. Louis Globe-Democrat*, January 11, 1899, 12.

137. Ibid.

138. Ibid. Although the building of the New Cathedral (the Cathedral Basilica of Saint Louis) would not begin until 1907, the archdiocese of St. Louis had built the St. Louis Cathedral Chapel to serve until the cathedral had been completed. The chapel stood on the southwest corner of Maryland and Newstead avenues, the site of the present-day rear parking lot of the New Cathedral.

139. Ibid.

140. *St. Louis Post-Dispatch*, January 5, 1899, 1.

141. Ibid. According to Primm, *Lion of the Valley*, 374, "boodle was the local term for the practice of bribing city officials or legislators to win utilities franchises, licenses, low tax assessments, garbage contracts, or other special privileges."

142. The account of the experiment is taken from the January 15, 1899, edition of the *St. Louis Post-Dispatch*, 1.

143. Ibid.

144. Ibid.

145. The account is taken from the January 18, 1899, edition of the *St. Louis Globe-Democrat*, 14.

146. Ibid.

Notes from Chapter 9

1. *St. Louis Globe-Democrat*, December 25, 1898, 11.

2. Ibid., January 4, 1899, 12.

3. Ibid.

4. This account taken from the *St. Louis Globe-Democrat*, January 5, 1899, 12.

5. Ibid.

6. Ibid.

7. Ibid., January 6, 1899, 4.

8. Ibid.

9. Ibid.

10. *Laws of the State of Missouri 1899* (Jefferson City, MO: Tribune Printing Co., 1900), 51–72.

11. *St. Louis Globe-Democrat*, February 16, 1899, 3.

12. Ibid., March 7, 1899, 2.

13. Ibid., February 22, 1899, 2.

14. Ibid., March 8, 1899, 12.

15. Ibid., 2.

16. Ibid. March 7, 1899, 9.

17. *Laws of the State of Missouri 1899*, 51.

18. *St. Louis Globe-Democrat*, March 11, 1899, 5.

19. Ibid.

20. *St. Louis Post-Dispatch*, April 26, 1899, 5.

21. Minutes of the Board, April 25, 1899.

22. *St. Louis Globe-Democrat*, April 26, 1899, 5.

23. Ibid.

24. Minutes of the Board, June 13, 1899.

25. Ibid., June 27, 1899.

26. *St. Louis Post-Dispatch*, June 1, 1899, 16.

27. Ibid., July 18, 1899, 4.

28. *St. Louis Globe-Democrat*, January 6, 1901, 12.

29. *The St. Louis Republic*, August 16, 1899, 7.

30. *The St. Louis Post-Dispatch*, August 15, 1899, 5.

31. *The St. Louis Republic*, August 16, 1899, 7.

32. *The State ex rel. Hawes et al. v. Mason*, 153 Mo. 23, decided December 19, 1899, 40–41.

33. Ibid., 41.

34. Minutes of the Board, August 21, 1899.

35. Ibid.

36. *Hawes v. Mason*, 41–42.

37. Ibid., 42.

38. Minutes of the Board, September 19, 1899.

39. Ibid., October 31, 1899.

40. Minutes of the Board, October 6, 1899.

41. *St. Louis Post-Dispatch*, October 15, 1899, 10.

42. Hyde and Conard, *Encyclopedia of the History of St. Louis*, vol. 3, 1,745–1,746.

43. *Hawes v. Mason*, 61–62.

44. Ibid., 62.

Notes from Chapter 10

1. Minutes of the Board, January 2, 1900.

2. Ibid.

3. *St. Louis Post-Dispatch*, March 26, 1900, 1.

4. Ibid.

5. Ibid.

6. Primm, *Lion of the Valley*, 380.

7. Ibid.

8. Minutes of the Board, May 9, 1900, 9:00 a.m. session.

9. Ibid., 2:00 p.m. session.

10. Ibid.

11. Ibid., May 14, 1900.

12. Ibid.

13. The account of the murder of Emergency Special MacRae was taken from p. 2 of the May 24, 1900, edition of *The St. Louis Republic*.

14. Primm, *Lion of the Valley*, 380.

15. According to Primm in *Lion of the Valley*, p. 380, the posse comitatus had been authorized by federal judge Elmer Adams because of the temporary stoppage of cars that carried mail. It is possible that the 1,500 additional men were authorized in response to the order of Judge Adams.

16. The account of the shooting is taken from the June 1, 1900, edition of the *St. Louis Post-Dispatch*, p. 2, and from Miksicek, MeElreath, and Pollihan, *In the*

Line of Duty, 29.

17. Minutes of the Board, June 26 and 28, 1900.

18. Primm, *Lion of the Valley*, 381.

19. *St. Louis Post-Dispatch*, July 6, 1900, 5.

20. Ibid.

21. Ibid.

22. Ibid.

23. Ibid., July 7, 1900, 8.

24. Ibid.

25. Ibid.

26. Ibid.

27. Ibid.

28. Ibid.

29. *St. Louis Post-Dispatch,* September 4–7, 1900; *St. Louis Globe-Democrat*, September 7–8, 1900.

30. *St. Louis Post-Dispatch*, September 4, 1900, 1.

31. *St. Louis Globe-Democrat*, September 6, 1900, 14.

32. Ibid.

33. Ibid.

34. Ibid.

35. *St. Louis Post-Dispatch*, August 27, 1900, 1. A mutoscope was a cabinet containing a series of still photographs. Peering into the cabinet eyepieces and turning a crank put the photos in motion, much like a motion picture.

36. Ibid.

37. Ibid., October 11, 1900, 1.

38. Ibid., October 12, 1900, 1.

39. *St. Louis Globe-Democrat*, December 17, 1900, 1; December 18, 1900, 7.

40. *St. Louis Globe-Democrat*, January 6, 1901, 12.

41. Ibid.

42. Ibid., February 5, 1901, 9.

43. Ibid.

44. Ibid.

45. Ibid., February 22, 1901, 14.

46. *St. Louis Post-Dispatch*, February 21, 1901, 1.

47. *St. Louis Globe-Democrat*, February 20, 1901, 14.

48. *St. Louis Post-Dispatch*, February 27, 1901, 1.

49. Mayor Ziegenhein later told a newspaper reporter that the other members of the board held a caucus before the meeting and "fixed everything up before the

board meeting commenced" (*St. Louis Post-Dispatch*, February 27, 1901, 1).

50. Minutes of the Board, February 26, 1901.

51. Ibid.

52. Ibid.

53. Ibid., February 27, 1901 (underlines in original).

54. *St. Louis Globe-Democrat*, March 30, 1901, 16.

55. Ibid., March 31, 1901, 1.

56. Ibid., June 30, 1901, 16.

57. *St. Louis Post-Dispatch*, March 29, 1901, 3.

58. *St. Louis Globe-Democrat*, March 31, 1901, 8.

59. Ibid.

60. Eugene J. Watts, "Black and Blue: Afro-American Police Officers in Twentieth-Century St. Louis," *Journal of Urban History* 7, no. 2 (February 1981): 131–167.

61. *St. Louis Globe-Democrat*, April 4, 1901, 7.

62. Ibid., October 21, 1903, 7.

63. *St. Louis Post-Dispatch*, March 11, 1901, 1.

64. *The St. Louis Republic*, April 16, 1901, 4.

65. *St. Louis Globe-Democrat*, April 20, 1901, 9.

66. Minutes of the Board, May 10, 1901.

67. The account of the shooting is taken from the June 16, 1901, edition of *The St. Louis Republic*, p. 8, and from Miksicek, MeElreath, and Pollihan, *In the Line of Duty*, 37.

68. Minutes of the Board, December 6, 1901.

69. Ibid.

70. Ibid., January 3, 1902.

71. *St. Louis Globe-Democrat*, December 19, 1901, 14.

72. Minutes of the Board, December 18, 1901.

73. Minutes of the Board, January 22, 1902.

74. Board of Police Commissioners, *Police Manual* (St. Louis: Con Curran Printing Co., 1902), table of contents.

75. *St. Louis Post-Dispatch*, June 27, 1902, 3.

76. Ibid.

77. Minutes of the Board, September 12, 1902.

78. Ibid., October 10, 1902.

79. *St. Louis Post-Dispatch*, October 27, 1902, 8.

80. Ibid., October 29, 1902, 4.

81. Geiger, *Joseph W. Folk*, 25.

82. *St. Louis Post-Dispatch*, March 3, 1903, 1.

83. *St. Louis Globe-Democrat*, March 31, 1903, 4.

84. Ibid.

85. Ibid., October 21, 1903, 1.

86. Ibid., March 31, 1903, 11.

87. This account was compiled from three sources: *The St. Louis Globe-Democrat*, May 31, 1903, 9; *St. Louis Post-Dispatch*, May 31, 1903, part 2, p. 3; and Miksicek, MeElreath, and Pollihan, *In the Line of Duty*, 45.

88. Primm, *Lion of the Valley*, 407.

89. *St. Louis Post-Dispatch*, August 31, 1903.

90. Board of Police Commissioners, *History*, 99.

91. *St. Louis Globe-Democrat*, October 17, 1903, 1.

92. Minutes of the Board, October 16 and 30, 1903.

93. *St. Louis Globe-Democrat*, October 21, 1903, 7.

94. *St. Louis Globe-Democrat*, December 5, 1903, 1.

95. Ibid.

96. Ibid.

97. Primm, *Lion of the Valley*, 374–375, describes boodle as "the local term for the practice of bribing city officials or legislators to win utilities franchises, licenses, low tax assessments, garbage contracts, or other special privileges."

98. Geiger, *Joseph W. Folk*, 78–79.

99. *St. Louis Globe-Democrat*, December 17, 1903, 1.

100. *St. Louis Post-Dispatch*, December 17, 1903, 1.

101. Ibid.

102. Ibid., December 27, 1903, 5.

103. Ibid., September 1, 1903, 3.

104. W. C. McCarty (or McCarthy), "St. Louis Police Department Will Make an Interesting Display at the Louisiana Purchase Exposition," typescript, Missouri History Museum, date unknown, 1–7.

Notes from Chapter 11

1. *The St. Louis Republic*, May 6, 1904, 2.

2. David R. Francis, *The Universal Exposition of 1904* (St. Louis: Louisiana Purchase Exposition Company, 1913), 634.

3. Ibid., 634–635.

4. *The St. Louis Republic*, May 6, 1904, 2.

5. Minutes of the Board, March 4, 1904.

6. Ibid., April 1, 1904.

7. *St. Louis Post-Dispatch*, April 2, 1904, 6.

8. *Forty-third Annual Report of the Board of Police Commissioners of City of St. Louis* (St. Louis: Board of Police Commissioners, 1904), 17, and *Forty-fourth Annual Report of the Board of Police Commissioners of City of St. Louis* (St. Louis: Board of Police Commissioners, 1905), 15.

9. McCarty, "Police Department Will Make Display," 1–7.

10. A *St. Louis Post-Dispatch* reporter posed as an "Indian" on this election day and described, in the March 13, 1904, edition of the newspaper (part 2, p. 1), what he did and saw. The Indians met at John Lavin's saloon on DeBaliviere before the polls opened. Lavin was the central committeeman from the Twenty-eighth Ward. They were transported to the First Ward and precinct in which they were to vote and given a slip of paper with the name and address of a voter there. This process continued throughout the day. They were paid, in this case $5, to cast votes in the name of the person listed on the slip of paper, for the favored candidate. They also intimidated voters from voting for the opposing candidate. Intimidation included being placed at the head of the line of voters; sometimes it included physical assaults.

11. *St. Louis Globe-Democrat*, March 13, 1904, 15.

12. Ibid., March 14, 1904, 3. Also, see *Globe-Democrat*, March 13, 1904, 15, and *St. Louis Post-Dispatch*, March 14, 1904, part 2, p. 1.

13. *St. Louis Post-Dispatch*, March 14, 1904, 1.

14. Ibid.

15. Ibid., March 15, 1904, 1.

16. Ibid.

17. Ibid., March 16, 1904, 1.

18. Ibid., March 31, 1904, 1.

19. Ibid.

20. *The St. Louis Republic*, April 1, 1904, 1.

21. Ibid.

22. Ibid.

23. Geiger, *Joseph W. Folk*, 71.

24. *The St. Louis Republic*, April 28, 1904, 6.

25. *St. Louis Globe-Democrat*, April 28, 1904, 6.

26. Ibid.

27. *The St. Louis Republic*, April 7, 1904, 1.

28. Ibid.

29. *St. Louis Post-Dispatch*, June 24, 1904, 1.

30. Ibid., June 5, 1904, 9B.

31. *St. Louis Globe-Democrat*, July 11, 1904, 1.

32. Ibid.

33. See, for example, the *St. Louis Post-Dispatch* editions of July 14, 1904, 14; July

20, 1904, 15; and July 28, 1904, 3.

34. Ibid.

35. Ibid.

36. The St. Louis Motor Carriage Company was begun by George P. Dorris and John French. The company would be moved to Peoria, Illinois, in 1905, but George Dorris would remain in St. Louis and found the Dorris Motor Car Company. Dorris automobiles would be built for the next twenty-five years.

37. *St. Louis Globe-Democrat*, August 10, 1905, 14.

38. Information obtained in a personal interview with Andrew S. Dorris, grandson of one of the cofounders of the St. Louis Motor Carriage Company, and Charles L. (Chuck) Rhoads, the owner of a 1903 "St. Louis" who, among other attributes, is a St. Louis Motor Carriage Company historian.

39. Ibid., July 11, 1904, 1.

40. Ibid.

41. Ibid., April 24, 1904, 6.

42. Minutes of the Board, April 29, 1904.

43. *The St. Louis Republic*, April 28, 1904, 6.

44. *St. Louis Globe-Democrat*, November 25, 1905, 2.

45. *Forty-fourth Annual Report of the Board*, 15.

46. Minutes of the Board, May 13, 1904.

47. *St. Louis Globe-Democrat*, March 15, 1904, 14, and March 16, 1904, 3.

48. *Forty-fourth Annual Report of the Board*, 47.

49. *St. Louis Globe-Democrat*, December 18, 1904, sporting section, 5.

50. Ibid.

51. Ibid., December 21, 1904, 1.

52. Ibid.

53. Ibid.

54. Ibid., October 30, 1904, 1.

55. Ibid., November 15, 1904, 1.

56. Ibid., 3.

57. *Forty-fourth Annual Report of the Board*, 46.

58. *St. Louis Post-Dispatch*, July 3, 1904, Sunday magazine, 5.

59. Ibid.

60. Ibid.

61. This account is taken from the *St. Louis Post-Dispatch* editions of July 20 through July 22, 1904. All were page 1 articles.

62. *St. Louis Post-Dispatch*, July 20, 1904, 1.

63. Cole, "Manufacturing Identity," 249.

64. Ibid., 252–253.

65. Ibid., 249.

66. J. Elbert Jones, *A Review of Famous Crimes Solved by St. Louis Policemen* (St. Louis: Moinster Printing, 1924), 292.

67. Julie K. Brown, "Tricks and Wiles of the Underworld: Crime-Fighting Technology at the World's Fair," *Gateway Heritage* 24, no. 4 (Spring 2004).

68. *St. Louis Globe-Democrat*, August 7, 1904, 6.

69. Ibid.

70. Ibid.

71. Board of Police Commissioners, *History*, 100.

72. Information taken from the confession of William Morris, one of the train robbers. Confession printed, verbatim, in the October 23, 1904, edition of the *St. Louis Globe-Democrat*, p. 12.

73. *St. Louis Globe-Democrat*, October 22, 1904, 1.

74. *St. Louis Globe-Democrat*

75. Ibid., 1 and 2.

76. Ibid., October 23, 1904, 12, and October 25, 1904, 1.

77. Miksicek, MeElreath, and Pollihan, *In the Line of Duty*, 56.

78. *St. Louis Globe-Democrat*, October 22, 1904, 2.

79. Ibid., October 25, 1904, 16.

80. *St. Louis Post-Dispatch*, October 25, 1904, 1.

81. Minutes of the Board, October 22, 1904.

82. Ibid.

83. Ibid., October 28, 1904, and *St. Louis Globe-Democrat*, October 28, 1904, 7.

84. *St. Louis Globe-Democrat*, November 5, 1904, 3.

85. Ibid.

86. Ibid.

87. Ibid.

88. Ibid., November 8, 1904, 4.

89. Ibid.

90. Ibid., November 9, 1904, 6.

91. Ibid., November 11, 1904, 4.

92. Ibid.

93. Ibid.

94. Geiger, *Joseph W. Folk*, 86.

95. *St. Louis Post-Dispatch*, November 13, 1904, 3.

96. Minutes of the Board, November 25, 1904.

97. Ibid., December 2, 1904.

98. *Forty-fifth Annual Report of the Board of Police Commissioners of the City of St. Louis* (St. Louis: Board of Police Commissioners, 1906), 14.

99. Minutes of the Board, December 9, 1904.

100. *St. Louis Post-Dispatch*, December 3, 1904, 1.

101. Ibid.

102. Ibid., December 8, 1904, 1.

103. Ibid.

104. Ibid.

105. *St. Louis Globe-Democrat*, December 14, 1904, 4.

106. Ibid., January 1, 1905, 5.

107. *The St. Louis Republic*, December 31, 1904, 14.

108. Ibid.

Notes from Chapter 12

1. The website of the Missouri Secretary of State (www.sos.mo.gov/archives/historicallistings/historicallistings.asp) lists Folk as the thirty-first governor of Missouri. A listing of all Missouri governors in *The St. Louis Republic* of December 26, 1904, p. 5, lists Folk as the twenty-ninth governor.

2. Geiger, *Joseph W. Folk*, 89–90.

3. Ibid.

4. *The St. Louis Republic*, January 21, 1905, 1.

5. Ibid.

6. Ibid.

7. Ibid., January 27, 1905, 2.

8. Ibid., January 21, 1905, 1.

9. Ibid., January 24, 1905, 3.

10. Ibid.

11. Ibid.

12. Ibid.

13. *St. Louis Globe-Democrat*, January 27, 1905, 2.

14. Ibid., January 30, 1905, 3.

15. Minutes of the Board, February 3, 1905.

16. *St. Louis Globe-Democrat*, February 4, 1905, 2.

17. Minutes of the Board, February 24, 1905.

18. Ibid.

19. Ibid.

20. *St. Louis Post-Dispatch*, February 4, 1905, 2.

21. Minutes of the Board, March 10, 1905.

22. *Forty-fourth Annual Report of the Board*, 15.

23. Minutes of the Board, April 7, 14, and 28, 1905.

24. Ibid., May 12, 1905.

25. Ibid.

26. *St. Louis Globe-Democrat*, August 10, 1905, 14.

27. Ibid.

28. *Forty-fifth Annual Report of the Board*, 6.

29. Minutes of the Board, October 9, 1905.

30. Ibid., December 1, 1905.

31. *St. Louis Globe-Democrat*, November 18, 1905, 18.

32. *St. Louis Post-Dispatch*, November 28, 1905, 1.

33. Ibid., November 23, 1905, 1.

34. Ibid., November 22, 1905, 1.

35. Ibid.

36. Ibid., November 23, 1905, 1.

37. Ibid.

38. Ibid., November 24, 1905, 1.

39. *The Republic*, November 18, 1905, 16.

40. *St. Louis Globe-Democrat*, November 25, 1905, 2.

41. Minutes of the Board, November 24, 1905.

42. *St. Louis Post-Dispatch*, November 25, 1905, 1.

43. *St. Louis Globe-Democrat*, November 18, 1905, 18.

44. Ibid., November 25, 1905, 2.

45. Ibid.

46. *St. Louis Post-Dispatch*, December 9, 1905, 7.

47. Ibid., December 2, 1905, 1.

48. Ibid.

49. Ibid.

50. Ibid.

51. Ibid.

52. Ibid.

53. Ibid.

54. Ibid.

55. Ibid.

56. Ibid.

57. Ibid., December 4, 1905, 1, and December 5, 1905, 2.

58. Ibid., December 4, 1905, 1–2.

59. Ibid.

60. Ibid., December 5, 1905, 1–2.

61. Ibid.

62. Geiger, *Joseph W. Folk*, 101.

63. *St. Louis Globe-Democrat*, December 19, 1905, 1.

64. Ibid.

65. Ibid.

66. *St. Louis Post-Dispatch*, December 23, 1905, 2.

67. *St. Louis Globe-Democrat*, December 23, 1905, 1.

68. Ibid., December 30, 1905, 2.

69. Ibid.

70. Ibid., 1.

71. Ibid.

72. Ibid., February 6, 1906, 1.

73. Ibid.

74. Ibid., February 4, 1906, 18.

75. Ibid.

76. Ibid., February 8, 1906, 3.

77. Ibid.

78. Ibid., February 17, 1906, 1.

79. Ibid.

80. Ibid., February 27, 1906, 1.

81. Minutes of the Board, February 27, 1906.

82. Ibid.

83. *St. Louis Globe-Democrat*, March 13, 1906, 1.

84. *St. Louis Post-Dispatch*, March 16, 1906, 3.

85. *St. Louis Globe-Democrat*, March 15, 1906, 2.

86. Ibid., March 13, 1906, 1.

87. Minutes of the Board, March 16, 1906.

88. Ibid., March 23, 1906.

89. Ibid.

90. Ibid.

91. Ibid., March 30, 1906.

92. *St. Louis Post-Dispatch*, June 3, 1906, part 3, 1.

93. Ibid.

94. *St. Louis Globe-Democrat*, June 23, 1906, 3.

95. Ibid.

96. Ibid., September 24, 1906, 3.

97. *Missouri Revised Statutes* (Jefferson City, MO: Hughes Printing Company, 1907), 113–115.

98. Ibid.

99. Ibid.

100. Board of Police Commissioners, *History*, 136.

101. *St. Louis Post-Dispatch*, January 16, 1939, 3A.

102. Ibid.

103. *St. Louis Globe-Democrat*, June 28, 1906, 1. A "bucket shop" was a saloon that (unlawfully) sold liquor in open containers such as small buckets.

104. Ibid.

105. Minutes of the Board, July 27, 1906.

106. *St. Louis Globe-Democrat*, July 28, 1906, 2.

107. Ibid.

108. *St. Louis Post-Dispatch*, August 3, 1906, 1.

109. Ibid., August 4, 1906, 2.

110. *St. Louis Globe-Democrat*, September 20, 1906, 1.

111. Ibid.

112. Minutes of the Board, September 19, 1906.

113. *St. Louis Globe-Democrat*, September 20, 1906, 1.

114. *The St. Louis Republic*, September 30, 1906, part 3, p. 8.

115. Ibid. Patrolman O'Leary's age was obtained from the burial records of the Calvary Cemetery website (www.stlcathcem.com).

116. Calvary Cemetery online burial records (www.stlcathcem.com).

117. *St. Louis Globe-Democrat*, October 5, 1906, 11.

118. *St. Louis Globe-Democrat*, November 1, 1906, 7.

119. Ibid., November 3, 1906, 2.

120. Ibid.

121. Ibid., November 4, 1906, 1.

122. Ibid.

123. Ibid., November 6, 1906, 1.

124. Ibid.

125. Ibid.

126. Ibid., November 7, 1906, 6.

127. Ibid.

128. Ibid., November 23, 1906, 3.

129. Ibid.

130. Ibid., December 15, 1906, 3.

131. Ibid., November 24, 1906, 3.

132. Ibid., December 29, 1906, 14.

133. Ibid., December 10, 1906, 11.

134. Ibid., December 8, 1906, 7.

135. Ibid., September 21, 1906, 8.

Notes from Epilogue

1. Victor G. Strecher, "Revising the Histories and Futures of Policing," in *The Police and Society: Touchstone Readings*, ed. Victor E. Kappeler (Prospect Heights, IL: Waveland Press, 1995), 71.

2. *St. Louis Post-Dispatch*, November 20, 1904, part 2, p. 8.

3. Ibid.

4. Ibid.

5. Lee Meriwether, *My Yesteryears: An Autobiography by Lee Meriwether* (Webster Groves, MO: The International Mark Twain Society, 1942), 169.

6. Ibid., 170.

7. Ibid.

8. Ibid., 171.

9. Strecher, "Revising the Histories," 72.

10. *Missouri Revised Statutes*, 113–115.

11. The St. Louis Metropolitan Police Department and the police department in Kansas City, Missouri, are the only police departments in the United States that continue under state control. The control of the police department in Kansas City has reverted to mayoral control and then returned to state control on different occasions, but the St. Louis department has continuously remained under state control since its inception in 1861.

Acknowledgments

"HOW MANY PEOPLE DOES it take to write a book?" It definitely takes more than the number to change a light bulb. It took more than twenty for this book. First, a thank you to my former boss, mentor, and friend, Dr. Victor G. Strecher, for his forty years of encouragement. Then, there was the inspiration and early help of my friend Joseph "Red" Menius.

Thanks to Dr. E. Terrence Jones, former dean of the College of Arts and Sciences and professor in the Department of Political Science at the University of Missouri–St. Louis, for his input and encouragement. Both Dr. Richard Wright, chair of the Department of Criminology and Criminal Justice (CCJ) at UM–St. Louis, and Dr. Scott Decker, now director of the School of Criminology and Criminal Justice at Arizona State University, read and critiqued early chapters of the manuscript. I thank them for their time and thoughts.

It was through Dr. Wright's efforts that I received a stipend from the CCJ department to defray some research expenses, and through Dr. Decker's and Dean Jones's that I was appointed a research fellow at the Missouri History Museum (MHM) for a semester. Thanks to Dr. Robert R. Archibald, president of MHM, for accepting the first non-historian for that honor. Dr. Eric Sandweiss, then director of research at MHM, was my guide to the rich resources available at that institution. That semester saw the beginning of this work. Thanks also to then–criminology and criminal justice graduate students Dennis Durso and Stephen Manley for assistance in the early stages.

Many people, some of whom I met for the first time, permitted me to use documents or photographs, or otherwise assisted in the development of this book. I thank the St. Louis Board of Police Commissioners, then presided over by Colonel Wayman Smith III;

Barbara Miksicek, librarian of the St. Louis Metropolitan Police Academy Library, for more than a decade of assistance; Assistant Chief of Police, Lt. Colonel Stephen Pollihan; Gloria Coyle and Jane Bickham, for providing me with a one-hundred-year-old police department photographic and historical publication; the late auto writer and historian Bob Francis; and Kirkwood, Missouri, Mayor Mike Swoboda and his Assistant Chief Administrative Officer, Georgia Ragland, for the sketch of the first Kirkwood City Hall.

George Dorris, the co-owner of the St. Louis Motor Carriage Company, built the first automobile used by the police department. My thanks to his grandson, Andrew S. Dorris, for his input and for introducing me to Charles L. (Chuck) Rhoads, who likely deserves the title of historian of the St. Louis Motor Carriage Company. Information provided by Bob Moore, the National Park Service historian in St. Louis, led me to the meeting with Andrew Dorris and Chuck Rhoads.

The staff at the State Historical Society of Missouri, in Columbia, assisted me in finding some original documents that proved quite useful. The staff at the Missouri State Archives in Jefferson City did yeoman's work in helping me to locate original documents confirming the earliest appointments to the Board of Police Commissioners.

My meeting with Debbie VanDyke provided me with information about her grandfather, Captain (and later Chief of Police) William Lee. Thanks to Benjamin Israel, who was a graduate student in the Department of History at the University of Missouri–St. Louis. Benjamin, who was researching a related topic, asked me many questions and provided many answers to my questions that kept us both on track.

Kevin Kerwin, of Ft. Lauderdale, Florida, provided me with a photograph and some biographical information on his great-grandfather, Daniel Kerwin. Thanks also to Harold G. Stratton of Cordova, Tennessee. He provided me with a copy of his painting, *St. Louis Dispatch*, depicting the arrival of the steamboat *J. C. Swon* in St. Louis in 1861. The cargo on the *J. C. Swon* played a part in the Camp Jackson affair in St. Louis later that year.

Once the manuscript had been accepted for publication by the Missouri History Museum, two individuals saw to it that the manuscript became a book: Victoria Monks, the Director of Publications, and Lauren Mitchell, the Senior Editor. Lauren deserves a very special thank you for all her hard work checking my every word and politely questioning things that apparently made sense only to me.

Despite my best efforts, I'm sure that I've forgotten others who have helped. I sincerely apologize to them.

Index

Sunday Sales schemes · pp 275 ff